DICTIONARY OF IDIOMS AND THEIR ORIGINS

Linda and Roger Flavell

M000279805

Kyle Books

This edition printed in Great Britain in 2016 by
Kyle Books, an imprint of Kyle Cathie Ltd.
192–198 Vauxhall Bridge Road
London, SW1V 1DX
general.enquiries@kylebooks.com
www.kylebooks.co.uk

First published in Great Britain in 1992 by Kyle Cathie Limited
Completely revised, updated and expanded in 2006

ISBN: 978 0 85783 401 0

A Cataloguing in Publication record for this title is available from the British Library.

Printed and bound at Gopsons Papers Ltd.

· Introduction ·

If I may be accused of encouraging or inventing a new vice – the mania, or 'idiomania', I may perhaps call it – of collecting what Pater calls the 'gypsy phrases' of our language, I have at least been punished by becoming one of its most careless and incorrigible victims
(Logan Pearsall Smith, *Words and Idioms*, 1925).

Our belief is that people turn to a book on idioms for two main purposes: for reference and to browse. We have tried to cater for both.

Reference

Each phrase dealt with in the body of the book is listed alphabetically in relation to a key word in it. As idioms are by definition phrases and not single words, there is necessarily a choice to be made of which word to classify the phrase by. We have exercised our judgement as to which is the key word (normally a noun or a verb) but, in case our intuitions do not coincide with the reader's, we have provided an index of the important words in each expression at the end of the book. Starting on page 317 there is also an Index of Themes, so that the reader interested in, say, idioms derived from Shakespeare or from the army and warfare can find any examples included here.

The head words are followed by a definition. This is the contemporary sense or senses – an important point, given that many idioms have a long history and have undergone marked changes in meaning during the centuries.

Quotations are listed in chronological order and provide a taste of how modern authors use idioms. We also try to give a idea of the different shades of meaning of the idiom, where possible. The contemporary illustrations are drawn from our internet searching and from the serendipity of our eclectic reading. We make no claims for comprehensive coverage of today's press – the quoting of the UK dailies simply means that we read them regularly!

The bibliography is there both to show our sources and to provide a point of extended reference. It is by no means complete: it contains some of the books we have referred to which are collections of idioms of one type or another. To have included all the books of idioms on which we have drawn – not to mention the hundreds of books of general language and wider reference we have consulted – would have produced a bibliography of unmanageable length. Our bibliography includes just one sort of title – if in the text of the book we refer to a specific source, the name of the author alone may be given (eg Walsh or Funk). Full details of Walsh, Funk and others may then be found at the back of the book.

Browsing

Our own love of the curious in language is, we have observed, shared by others. For them, and for ourselves, we have written the parts of this book that aim to please the browser.

The entries have been selected because they have a tale to tell. Many idioms were rejected because there was nothing interesting to say about them. Plenty more have had to be excluded because of pressures of time and space, but we hope that what remains is a satisfying cross-section of the vast range of idioms which occur in everyday English, even if it cannot claim to be a comprehensive list.

The etymology – or etymologies, since there are often alternative accounts – tries to go back to the earliest origins. We endeavour to give dates, but it is often impossible to do this with any confidence. Phrases have literal meanings, then they generally develop metaphorical uses and ultimately, in typical cases, acquire an idiomatic sense that is separate from the literal one. The form a phrase takes may also vary considerably over the years. It is therefore extremely difficult to state accurately when the idiom as such was first used. Wherever possible, we make the best estimate we can. We have also sometimes selected quotations to show the historical change in the use or form of phrases, as well as for their intrinsic interest.

The stories behind the expressions are in part those that authorities suggest. Our own researches have added to or replaced these, where we felt it was necessary. Quite often it is impossible to say with certainty what is the best source; in these instances, we have not hesitated to admit that doubt exists.

There are various essays strategically situated throughout the book (usually near entries on a connected theme). These are of various kinds – linguistic, historical, just plain curious – and are intended to inform and entertain. A list of these essays appears on the next page. One of them is entitled *The Old Curiosity Shop of Linguistics* (see page 198). This could also serve as the watchword for all that we have tried to provide for the browser!

In conclusion, our aim has been to provide a balance of reference information and a rich, varied diet for the curious; we have striven for scholarly accuracy without falling into academic pedantry.

We have certainly made mistakes and would welcome comments and corrections. We were delighted to receive very well-informed comments from a number of sources on the publication of earlier editions of this book. One correspondent even devoted much of Christmas Day to the task! For this very greatly changed and enlarged edition, we have also benefited from e-mail information and advice from an author who has published his own collection of idioms on the internet, from another author willing to be quoted in this book, from experts on issues ranging from women at sea to Yorkshire dialect, from local librarians, and from a student friend who hunted out references in the local University library. We owe a particular debt to our friend Ann Mason for her detailed and perceptive comments on our revised text. We would also like to thank Catherine Varley for her help.

Linda and Roger Flavell
YORK
NOVEMBER 2005

MAIN ESSAYS

A

aback: taken aback
surprised, shocked

Known at least a thousand years ago, the term *aback*, meaning 'backwards', 'behind', slipped from use during the second half of the nineteenth century. It survives only as a nautical term referring to a ship facing into a headwind whose sails are pressed hard against the mast. The nautical phrase *to be taken aback* emerged in the eighteenth century to describe situations where this happened unexpectedly, either through faulty steering or a swift change in wind direction, thus abruptly halting the ship's progress and putting her in danger. Around 1840 the phrase began to be applied figuratively to a person's reaction when suddenly stopped short by a piece of news or a surprising event.

An American woman on a business trip to China was **taken aback** *when she tried to book into her hotel after a long, tiring flight from New York.*
The White Swan in Guangzhou was fully booked and had no record of Claudia Niera's internet reservation. When she checked, she found that she had booked a room at the White Swan at Pickering, thousands of miles away in North Yorkshire. She had confused the hotels' websites.
THE DAILY TELEGRAPH, 23 APRIL 2001

He said MPs from across the political spectrum had demanded action after being **'taken aback'** *by the controversial presenter's personal questions.*
DAILY EXPRESS, 19 JULY 2002

For other nautical idioms, see A LIFE ON THE OCEAN WAVES, page 24.

above board
honest, straight

The sixteenth-century term *under board* literally meant 'under the table', the place for dogs, food scraps and gentlemen who had drunk too much. But before long the dishonest practices of gamesters who would drop their hands below the board, or tabletop, to exchange unfavourable cards brought about the figurative sense of 'in an underhand way, dishonestly'. (The modern idiom is *under the table*.) The insistence was that players should keep their hands above the board to ensure fair play. Thus *above board* came to mean 'honest, open to scrutiny': *All his dealings are square, and above the board* (Joseph Hall, *Virtues and Vices*, 1608).

I am not, I should point out, in the habit of gatecrashing celebrity weddings. My presence here is entirely **above board**. *The embossed invitation in my jacket pocket reads: 'Donatella Versace has the pleasure of inviting Jess Cartner-Morley to a dinner celebrating the wedding of Jennifer Lopez and Chris Judd. Tuesday October 2, 9.30pm, Villa Fontanelle, Lake Como.'*
THE GUARDIAN, 4 OCTOBER 2001

Achilles' heel
a weak or vulnerable spot in someone or something that is otherwise strong

According to Greek mythology, Thetis held her baby son Achilles by the heel while dipping him into the river Styx to make him invincible. Achilles' heel, however, remained dry and was his only weakness. After years as a brave and victorious warrior, Achilles was killed during the Trojan war by an arrow which pierced his heel. His deadly enemy Paris had learned of his secret and aimed at the weak spot. The full story is told in Homer's *Iliad* (c. eighth century BC).

In an 1810 issue of *The Friend*, Coleridge referred to Ireland as *that vulnerable heel of the British Achilles!* His inspiration was subsequently imitated by Thomas Carlyle who dubbed Hanover *the Achilles'-heel to invulnerable England* (*Frederick the Great of Prussia*, 1865).

Achilles heel is still alive and kicking – even if it has a somewhat literary flavour – despite George Orwell's assertion just after the Second World War that it was a dying turn of phrase.

I was just appalling at interviews – I used to get so nervous. Normally I'm not a nervous person, I'm confident in all sorts of ways. For instance, I can speak to public audiences. But interviews were always my **Achilles heel**.
THE TIMES EDUCATIONAL SUPPLEMENT, 8 FEBRUARY 2002

The mistakes will have been a bitter blow to Ferguson, not just because they cost United the chance of recapturing the FA Cup which he first won against Crystal Palace in 1990, but because they meant that a weakness that he thought was a thing of the past does, in fact, remain their **Achilles heel**.
THE DAILY TELEGRAPH, 26 JANUARY 2002

For other idioms derived from ancient legends, see page 317.

acid test, the
a foolproof test for assessing the value of something

Although the secret of *aqua regia* had been known for some time, the German alchemist Andreas Libau was the first to describe its preparation in his *Alchemia* (1597), a work noting all the major discoveries of alchemy to date. Gold is not affected by most acids but reacts to *aqua regia*, so a sure way to find out whether a metal is pure gold is to test it with this three-to-one mixture of hydrochloric and nitric acids. The Latin name, which means 'royal water', was given to the preparation because gold was the 'royal metal'. An alternative was to use a drop of nitric acid on a specimen. If it were pure gold, and not *fool's gold*, then there would be no reaction. The big advantage from the gold prospector's point of view was that the sample was not destroyed!

It is claimed in many American sources that the term *acid test* was first used in the Gold Rush days of the mid-nineteenth century; its use in England goes back to at least the late nineteenth century. Its figurative sense of 'a rigorous test' dates from the early twentieth century.

The irony for Henry, as he contemplates seven weeks of hard work being distilled into 80 minutes on Saturday, is that he is now going to have to turn to some of the mid-week team…This is Henry's **acid test**.
THE GUARDIAN, 9 JULY 2001

And now the **acid test***. I wondered whether he saw himself as a caretaker prop, awaiting the return from injury of Phil Vickery and Julian White, or England's numero uno.*
THE SUNDAY TELEGRAPH,
27 MARCH 2005

Adam's apple
the lump on the front of the throat formed by the thyroid cartilage

The rigid bulge of the thyroid cartilage in the throat protects the rest of the larynx, and the vocal cords inside it.

Although both men and women have these bulges, the lump is more noticeable in men simply because they have longer vocal cords. But why is the bump called an *Adam's apple*? When Adam ate the forbidden fruit in the Garden of Eden (the biblical account in Genesis, chapter 3, does not mention any specific fruit), a piece of it became lodged in his throat. Legend has it that it was an apple, although a quince or fig is more likely. It serves as a reminder of his disobedience.

When Mr Anderson, aged 64, lost his larynx, a hole was cut in his neck, near the **Adam's apple**, *to allow him to breathe.*
THE DAILY TELEGRAPH,
29 NOVEMBER 2000

He would set the reel on the projector and start it up. A face would fill the screen... someone I didn't know, or perhaps a friend...and sometimes a celebrity, such as Salvador Dalí. Peter and I would sit there staring at the two spires of Dalí's moustache, and then suddenly he would swallow, his **Adam's apple** *going up and down, and it was as if the screen had exploded.*
THE GUARDIAN, 27 JANUARY 2002

albatross: an albatross around one's neck
a heavy burden, a constant trial

> *Ah! well a-day! what evil looks*
> *Had I from old and young!*
> *Instead of the cross, the Albatross*
> *About my neck was hung.*

Coleridge's narrative poem 'The Rime of the Ancient Mariner' (1798) tells of a sailor who defies superstition by cruelly killing an albatross, thereby bringing a curse upon his ship. When ill fortune strikes the vessel, the rest of the crew hang the albatross around the sailor's neck to mark the culprit. It takes the death of all his shipmates and

his own final true repentance before the burden is lifted from the unfortunate Ancient Mariner.

The figurative use of the expression did not become widespread till the 1930s. In fact, another poet, Dylan Thomas, had a hand in this through his use of it in a periodical publication of that decade:

> *The old forget the grief,*
> *Hack of the cough, the hanging albatross,*
> *Cast back the bone of youth...*
> ('Grief thief of time',
> *First Comment Treasury*, 1937)

Ankinci is typical of the progressive, pro-European voices that are being heard all the more in Turkey; the same voices that have begun to see 'little Cyprus' not only as **an albatross** *but as the obstacle that might even obstruct the Turkish nation's own entry into the EU.*
THE GUARDIAN, 29 NOVEMBER 2001

'My foster mother died and I did not have a relationship with my real parents. I know who they are. It's not upsetting; it's just the way it is. You cannot change things. My childhood isn't like **an albatross around my neck**.*'*
THE GUARDIAN, 20 NOVEMBER 2004

See also *a* MILLSTONE *around one's neck.* For other idioms drawn from literature, see page 319.

alive and kicking
very active, lively

This phrase dates back to at least the early 1830s. The general consensus is that fish vendors used it to advertise their wares. The fish are so fresh that they are still jumping and flapping about. Although there is no known written example of its use in this context, it bears comparison with (*all*) *alive oh* for which there is ample evidence, notably in James Yorkston's popular song 'Cockles and Mussels' (1884):

What is an idiom?

Language follows rules. If it did not, then its users would not be able to make sense of the random utterances they read and hear and they would not be able to communicate meaningfully themselves. Grammar books are, in effect, an account of the regularities of the language, with notes on the minority of cases where there are exceptions to the regular patterns. In English, for example, nearly all verbs add an *s* to the third person singular, present tense (*he walks, she throws, it appeals*). There are obvious exceptions to this basic 'rule' (*he can, she may, it ought*).

One of the interesting things about idioms is that they are anomalies of language, mavericks of the linguistic world. The very word *idiom* comes from the Greek *idios*, 'one's own, peculiar, strange'. Idioms, therefore, break the normal rules. They do this in two main areas – semantically, with regard to their meaning, and syntactically, with regard to their grammar. A consideration, then, of the semantic and syntactic elements of idioms leads to the question *What is an idiom?*

Meaning

The problem with idioms is that the words in them do not mean what they ought to mean – an idiom cannot be understood literally. A *bucket* is a 'pail' and *to kick* means 'to move with the foot'. Yet *to kick the bucket* probably does not mean 'to kick the pail with one's foot'. It is more likely to be understood as 'to die'. The meaning of the whole, then, is not the sum of the meaning of the parts, but is apparently something quite unconnected to them. To put this another way, idioms are mostly phrases that can have a literal meaning in one context but a totally different sense in another. If someone said, *Alfred spilled the beans all over the table*, there would be a nasty mess for him to clear up. If it were *Alfred spilled the beans all over the town*, he would be divulging secrets to all who would listen.

An idiom breaks the normal rules, then, in that it does not mean what you would expect it to mean. In fact the idiom is a new linguistic entity with a sense attached to it that might be quite remote from the senses of the individual words that form it. Although it is in form a phrase, it has many characteristics of a single word.

Grammar

The second way idioms are peculiar is with regard to their grammar. There is no idiom that does not have some syntactic defect, failing to undergo some grammatical operation that its syntactic structure would suggest is appropriate.

In Dublin's fair city,
where the girls are so pretty
I first set my eyes on sweet Molly Malone
As she wheel'd her wheel barrow
Thro' streets broad and narrow
Crying Cockles and Mussels alive, alive O!
Alive, alive O! Alive, alive O!
Crying Cockles and Mussels
Alive, alive O!

Nevertheless, the *Dictionary of Slang* (Farmer and Henley, 1890–1904) states that the phrase alludes to the months of pregnancy following 'quickening', when the mother is able to feel the child she is carrying moving in her womb.

*Recent research…reveals that while being blonde may boost your social life, it can also damage your career prospects… And at the heart of it is the stereotype of the dumb blonde – a stereotype that is still **alive and kicking**. Basically, men rate blondes as more feminine but less intelligent than brunettes.*
THE GUARDIAN, 29 JULY 2001

Different types of idiom suffer from different restrictions. With *a hot dog* the following are not possible: *the dog is hot, the heat of the dog, today's dog is hotter than yesterday's, it's a very hot dog today*. Yet with the superficially identical phrase *a hot sun*, there is no problem: *the sun is hot, the heat of the sun, today's sun is hotter than yesterday's, it's a very hot sun today*. Idioms that include verbs are similarly inflexible in the manipulations that they will permit. For instance, why is it that you cannot take the separate parts of *to beat about the bush* and substitute for them a near synonym? There is no way you can say *hit about the bush* or *beat about the shrub*. Nor can you change the definite article to the indefinite – you can't *beat about a bush*. It's not possible to make *bush* plural. Whoever heard of *beating about the bushes*? *The bush was beaten about* is as strange as the passive in *the music was faced*. Some idioms go further, exhibiting a completely idiosyncratic grammatical structure, such as intransitive verbs apparently with a direct object: *to come a cropper, to go the whole hog, to look daggers at*.

The best examples of idioms, therefore, are very fixed grammatically and it is impossible to guess their meaning from the sense of the words that constitute them. Not all phrases meet these stringent criteria. Quite often it is possible to see the link between the literal sense of the words and the idiomatic meaning. This is because a route by which many phrases become idioms involves a metaphorical stage, where the original reference is still discernible. *To skate on thin ice*, 'to court danger', is a very obvious figure of speech. The borderline between a metaphor and an idiom is a fuzzy one. Other idioms allow a wide range of grammatical transformations: *My father read the riot act to me when I arrived* can become *I was read the riot act by my father when I arrived* or *the riot act was read to me by my father when I arrived*. Much more acceptable than *the bush was beaten about*!

In short, it is not that a phrase is or is not an idiom; rather, a given expression is more or less 'idiomaticky', on a cline stretching from the normal, literal use of language via degrees of metaphor and grammatical flexibility to the pure idiom. To take an analogy, in the colour spectrum there is general agreement on what is green and what is yellow but it is impossible to say precisely where one becomes the other. So it is hard to specify where the flexible metaphor becomes the syntactically frozen idiom, with a new meaning all of its own.

*...the author herself is ample proof that individuality is **alive and kicking**.*
THE INDEPENDENT, 20 SEPTEMBER 2003

all systems go
everything is ready for action

All systems go, the phrase used by ground control at Cape Canaveral to indicate that a spacecraft is ready for launching, became current in the 1960s when launches began to be televised worldwide. It is typical of so many originally jargon phrases that gain a wider currency from their colourfulness or appropriacy. *Countdown* and *lift off* are others from the heyday of space flights in the 1960s.

*Meanwhile, at John Lewis it's **all systems go** for a huge surge in demand in school uniform in the weeks and months ahead. Not child-size uniforms, though – the summer holidays have been dominated by adults trying to buy skirts, shirts and*

school ties as the old school disco phenomenon takes hold.
THE GUARDIAN, 11 SEPTEMBER 2001

He will not reveal how much is in the bag, but says that once all the investors have confirmed, the paper will be on the newsstands in little more than six months. 'We have a professional management team on board, and it's all systems go,' he says.
EVENING STANDARD, 24 MARCH 2004

It's all systems go at the Ricoh Arena with the landmark development set to open its doors for the first time nine weeks today.
COVENTRY EVENING TELEGRAPH, 18 JUNE 2005

amok: to run amok (amuck)
to become frenzied, out of control

In the early sixteenth century the Portuguese in search of valuable spices penetrated as far as the Malay archipelago. There they observed, with a degree of disquiet, that some of the people were capable of gradually working themselves up into a state of delirious fury before rushing out into the streets where they would indiscriminately murder anyone they came across. The Malayan adjective for this frenzied state of mind is *amoq*. This was taken into Portuguese as *amouco*, a noun used to denote a person in the grip of such a fury. This term had made its way into English by the second half of the seventeenth century through popular translations of Portuguese travellers' tales. The earliest recorded use of the phrase *to run amok* comes in Andrew Marvell's *The Rehearsal Transpros'd* (1672): *Like a raging Indian...he runs a mucke (as they cal it there) stabbing every man he meets*. Almost contemporaneously, the earliest recorded non-literal use is in Edmund Hickeringill: *Running a Muck at all Mankind* (*A speech without doors*, 1689).

A man ran amok with a samurai sword after his address was accidentally leaked in a report into the murder of Stephen Lawrence, a jury heard yesterday.
The defendant exploded into violence on June 13 last year...Wearing pyjamas and a dressing-gown, he stood in the middle of the A20 outside his former home in Eltham...brandishing the sword, his eyes bulging and a manic expression on his face.
DAILY MAIL, 14 MARCH 2000

The owner's enthusiastic description of this morning's valuation led me to expect an idyllic country cottage with roses around the door. I was unprepared for the 16 or so crazed goats that ran amok between chicken huts and piles of rotting vegetables.
THE SUNDAY TELEGRAPH, 16 SEPTEMBER 2001

See also *to go* BERSERK.

angel: to write like an angel
to be a gifted writer of poetry or prose

Isaac Disraeli, English critic and historian and father of Benjamin Disraeli, gives the origins of this phrase in *Curiosities of Literature* (1791–1834), an anthology of literary and historical anecdotes:

There is a strange phrase connected with the art of the calligrapher which I think may be found in most, if not in all, modern languages, to write like an angel!...This fanciful phrase, however, has a very human origin. Among those learned Greeks who emigrated to Italy, and some afterwards into France, in the reign of Francis I, was one Angelo Vergecto [Vergece or Vergezio], whose beautiful calligraphy excited the admiration of the learned. The French monarch had a Greek fount [font] cast, modelled by his writing. The learned Henry Stephens, who was one of the most elegant writers of Greek, had learnt the practice from Angelo. His name became synonymous for beautiful writing, and gave birth to the phrase to write like an angel.

From this explanation it is evident the phrase was originally descriptive not of a person's style of writing, but of his handwriting. This critic, therefore, excited by the award of the Nobel Prize for Literature to W B Yeats, shows a modern shift of meaning for the idiom: *He is a poet of real greatness; prose, too, he can write like an angel* (*The Manchester Guardian*, 4 November 1929).

As so often happens, a fixed expression can be overused and become a cliché. Roger Whitehead deftly parodied this and many other expressions in his stylistic advice to British Home Office Civil Servants (personal communication): *First and foremost, the bottom line is that the difference between good and bad writing has to be like chalk and cheese – it's a whole new ballgame of checks and balances. Bear in mind, though, that the way you seamlessly set out your stall is not a question of rules and regulations – these are just the tip of the iceberg – more of custom and practice. If you are to write like an angel, your purple prose has to be to die for; it has to be awesome. This is not negotiable.*

*Not only does Kate Cohen **write like an angel**, she offers an unusual blend of intense and scrupulously honest self-scrutiny with an extremely scholarly and comprehensive storehouse of knowledge about the customs of weddings. From Dante and Milton to* Brides *magazine, she presents information that is fascinating and often hilarious.*
AMAZON, CUSTOMER ONLINE REVIEW, 28 MAY 2001

angels: on the side of the angels
in agreement with orthodox views or authorities

The phrase is from a speech given by Benjamin Disraeli at the Oxford Diocesan Conference in 1864. Entering the dispute on evolution that currently raged, Disraeli declared himself opposed to the theory that our early ancestors were apes and maintained that man was created by God: *What is the question now placed before society with the glib assurance which to me is most astonishing? That question is this: Is man an ape or an angel? I, my lord, am on the side of the angels.*

Tom Mangold's investigation of the scandal of the Erika, *a 25-year-old rustbucket of a tanker which, in 1999, caused one of the worst oil spills Europe has ever seen, was a shining example of intelligent, impartial and thorough investigative journalism, journeying from Paris to Bombay in search of answers. Non-partisan yet **on the side of the angels**, it was exemplary TV news journalism.*
THE GUARDIAN, 21 AUGUST 2000

*Another TV megastar is Nigella Lawson... She's a wealthy and beautiful widow who cooks in a denim jacket. While she may not look like too many cooks I know, she does seem to cook a lot of exuberantly cheesy, fatty, greasy stuff – not shying away from the butter and cream – which puts her **on the side of the angels** in my book.*
THE GUARDIAN, 30 NOVEMBER 2001

'SIMPSONS' ON THE 'SIDE OF THE ANGELS'
*[Rowan] Williams, enthroned as arch-bishop last year and known for having a finger on the pulse of modern life, has called the show 'one of the most subtle pieces of propaganda around in the cause of sense, humility and virtue'. In an interview to be broadcast on Britain's ITV network next Sunday, he says of the program: 'It's generally **on the side of the angels** and on the side of sense. It punctures lots of pompous fictions about how the world works.'*
REUTERS, 20 JUNE 2004

apple: an apple of discord
something which causes strife,
argument, rivalry

In a fit of pique because she had not
been invited to the marriage of Thetis
and Peleus, Eris, goddess of Discord,
threw a golden apple bearing the
inscription 'for the most beautiful'
among the goddesses. Pallas, Hera and
Aphrodite each claimed the apple and
a bitter quarrel ensued. Paris, who was
chosen to judge between them,
decided upon Aphrodite, whereupon
Pallas and Hera swore vengeance upon
him and were instrumental in bringing
about the fall of Troy.

*Books examining the fraught Franco-
American relationship are already a
growing cottage industry in France...
It is not surprising that Iraq would
eventually become such **an apple of
discord**... It may well be that France
and the U.S. would have collided, even
without the convenient excuse of Iraq.
Over the past 20 years, economic policies
have been increasingly diverging, as have
the two countries' approaches to key
social questions such as capital
punishment.*
BUSINESS WEEK, 3 MAY 2004

For other idioms derived from ancient
legends, see page 317.

apple: in apple-pie order
everything neatly arranged, in its
proper place

Two folk corruptions from French are
suggested to account for this phrase.
   The notion behind the old French
phrase *cap à pie*, 'from head to foot', is
that of a fully armoured knight, perfectly prepared for battle. Those who
argue in favour of this origin point
out that the phrase was once common
in English and that, with anglicised
pronunciation, it is phonetically not so
very different from *apple pie*.

Unfortunately, no examples of *cap à pie*
order have yet come to light.
   Nappes pliées, on the other hand,
means 'folded linen' and conveys the
idea of neatness and tidiness. (This last
is also a candidate for the origin of
apple-pie bed, the schoolboy jape where
bedsheets are folded in such a way as
to prevent the dupe from lying down.)
Again, evidence for this is wanting.
   The origins of this homely phrase,
current in English since the second
half of the eighteenth century, are
shrouded in mystery. And where there
is mystery (especially such a long-
standing one), then speculation
abounds. There have been many other
attempts to explain the origin of the
phrase – a cored apple, neatly cut into
quarters, for example, or a mispronun-
ciation of *alpha, beta* to represent the
ordered sequence of the alphabet. And
so they go on...

*The Spice Market (also known as the
Egyptian Bazaar) is housed in a handsome
building almost on the waterfront. Inside,
everything is arranged **in apple-pie order**,
reminiscent of old-fashioned chain grocers.*
THE GUARDIAN, 6 MAY 2000

*Poska Villa...is a charming wooden
house...The ladies who run it seem a touch
fierce at first, but they soon warm up, and
they keep the eight rooms **in apple-pie
order**, with local wooden furniture, floaty
curtains and sparkling shower rooms...*
THE SUNDAY TELEGRAPH, 10 APRIL 2005

apple: the apple of one's eye
anyone or anything loved and protected

In the time of the great West Saxon
king, Alfred (848–99), the pupil at the
centre of the eye was known as the
apple (Old English *æppel*) since it was
erroneously thought to be an apple-
shaped solid. (Indeed this use, if not
the concept behind it, persisted into
the first half of the nineteenth century.)

Since the delicate pupil of the eye is essential for vision, it is a part that is cherished and protected at all costs. Thus *apple of the eye* was used as a figure for a much loved person or thing. King Alfred used the phrase in this sense in his translation of Gregory's *Curia Pastoralis* (c. 885).

When the Bible was translated into English, William Tyndale used the phrase to render a number of texts such as Deuteronomy 32:10, where the Lord's care for Israel is described thus: *He found him in a desert land, and in the waste, howling wilderness; he led him about, he instructed him, he kept him as the apple of his eye.*

Scores of current English idioms come from the Bible and use of this particular ancient expression was doubtless reinforced by familiarity with such texts.

Trevor Bentham, the writer and long-term partner of the late Sir Nigel Hawthorne, sits alone in the drawing room of their 15th-century manor house. As dark falls, he rumples the wiry hair of Seamus, their terrier and **apple of Sir Nigel's eye** *– 'like a son to him,' says Trevor wryly.*
THE MAIL ON SUNDAY, 20 JANUARY 2002

'She was **the apple of my eye**,*' her husband said. 'We had a good marriage…a lot of hard knocks, but through thick and thin we stuck together. We accepted life on life's terms.'*
PORTLAND PRESS HERALD,
23 MARCH 2005

For other idioms from the Bible, see page 317.

apple: to upset the apple cart
to spoil a plan, to make things go wrong

The Roman expression had a simple cart: *plaustrum perculi*, 'I've upset the cart', that is 'I've made a mess of things'. Thomas Fuller, who enjoyed aphorisms, records a vindictive *If I ever catch his cart overthrowing, I'll give it one*

shove in his *Gnomologia* (1732). But it was not until the end of the eighteenth century that the heavily laden *apple cart* hove into view, providing a much more satisfying image of disarray: apples rolling in all directions, inconveniencing everyone and becoming bruised and spoilt into the bargain.

Soon they had a location for their restaurant on Kensington High Street…The budget was set at £1.1m – £700,000 to come from investors, the rest from the bank. That was how much Iqbal reckoned his dream would cost.

Then, a few months later, **he kicked over his own apple cart**. *He wrote a column for* Tandoori *magazine, which serves the Indian restaurant sector, in which he criticised the standard of service at most curry houses… The effect was almost instantaneous. 'One guy wanted to invest £500,000 but he said he couldn't now because he was Bangladeshi and the community had turned against me.'*
THE GUARDIAN, 11 MARCH 2002

So we embark upon 2005 with the outlook set fair and the expectation that little will emerge **to upset the apple cart**.
THE JOURNAL, 5 JANUARY 2005

For other idioms drawn from Greek and Roman writers, see page 318.

apron: tied to his mother's apron strings
said of a young man who is still kept strictly under his mother's control and authority

'Apron string tenure' was a legal arrangement in the seventeenth century whereby a man was granted tenure over his wife's estate only during her lifetime. In this sense he was tied to her. During the nineteenth century the expression *tied to the apron strings* came to denote any man who was firmly under the thumb of a dominant wife or mother. Nowadays it is more usually applied to a grown-up son and *cutting* or *letting go of the apron strings* is the act of liberation.

This said, an earlier figurative use of *apron strings*, dating from the end of the seventeenth century, does not describe a family relationship at all. In his *New Account of East India and Persia* (1689) John Fryer, a surgeon for the East India Company, wrote of being *harness'd witte the Apron-strings of Trade,* and the figure is still widely used today for objects or institutions which have a hold over one or with which one feels an emotional bond that is difficult to break. The monarchy, for instance. This example is from *The Guardian*, 11 November 2001: *It is with sympathy for the royal family's position – and not a keenness to criticise their failings – that the* Observer *resolved a year ago that it was time for Britain to consider letting go of our current constitutional apron strings to monarchy once the current Queen's reign ends.*

Yet, away from the ring, [Lennox] Lewis epitomises the cliché 'a gentle giant' and, astonishingly in this brutal sport, is happy to admit he is still **tied to his mother's apron strings**.
EVENING STANDARD, 19 APRIL 2001

Aunt Sally
a scapegoat, an easy target of blame

Aunt Sally originated as a game common to fairs and racecourses around Britain in the middle of the nineteenth century. The wooden head of an old woman would be mounted on a pole in the ground. Players standing at a distance of twenty or thirty yards would then throw sticks to try to smash the clay pipe she held in her mouth. By the end of the century poor abused *Aunt Sally* had slipped into idiomatic use to denote 'an object of unreasonable criticism'.

Aunt is a term used both to express a particular form of kinship and, more likely here, to denote any elderly woman. But the origin of the effigy itself is a mystery. There has been speculation since the late 1800s that it evolved from a black-faced doll, also known as Aunt Sally, which was popular in the early nineteenth century and which was also frequently hung outside the premises of marine stores and second-hand clothes dealers. According to Jonathon Green (*Cassell's Dictionary of Slang*, 1998), the doll represented Black Sal, a character from Pierce Egan's sensational *Life in London* (1821–28), racy accounts of the pleasures of Regency London. Indeed, Black Sal was widely known in a variety of other contexts in the nineteenth century and earlier. She was, and still is, the companion of the Green Man in the pagan festival of Beltane on 1 May each year. Jack-in-the-Green, covered in luxuriant green foliage, parades with his black-faced consort and is ultimately killed, in order to release the spirit of summer. And Black Sal is also a nineteenth-century dance.

Black Sal, then, was undoubtedly well known, in one guise or another, in the nineteenth century, and it is a relatively easy step to connect her with the various realisations of *Aunt Sally* in the same period.

Uncertain though the origin might be, *Aunt Sally* is still alive and well as a game. In Oxfordshire there is an Aunt Sally Association that looks after the 2,000 players of the pub game in the area.

Wherever change is proposed, there is a familiar pattern. First opponents of change construct an **Aunt Sally** *grossly misrepresenting it; then a great campaign is mounted against the Aunt Sally; then we defend ourselves; then those who created the Aunt Sally ask us why we keep talking about*

it. *Then, after the change goes through, people wonder what the fuss was about.*
THE GUARDIAN, 12 SEPTEMBER 2001

*'If we construct this **Aunt Sally** of the so-called European superstate, gnawing away at Britain's sacred birthright, then I think we turn electors off by the ten thousand; the political equivalent of the machine-gun corps in the First World War mowing down potential supporters.'*
THE INDEPENDENT, 6 MAY 2002

axe: to have an axe to grind
to have a secret motive, a personal stake in something

Benjamin Franklin is generally considered to be the originator of this phrase. His writings laid the groundwork for it, but the origin of the actual wording lies elsewhere. Franklin, like many comedians, preachers and writers, was happy to use a story on one occasion, and then re-work it to a rather different end on another. In 1784, writing an account of his life, he readily admitted to his difficulty in sorting his papers efficiently, and to relying on his memory instead. With advancing years, however, proper order had become more necessary, but even more difficult to achieve.

He illustrated his decision to settle for the second best of imperfectly ordered papers by the story of a man who wanted to have the whole surface of an axe he was buying ground as bright as the edge. The smith agreed, providing the man turned the wheel, on which the smith leaned heavily with the axe. This hard work caused the man to compromise on a speckled axe, rather than a shiny one. Franklin concludes: *And I believe this may have been the case with many, who…have given up the struggle, and concluded that 'a speckled ax was best'.*

Franklin, a journalist in his early career, also wrote a story entitled 'Too Much For Your Whistle'. It contains a similar account of a young man who wants his whole axe as shiny as the cutting edge. The smith agrees to do it, providing the young man turns the grindstone. This time, the moral Franklin draws is that of taking on more than one can cope with.

There is no mention of the specific phrase *to have an axe to grind* in either version of Franklin's story. Instead the idiom originates in *Who'll Turn the Grindstone?*, a reminiscence by Charles Miner, which bears startling similarities to Franklin's tale. Miner was the editor of *The Gleaner and Luzerne Federalist* in Wilkes-Barre, Pennsylvania. In the publication of 7 September 1810, he recounts how he was flattered into turning the grindstone for a man wanting to sharpen his axe. The tale continues:

Tickled with the flattery, like a little fool, I went to work, and bitterly did I rue the day. It was a new axe, and I toiled and tugged, till I was almost tired to death. The school bell rung, and I could not get away; my hands were blistered and it was not half ground. At length, however, the axe was sharpened, and the man turned to me with, 'Now, you little rascal, you've played the truant – scud to school, or you'll rue it.' Alas, thought I, it was hard enough to turn the grindstone, this cold day; but now to be called 'little rascal' was too much. It sunk deep in my mind, and often I have thought of it since.

The experience sowed seeds of suspicion in Miner's mind; he ends his anecdote thus: *When I see a merchant, over polite to his customers – begging them to taste a little brandy, and throwing half his goods on the counter – thinks I, that man has an axe to grind.*

Honourable Members of Parliament are, as we know, honourable…They promise that they will be as open as possible with us, the people who voted them into power. We will

always be told when an honourable member **has an axe to grind***. If he or she seems particularly keen on promoting the interests of widget manufacturers, then we will at least know why: the MP concerned will have declared that he or she is a paid consultant to the British Widget-Makers' Association.*
EVENING STANDARD,
18 NOVEMBER 2001

Needless to say, in providing these neat contrasts, the programme may have been **grinding an axe** *of its own... For my money, it made a suitably strong case that 11 is too early an age to have your future prospects mapped out.*
THE DAILY TELEGRAPH, 2 MARCH 2005

For other idioms drawn from literature, see page 319.

· B ·

backroom boys

researchers, scientists, etc, whose hard work is essential but is not brought to public notice

The phrase was coined by Lord Beaverbrook, then British Minister for Aircraft Production, in a speech given on 24 March 1941 in honour of the 'unsung heroes' of the war effort: *To whom must praise be given? I will tell you. It is the boys in the back room. They do not sit in the limelight but they are the men who do the work.*

*Excitingly, it was up to some **backroom boys** in a lab somewhere in leafy Berkshire to find the key to the mystery – not a submarine collision at all, according to the seismologists, but a small internal explosion of hydrogen peroxide that triggered a fire that set off the Kursk's huge arsenal of torpedoes.*
THE GUARDIAN, 9 AUGUST 2001

*And a word for the **backroom boys**. The ring crew are so good you won't notice them and the production values are as spot-on as any theatre could deliver – excellent lighting, split-second sound cues and all the rest.*
BIRMINGHAM POST, 2 AUGUST 2004

For other idioms derived from the army and warfare, see page 317.

bacon: to bring home the bacon

to earn enough to support oneself and one's family; to succeed in something

Two possibilities are suggested as origins of this idiom.

The first proposes a connection with the Dunmow Flitch, a side of bacon awarded to any couple from any part of England who could humbly kneel on two stones by the church door in Great Dunmow, Essex, and swear that for twelve months and a day they had never had a household brawl or wished themselves unmarried. The bacon was not easy to win. The great fourteenth-century writer William Langland noted in *Piers Plowman* that many lied about their state of marital harmony, and:

> *Though they go to Dunmow*
> *(Unless the devil help them)*
> *To try for the flitch*
> *They will never steal it...*

And Matthew Prior remarked that *Few married folk peck Dunmow-bacon* (*Turtle and Sparrow*, 1708). Between 1244 and 1772 only eight flitches were awarded. The custom still takes place every four years, contestants appearing before a jury of six bachelors and six spinsters and the winners being carried shoulder-high through the town by local residents dressed in peasants' smocks.

Delightful as this story is, records of the idiom date back only as far as the 1920s and the second etymology is more likely. This concerns the sport, popular at country fairs, of catching a greased pig. The winner kept the pig as the prize and so successfully *brought home the bacon*.

*All our research shows that men don't like commercials where they **bring home the bacon** and the stay-at-home woman cooks the tea.*
THE GUARDIAN, 28 MAY 2000

*Last fall, Olivia waddled into bookstores and the world swooned. Her debut earned Ian Falconer a Caldecott Honor, and the book sold like hotcakes. A mere 12 months later, Falconer has rushed his piggy back to market with 'Olivia Saves the Circus.' Despite the haste, he **brings home the bacon**. What a delightful book! The text is droll, the story charming, the pictures marvelous.*
NEW YORK TIMES, 18 NOVEMBER 2001

*In 23-year-old Jamie Lyon, Millward has procured the services of a powerhouse centre who will go some way to help the Saints **bring home the bacon** this season. Along with skipper Paul Sculthorpe and emerging talents James Graham and James Roby, the former Parramatta player will help eradicate the memory of last year's paltry fifth-place finish.*
LIVERPOOL ECHO, 11 FEBRUARY 2005

bacon: to save one's bacon
narrowly to escape injury or difficulty

Brewer hazards a guess that the idiom refers to the need to preserve bacon stocks from the household dogs during the hard winter months, thus guarding against starvation. A more scholarly approach is the explanation that the English words *bacon* and *back* probably share the same Germanic root, bacon being meat taken from the back and sides of the pig. From this linguistic base some argue that the *bacon* in the idiom is really a corruption of the Old English word *bæc*, 'back', while others maintain that, when it came into English in the fourteenth century, the word *bacoun* was applied first to the pig's carcase and then by extension to the human body.

The problem here is that there is no written evidence of either interpretation before the appearance of the idiom around the middle of the seventeenth century. What *bacon* had come to mean by that time, however, was 'a thief's booty'. The term is recorded as slang in *Dictionary of the Canting Crew* (c. 1698) and again in *A New Canting Dictionary* (1725), where the entry reads:

Bacon: in the Canting Sense is the Prize, of whatever kind, which Robbers make in their Enterprizes. He has saved his Bacon; i.e., he has himself escap'd the Hue-and-Cry, and carry'd off his Prize to boot: Whence it is commonly us'd for any narrow Escape.

*Most of us are in jobs in which our occasional glaring clanger can be covered up or corrected by associates... It is why I am always grateful to Sportsmail's sharp-eyed sub-editors, who have **saved my bacon** more than thrice.*
DAILY MAIL, 21 AUGUST 2002

*He's on riotous form here as the servant Castano, who, in order to **save his bacon**, has to clamber into Dona Leonor's clothes.*
THE INDEPENDENT, 19 JULY 2004

bag and baggage
with all one's possessions

This was originally a military phrase denoting 'the baggage train, the entire property of an army, including the personal belongings of the individual soldiers'. In the fifteenth century any army that returned from war with *bag and baggage* had waged a successful campaign: none of its property had fallen into enemy hands. An issue of the *London Gazette* newspaper for 1667 captured the spirit of the phrase when it spoke of an army leaving *Upon honorable conditions, marching off with Bag and Baggage, Drums beating, Colors flying.*

Later, Shakespeare played with the phrase in *As You Like It* (1599) where Touchstone says: *Come, shepherd, let us make an honourable retreat; though not with bag and baggage, yet with scrip and scrippage* – scrip and scrippage referring to 'the purse and its contents'.

The seventeenth century also saw the first instances of the phrase being used to describe less commendable departures, military or otherwise, tainted with the sense of 'good riddance'; and that is the tone the idiom carries today.

*In the 17th century the Turks were barely stopped from taking Vienna. But soon it was much more the turn of Western expansionism to push Eastwards. North Africa fell under the domination of France; France and Britain competed for Egypt; the Turk was bundled, **bag and baggage**, out of Europe, and Turkey was declared a Sick Man...*
THE SPECTATOR, 27 OCTOBER 2001

*If these relationships were silly indiscretions and you both want to put them behind you, I suggest you move **bag and baggage** to Spain for one year, learn Spanish, study or work for charity, make a grown person's life rather than subscribing to the critically immature belief that you can have everything.*
THE INDEPENDENT, 10 APRIL 2004

For other idioms derived from the army and warfare, see page 317.

bag: in the bag
virtually guaranteed; victory or success assured

The *bag* in the idiom is the *game bag* used to collect small game – rabbits or birds for instance – on hunting trips. The figurative application of the phrase to the virtual certainty of success arose in America in the first half of the twentieth century.

During the nineteenth century when British hunters in the colonies were shooting quantities of big game, *bag* came to refer not to the contents of the game bag but to the total produce of a day's shooting. It is from this that the slang term *bags* to mean 'much', 'many' or 'plenty' – as in *he has bags of confidence* – originated.

*Peers vote on the bill tomorrow and supporters of an outright ban believe they already have more than 100 votes **in the bag** to support a clause sponsored by a group of anti-smacking peers and the Bishop of Portsmouth, which would give children the same protection from assault as adults.*
THE GUARDIAN, 4 JULY 2004

Chelsea captain John Terry refused to accept the Premiership trophy is headed towards Stamford Bridge despite the Blues extending their lead at the top of the table with the win over Albion.
*'It is not **in the bag** – there is still a long way to go,' said Terry. 'Manchester United are pushing us all the way. We still need a few wins.'*
BIRMINGHAM EVENING MAIL,
16 MARCH 2005

baker's dozen, a
not twelve but thirteen

The first, quite plausible suggestion for *baker's dozen* claims that bakers, when not selling direct to the public, would include a thirteenth loaf with every batch of twelve. This constituted the middleman's profit. However, most authorities, together with the Worshipful Company of Bakers in London, say that the phrase arose from a piece of thirteenth-century legislation, the Assize of Bread and Ale of 1262. Bakers of the period had a reputation for selling underweight loaves and so strict regulations were introduced to fix a standard weight. A spell in the pillory could be expected if short weight were given. To avoid this, bakers started to give an extra piece of bread away with every loaf (the *in-bread*) and a thirteenth loaf away with every dozen (the *vantage loaf*).

Such was the medieval baker's unpopularity that he became the subject of a traditional puppet play in which he was shown being hurried into the flames of hell by the devil for keeping the price of bread high and giving short weight. Despite the long history of this practice, it is only as late as 1599 that the phrase itself is first recorded.

The Chartered Institute of Taxation was recently asked to identify a dozen important tax dates for small businessmen and women. Not wishing to appear ungenerous, we came up with **a baker's dozen**.
THE INDEPENDENT, 29 JANUARY 2002

A baker's dozen of top cops, charged with stopping anti-social behaviour, were paraded by Durham Police. The 13 police inspectors are spearheading the Durham force's major campaign against anti-social behaviour and disorder.
NEWCASTLE EVENING CHRONICLE,
15 NOVEMBER 2003

balloon: (when) the balloon goes up

(when) the trouble/excitement/action is about to begin

This informal British phrase refers to the observation balloons used in the First World War. The sight of a balloon going up was the first visible sign of an impending action. The Royal Navy, on its website, claims the expression to be of naval origin, but it also applied to the artillery in the trenches. The phrase passed into civilian speech soon after the war and usage was doubtless reinforced during the Second World War when barrage balloons, hauled up to impede the passage of low-flying enemy

aircraft, alerted the population to an imminent air-raid.

Peter Oxley, the leading British bow-maker, is more forthcoming. If **the balloon goes up**, *he says, it will happen in late 2002, when the Convention on International Trade in Endangered Species puts pernambuco into a category that makes its import illegal in Europe.*
THE INDEPENDENT, 27 OCTOBER 2000

So look for North Korea to commence reprocessing plutonium at its Yongbyon plant **as soon as the balloon goes up** *in Iraq and to provoke incidents along its borders in the hope of reaping American hostages.*
TIME INTERNATIONAL, 24 MARCH 2003

For other idioms derived from the army and warfare, see page 317.

bandwagon: to climb/hop/jump on the bandwagon

to support a cause or enterprise that looks as if it will succeed, often for personal profit or advantage

Dan Rice (1823–1901) was a touring clown at the time of the American Civil War whose act included humorous comment and topical songs about political and current affairs. Whenever Rice and his troupe came to town they would parade through the streets, Rice the showman aboard the circus bandwagon. The story goes that on one occasion in Baton Rouge, Louisiana, in 1848, Rice invited Zachary Taylor, his preferred presidential candidate, to join him on his bandwagon to promote his campaign. The blend of razzmatazz and politics proved a winning formula: Taylor, known as Old Rough and Ready, won the election the following year.

From then on, parades with a bandwagon were a regular feature in election campaigns, particularly in the southern

States. The candidate would be up there with the band and, as the excitement mounted, he would be joined by local politicians pledging support and taking advantage of the publicity.

The practice dates back to the mid-1800s, and by the last decades of the century *to get aboard the bandwagon* was in use as a metaphor for a political campaign. Theodore Roosevelt uses it thus in a letter of 1899. A few years later the expression described the second presidential campaign of William Jennings Bryan.

The term *bandwagon* now also stands alone to denote 'a party or cause that attracts increasing numbers of supporters'.

Following the success of the Mirror's *3 a.m. girls column, the* Guardian *has decided* **to jump on the bandwagon** *with a blatant copy.*
THE GUARDIAN, 8 FEBRUARY 2002

But Harry Potter is a phenomenon in itself – it hasn't set a trend that others can easily follow. The danger of publishers encouraging writers **to jump on a bandwagon** *is that they end up killing the genre.*
GOOD HOUSEKEEPING, JULY 2002

John Prescott, the Deputy Prime Minister, said the toughest decision the Conservative leader faced each day was '**which bandwagon to jump on** *once he gets out of bed'.*
THE DAILY TELEGRAPH, 25 MARCH 2005

bandy: to bandy words with someone
to wrangle, to argue with someone

In *Pierce Penniless, His Supplication to the Divell* (1592) satirist Thomas Nashe paints a picture of Hell where they *bandy balles of Brimstone at one anothers head*. *Bandy* in the sixteenth century meant 'to hit a ball back and forth' – in tennis, for example. Before long the term was being applied figuratively and

words and ideas were also being *bandied about*. Since ball games are often played with dogged determination, *to bandy words* doesn't just mean 'to exchange reproaches' but 'to argue obstinately'.

During the seventeenth century a game evolved in Ireland which involved striking a ball to and fro with a curved stick. This precursor of hockey was known as *bandy* because of the way that the ball was *bandied about*. Thereafter people with bowed legs came to be described as *bandy-legged* or *bandy*, the shape of their legs being reminiscent of the curved bandy stick.

Let's not **bandy words**, *this crime was committed by terrorists, murderers, cowards who use the Muslim faith to hide behind.*
SOUTH WALES ECHO, 19 SEPTEMBER 2001

…it may not be wise **to bandy words** *with Syed, a veritable Jeremy Paxman with a western shake-hands grip.*
THE INDEPENDENT, 2 AUGUST 2002

He's turned back into an indispensable pillar of the team, speeding up England, slowing down the opposition at the same time, and still finding the energy **to bandy words** *with the referee.*
THE GUARDIAN, 31 MARCH 2003

baptism of fire, a
a harsh initiation into a new experience

Baptism by fire originally meant 'martyrdom', specifically that achieved by Christian believers who were burnt at the stake for their faith. The phrase took an equally unpleasant twist during the nineteenth century when the French used *baptême de feu* to denote a soldier's first experience of enemy fire. According to his Irish physician, Barry O'Meara, Napoleon used it as he reflected on his life and government while in exile on St Helena in 1817: *I love a brave soldier who has undergone le baptême du fer* [sic], *whatever nation he may belong to* (*Napoleon in Exile*, 1822). (The substitution of *fer*, 'iron', for *feu*, 'fire', here was possibly O'Meara's error.)

Napoleon's 'brave soldier' was often a young one: during the Franco–Prussian war of 1870, Napoleon III sent his fourteen-year-old son into battle at Saarbruck. *Louis has just received his baptism of fire,* the Emperor wrote to his wife Eugénie when the lad came back safe and sound. There is a poignant end to the tale. Napoleon III was defeated and captured soon afterwards and, on his release, came to England with his family. His son joined the British army and died fighting the Zulus at the still tender age of twenty-two.

The phrase continues to be used in military contexts for a soldier's first experience of hostile fire or for a regiment's first engagement with the enemy, but now also much more widely for any demanding initiation.

Jonathan Kaplan describes both the honour and the horror of a surgeon's work – and recalls his **baptism of fire** *after a police attack on a South African township.*
THE SUNDAY TELEGRAPH,
9 SEPTEMBER 2001

The night we opened Sitting Pretty *at the Nuffield Theatre, Southampton, was the night of the terrorist attacks in America… My daughter, Amy, who wrote* Sitting Pretty, *couldn't have had more of* **a baptism of fire** *to start her career in the theatre.*
MAUREEN LIPMAN IN GOOD
HOUSEKEEPING, JANUARY 2002

For more on Napoleon, see *to* BEAT *a retreat* and *to meet one's* WATERLOO. For other idioms derived from the army and warfare, see page 317.

bargepole: wouldn't touch it with a bargepole
used of someone or something one loathes or distrusts, from which one wants to keep one's distance

Without a payre of tongs no man will touch her, protested an unknown author in the seventeenth century (*Wit Restor'd*, 1658), and in the mid-nineteenth century Dickens wrote: *I was so ragged and dirty that you wouldn't have touched me with a pair of tongs* (*Hard Times*, 1854). This was the original expression and the allusion is clear: tongs are used to pick up objects which are dirty or potentially harmful. Our present-day variant, *wouldn't touch it with a bargepole*, is much more recent, originating from the end of the nineteenth century. A bargepole is the very long pole used for propelling a barge along a canal and the idiom emphasises one's detestation for someone or something by the desire to keep them or it at a great distance.

Diseased Belgian chickens and soiled French nappies are the sort of things most people **wouldn't touch with a bargepole**, *but the world's cement makers can't wait to get their hands on them.*
THE INDEPENDENT, 22 OCTOBER 2000

As far as I'm concerned, chintz as soft furnishing joins tapestry ottomans in the **Don't Touch With A Bargepole** *class.*
GOOD HOUSEKEEPING,
SEPTEMBER 2002

bark: to bark up the wrong tree
to follow a wrong line of enquiry

This is a nineteenth-century American phrase from raccoon hunting. Raccoons were hunted at night because of their nocturnal habits. Hunting dogs chased the quarry up a tree and then waited down below barking until the huntsman arrived with his gun. A dog who mistook the tree in the darkness, or was outwitted by the prey scrambling across to an adjacent tree, wasted time and energy barking up the wrong one: *He reminded me of the meanest thing on God's earth, an old coon dog, barking up the wrong tree* (Davy Crockett, *Sketches and Eccentricities*, 1833). The idiom itself dates back to at least the early 1830s and, during the 1940s' vogue for crime fiction, was worked to death on both sides of the Atlantic.

*The Government may be **barking up the wrong tree** by trying to attract more men into primary teaching, according to new research. One study shows that children's security at home, not the sex of their teacher, determines their early achievement at school.*
THE TIMES EDUCATIONAL SUPPLEMENT, 28 SEPTEMBER 2001

*Which leads us to the question of which language is the most useful to learn. Leo might be **barking up the wrong tree** with French. Spanish is now the fastest growing tongue on earth and is set to overtake English. It is the official language of 20 countries and 11% of Americans now speak it as their first language.*
THE GUARDIAN, 5 DECEMBER 2001

barrel: over a barrel
helpless to act, at the mercy of others

At one time a person who had almost drowned would be draped, face down, *over a barrel*, the head lower than the rest of the body, until all the water had drained from the lungs. This happens, for instance, to a certain Dan Grin, following a canoeing accident in H Irving Hancock's *The High School Boys' Canoe Club* (1912): *By the time Dalzell had been hustled ashore the barrel was in readiness. Dan received an energetic rolling. Three or four little gushes of water issued from his mouth.*

Dan was, of course, in no fit state to act for himself and was totally dependent on his rescuers. And this is the theory for the phrase's origin advanced by the OED. But forcing someone to lie *over a barrel* has also been a form of punishment or humiliation over the years, sometimes as a means of holding a victim down for a flogging. The sense of the idiom, that of a victim at the mercy of others, is better explained by the latter. The phrase dates from the late nineteenth century.

*Complications remain, however. The French and, to a lesser extent, the Germans are playing it tough, aware that they have Bush **over a barrel**, British sources say. 'They can squeeze more concessions out of Bush at the moment and they know it,' one source said.*
THE OBSERVER, 7 SEPTEMBER 2003

*One analyst said: 'Jarvis is in a right mess. If you are a subcontractor, you'd only work for Jarvis if they pay you upfront and the clients have got them **over a barrel**, refusing to pay until they are completely satisfied with their work. So they've got no cash flow.'*
THE DAILY TELEGRAPH, 24 MAY 2005

basket case, a
an infirm person, one unable to care for himself; a lost cause

This slang expression originated with the United States army during the First World War and referred to a soldier who had had both arms and legs amputated. The 'basket' was the wickerwork wheelchair in which he sat. The term is no longer confined to the physically disabled but also describes those with emotional or mental instability. Since the early 1980s it has frequently been applied to politicians, companies, institutions or even countries that have ceased to function as they should.

Even if he weren't who he is, [Prince]
William would turn heads and break hearts.
But, given his uniquely storm-tossed life so
far, and the fragile, mildly depressive psycho-
profile of both his parents, it seems a miracle
that he isn't a gibbering basket-case.
THE OBSERVER, 4 JUNE 2000

It is not our fault that Africa is a basket
case. It is far too late to blame colonialism,
not when you compare the post-war
economic performances of, say, Malaysia
and Ghana.
THE DAILY TELEGRAPH,
24 JANUARY 2002

For other idioms derived from the
army and warfare, see page 317.

batten: to batten down the hatches
to prepare for trouble

When a storm was imminent, sailors
would cover the ship's hatches with
tarpaulin secured at the edges by
battens of wood. The nautical phrase
dates from the early nineteenth
century and passed into general use in
the late 1800s.

The clocks have yet to go back, but the
seasons move on and while autumn
continues to be windswept and raw, winter
will be more so and there is every excuse
now to batten down the hatches and pile
up the logs round the hearth.
THE GUARDIAN, 17 SEPTEMBER 2001

WIRELESS SCRAMBLES TO
BATTEN DOWN THE HATCHES
Defending Wi-Fi networks against hackers
and freeloaders has some IT guys pining for
good, old-fashioned wires.
FORTUNE, 4 OCTOBER 2004

For other nautical idioms, see A LIFE
ON THE OCEAN WAVES, page 24.

battle royal, a
a free-for-all, a general quarrel

From the fifteenth century, the adjective
royal was applied to military nouns
(joust, siege, war, etc) to give the sense
'done on a great scale'. *Battle royal* was
used particularly in the now outlawed
sport of cockfighting to describe a contest where a large number of birds were
pitted against each other until a victor
remained. In the second half of the seventeenth century it began to be used
figuratively to mean 'a general quarrel'.

A lobbying battle royal is shaping up in
Washington over what could be one of the
decade's biggest overseas contracts for a
U.S. defense firm.
TIME, 14 AUGUST 2000

'People will not tolerate a two-tier system.
I am sure there is a battle royal going on
between the different interest groups now in
Downing Street.'
THE INDEPENDENT, 18 JANUARY 2003

bay: to keep something/ someone at bay
to keep something/someone out, at a
safe distance

The Old French verb *abaiier* is the source
of the English *to bay* which describes the
continuous howling of hunting hounds
in pursuit. The *-bai-* sound in the word is
probably imitative of that cry. From this
verb comes the Old French *abai*, borrowed into English in the early
fourteenth century as *at bay*, which
referred to the moment when a hunted
animal was finally cornered or wearied
and turned to face the hounds: *Yonder*
stagge is almoste yelden, I here the houndes
holde hym at a beye (John Palsgrave,
Lesclarcissement de la langue francoyse,
1530). At this point the stag is both *at*
bay itself and also holds the dogs *at bay*.
   Only a few years later this ambiguity of sense in hunting contexts was

used more widely. *Foxe's Book of Martyrs* (1553–87) has: *Whereat the Chancellor was much offended: but Bradford still kept him at the bay* (Bradford was fending off the angry Chancellor). Conversely Tomson's translation (1579) of Calvin's *Sermons on Timothy* has: *He shall be sette uppon on all sides, they make a bay at him* (the victim has been cornered). This ambiguity of sense has been resolved subsequently, in that the predominant general meaning is 'to maintain at a distance'.

*Like many older women I was also worried about the onset of conditions such as osteoporosis and rheumatism. It's great to get specific exercise advice on how **to keep these at bay**.*
ESPORTA NEWS, SUMMER 2001

*An alarmingly large number of my crop of unsolicited emails come from the very undergraduates I did my best to avoid during their time at university. But whereas they could then be **kept at bay** by a locked door, now they can electronically burst into my office at will and regale me with crudely critical accounts of the irrelevance of my courses to their present employment.*
THE TIMES HIGHER EDUCATION SUPPLEMENT, 13 FEBRUARY 2004

*But sexism is hard to **keep at bay** if a candidate is happy to be described as, say, 'Britain's leading woman mycologist' and pontificate on the dangers of eating magic mushrooms.*
THE TIMES HIGHER EDUCATION SUPPLEMENT, 5 MARCH 2004

beam: broad in the beam
having wide hips

The width of a ship was measured at the beam, one which was *broad in the beam* being particularly wide. The phrase was put to unflattering use from the early twentieth century to describe a person with ample hips.

*The average European may be surprised to find a US city with such trim-looking and healthy citizens as those of Denver. Don't expect, as you board a bus or go into a bar, to see a wide variety of shapes and sizes. In this town, very few people are **broad in the beam**.*
THE GUARDIAN, 16 OCTOBER 2001

*Chronic lack of sleep could be one reason people in the United States are getting so **broad in the beam**, suggest the authors of two new studies. Their research found that going without sleep seems to elevate blood levels of a key appetite-stimulating hormone, ghrelin. It causes levels of a 'stop eating!' hormone, known as leptin, to drop. The likely net effect is an increase in appetite.*
CHARLOTTE OBSERVER, 10 JANUARY 2005

See also on one's beam ends. For other nautical idioms, see A LIFE ON THE OCEAN WAVES, page 24.

beam: on one's beam ends
in a difficult financial position; in a predicament

In a wooden sailing ship *the beams* were the vast cross-timbers which spanned the width of the vessel to hold the ship together and to support the deck. So, if a ship were *on its beam ends*, it was listing at a dangerous angle, almost on its side. The sense of a ship being in this alarming state transfers to a person in financial jeopardy.

*My accent gave me away as a bit of a toff and, therefore, an easy mark. On the plus side, I was not desperate for money, unlike most of the players up there, playing **off their beam-ends**.*
THE INDEPENDENT, 21 OCTOBER 2000

*And yet, without Middle East oil, the US economy would be **on its beam ends**, as would other energy-hungry Western economies.*
THE SCOTSMAN, 12 SEPTEMBER 2001

See also *broad in the* BEAM. For other nautical idioms, see A LIFE ON THE OCEAN WAVES, page 24.

beanfeast, a
a celebration

In past centuries it was customary for employers to hold a dinner, a *beanfeast*, for their workers once a year. Opinions differ as to what was on the menu. One authority suggests it was a *bean goose* (the bird's name coming from a bean-shaped mark on its beak) and others that copious quantities of beans supplemented the fare. An account of the occasion in an 1805 issue of the *Sporting Magazine* speaks of a table *groaning with bacon* while a text written in the 1870s states that beans were *an indispensable dish*. Whatever the feast consisted of, it was a rowdy and somewhat vulgar occasion but much looked forward to throughout the year.

An older term for an entertainment of this kind, which dates from the second half of the seventeenth century, was *waygoose*, whose origins are equally perplexing. A waygoose was a festivity offered by the master-printer to his workforce and took place towards the end of August when the season of working by candlelight was about to begin. The term was common until the end of the nineteenth century but gradually lost out to *beanfeast*, which the printers abbreviated to *beano*, also meaning 'a spree'. This shortened form had a considerable vogue in the 1920s and '30s: *This was news to me, that Bicky's uncle was a duke. Rum, how little one knows about one's pals! I had met Bicky for the first time at a species of beano or jamboree down in Washington Square, not long after my arrival in New York* (P G Wodehouse, *My Man Jeeves*, 1919).

Traditionally, City spending sprees happen around one of three events: the signing of a big deal with a client, the successful completion of a mega-money event such as a flotation or buyout, or the payment of an annual bonus.

*Of these, the client **beanfeasts** tend to be more sedate affairs, because the client may not be too impressed by excess – drunken or monetary – being paid for out of their fees.*
THE GUARDIAN, 10 JULY 2001

The Federal Communications Commission, has brought in a suite of new regulations intended to address the new problems posed by reality TV... Temptation Island... features 'couples who are at a crossroads in their relationship' on a romantic holiday island. They are set up with dates with single men and women whilst the audience waits for the 'holiday romance bonking' to begin. Injury (if not divorce) seems inevitable.

*Can you really consent to such an injury is a question the courts will undoubtedly wrestle with soon after the couples err rather than later. Whatever the outcome, a **beanfeast** for lawyers seems assured.*
THE TIMES, 24 JULY 2001

beans: full of beans
in high spirits, in the peak of condition

This is a horsey idiom, originally a piece of nineteenth-century stable slang referring to the condition and liveliness of a horse fed on beans. It was an effect that the Romans were well aware of. As to the beans themselves, they are variously called horse beans or field beans or broad beans, but are all seeds of the species *Vicia faba*.

*However, when I met him he was **full of beans**. He laughed, joked and answered questions from all sides with enthusiasm.*
EVENING STANDARD,
7 FEBRUARY 2002

*It felt almost impertinent to watch as the Scot, so **full of beans** the day before, was reduced to a grim acceptance of his lot. Another year, and another chance lost.*
DAILY MAIL, 22 JULY 2002

For other horsey idioms see page 319.

beans: to spill the beans

to let out a secret, to disclose confidential information

This idiom originated in America in the second decade of the twentieth century. Its origin is obscure but the expression may be cobbled together from other bits of US slang. The verb *to spill* meaning 'to divulge facts' had come into use in the previous decade. *Beans*, on the other hand, occurs in the earlier phrase *to know beans*, meaning 'to be well-informed'. Thus *to spill the beans* means 'to disclose confidential information'.

Mark my words: that hussy Siobhan Hathaway is going to topple the wisteria-covered pillows of Home Farm with the same catastrophic consequences as Electra wreaked on the house of Agamemnon. Any minute now she's going **to spill the beans** *to Elizabeth Pargetter, who has been trying to winkle the information out of her for weeks.*
THE OBSERVER, 5 MAY 2002

We all know that Diana was hardly sparing with her affections but the reason her lovers are not all queuing up **to spill the beans** *on CNN is that they are surgeons and art dealers, not jobless, friendless and desperate for a leg-up.*
EVENING STANDARD, 10 JANUARY 2003

There was a fascinating exposé in one of the Sunday newspapers last weekend, revealing that MPs have been claiming tax credits targeted at hard-up families, despite their salaries of almost £60,000…the whistle-blower is Liberal Democrat MP, Steve Webb…When I called Webb yesterday, he refused to elaborate. 'I don't talk about my personal finances as a matter of principle.'
Unless, it seems, he is guaranteed anonymity by a newspaper before **spilling the beans**.
THE DAILY TELEGRAPH, 30 JUNE 2005

beat: to beat a (hasty) retreat

to leave, usually in a hurry; to suddenly abandon an undertaking

Drums were once very much a part of the war machine as soldiers on the battlefield took their orders from its beat. *Retreat* was one such order used to recall an army facing defeat or, tactically, to avoid an encounter. However, the earliest examples of this military phrase have *to blow* or *sound the retreat*, showing that the command was formerly given by bugle. It appears thus in *The Bruce* (1375), an epic work by the Scottish poet John Barbour.

Idiomatic use of the phrase *to beat a retreat* dates from around the middle of the nineteenth century.

The door opens and this larger-than-life character emerges, clad in a skimpy towel and a beaming smile, carrying a glass of champagne. He has had a last-minute change of plan and stayed in London after all. Would we like to join him for a massage? The invitation is sincere but we **beat a hasty retreat**.
THE SUNDAY TELEGRAPH,
9 SEPTEMBER 2001

Then the team **beat a retreat** *– Number One Liberty Plaza, came the warning, was about to fall on top of them.*
THE OBSERVER, 16 SEPTEMBER 2001

But in fact my lowest point came one day soon after [the triplets] had started to crawl. I misjudged someone's tears and took too long to settle them, so the others kicked off. Round went the deafening screams all afternoon… Because they could crawl, I couldn't even **beat a retreat** *to the bedroom.*
GOOD HOUSEKEEPING, MARCH 2002

For other idioms derived from the army and warfare, see page 317.

A life on the ocean waves

Each kind and area of human activity has its own vocabulary of words, metaphors and idioms. Sportsmen, musicians, agricultural workers, managers, lawyers, sailors, all have terms peculiar to themselves to describe their own particular domain of interest. Some of their expressions find a wider use in analogous but non-specialist situations; the farmer talks of life in general in terms of farming and the sportsman in terms of training, racing and winning. Similarly, the seaman uses his nautical vocabulary to describe the problems he comes across ashore. The most striking or useful of these images and phrases from the subgroups are often taken up by the general population, and so new fixed expressions join the standard language. PACKING A PUNCH (page 45) and IT'S NOT CRICKET (page 252) look at how sport has enriched the general stock of idioms.

Britain is an island, a seafaring nation. It is not surprising, therefore, that over the centuries nautical terms and the parlance of sailors have been absorbed into everyday, idiomatic English. *To trim the sails by, on* or *to the wind*, for instance, has meant 'to adjust a ship's sails in order to take best advantage of the wind' since at least the first half of the seventeenth century. Used figuratively since the early nineteenth century *to trim one's sails (to the wind)* means 'to adapt to circumstances'. *Aloof* is another nautical term, probably of Dutch origin (the Dutch were another great seafaring nation). It was borrowed into English maritime vocabulary in the sixteenth century as a command to steer the ship into the wind. The now obsolete order from the captain meant that the ship did not drift before the wind, and so steered clear of danger. Hence the figurative phrase *to stand, keep aloof*, meaning 'to keep one's distance, to refuse to join in', which came into use in the late sixteenth century. *I stand aloofe*, says Shakespeare's Hamlet (1604), *and will no reconcilement*.

Some nautical phrases come from life on board ship – *to* PIPE *down*, for instance. Others, such as *tell it to the* MARINES (I don't believe you) or *three* SHEETS *to the wind* (drunk), are sailors' cant.

There follows a list of just a few of the nautical idioms in common use, some described in this book, others not. Some of the terms in the list are clearly nautical metaphors; others' maritime origins are genuine but not superficially obvious. The dates refer to their earliest idiomatic use beyond a nautical context.

taken ABACK C19	astounded, nonplussed
to BATTEN *down the hatches* late C19	to prepare for a difficult time
broad in the BEAM early C20	wide in the hips
to be on one's BEAM *ends* C19	to be hard up
to give a wide BERTH C19	to avoid close contact
to the BITTER *end* mid C19	to the very end of endurance
to go by the BOARD mid C19	to be discarded, neglected
CHOCK-A-BLOCK C19	full to bursting, wedged in close
to be at CLOSE *quarters* C20	to be very close

beat: to beat a path to someone's door

to seek someone out, as an expert or authority

This expression comes from what is known as 'the mouse-trap quotation', attributed to American philosopher and poet Ralph Waldo Emerson. The question is, did he actually say it, or just something rather like it?

In 1871 Emerson gave a lecture in Oakland, California. In the audience

COPPER-*bottomed* C19	guaranteed
to CUT *and run* C19	to abandon a project, to run away
the CUT *of someone's jib* early C19	a person's character (and appearance)
between the DEVIL *and the deep blue sea* C17	caught between two difficulties
HAND *over fist* C19	swift progress
HARD *and fast* C19	inflexible (of a regulation, etc)
to be left HIGH *and dry* C19	to be stranded, left out
in the OFFING C18	to be imminent
tell it to the MARINES C19	I don't believe you
PLAIN *sailing* C19	uncomplicated, easy
to know/learn the ROPES C19	to know exactly how to do something
three SHEETS *to the wind* C19	very drunk
(all) SHIPSHAPE *and Bristol fashion* C19	neat and tidy
to SHOW *a leg* mid C19	get up
all at sea C18	uncertain, perplexed (after a ship that has lost its bearings)
to bear down upon early C18	to advance with determination towards
to cut adrift mid C18	to abandon to fate
in deep water C19	in trouble
first rate C17	among the best (from the rating of warships according to size and number of guns)
to forge ahead C19	to make swift progress
to keep one's weather eye open C19	to keep alert, on the lookout
to make headway C19	to make progress
to make (up) leeway C19	to endeavour, to make up lost time
to put one's oar in C17	to meddle
to sail close to the wind C19	to risk moral error or offence
in the same boat C19	in similar circumstances
to see how the land lies C17	to assess the state of affairs
to steer clear of C18	to stay well away from
to take the wind out of someone's sails early C19	to halt someone's progress
in the wake of early C19	following close behind
to weather the storm late C18	to come through difficult experiences/times

Extensive though this list is, it is by no means comprehensive. Clearly the influence on the national culture and language from this source is very pervasive, rivalling that of the Bible and Shakespeare (see the list of Idioms from the Bible, page 317, Idioms from Shakespeare, page 320, and the boxes on WILLIAM TYNDALE, page 270, and WILLIAM SHAKESPEARE, page 154).

was a Mrs Sarah Yule who afterwards made notes on what she had heard. Many years later, in 1889, Mrs Yule, together with other ladies of the First Unitarian Church of Oakland, published a little book entitled *Borrowings* which they sold to raise money for church funds. One of Mrs Yule's contributions was the following, which she attributed to Emerson: *If a man can write a better book, preach a better sermon, or make a better mouse-trap, than his neighbour, though he builds his house in the woods, the world will make a beaten path to his door.*

Were these Emerson's words, in no way corrupted by Mrs Yule's jottings or memory? Enthusiasts scoured Emerson's works in vain for the exact phrasing but found only the same notion differently expressed in a journal of 1855: *I trust a great deal to common fame, as we all must. If a man has good corn, or wood…or can make better chairs or knives, crucibles, or church organs, than anybody else, you will find a broad, hard-beaten road to his house, though it be in the woods.* Nevertheless, it is the version from *Borrowings* that has produced the current idiom.

*Sadly, this inspirational building can find no organist, so the ever-resourceful incumbent has found a digital machine to accompany the singing. Let's hope an organist will soon **beat a path to his door**. This church cries out for real music.*
THE OBSERVER, 21 MAY 2000

*Her intelligence and charm were, without a doubt, one of the chief attractions for the astonishing numbers of the great who **beat a path to** Chelsea and the foremost intellectual London salon of the age, or perhaps any other.*
THE SPECTATOR, 26 JANUARY 2002

*I saw him being interviewed on TV this week and I think it's fair to say that Mensa won't be **beating a path to his door**.*
DAILY MAIL, 7 MARCH 2002

For other idioms drawn from literature, see page 319.

beat: to beat about the bush

to go about something in a roundabout way; to avoid coming to the point

In a hunt *beaters* are employed to thrash the bushes and undergrowth in order to frighten game from its cover. It is they who *beat about the bush*; the huntsman is more direct. In the words of George Gascoigne (1525–77) *He bet about the bush whyles others caught the birds.*

*'I've only got this season and next season at Old Trafford and I won't **beat about the bush** if I think the time is right to leave United or football.'*
THE OBSERVER, 2 SEPTEMBER 2001

*Those guys were influential. They didn't **beat around the bush**; they were straight down the line, and that's all you can ask for in a teacher.*
THE TIMES EDUCATIONAL SUPPLEMENT, 9 NOVEMBER 2001

*Let's not **beat about the bush**. Lisa Jewell is Enid Blyton for those who have progressed through Kirrin Island and Malory Towers and now go to Greenday concerts between episodes of Big Brother. She thinks the thoughts, talks the talk and her pulse beats to the same rhythms as modern, metropolitan, nice but trite everyperson.*
THE SPECTATOR, 12 JANUARY 2002

beat: to beat (someone) black and blue

to beat someone viciously until they are covered in bruises

The colours *blak* and *blae* have been coupled together since at least the beginning of the fourteenth century. *Blak* is straightforward enough. *Blae*, on the other hand, describes a blackish blue shade. *Blaeberry*, for instance, was an old name for the bilberry or whortleberry after the colour of its fruit. *Blae* was also descriptive of the human body when it was cold or bruised. A fourteenth-century text describes Christ's crucified body as *alle bla and blody*. Used together to describe livid bruising on the human body, *blak and blae* intensify one another, while the words roll easily off the tongue. Thus, even when *blae* became obsolete in the second half of the sixteenth century, the idiom was retained by adapting the term to the more familiar *blue*.

*Kershaw was also an aggressor, who, when he was not feeding Savitch cocaine, regularly **beat her black and blue**.*
THE GUARDIAN, 3 MARCH 2000

*All I could think was that I had to get down the mast, quickly… It was exhausting and I was **black and blue** when I reached the deck.*
GOOD HOUSEKEEPING, DECEMBER 2002

bed of roses, a

a pleasant place; an easy or untroubled existence

There is no rose…in garden, but there be sum thorne wrote the poet John Lydgate in the fifteenth century. Quite so; *a bed of roses* would seem far from comfortable or desirable. It must have been the rose's other qualities then, its fragrance, beauty and rich colour, which Christopher Marlowe's Passionate Shepherd (c 1593) had in mind when he told his love

And I will make thee beds of roses
And a thousand fragrant posies…

From the poetic imaginings of the lover, then, comes the phrase *bed of roses*, a delightful place to be. By the mid-seventeenth century, however, the expression was being used in a much more tetchy tone: *Think'st thou I lie on beds of roses here* wrote Dryden in *The Indian Emperour* (1665). And this is how the idiom is often used today, in a negative context with the sense that the situation, or life in general, is not easy: *Living at home with the parents is no bed of roses: moods have to be negotiated, and parents have to discover that they can learn from their children (The Guardian, 7 March 2001). Indulged children are often less able to cope with stress because their parents have*

*created an atmosphere where their whims are indulged, when they have always assumed that they're entitled and that life should be **a bed of roses**.*
THE OBSERVER, 5 AUGUST 2001

bee: as busy as a bee

very busy, industrious

Bees are never seen at rest: they are either gathering pollen or busily occupied with the hive. It is not surprising, therefore, that someone who is always working should be compared to this industrious insect. The earliest mention of the simile *busy as a bee* comes in Chaucer's Epilogue to *The Merchant's Tale* (1386), while in his *Second Nun's Tale* is the earliest reference to *a busy bee*, meaning 'an industrious person': *Lyk a bisy bee, with-outen gyle.*

Perhaps busy-ness, as well as cleanliness, is next to godliness. Isaac Watts, the great hymn writer of the first half of the eighteenth century certainly recognised the moral value of the busy bee:

How doth the little busy bee
Improve each shining hour,
And gather honey all the day
From every opening flower!

*My tentacles spread far and wide – checking on the menu, bossing the cook, keeping my beady eye on badly behaved guests (snack stealers and suchlike) and, in the evenings, re-writing all the promo material. I'm **busy as a bee** and loving every minute.*
THE OBSERVER, 16 SEPTEMBER 2001

*Idle hands never were a problem for Rosalee Blount. 'She was **busy as a bee**. She wouldn't ever sit down long enough to eat. She loved to be on the go,' said her granddaughter, Debbie Holman of Buford.*
ATLANTA JOURNAL AND CONSTITUTION, 18 AUGUST 2004

See ALLITERATIVE SIMILES, page 237.

bee: to have a bee in one's bonnet

to be obsessed by an idea

Back in the early sixteenth century someone in the grip of an eccentric fancy was said to *have bees in the head*. Whether the metaphor alluded to the frenetic buzzing of thought, like the protests of the trapped bees, or to the frenzied behaviour of the afflicted person, is open to debate. During the following century, in an age when bonnets were brimless headgear worn by both men and women, bees began to enter bonnets to the same effect:

> *Ah woe is me, woe, woe is me,*
> *Alack and welladay!*
> *For pitty, Sir, find out thet Bee,*
> *Which bore my Love away.*
> *I'le seek him in your Bonnet brave,*
> *I'le seek him in your eyes.*
> (Robert Herrick, 'The Mad Maid's Song', 1648)

Gradually the idiom evolved until, in the nineteenth century, it achieved its modern form, an early written appearance being in Walter Scott's *The Pirate* (1821).

*Bill Dear is no Humphrey Bogart. But as a tenacious private detective from Dallas, Texas, he certainly proves that all those American crime novels got one thing right: one private eye with **a bee in his bonnet** and apparently boundless energy can get a whole lot further in coming up with new leads than an American city police department.*
THE GUARDIAN, 4 OCTOBER 2000

*Unlike many of the rich men who stumble into the world of political donation, Mr Wheeler is not a political junkie and has no discernible **bee in his bonnet** other than to see a Tory government re-elected.*
THE GUARDIAN, 19 JANUARY 2001

beeline: to make a beeline for

to travel (with determination) in a straight line, to take the direct route

It has long been thought that bees were single minded in their work and always flew in a straight line back to the hive, a piece of country lore which seems to have arisen in America and was published abroad in the first half of the nineteenth century. One might even hazard a guess as to the home state of this proverbial wisdom, for the first recorded appearance of *bee line* is in an 1830 edition of *The Massachusetts Spy*. The phrase was subsequently used by Edgar Allan Poe (1843), Henry David Thoreau (1852) and Ralph Waldo Emerson (1870), all sons of Massachusetts. Alternatively, of course, one borrowed from the other.

Science has progressed apace since the nineteenth century, and it seems that the old country people might have got it right. One recent researcher had this to say. He is talking of a 'recruit', a bee which has seen the dance of the initial forager and now is trying to get to the same food source:

The experienced forager flies directly back and forth between the hive and food source. The recruit flies out from the hive in expanding circles until it encounters the plume of odor molecules emanating from the food source that match the odors on the dancing bee. Then the recruit flies upwind into an ever increasing concentration of the odor until it reaches the food source. After learning the food source location (and the location of the hive) the recruit can also fly the bee-line (Edward E Southwick, *Bee Research Digest,* October 1992).

But no two experts agree. More recent research, which included tracking by radar minute radio transponders on bees' backs, shows that the critical issue is the 'waggle dance' performed by returning foragers, instructing others in how to fly directly in a straight line to the food source. Only when they get there does the issue of scent come into question.

So the country folk definitely had it right. Bees do go absolutely straight to their goal. Another piece of rural wisdom (English, this time) concerns crows which are supposed to fly directly to their intended destination, giving rise to the expression *as the* CROW *flies*.

Lovers of German wine should **make a bee-line for** *Majestic. Their buyers have secured small parcels of surplus stock from the Swedish state monopoly, and are able to offer a range of mature wines...at amazingly low prices...*
BIRMINGHAM POST, 30 MAY 2001

I cannot pass a bookshop. I have to go in and **make a bee-line for** *the cookery section; I rarely re-emerge on the pavement empty handed. I am obsessed with cookbooks.*
THE OBSERVER, 10 JUNE 2001

At the Warner Music party at the Grammy Awards in Los Angeles last year, a senior private-equity executive **made a beeline for** *Madonna's publicist. He took her by the arm and demanded that she introduce his daughter to the singer.*
THE ECONOMIST, 24 FEBRUARY 2005

bee's knees, the
undisputedly the best

Amongst the shocking and fun-loving flappers of America in the 1920s there was a vogue for concocting bizarre phrases that compared something deemed to be 'the best' with improbable or non-existent parts of animal anatomy: *the gnat's elbows, the flea's eyebrows, the snake's hips, the elephant's instep* and *the cat's miaow* are just a few of dozens. A main instigator of this fad for whimsical expressions of enthusiasm was Tad Dorgan, an influential

American cartoonist and newspaper columnist. *The bee's knees* probably survives on the strength of its pleasing rhyme. Less common, but still occasionally heard, are *the cat's whiskers* and *the cat's pyjamas* (which, along with *the gnat's garters*, is one of the few phrases to mention clothing rather than a body part).

The latest wheeze is synthetic phonics, which claims to get children reading within weeks. It is said to be **the bee's knees** *with boys, dyslexics and ethnic-minority children. It also cures the plague and makes children eat their greens. Allegedly.*
THE TIMES EDUCATIONAL
SUPPLEMENT, 26 OCTOBER 2001

This is not to say he has no sex appeal at all. Teenage girls and gay men think he's **the bee's knees**.
DAILY MAIL, 7 MARCH 2002

bell: to bell the cat
to undertake a difficult mission at great personal risk

An ancient fable, related by Langland in *Piers Plowman* (1377), tells of a colony of mice who met together to discuss how they could thwart a cat who was terrorising them. One young mouse suggested hanging a bell around the cat's neck so that its movements would be known. This plan delighted the rest until an old mouse asked the obvious question, 'Who will bell the cat?'

Scottish history records a very pertinent instance of the expression in action. Members of the nobility at the court of James III were mistrustful of the king's low-born favourites and, in particular, an architect named Cochran. The nobles met together secretly and determined to get rid of him, whereupon Lord Gray inquired who would be bold enough to enter the king's presence and *bell the cat*. After a pause, Archibald Douglas, Earl of Angus, replied, 'I will bell the cat.' He was as good as his word, seizing Cochran and hanging him over the bridge at Lauder, an act which earned him the nickname 'Bell-the-Cat Douglas'.

*Every so often the other shareholders (he was the biggest) squeaked and chattered but none of them dared **bell the cat**.*
THE DAILY TELEGRAPH, 24 JULY 2002

*Every week the party makes yet another statement about how it's turned the corner, got over the worst, made the breakthrough, **belled the cat**, neutered the budgie, whatever the latest limp slogan it conjured up to have us believe that it matters.*
THE SUNDAY TIMES, 23 FEBRUARY 2003

For other idioms derived from fables, see page 318.

belt: below the belt
unfairly

In 1865 lightweight boxer John Chambers rewrote the code of conduct for the sport of boxing, which was eventually published in 1867 under the patronage of John Sholto Douglas, eighth Marquis of Queensberry. One of the twelve 'Queensberry rules' forbade contestants from hitting one another below the belt line on their trunks – a thoroughly understandable requirement for any gentleman. The expression *below the belt* to denote 'unfair conduct' was first used figuratively in the 1890s. A few years later it was used to criticise Prime Minister David Lloyd George, who had a certain reputation for low cunning. *He couldn't see a belt without hitting below it,* Margot Asquith is said to have remarked.

*The Leader of the Opposition was extremely aggressive and, by the end of the bout, he looked extremely angry but he never tried to hit **below the belt**.*
THE DAILY TELEGRAPH, 1 APRIL 2004

*For rapper-turned-actor Ice Cube, the 15-year transformation from pariah to family entertainment hero begins and ends in the same place: **below the belt**. Only now, instead of delivering manly blows, he's taking blows to his manliness. Over and over and over again.*
WASHINGTON POST, 19 JANUARY 2005

For other boxing idioms, see
PACKING A PUNCH, page 45.

berserk: to go berserk
to be in a state of uncontrollable fury, deranged

The *berserkers* were bands of elite Viking warriors, devoted to the god Odin, who would work themselves up into a murderous frenzy before plunging into battle. The word *berserker* is derived from *björn* (stem *ber-*) 'bear' and *serkr*, 'shirt'. It refers to the fact that the warriors fought without armour, clad only in bearskins in the belief that they would then be possessed by the strength and ferocious spirit of the animals.

The scene now shifts to nineteenth-century Britain where, in 1821, the erudite and popular novelist Sir Walter Scott added the following footnote to a page in his new novel, *The Pirate*: *The berserkars were so called from fighting without armour*. Thereafter references to *berserkers* and the *berserker rage* began to appear in the works of other distinguished writers. By the middle of that century the derived adjective *berserk* was in use and by the early twentieth century the first instances of the modern idiom *to go berserk*, meaning 'to be violently angry', were to be found. This example comes from Rudyard Kipling's *Regulus* (1917).

Meantime Winton, very penitent and especially polite towards Vernon, was being cheered with cocoa in Number Five Study. He himself pointed out to Vernon that he had attacked a sub-prefect for no reason

whatever, and, therefore, deserved official punishment...
    'You went Berserk. I've read all about it in Hypatia.'
    'What's "going Berserk"?' Winton asked.
    'Never you mind,' was the reply...
'You've gone Berserk and pretty soon you'll go to sleep. But you'll probably be liable to fits of it all your life,' Beetle concluded. 'Shouldn't wonder if you murdered some one some day.'

The vicar was conducting an evening service and on his knees saying, 'Lord forgive us,' whereupon the angry husband **went berserk***. He stormed up the aisle and shouted: 'You are a fornicating adulterer. You disgust me. You cannot even be honest about your sins when you are before God.'*
DAILY MAIL, 12 SEPTEMBER 2001

See also *to run* AMOK (AMUCK).

berth: to give something/ someone a wide berth
to stay at a distance, to keep away from

The word *berth* is a nautical term which first came into use around the end of the sixteenth century to denote 'the distance a ship under sail should maintain from any obstacle to avoid collision'. It was frequently found in the expression *to give a good* or *clear berth to*: *Giving the Lighthouse a clear birth of 50 fathoms to the southward* (John Smeaton, *The Eddystone Lighthouse*, 1793).
    To give a wide berth to therefore means 'to steer well away from'. The phrase became an idiom in the first half of the nineteenth century: *Giving the apparent phantom what seamen call a wide berth* (Sir Walter Scott, *Letters on Demonology and Witchcraft*, 1830).

I thought 7pm would be safe enough, but when I arrived in Manchester city centre there were six spectacularly drunken youths at the tram stop... It seemed best not to make eye contact. I **gave them a wide berth** *and hurried into the civilised confines of the Atlas Bar at the bottom of Deansgate. They followed me in.*
THE INDEPENDENT, 5 MAY 2001

For other nautical idioms, see A LIFE ON THE OCEAN WAVES, page 24.

besetting sin, a
a characteristic failing

One of the meanings of the verb *to beset* was 'to encircle with hostile intent'. It was used of armies and enemies but also figuratively of vices, obstacles and difficulties. It was the word chosen by Bible translators of 1611 to express the text of Hebrews 12:1: *...let us lay aside every weight, and the sin which doth so easily beset us, and let us run with patience the race that is set before us...* Hence the phrase *besetting sin*, current since the late eighteenth century, to denote 'a failing to which one is particularly prone'.

Meanness is the only true **besetting sin***. A good person cannot be mean. I'm not talking about only the rich here, because generosity has nothing to do with bank balance, and everything to do with personality. People who are mean are mean not just with money, but with emotions, themselves, and to themselves as much as to others.*
THE OBSERVER, 19 NOVEMBER 2000

'I knew too little about so many things,' Pound once told his friend Daniel Cory. 'I picked out this and that thing that interested me, then jumbled them into a bag. But that's not the way...to make a work of art.' Hard-core Poundians can explain this away as late-life depression, but its stern lucidity sounds like that fierce young teacher and theorist who did his damnedest to purge poetry of artiness – which he hated in part because it was always his own **besetting sin***.*
NEW YORK TIMES, 1 FEBRUARY 2004

For other idioms from the Bible, see page 317.

better half, my
my wife

The expression dates back to Roman times: Horace and then Statius used it fondly to mean 'a dear friend'. During the seventeenth and eighteenth centuries it was used to describe the soul, which the Puritans believed to be the better part of a man. But it was Elizabethan poet Sir Philip Sidney in his prose romance *Arcadia* (1580) who first used the phrase to mean 'a spouse'. Here Argalus addresses his wife, Parthenia as *My deare, my better halfe*. Thereafter and until the nineteenth century the term was used with affection to denote either 'a husband' or 'a wife'.

It did invite flashes of wit or sarcasm, however. *It is not fit my better-half should be ignorant of the state of her worse-half,* wrote Horace Walpole in a letter to Lady Browne dated 19 October 1783, while a century later the novelist Florence Marryat wrote: *The preparations would serve to occupy our time, whilst our worse halves are out shooting* (*Under the Lilies and Roses*, 1884).

In modern English the idiom is usually a jocular reference to a wife, which has been a rich source of humour for cartoonist Randy Glasbergen in his strip *The Better Half.*

Meanwhile, the French have released a study showing that Saturdays and Sundays are the riskiest days of the week for fatal heart attacks among men. Sacré Dieu! *It would seem that all that DIY, being stuck in traffic jams, and making conversation with* **your better half** *cranks up the stress level to a degree that leaves you longing for Monday's memo from the boss.*
THE OBSERVER, 26 AUGUST 2001

Nine years ago I managed to persuade **my better half** *to name our second daughter Lara after the West Indian cricketer who had then just scored a world record 501 for Warwickshire.*
SPORTS ARGUS, 20 MARCH 2004

For other idioms drawn from Greek and Roman writers, see page 318.

bib: best bib and tucker
one's best clothes

Bib brings to mind the cloth tied under a baby's chin to absorb the dribbles. From the late seventeenth century onwards, bibs of a sort were also worn by women. They were pieces of cloth that covered the breast or formed part of an apron. A *tucker* was another woman's garment of the same period, this time a flimsy piece of lace or muslin worn around the top of the bodice.

The expression *best bib and tucker* to denote 'best clothes' arose in the mid-eighteenth century, properly to describe a woman's finery but, as time passed, fashions changed and the fixed phrase lost its connection with its first meaning, it also came to describe a man's special attire.

Students at Rugby College will be wearing their **best bib and tucker** *at their first student ball tonight.*
COVENTRY EVENING TELEGRAPH, 30 JUNE 2000

I did and do intensely admire the professional nurserymen running tiny business [sic] that work all year for the show, awkward in **best bib and tucker** *like farmers at a show.*
THE OBSERVER, 20 MAY 2001

big cheese, a
an important person

It was around 1840 that the word *cheese* became a popular slang term to denote 'anything excellent, tasteful or pleasant'; in other words, 'the real thing'. Plain-speaking Sam Slick gives an early instance in *The Clockmaker* (1837–8): *Whatever is the go in Europe will soon be the cheese here.* Sometimes the name of a particular cheese would be substituted for the word itself. Stilton was obviously highly thought of, for Hotten's *Slang Dictionary* of 1859 has: '*That's the stilton*', or '*it is not the stilton*', i.e. *that is quite the thing, or that is not quite the thing; – polite rendering of 'that is not the cheese*'.

In fact the word *cheese* in this context has nothing at all to do with dairy produce; rather it is thought to be a corruption of the Persian and Urdu word *chiz*, 'thing', which young Anglo-Indians apparently bandied about as a slang term of approval, rather as *ace* has been used recently: *My new Arab is the real chiz* (Yule and Burnell, *Hobson-Jobson*, 1886).

By the 1920s *cheese*, often qualified by *big*, was being used to denote 'an important or self-important person', particularly in American slang. The first recorded use is by Ring Lardner in his story 'Horseshoes', first published in *The Saturday Evening Post*, 15 August 1914. One player in a Baseball World Series is moaning about another:

'*Did you see the serious?*'
'*No,*' *I lied glibly, hoping to draw from him the cause of his grouch.*
'*Well,*' *he said,* '*you sure missed somethin'. They never was a serious like it before and they won't never be one again. It went the full seven games and every game was a bear. They was one big innin' every day and Parker was the big cheese in it.*'

The term is at best neutral but usually carries derogatory overtones; no captain of industry or head of state would be flattered by being referred to as *the big cheese*.

They liked to show off back then, make a splash… Play **the big cheese**.
MARGARET ATWOOD,
THE BLIND ASSASSIN, 2000

Bringing **the big cheeses** *in your company up to speed with technology could benefit your IT department in the long run.*
COMPUTING, 1 MARCH 2001

See also *a* BIGWIG and, for more on Sam Slick, see UPPER *crust*.

bigwig, a
a person of importance

When Louis XIV of France (1638–1715), at the age of 32, took to wearing wigs to conceal his bald spot, he set a fashion not only for his own courtiers but for the royal courts of Europe. The favoured style was the long full-bottomed wig that curled and draped over the shoulders. During the eighteenth century wigs became more and more elaborate and could be styled in at least a hundred different ways. Very large wigs were made up of several heads of real hair. They were extremely expensive to buy and maintain, and so the bigger the wig, the more important the man. Thus it was that, by the 1730s, people of rank and importance, such as the aristocracy and key figures in the judiciary and the church, had come to be known humorously or contemptuously as *bigwigs*.

In Britain, some people of importance still traditionally wear a wig, although contemporary *bigwigs* are becoming disenchanted with their hot and heavy headgear. The first woman Speaker of the House of Commons refused to wear her wig on the grounds of comfort at work, a practice that has been continued by her male successor: *Michael Martin doesn't mind getting dressed up, but he draws the line at a traditional full-bottomed wig, ceremonial gown, knee breeches, black silk stockings, and silver-buckled shoes…That's an almost revolutionary stance in tradition-strapped Britain, but one that nevertheless appears to be catching on (Christian Science*

Monitor, 31 October 2000). And the Lord Chief Justice, Lord Woolf, would prefer British judges to go wigless, like their American counterparts.

*Of all the horrors to emanate from the Continent, here was the final humiliation: British ministers ordered around by the **bigwigs** of European justice.*
THE SPECTATOR, 10 NOVEMBER 2001

*The Tories have been mercilessly ridiculed for the poor calibre of their showbiz supporters (i.e., Jim Davidson and Patti Boulaye) but Iain Duncan Smith should add another famous name to the list. Tony Hadley was spotted with party **bigwigs**, including chairman David Davis, in a House of Commons dining room on Tuesday.*
DAILY MIRROR, 27 JUNE 2002

*But now war had broken out in Europe they had to go somewhere, and whoever thought of the Bahamas ensured that the biggest of **bigwigs** now found themselves in the smallest of small towns: the Duke and Duchess must have looked around them in dismay and incredulity.*
THE DAILY TELEGRAPH, 12 APRIL 2003

For another idiom about wigs see to *pull the* WOOL *over someone's eyes*. For another idiom meaning 'important person' see BIG *cheese*.

billio: like billio/billyo/billy-o
with enthusiasm, with gusto; excessively

This expression of exuberance seems to have originated in the second half of the nineteenth century and has spawned a clutch of eponymous explanations. The first is that it makes reference to the action of Stephenson's steam engine, the Puffing Billy. The second links it to Nino Biglio, a lieutenant under Garibaldi, who would plunge into the fray exhorting his men to *follow me and fight like Biglio*. The third claims that the phrase comes from the name of Joseph Billio, a particularly

zealous Puritan and founder of the Independent Congregation at Maldon, Essex in 1682. This last would seem inappropriate for a late nineteenth-century term unless the energetic Joseph managed to inspire a revival in Maldon from beyond the grave.

More likely is that the intensive phrase *like billy-o* was a euphemism for the much older 'like the devil'. There is support for this argument for, according to Jonathon Green's *Dictionary of Slang* (1998), *billy* was used to mean 'devil' in two American slang phrases dating from the mid-nineteenth century: *billy-be-damned*, meaning 'hell' (e.g. *as hot as billy-be damned*) and *billy hell*, referring to an imagined place of intense gloom and depression (e.g. *as miserable as billy hell*).

*The key is not to let grime get too attached to pots in the first place. Almost as soon as you've thrown away whatever you were cooking, get the pots into hot water and scrub **like billio**. Then, when you've got them pretty much pristine, they'll be ready for the dishwasher.*
THE GUARDIAN, 16 JUNE 2001

*The truth of the matter is that though they complain **like billio**, the big battalions of business represented by the CBI are much better able to cope with the rising tide of red tape and taxes than the little guy.*
THE INDEPENDENT ON SUNDAY,
3 FEBRUARY 2002

For other satanic names, see THE DEVIL, page 97.

bird: a little bird told me
a secret source told me

Most authorities subscribe to the view that this phrase's origin is a biblical one and can be found in Ecclesiastes 10:20: *Curse not the King; no not in thy thought; and curse not the rich in thy bedchamber; for a bird of the air shall carry the voice, and that which hath wings shall tell the matter.*

There is a story which, although an unlikely origin, is worth telling for its charm. All the birds were summoned to appear before Solomon. Only the Lapwing did not appear. When questioned on his disobedience, Lapwing explained that he was with the Queen of Sheba and that she had resolved to visit King Solomon. The king immediately began preparations for the visit. Meanwhile Lapwing flew to Ethiopia and told the queen that King Solomon had a great desire to see her. The magnificent meeting, as we know, then took place. Idiomatic little birds have been English messengers since the middle of the sixteenth century.

'I hear you like animals.'
'Who told you that?'
'A little bird told me,' I replied.
'I'll kill that bleeding bird...'
GERVASE PHINN, HEAD OVER HEELS IN THE DALES, 2002

For other idioms from the Bible, see page 317.

bird: to give someone the bird/to get the bird

to boo or hiss at an actor/to be hissed at

Just as geese when provoked hiss in warning, similarly an unimpressed audience might hiss an incompetent actor or performer. In the theatrical slang of the early nineteenth century they would *give him the goose* or *give him the big bird*: *To be goosed, or, as it is sometimes phrased 'to get the big bird,'* is occasionally a compliment to the actor's power of representing villainy, but more often is disagreeably suggestive of a failure to please (*The Graphic*, April 1886). The phrases were current throughout the century with the modern variant *to give someone the bird* dating from the 1890s.

Astoundingly, in the light of the fact that Cúper has brought more glory to Valencia in 18 months than anyone had imagined possible in 10 years, the fans **gave him the bird** *at a home game a month ago.*
THE INDEPENDENT, 11 FEBRUARY 2001

Alastair Campbell isn't held in universally high regard by the rank and file of the Labour Party. Interesting, therefore, to hear that the PM's controversial former spin doctor has been booked as the main after-dinner speaker for Labour's huge annual fund-raising dinner at the Hilton next month.
'The tickets are £500 each, so Alastair had better put on a good show,' says my man with the red rosette. 'I'd hate to see the audience **give him the bird***.'*
THE DAILY TELEGRAPH, 13 MARCH 2004

biscuit: to take the biscuit

to take the prize; to be the most outstanding or outrageous example of something

See under *to take the* CAKE.

Chocolate labradors **take the biscuit** *as the most accident-prone dogs, according to figures released yesterday. More than half the chocolate labradors insured become the subject of a claim to cover the cost of treatment for accident or illness, it is calculated, making them twice as bad an actuarial risk as their close relatives, black labradors.*
THE TIMES, 9 AUGUST 2001

Perhaps a more striking distinction of 19th-century Russians is their impressive knack of dying grotesque and dramatic deaths: Pushkin in a duel; Tolstoy at a railway station in a doomed attempt to escape his family; Tchaikovsky deliberately contracting cholera to erase a debt of honour. Griboyedov, however, **takes the biscuit***...his extraordinary dramatic and violent life would make an enthralling story even if he had never written a word.*
THE SPECTATOR, 12 JANUARY 2002

bit: to have/take the bit between one's teeth

to be so keen to do something that one cannot be restrained, to pursue one's own course relentlessly

The bit is the metal mouthpiece on a horse's bridle that enables the rider to direct the animal. The horse is only sensitive to the rider's direction while the bit is in the right place in his mouth. If he *takes the bit between his teeth* he can no longer feel the pull of the reins and the rider has lost control of him.

The expression is a very old one, dating back in Greek culture to Aeschylus in 470 BC: *You take the bit in your teeth like a new harnessed colt* (*Prometheus Bound*). Some 420 years later it was also used by the Roman writer Cicero. The phrase may have been introduced into England by the influential Renaissance scholar Erasmus, who included it in his *Adagia* (1500).

The meaning through millennia had been of obstinate self-will. Comparatively recently it has developed the sense of determinedly setting out on a task, not necessarily with negative overtones.

There was no stopping Schumacher once he **had the bit between his teeth** *and at one stage he roared ahead of Barrichello.*
DAILY MAIL, 19 MARCH 2001

Graham Thorpe's grit served England well as the tourists stayed afloat on a rain-shortened third day of the final Test against South Africa at Centurion...
　'I **had the bit between my teeth** *when I went out to bat. But it is tough coming off (when bad weather intervenes) and then having to go back on and start again,' he said. 'It means the bowlers keep coming back fresh, but I just tried to concentrate hard.'*
DAILY MAIL, 23 JANUARY 2005

For other horsey idioms see page 319. For other idioms drawn from Greek and Roman writers, see page 318.

bite: to bite the bullet

to face up to a difficult or unpleasant situation, to screw up one's courage; to embark upon an unpleasant task

There are two suggested origins for the phrase, both from the battlefield.

The first refers to nineteenth-century soldiers who with their rifle in one hand and ammunition in the other would have to use their teeth to rip off the end of the sealed paper cartridge before the weapon could be loaded and the spark ignite the gunpowder inside.

The second claims that wounded soldiers, about to be operated on without the benefit of an anaesthetic, were encouraged to bite on a bullet to help them forget their intense fear and pain. Some quote Rudyard Kipling's *The Light that Failed* (1890) to support the theory: *Bite on the bullet, old man, and don't let them think you are afraid.* Unfortunately the surrounding text fails to mention an actual bullet, so it remains possible that Kipling's character was using an established idiom and exhorting his wounded friend to be brave, rather than encouraging him to bite on a literal bullet to ease his pain. Nevertheless it is a fact that, before the discovery of anaesthesia, patients in general were often given things to bite upon when enduring surgery without anaesthetic, so it would seem logical to offer a soldier on the battlefield a bullet. In a not dissimilar context, this time one of painful military discipline, Grose, in his *Dictionary of the Vulgar Tongue* (1785), has this entry for *nightingale*:

NIGHTINGALE: *A soldier who, as the term is, sings out at the halberts. It is a point of honour in some regiments, among the grenadiers, never to cry out, become nightingales, whilst under the discipline of the cat of nine tails; to avoid which, they chew a bullet.*

*Because the real crunch is two or more
decades away, it's tempting to leave the
problem for another government and
another day...but if politicians in countries
like Germany and France remain too
scared of voters **to bite the bullet** on
pensions, then when the final reckoning
inevitably arrives, it will be more painful –
and the political fallout far worse.*
TIME, 29 MAY 2000

*So, if you genuinely believe you can give
your mother more respect – patience,
kindness, devotion – if the two of you live
apart, tell her that and make arrangements
to soften the blow. But if you know deep
down that the most respectful way to treat
your mother is have her live with you, then
bite the bullet.*
GOOD HOUSEKEEPING, AUGUST 2001

*Q: It's almost bank holiday garden party
time and I'm dreading the annual
invitation from the neighbours. The
husband is hopeless on the barbecue and
I'm worried I'll be poisoned. How can I
avoid it without having to spend the day
indoors?
A: **Bite the bullet** and go to their party,
but with carrot batons to back up your claim
of being on a low-cholesterol, raw veg diet.*
GOOD HOUSEKEEPING, JUNE 2002

For other idioms derived from the
army and warfare, see page 317.

bite: to bite the dust
to die, to be finished, to be worn out

Although this idiom was popularised
by the American western genre, especially in the Nick Carter Library at the
turn of the twentieth century, it has a
classical origin going back to Homer's
Iliad (c. eighth century bc). We have
the translation of the American poet
William Cullen Bryant (1870) to
thank for the modern expression:

*May his fellow warriors, many a one,
Fall round him to the earth and bite the dust.*

English writers and translators before
Bryant used other words for 'dust':
ground (Thomas Gray, Lord Byron) and
sand (Alexander Pope). The highly
authoritative King James Version of
the Bible (1611) uses a similar phrase
three times, and may have helped
prepare the way for the modern idiom.
Psalm 72:9 says: *They that dwell in the
wilderness shall bow before him; and his
enemies shall lick the dust.*

The original meaning of the expression was 'to fall in battle' but modern
usage has extended this and now
almost anything that has succumbed
to disrepair or failure, from a lawn-
mower to a business venture, is said to
have *bitten the dust*.

*If Martina Hingis had as much trouble
breaking in horses as breaking in her new
racket, she would **bite the dust**.*
THE INDEPENDENT, 24 FEBRUARY 2001

*Cruel January will no doubt claim its
victims as our personal new year vows **bite
the dust**. Already the gin bottle seems to be
winking at me quite confidently from its
space on the high-up shelf.*
THE TIMES EDUCATIONAL
SUPPLEMENT, 11 JANUARY 2002

For other idioms drawn from Greek
and Roman writers, see page 318.

bitter: to the bitter end
(persevering) to the very last moment,
until a struggle is finally resolved one
way or the other

Although the etymology of this idiom is
uncertain, it is generally considered to
be a nautical phrase. On sailing ships
ropes were fastened to and then coiled
around *the bitts*, pairs of stout posts set
in the deck. The last portion of cable
was known as *the bitter end: When a chain*

or rope is paid out to the bitter-end, no more remains to be let go (Admiral William Smyth, *Sailor's Word-book,* 1867).

Just as a rope *let out to the bitter end* can go no further, so a person who endures *to the bitter end* perseveres to the very last. The phrase has been in use since at least the mid-nineteenth century.

So far, the biggest beneficiaries are the Montana shareholders who bravely hung on **until the bitter end** *of the battle to gain a bonus payout.*
NEW ZEALAND HERALD, 8 APRIL 2002

The rest of the Nazi upper echelon – the so-called 'Golden Pheasants' – were no better. As Berlin's fall became imminent, some 2,000 of them caught trains to the south. Of those who stayed, Hitler's No 2, Martin Bormann, and SS General Mohnke ordered the execution of any Germans who failed to stay right **to the bitter end.**
THE SCOTSMAN, 20 APRIL 2002

For other nautical idioms, see A LIFE ON THE OCEAN WAVES, page 24.

black: in black and white
in print; in simple terms

In Shakespeare's *Much Ado About Nothing* (1598), constable Dogberry, having accused Borachio of a terrible crime, is anxious that the villain should answer for all his misdeeds: *Moreover sir, which indeed is not under white and black, this plaintiff here…did call me ass.* The good constable will have to be taken at his word, since the accusation is not *under white and black*, that is, not in black characters on white paper, not down in writing. The idiom had changed to the familiar *in black and white* by the early eighteenth century. Its sense now allows for use in non-literal contexts.

Never has an account sheet looked so depressing when its actual aim was to portray a healthy picture of royal life. For there, **in black and white,** *either by accident or design, a new 'family unit' has sprung from the profit and loss pages: Prince Charles, Prince William, Prince Harry. And now Camilla Parker Bowles.*
DAILY MIRROR, 1 JULY 2004

Even some who admire Mr. Zhao say that the main impetus for China's economic and modest political liberalization came from Mr. Deng… Mr. Zhao's conversion to the cause of the protesters came only after he lost an internal party battle for control.

But those are shades of gray in a propaganda battle waged **in black and white** *for the nation's memory and loyalty. In effect, the Communist Party abandoned Mr. Zhao and the opposition adopted him, making him an unlikely icon of resistance.*
NEW YORK TIMES, 23 JANUARY 2005

See also BLACK AND WHITE, page 311.

black: in the black
in credit, showing a profit

See *in the* RED

But the real story is that RMC's German business is showing signs of revival, with price rises sticking and forecasters saying the division will be back **in the black** *by 2005.*
THE OBSERVER, 20 JUNE 2004

See also BLACK AND WHITE, page 311.

black: like the Black Hole of Calcutta

in cramped, airless conditions

The British East India Company had established Calcutta as a trading station in 1690. In 1756 Nawab Siraj-ud-daulah of Bengal, concerned at the growth of the settlement, demanded that the new fortifications there, designed to be used against him, be demolished. When nothing happened the Nawab marched on Calcutta, where he attacked the Company's headquarters. His forces allegedly took 146 prisoners who were crammed overnight into a tiny, airless cell in the barracks at Fort William. As the temperature inside the room soared the captives, forced to stand for lack of space, began to faint for want of air and water. Only 23 of them survived until morning.

That, at any rate, was the British side of the tale, and almost all the available evidence is written from the British perspective. Indian nationalists, on the other hand, have claimed that the incident was an Imperialist fabrication to justify subsequent military action in Bengal; modern historians think the details of the imprisonment were somewhat exaggerated. Whatever the truth, the incident was referred to as the Black Hole of Calcutta and, since the nineteenth century, any unbearably cramped surroundings have been compared with it.

*There is no doubt that the old place needed rebuilding. The backstage conditions were a disgrace to a so-called civilised society, the chorus accommodation bore a strong resemblance to **the Black Hole of Calcutta**, and storing the sets was a nightmare.*
THE SPECTATOR, 7 OCTOBER 2000

Everyone piled into the Wimbledon train, but for every would-be Circle Line passenger who dismounted at Earl's Court, *two others got in, and as the train waited, and waited, and waited for some gesture from the signalman, by the time the doors eventually closed and the train moved off, conditions were akin to those of **the Black Hole of Calcutta**.*
EVENING STANDARD,
18 SEPTEMBER 2001

black: to be in someone's black book(s)

to be out of favour with someone, to be in disgrace

Black-bound books of officialdom have a very long history. The earliest, dating from the second half of the twelfth century, was that kept by the Exchequer to record royal revenue. In the fourteenth century a similarly black-bound volume contained rules relating to naval affairs. The *black books* referred to in the idiom, however, were official reports on investigations into alleged corruption within the monasteries, compiled as evidence of *manifest sin, vicious, carnal, and abominable living* during Henry VIII's struggle to sever his kingdom from Papal authority. In the light of this 'evidence' Parliament was persuaded in 1536 to dissolve the monasteries and assign their property to the king. Thereafter any book containing the names of persons who had committed offences was known as a *black book*: *Ned Brownes's villanies...are too many to be described in my Blacke Booke* (Robert Greene, *Black Bookes Messenger*, 1591).

Later, Proctors at the University of Oxford took to keeping *black books*. So did military regiments. Such a listing debarred the culprit from his degree or a higher rank. The practice continues to this day, with everyone from sports officials to media manipulators keeping lists of names and offences.

Little black book is a twentieth-century development of the original phrase. It refers to the list of past loves and sexual conquests that men are reputed to carry with them. However, the film *Little Black Book*, released in 2004, required some updating to keep in tune with the times. When a daytime talk-show producer, a little too curious about her new boyfriend's past, digs into the files on his handheld Palm Pilot, she discovers more about him than she cares to know, including information about his ex-girlfriends.

*Diary learns that spin supremo Max Clifford has been approached by a rival media firm wanting to buy his business... But our Max is not for selling at this price apparently. His **black book** – with which he could bring down half of London – must alone be worth squillions.*
THE OBSERVER, 23 MARCH 2003

*Calls to reconsider Bush's visit here are based on the misguided assumption that Al-Qaeda has compiled a list of western goodies and baddies...that we might yet join the Yanks and the Spaniards in **their black books**. But we're already there, along with the French and the Germans and the Norwegians and the Andorrans, and any western country that enjoys the freedom and democracy that these terrorists abhor.*
THE SUNDAY TIMES, 21 MARCH 2004

See also BLACK AND WHITE, page 311.

black sheep (of the family), the

a member of a group (or family) who has fallen foul of the others, who is in disgrace

Shepherds disliked black sheep since their fleece could not be dyed and was therefore worth less than white. Shepherds in earlier times also thought that black sheep disturbed the rest of the flock. A ballad of 1550 tells us that *The blacke shepe is a perylous beast* and

Thomas Bastard, writing in 1598, accuses the poor animal of being savage:

Till now I thought the prouerbe did but iest,
Which said a blacke sheepe was a biting beast.

Market forces, superstitions and prejudice prevailed so that, by the late eighteenth century, the term *black sheep* was being applied to anyone who did not behave as the rest of the group thought fit: *You are a black sheep; and I'll mark you* (Charles Macklin, *The Man of the World*, 1782).

The expanded expression *black sheep of the family* dates from the mid-nineteenth century.

*Rob was **the black sheep of a local Irish family** and was always in trouble with the police.*
THE OBSERVER, 19 MAY 2002

*Angelozzi...had broken ties with his family after an inheritance dispute. 'I thought he was dead,' said his sister Giulia in a newspaper interview. 'I have had no contact with him for years. He was **the black sheep of the family**.'*
CHRISTIAN SCIENCE MONITOR,
22 JUNE 2005

See also BLACK AND WHITE, page 311.

blackball, to

to exclude someone from a social group or club

In the eighteenth century applications for membership of exclusive clubs were submitted to the vote. Existing members would drop either a white or a black ball into an urn. A white ball meant 'yes' and a black 'no'.

The practice was still widespread in Victorian England:

The club numbers a thousand members; the entrance fee being fifty guineas, and the annual subscription twelve. Elections take place by general ballot of the members; and, on the whole, the Senior Jupiter is a club rather difficult to get into. For example, certain prejudices exist in certain cliques among the members, against stockbrokers, solicitors, wine-merchants, Turks, Armenians, educated Baboos studying at the Inns of Court, paragraphists of society papers, retired majors of the 96th Lancers, and Chinese 'bucket-shop' keepers, who are too accomplished proficients at fan-tan, euchre, and poker. Proprietors of quack medicines are also looked upon askance; and a lion comique, or the landlord of an East-End gin-palace, would have but a very faint chance of election in this equally select and sumptuous place of resort for the aristocratic, the cultured, and the wealthy. As for artists, men of letters, and journalists, the sky would rain blackballs if such 'poor white trash' dared to come up for ballot (George Augustus Sala, *Five P.M.: A ballot at a Pall Mall Club*, 1895).

One wonders how anyone ever became a member at all.

*A heated meeting of club members yesterday finally overturned last month's decision to **blackball** the famous soprano and nine other women who had applied to join.*
THE GUARDIAN, 5 APRIL 2001

*After turning down a co-starring role with Bogart in 1947 she was duly suspended by Warner Bros – which meant that she was effectively **blackballed** by every Hollywood studio.*
THE GUARDIAN, 22 APRIL 2002

See also BLACK AND WHITE, page 311.

blacklist, to
to list the name of someone contravening rules or conventions, to ostracise

According to John Milton's pamphlet *First Defense of the English People* (1651), the original *Black List* was drawn up by the future Charles II as he languished in exile. It contained the names of those men responsible for the trial and execution of his father, Charles I, in 1649. Milton says: *If ever Charles his Posterity recover the Crown…you are like to be put in the Black List.* And indeed on his restoration to the throne in 1660, Charles II hunted out all those on the list, executing thirteen and imprisoning many others.

A *black list* thus became a list of persons deemed undesirable or in need of correction for one reason or another: ships had *black lists* to keep the crew in check and, during the reign of Edward VII, magistrates kept *black lists* of habitual drunkards. The police were trained in how to deal with such miscreants. This example is from H Childs' *'Police-Duty' Catechism and Reports* (1903):

QUES: *If you see a person who is on the 'black list' go into a public house or registered club to obtain drink, what should you do?*
ANS: *Warn the publican not to serve him with intoxicating drink.*
QUES: *May a publican serve a person who is on the 'black list' with non-intoxicating liquors?*
ANS: *Yes; no offence if the man is sober…*
QUES: *If you saw a man go into a public-house, procure intoxicating liquor, and bring it out into the roadway to a person who you know is on the 'black list,' and who drinks it, the landlord being ignorant of the transaction, what steps would you take?*
ANS: *Take names and addresses of both men and report for summons.*

Since the late nineteenth century the principal use has been in relation to management and union affairs. The OED cites J D Hackett's definition of *blacklist* in his *Labour Terms in Management Engineering* (1923): *a list of union workmen circulated by employers to prevent such workers from being hired.*

Conversely, unions also produced *black lists* of firms they refused to deal with. Laws, litigation and considerable industrial strife regularly resulted. A particularly famous case was that of the McCarthy witch hunt against communists in the 1950s American film industry. As a direct result of hearings and a *blacklist* that developed from them, 324 people lost their jobs in the Motion Picture Industry. Wider uses are reasonably common. Libraries, for instance, can hold *black lists* of borrowers who abuse the system.

*The first step was to tell him I wasn't going to allow people in the house who constantly criticised or complained or put other people down – I even **blacklisted** a couple of our acquaintances.*
GOOD HOUSEKEEPING, OCTOBER 2001

*Teachers have **blacklisted** 78 of the country's most violent and disruptive pupils.*
DAILY MAIL, 28 MAY 2002

See also BLACK AND WHITE, page 311.

blank: to draw a blank

to fail in attempts to discover or remember something

Lotteries are centuries old. The first in England was held under the patronage of Elizabeth I, the proceeds going towards the repair of ports and the strengthening of defences. In past centuries lotteries were organised differently. There were two jars or lot-pots, one containing the entrants' tickets, and the other an equal number of tickets, some with prizes written on them and the rest blank. First a named ticket would be drawn, and then a prize. Of course, since many of the prize tickets were blank, a lottery player might win nothing at all. The phrase *to draw a blank* dates from the first quarter of the nineteenth century.

*Dr Hazel Wilkinson, a senior research fellow at Kew Gardens, was sent magnified pictures of what police believed were plant cells. After extensive analysing of the cells, she initially **drew a blank**.*
EVENING STANDARD, 16 OCTOBER 2003

*An attempt to find a listing for the firm at Companies House also **drew a blank**.*
DAILY MIRROR, 28 JUNE 2004

blind: the blind leading the blind

someone with no knowledge or experience attempting to teach another

Jesus warned his disciples against the legalistic teaching of the Pharisees; they were blind to God's truth and, therefore, ill-equipped to help others find the way to Him. *They be blind leaders of the blind*, he said, *and if the blind lead the blind, both shall fall into the ditch*. The teaching is found in both Matthew 15:14 and Luke 6:39. During the first half of the sixteenth century, Jesus's words became proverbial in English, which may in part be a result of the lifting of censorship in 1537 of the Bible in English: *Where the blynd leadeth the blynd, both fall in the dyke* (John Heywood, *Proverbs*, 1546).

In 1568, the famous Dutch painter, Pieter Bruegel, painted a compelling picture entitled *The Parable of the Blind leading the Blind*, a shortening which prefigured the present-day form, mainly found from the nineteenth century.

I fear that Birt and Hussey did indeed share the same kind of non-vision: **the blind leading the blind** *into a cul-de-sac...*
THE TIMES, 16 NOVEMBER 2001

For other idioms from the Bible, see page 317.

blind: to turn a blind eye
to choose to ignore an unpleasant situation

In 1801 Britain, in response to the threat of a perceived coalition between France and the Baltic powers, assembled a fleet under the command of Admiral Hyde Parker with Vice-Admiral Lord Nelson as second-in-command. The English fleet was stationed off Copenhagen with the intention of intimidating Denmark into withdrawing from any agreements with its Baltic neighbours. When the Danes refused to negotiate, it was decided that Nelson should mount an attack with some of the fleet.

The task was formidable and the battle began disastrously. From a distance Parker, noting that two of Nelson's ships were flying distress signals and that another had run aground, decided to signal retreat. Nelson had famously lost sight in one eye during action at Calvi. When alerted to the retreat signal, he is reported to have said *I have only one eye – I have a right to be blind sometimes*. Then, lifting his eyeglass to his blind eye he calmly uttered the words: *I really do not see the signal*. The fleet fought on to victory.

The phrase was in idiomatic use some twenty years after the Battle of Copenhagen.

But leaving a large, dangerous minority of teenage boys out in the cold – jobless, bored and resentful – is a blueprint for social unrest, of which this summer's riots were

but a nasty foretaste. There are no easy answers. **Turning a blind eye,** *however, is no answer at all.*
THE TIMES, 15 AUGUST 2001

Who wouldn't try to keep love alive by **turning a blind eye** *to gossip, even to hard evidence, that their man is cheating on them?*
DAILY MIRROR, 25 JUNE 2004

blood, sweat and tears
gruelling hard work

Thou knowst how drie a Cinder this world is.
And learn'st thus much by our Anatomy.
That 'tis in vaine to dew, or mollifie
It with thy teares, or sweat, or blood.

Thus wrote John Donne in his poem 'First Anniversary' (1611). Other poets, such as Byron and Robert Browning, subsequently used the grouping *tears, sweat, blood*, though not necessarily in that order. The phrase with its cumulative force proved irresistible to politicians. A speech by Theodore Roosevelt, addressed to the Naval War College in 1897, spoke movingly of *the blood and sweat and tears, the labour and the anguish, through which, in the days that have gone, our forefathers moved to triumph*. But it was Winston Churchill who most famously employed it in his acceptance speech as Prime Minister on 13 May 1940, aware that, as he spoke, the British army on the Continent was retreating from the sudden onslaught of Hitler's forces: *I would say to the House, as I said to those who have joined this Government: I have nothing to offer but blood, toil, tears and sweat.*

Interestingly, this speech by Churchill was included in the record of his public pronouncements from 1938 to 1941 – the book was entitled *Blood, Sweat and Tears*, published in 1941. This suggests that the formulation of the phrase we know today was in Churchill's mind – or at least his publisher's – soon after the date of the speech itself.

Don Merton, from New Zealand's Department of Conservation, told New Scientist: *'After all the years of **blood, sweat and tears**, it's fantastic to know that the kakapo is not going to die out in a hurry. In fact, it now has an excellent chance of surviving.' But the survival has only been achieved by having humans guard the nests and watch the parrots 24 hours a day and provide them with a special diet to keep them healthy.*
THE INDEPENDENT, 30 MAY 2002

For other idioms drawn from literature, see page 319.

blow by blow
scrupulously detailed

The idiom originated in America around the 1930s. Radio reporters at the ringside of a big fight would describe the boxing match to their listeners literally *blow by blow* as it happened. By the 1940s the phrase was in use outside the boxing context: crime writer Hilda Lawrence has *blow by blow description* (*Death of a Doll*, 1948). The expression also precedes words such as *report* and *account*.

*Endless secret meetings took place, usually in Downing Street, lasting many hours. One grows to trust Ashdown's **blow by blow** versions of these conversations.*
THE SPECTATOR, 22 SEPTEMBER 2001

*We had a guide show us around for a couple of hours. Richard Hohmann, a retired teacher, gave us a **blow by blow** account of how the battle raged for those three days in which 170,000 men took part.*
THE GUARDIAN, 17 JUNE 2002

For other boxing idioms, see PACKING A PUNCH, opposite.

blow: to blow one's own trumpet/horn
to proclaim one's own merits or successes, to boast

The expression is a very old one and refers to the practice of announcing the arrival of an important person by blowing a horn. *Blowing one's own trumpet* is amongst those proverbs gleaned from the writings of the ancients by the Greek Diogenianus for his *Adagia* (c. AD 125), although he does not give his specific source.

Nevertheless, the phrase made a re-appearance during the Renaissance when interest in the ancient world was renewed. *I will...sound the trumpet of mine own merits*, wrote Abraham Fleming (*A Panoplie of Epistles*, 1576) and Shakespeare, whose plays are full of idiom contemporary to Elizabethan England, uses it in *Much Ado About Nothing*: *It is most expedient for the wise, ...to be the trumpet of his own virtues.*

The idiom settled down in the form we recognise today during the nineteenth century. The variant of the same period *blow one's own horn* is chiefly American. According to his biographer, Hesketh Pearson, the phrase was subject to a delicious play on words by W S Gilbert who, listening one day to a theatrical manager fulsomely praising his mistress, commented: *The fellow is blowing his own strumpet.*

*If you haven't heard of Fitzgerald that is most likely down to his niceness, too... As one of the solicitors who briefs him says: 'He does 20 times more human rights work than [he names another well known barrister] but he doesn't **blow his own trumpet**.'*
THE GUARDIAN, 11 DECEMBER 2000

Packing a punch

Nearly every sport played or enjoyed by a large section of the population has provided the language with a stock of idioms. Boxing has been particularly prolific, a testimony to its popularity from its beginnings in the early eighteenth century, when it enjoyed aristocratic patronage, to the present.

The term *boxing* was coined to distinguish a sporting bout from a regular fist fight to settle a quarrel. It was derived from the verb *to box*, meaning 'to strike with the fist', which in turn came from the fourteenth-century noun *box*, meaning 'a blow'. Early boxing matches were bare-knuckle fights.

It was Jack Broughton, English boxing champion from 1727 to 1750, who introduced the first rules to this violent sport after mortally injuring an opponent. For the first time, fights were split into rounds, a round being over when a fighter was knocked down but managed to get up again before a count of ten. If he remained on the ground he was *out for the count*, 'unconscious'. After a rest of thirty seconds, contestants had *to come up to (the)* SCRATCH, a mark on the ground, to begin a new round. Thus rounds differed greatly in length and, surprisingly, fights were often more than sixty rounds long as opponents sought to *beat the living* DAYLIGHTS out of each other. All the blood would be wiped away with a sponge and, if a fighter were not *a* GLUTTON *for punishment*, his manager could *throw in the* SPONGE *or* TOWEL and signal defeat.

Not until 1867, when John Chambers devised new rules, published under the patronage of the Marquess of Queensberry, were rounds limited to three minutes with a rest of one minute between. At the end of every round a bell rang, and many a struggling fighter was quite literally *saved by the bell* from worse punishment. Under the Queensberry rules, however, no one was permitted to punch *below the* BELT and cause unnecessary injury. Instead, contestants had to be brave and *take it on the chin*.

The best seat in the house for any spectator was *a ringside seat*, where all the action was. This was also where the broadcasters would be situated, giving BLOW *by blow* accounts of the fight to their listeners. After the introduction of the Queensberry rules, however, it was unlikely that any onlooker would want *to throw his* HAT *into the ring* and challenge the winner.

'Admittedly not our favourite recording,' *they say of one piece; of another they 'did a better version of this at the BBC, but it was accidentally erased'; while another is shrugged off with, 'Mimi wrote this in five minutes while washing the dishes'.* *Don't **blow your own trumpet** too hard, guys!*
THE INDEPENDENT, 17 DECEMBER 2004

For other idioms drawn from Greek and Roman writers, see page 318.

blue: like a bolt from/out of the blue

totally unexpected

The blue has been used rather poetically to denote 'a clear sky' since around the middle of the seventeenth century. The idiom alludes to the unlikely event of a bolt of lightning coming from a cloudless sky. It would be shocking indeed. It is not known how long the phrase has been in the spoken language but Thomas Carlyle used it in *The French Revolution* in 1837: *Arrestment, sudden really as a bolt out of the Blue, has hit strange victims*. The idiom *out of the blue*, which means exactly the same, dates from the early twentieth century.

The deaths of Robert, 23, and Richard, 20 – which came as Mr Turnbull was visiting Kent to seek new accommodation for the family – were 'a bolt out of the blue', said the report, by the community care development centre at King's College, London.
THE GUARDIAN, 26 JUNE 2001

Prevention is difficult; depression can strike **out of the blue**.
THE TIMES, 11 JUNE 2002

He'd just started a new school program and was struggling daily to remain there. Every day they told us how Nat had become aggressive **'out of the blue,'** *and that they did not know what to do for him... By April he had been expelled, sent home until a new placement opened up.*
WASHINGTON POST, 16 JANUARY 2005

blue-blooded
born into a royal or aristocratic family

In 711 the Iberian peninsular was invaded by the Moors, who pressed northwards as far as the Pyrenees. There remained, nevertheless, a remnant of Christian rule in the north which gradually regained territory, although it was not until 1492 that the Moors were finally expelled from Spain. Inevitably, relationships forged between the races over centuries of occupation produced many citizens of mixed blood. It was the proud boast of some of the ancient aristocratic families of Castile that their family lines had never been contaminated. Proof of their racial purity was evident in the fairness of their skin through which the veins showed blue. They were said to be of sangre azul, 'blue blood'. The darker complexions of those who had consorted with the Moors did not show off the blueness of the veins. The expression blue blood to denote 'a person of aristocratic birth' was borrowed into English in the 1830s.

And today, it [Ipswich] has a touch of **blue blood**... *The mother of king Abdullah of Jordan, Princess Muna, was once plain Toni Gardiner, an Ipswich typist.*
THE TIMES, 30 MAY 2000

A £300 million **blue-blooded** *bid battle for London's world famous Berkeley Square will be fought out between Middle Eastern royalty and Britain's richest aristocrat over the next two weeks.*
EVENING STANDARD, 29 MARCH 2001

Later today, a member of the aristocracy is coming to view the property. Did you hear that? None of your bloody middle-class, arriviste trash: proper **blue bloods** *with inherited furniture, speech impediments and good breeding.*
THE SUNDAY TIMES, 18 MAY 2003

blue chip
reliable, giving the highest return

In the game of poker counters, or *chips*, of different colours are used to represent money, with the *blue chip* having the highest value. In the early twentieth century Wall Street, doubtless reasoning that most people will only bet on a certainty, began to describe stocks with stable growth and a history of paying dividends as *blue chip*. Thus a *blue chip investment* is one that promises a good return while a *blue chip company* is nationally or internationally known and considered financially secure.

Switzerland's role as one of the world's more defensive stock markets in turbulent times has been thrown into question over the last few weeks as shares of some of its best-known **blue chips** *have taken a pounding.*
FINANCIAL TIMES, 27 JUNE 2002

For other idioms derived from poker, see page 320.

blue ribbon

the highest distinction or quality, the pick of the bunch

The most coveted order of knighthood in Britain, established by Edward III in about 1348, is the Most Noble Order of the Garter, whose emblem is a blue velvet ribbon. The story goes that the Countess of Salisbury's garter slipped from her leg while she was dancing at a ball. It was retrieved by the king who, mindful of her embarrassment, gallantly put it about his own leg, silencing sniggering onlookers with the words *Honi soit qui mal y pense* (Shame on him who thinks evil of this). The story, charming as it is, is not given much credence by the official royal website.

A theory of recent date suggests that the Order was originally a Marian cult, the Virgin's act of giving birth to the saviour being commemorated in that most intimate of symbols, the garter. The garter's legend forbids lewd comment at Our Lady's expense.

The honour is in the gift of the sovereign and, apart from senior royals, is bestowed upon just 24 Knights of the Garter. It is so highly esteemed that, since the mid-nineteenth century, the term *blue ribbon* has come to denote 'the highest possible achievement' in any field.

There is an interesting parallel in France. *L'Ordre du Saint Esprit* (the Order of the Holy Spirit), established in 1578, was the most prestigious in the land. Members wore a Cross, which hung from a *cordon bleu*, a 'blue ribbon'. In consequence, these *chevaliers* became known as *cordons bleus*. They had a reputation for getting together and enjoying excellent dinners, so *un repas de cordon bleu* was a real culinary feast. English borrowed the term in the early nineteenth century and *cordon bleu* now describes first-class cooking and chefs.

From about 1860 to 1960, there was intense rivalry between cross-Atlantic shipping companies to do the journey in the fastest possible time. It was a matter of great pride for the shipping line to have the fastest ship in its fleet and to be able to fly a blue pennant in its topmast. This was the *Blue Riband* of the Atlantic. In similar fashion, the *Blue Riband* of the Turf is horse racing's greatest prize, the Derby at Epsom. This alternative spelling goes back to the fifteenth century, and is still found quite widely in varied contexts.

As for the Brits, the organisers are preparing for a staggering eight hours of additional broadcasting leading up to the music industry's **blue ribbon** *event – showing just how highly valued the event has become to advertisers.*
THE OBSERVER, 17 FEBRUARY 2002

My grandparents loved shuffleboard so much that they built a court at their summer home up north in New Jersey. Therefore, I grew up in a family of very competitive shufflers, who for decades staged an annual Fourth of July tournament. I am the former champion of that tournament – I still have the **blue ribbon** *to prove it, and my name is etched on a shuffleboard plaque that's packed away somewhere in my parents' basement.*
WASHINGTON POST, 23 JANUARY 2005

I have long prided myself on being a connoisseur when it comes to refrigerator art. I'd like to think my collection is right up there with the Getty. Maybe even a bit more imaginative. My mother's fridge takes the **blue ribbon**, *however, because on hers she displays what might possibly be the largest photo of me ever made.*
USA TODAY, 25 JANUARY 2005

bluestocking, a
an erudite, literary woman

In the early 1750s a group of society women, most notably Mrs Montague, Mrs Vesey and Mrs Boscawen, tired of the trivial social round of cards and gossip, began to open their houses to like-minded intellectuals and prominent literary figures of the day for the purpose of intelligent conversation. Regular guests included Dr Johnson, James Boswell, actor David Garrick, novelist Samuel Richardson, writer and politician Horace Walpole and artist Sir Joshua Reynolds.

One evening Mrs Vesey invited Benjamin Stillingfleet to one of her soirées. Stillingfleet, a struggling botanist, poet and philosopher, felt unable to attend, being too poor to afford formal evening wear, but Mrs Vesey waved his hesitations aside, telling him to come just as he was. From then on Stillingfleet regularly turned up wearing his everyday attire and blue worsted stockings. It is said to be Admiral Boscawen who, eyeing Stillingfleet, laughingly dubbed the select group *The Blue-Stocking Society*. The quip caught on. Ladies who met thus for stimulating conversation were called *Blue Stockingers* or *Blue Stocking Ladies* and, by the end of the century, *Blue Stockings*. Throughout its life, the phrase has had an attached tone of contempt and ridicule. From the nineteenth century the term widened in meaning to apply to any lady who had or affected scholarship, whether she attended literary salons or not.

Bluestocking or bimbo? It may sound crude, but that is, in essence, the choice that women are repeatedly asked to make.
EVENING STANDARD,
3 NOVEMBER 2000

There is an awful lot to like about Dame Gillian Beer, who is a professor of English Literature at Cambridge. Her expansive donnishness for one thing – in an age of would-be totty academics, she looks like everyone's idea of a bluestocking – and her agreeable diction.
THE DAILY TELEGRAPH, 12 JUNE 2002

bluff: to call someone's bluff
to test someone's claims on suspicion of falsehood

This phrase was coined around the poker tables of nineteenth-century America and is all to do with deception. In poker, when a player makes a bet upon the cards he holds, he might try *to bluff*, 'to trick', his opponents into believing that his hand is better than it really is, by his body language, voice tone or by betting heavily upon it. If his *bluff is called*, he is forced to expose his cards and show himself true or false.

*[President Bush's] refusal yesterday to dispatch a team of US congressional leaders to Baghdad for talks about sending weapons inspectors to Iraq is another of the increasingly clear signals that nothing will deflect the Americans from a war aimed at toppling Iraq's regime... Mr Bush was right to dismiss the Iraqi move, **call Saddam's bluff** and declare that Saddam has to disarm his weapons of mass destruction before any further negotiations can resume.*
EVENING STANDARD, 6 AUGUST 2002

For other idioms derived from poker, see page 320.

board: to go by the board
to be cast aside, to be irretrievably lost

The *board* is the side of a ship and something which goes *by the board* falls over the side (over*board*) and is probably lost forever. The nautical phrase, current since the seventeenth century, was put to figurative use in the middle of the nineteenth century and applied to ideas, projects or values which are discarded or neglected.

*Finally...these novels are totally absorbing. Once I start reading one, all else **goes by the board** till I have finished it. Which is after all one of the things you want from a novel.*
THE SPECTATOR, 12 JANUARY 2002

For other nautical idioms, see A LIFE ON THE OCEAN WAVES, page 24.

boat: to push the boat out
to be generous, to spend freely

The term, which began as naval slang in the 1930s, originally meant 'to buy a round of drinks' at a shore party before setting sail. It has since developed a sense of spending extravagantly on a treat or special occasion.

FREE-SPENDING BRITONS **PUSH THE BOAT OUT** – BLOWING £100BN ON HOLIDAYS
HEADLINE, THE SCOTSMAN,
28 JULY 2004

He arrived by private jet, with three days of shooting booked, starting on the Glorious Twelfth, paying £34,000 a day. Sadly, the 12th was so foggy that it was impossible to shoot. Insurance only covers the costs of a day lost to bad weather if you stay out till midday. The Magnum PI star and his party, presumably, didn't mind the expense. For Spy hears they packed up and left for lunch at 11am.

*An extravagant mini-break it certainly was, but Selleck didn't exactly **push the boat out** with his accommodation – he stayed at a nearby pub.*
THE DAILY TELEGRAPH,
19 AUGUST 2004

Bob's your uncle
everything turns out well; no problem; there you are; it's as simple as that

A political scandal is suggested as the source for this British quip. In 1887 (contemporary with the early use of the phrase) Arthur Balfour was appointed Chief Secretary for Ireland by the Prime Minister, Robert Cecil, his uncle. Mr Balfour's abilities were considered inappropriate for the post and nepotism was suspected. Popular opinion suggested that he had been selected purely because Bob (short for Robert) was his uncle. In the event, Cecil's judgement was vindicated as Balfour turned out to be an outstanding politician and ultimately became Prime Minister himself from 1902 to 1905.

As with many etymological stories, there is some doubt as to the truth of this one. The biggest difficulty is that there is no written record of the phrase till 1937, when Partridge, in his *Dictionary of Slang and Unconventional English*, dates it to around 1890. A likely influence, if not the direct source, is another phrase, *all is Bob*, meaning 'everything is fine'. This has a long history, going back to Francis Grose's *Dictionary of the Vulgar Tongue* in 1785, and beyond to the sixteenth century.

The first sense of the idiom was an ironic comment on a situation that hinted of favouritism. Later the expression developed a range of meanings. It is essentially a conversational fill-in, with no very precise sense, but carrying with it the ideas of simplicity and success.

*Right, I'm back for a few days so we're going up north. Ah, it's the rainy season. I hadn't thought of that. So Cairns is as far as I get. Let's take the plane to Darwin (not very nice) and drive to Alice Springs. Now, I'll just nip to Ayers Rock for a couple of hours as I've forgotten to book a hotel, then it's over to Perth for a suntan and **Bob's your uncle**. My cheque's in the bank.*
THE GUARDIAN, 4 AUGUST 2000

*I bet her that no one at school had a cat called Montefiore. We giggled over the name a bit and **Bob's your uncle** and Montefiore's your cat.*
ANN WIDDECOMBE,
THE CLEMATIS TREE, 2000

bold: as bold as brass
overly bold in manner, impudent, brazen

In the sixteenth century the word *brazen*, 'made of brass', began to be used figuratively to mean 'shameless, impudent'. From this came *brazen-faced*, the figurative allusion to a countenance that is hardened and incapable of registering shame, as if cast in brass. Towards the end of the sixteenth century Shakespeare wrote the line *Can any face of brasse hold longer out?* (*Love's Labour's Lost*, 1595) to express the same idea, and during the seventeenth century *brass* came to be used to mean 'effrontery, shamelessness'.

The simile *as bold as brass* dates from towards the end of the eighteenth century, when George Parker, in his *Life's Painter of Variegated Characters* (1789), described it as *an expression commonly used among the vulgar after returning from an execution*.

It is possible that the Lord Mayor of London from 1770, one Brass Crosby, may have influenced the development of the phrase. In 1771 he had brought before him as Chief Magistrate a printer who had illegally produced records of Parliamentary proceedings. He let him off, for which action Brass was called before the House of Commons to explain his decision. He was incarcerated in the Tower of London for treason. However, several judges refused to hear his case and he gained considerable public support. In the light of this, he was released.

Since that landmark decision, there have been no further interruptions in reporting parliamentary proceedings, a service that is today known as Hansard. For his bravery in facing Parliament and the Tower, Brass Crosby may have gained some immortality in being a trigger for the wide adoption of the phrase *as bold as brass*.

*There, **bold as brass**, is a photograph of two members dressed up in civil war gear...*
THE TIMES EDUCATIONAL
SUPPLEMENT, 22 FEBRUARY 2002

See ALLITERATIVE SIMILES, page 237.

bombshell: a blonde bombshell
a glamorous blonde

Curvaceous, vivacious, peroxide-blonde actress Jean Harlow was nicknamed the *blonde bombshell* when her 1933 Hollywood hit *Bombshell* was released in Britain as *Blonde Bombshell*. Rees suggests the title was changed to show that the film was not about war. Miss Harlow's beauty created an immediate impact on those who saw her, and a longer-lasting one on English, through the set phrase now associated with her.

*If anyone had mentioned the words 'Cover Girl' to a young fellow of my wartime generation his mind would have immediately conjured up the image of some **blonde bombshell** like Betty Grable posing on the front page of a saucy movie magazine.*
THIS ENGLAND, SUMMER 2002

bombshell: to drop a bombshell
to disclose disturbing news or information

I saw a trial of those devilish murdering, mischief-doing engines called bombs, shot out of the mortar-piece on Blackheath. The distance that they are cast, the destruction they make where they fall, is prodigious, wrote John Evelyn in his *Diary* for 16 March 1687. Military engineers went on to perfect their weaponry to devastating effect but it was not until the second half of the nineteenth century that *bombshell* began to be used figuratively to describe unwelcome news. The idiom really took off in the wake of World War I and has been current ever since.

However, last Sunday Caroline **dropped a bombshell** *that revealed our marriage won't be quite as conventional as I'd hoped. After we're married, she announced, she won't be changing her name to Young. On the contrary, she wants me to change my name to Bondy, which is her surname.*
THE SPECTATOR, 20 JANUARY 2001

For other idioms derived from the army and warfare, see page 317.

bone: to have a bone to pick with someone

to have something disagreeable to discuss, a matter to settle, a complaint to raise

To have a bone to pick or *gnaw* had been in English since at least the 1560s and meant 'to have something to think over, a problem to solve'. The figure was that of a dog engrossed with its bone. *To have a bone to pick with someone*, the contemporary form, did not enter English until the mid-nineteenth century.

There have been various attempts to link the earlier phrase to the modern one. Possibly the best suggestion is that a bone is thrown to a couple of dogs, creating a dispute, but both persevere until one wins out. This parallels the sense of 'an issue to be discussed until the participants come to a resolution'. A second proposition is that, given that BONE *of contention* is of the same date, *to have a bone to pick* is a contraction of *to have a bone of contention to pick* (with someone). The *bone of contention* is shortened in another idiom, *to cast a bone [of contention] between*, 'to set people at loggerheads', so the same process may be in train here.

He had a bone to pick with me. In one of my novels, I had quoted a witticism of his that had been repeated to me by a mutual friend, and Gore was pissed off. What I had thought of as a tribute to his wit, he had thought of as a deliberate misquotation or attack and we were off to a bad start.
THE GUARDIAN, 26 OCTOBER 2000

See also *a* BONE *of contention* and *to make no* BONES *about something*.

bone of contention, a
something that causes disagreement

Great mischief is caused by throwing a single bone amongst dogs. *The diuell hath cast a bone to set stryfe Between you*, John Heywood quoted in his *Proverbs* (1546). The metaphorical *bone*, the matter in dispute, was sometimes referred to as *a bone of dissention* but by the early eighteenth century had become *a bone of contention*.

BONE OF CONTENTION
Who converted Paul McCartney to vegetarianism? Was it Jane Asher in an ashram, or, as Sir Paul has always claimed, his wife Linda over a roast lamb?
THE GUARDIAN, 25 SEPTEMBER 2001

In most relationships, money will be **a bone of contention** *at some point – between 80% and 85% of couples have problems with financial responsibility.*
GOOD HOUSEKEEPING, OCTOBER 2001

See also *to make no* BONES *about* and *to have a* BONE *to pick with someone*.

bone: to bone up on
to study for an exam, to swot up on

Henry George Bohn (1796–1884) was an English publisher, bookseller and translator. His libraries of standard works (Standard Library, Scientific Library, Classical Library, etc) were inexpensive and became very popular with students. Indeed, according to J S Farmer and W E Henley in their *Dictionary of Slang* (1890), volumes of his Classical Library were so widely used among undergraduates in American colleges that *Bohn* had come to mean 'a translation'. The foreign *Bohn* was soon made more familiar as *bone* and, during the mid-1800s, became a verb with the sense 'to study hard', often with additional prepositions such as *in, down, up on.*

For children wishing **to bone up on** *all things Roman without having to trawl through the usual, boring history books try* The Lost Diary of Julius Caesar's Slave, *which gives an eyewitness peek at life in Roman times.*
EVENING STANDARD, 5 JULY 2001

To bone up on packaging symbols visit the website www.recycle-more.co.uk, where you'll also find details of nationwide recycling banks for paper, metals, plastics and more.
GOOD HOUSEKEEPING, JANUARY 2003

bones: to make no bones about something
not to shrink from voicing one's misgivings or scruples about a matter

One theory for the etymology of the phrase is connected with gaming. Even today, one might hear *roll those bones*, meaning 'roll those dice'. *Bones* with this sense goes back to the fourteenth century. A suggestion is that if you *make no bones* you are not trying to influence the dice with all the different superstitious practices (blowing on them, rolling them in the hands, etc) of

ardent gamblers. However, this still leaves an unexplained, semantic step to the current meaning.

Proverbial *bones* are generally problems and difficulties (see *to have a* BONE *to pick* and *a* BONE *of contention*). A fifteenth-century phrase for 'to hit upon difficulties' was *to find bones in*, an allusion to coming across bones in one's broth that make it difficult to eat. The derived expression *to make bones about*, which dates from the sixteenth century, therefore meant 'to make objections, to have misgivings'. The phrase is now usually found in its negative form *to make no bones about* which means 'to have no hesitation in raising objections (with a view to airing them and dealing with them)'.

[Catherine Deneuve] **makes no bones about** *the sustaining value of family life. 'Unless you're Simone de Beauvoir I think the most difficult thing for a woman is to grow old alone.'*
GOOD HOUSEKEEPING, MARCH 2002

Most journalists are morally bankrupt. I make no bones about this. That is how the public sees us.
THE SPECTATOR, 20 JULY 2002

John, dear, there's nothing disgraceful about manual labor and having to work for a living. What's disgraceful is the fact many thousands choose to sit on their butts and collect welfare. Some of my co-workers **make no bones** *about wanting to sit home and have a paycheck come in the mail.*
WASHINGTON POST, 28 JANUARY 2005

See also *a* BONE *of contention* and *to make no* BONES *about something.*

bow: two strings to one's bow

resources in reserve, more than one option

The phrase dates from the second half of the fifteenth century and alludes to the spare string that archers would carry in case the first broke. *It is always good to haue two stringes to a bowe*, wrote John Florio in *Firste Frutes* (1578), his book of Italian–English dialogues. From the late eighteenth and into the twentieth century the *two strings* were often a lady's lovers. In Jane Austen's *Mansfield Park* (1814) it was Maria Bertram who was said to have *two strings to her bow* when she was unable to resist flirtation with Henry Crawford, although she was already engaged to Mr Rushworth. Nowadays *two strings to one's bow* has largely been replaced by *another* or *a second string* and often refers to an occupation or career. In this sense *second string* dates back to the mid-seventeenth century.

*The project has been several years in gestation; and while Mr Pickard waits, and waits, for the last few technicalities to fall into place, he has **other strings to his bow**. He has a little sideline in providing building services... This, and an insurance brokerage, features heavily in the other main leg of his business: a glossy colour quarterly magazine called* The Ukrainian.
THE ECONOMIST, 11 MAY 2000

*He is now anxious to make his own way, and although the graphic design firm he started last year with friends has had its problems, he has **another string to his bow** as a DJ in clubs in Long Beach, Orange County and in LA, where he plays a mix of 1980s music and rap.*
THE GUARDIAN, 5 SEPTEMBER 2003

brand new

entirely new, completely new

Here *brand* has nothing to do with the mark of workmanship but means 'the result of burning'. In *brand new* the allusion is to a metal object which has just been lifted from the furnace – it is so new it has not yet cooled. The phrase goes back to the sixteenth century, as does Shakespeare's more explicit variant *fire-new* used in *Richard III* (1597) and *Love's Labours Lost* (1595):

> *Armado is a most illustrious wight,*
> *A man of fire-new words, fashion's*
> *own knight.*

*Just down the road from the BMW car dealership, razed in last summer's race riots, optimism and hope are getting a rare airing at the launch of a **brand new** Bradford secondary school.*
THE INDEPENDENT, 25 JULY 2002

brass: cold enough to freeze the balls off a brass monkey

extremely cold

There is a quaint naval yarn to explain this phrase. In the days when warships carried cannon, shot was stacked on a brass tray, or *monkey*, beside each gun. In very cold conditions the metal tray would contract and cannonballs roll off the pyramid. Of course this raises the question why sailors continued to use inconvenient metal trays. The answer is that they probably never did, for any evidence to support the story is lacking.

An alternative theory has an ornament, commonly found in drawing rooms in both Britain and America in the nineteenth century, as the source of the idiom. The ornament was of three brass monkeys, one covering his eyes, one covering his ears, and the third covering his mouth – 'See no evil, hear no evil, speak no evil'. The monkeys originated in China and were introduced to Japan by a Buddhist monk in the eighth century, the most notable representation being a set of carvings in the Nikko Toshogo Shrine.

Whether or not the phrase was inspired by the ornament, in America around the middle of the nineteenth century *brass monkey* began to appear in statements about the weather. Herman Melville used it in *Omoo: A Narrative of Adventures in the South Seas* (1847) to describe weather that was *'ot enough to melt the nose h'off a brass monkey*. By the late nineteenth century, however, the term was largely confined to cold conditions: *Mr. Banks, who was known to have spoken to him, could only remember that one warm evening, in reply to a casual remark about the weather, the missing man, burying his ears further in the turned-up collar of his pea-jacket, had stated, 'It was cold enough to freeze the ears off a brass monkey,'—a remark, no doubt, sir, intended to convey a reason for his hiding his own'* (Bret Harte, *The Crusade of the Excelsior*, 1887).

The monkey in Harte's novel loses its ears; in that of Ralph Connor its tail falls off: *'Begob, but it's cowld enough to freeze the tail aff a brass monkey…'* (*The Doctor: a Tale of the Rockies*, 1906). In yet another variant, it is the monkey's whiskers that are subject to the cold. Nose, tail, ears, whiskers, what else could possibly fall off the creature?

The answer came around the turn of the twentieth century, when the term was coarsened. The weather became *cold enough to freeze the balls off a brass monkey*, a variant that was subsequently shortened to *brass monkey weather* or, shorter still, *it's brass monkeys*.

Meanwhile, during the early twentieth century, the politer versions of the phrase gave rise to a flurry of alternative *brass monkey* idioms, and phrases such as *talk the tail off a brass monkey* or *have the gall of a brass monkey* were

heard. But it is the more risqué phrase that has eventually won out, and the brass monkey now loses his balls in every English-speaking country where the temperature drops below zero.

If you quite liked Cool Runnings, *the wacky comedy about the Jamaican bobsleigh team at the Winter Olympics, then you'll quite like* Snow Dogs, *the wacky comedy about a dentist in sunny Florida…who journeys to Alaska to find his real dad, and gets caught up in the world of dog-sled racing in the **brass-monkey-freezing** weather.*
THE GUARDIAN, 31 MAY 2002

brass: to get down to brass tacks

to consider the essential facts, to get to the heart of the matter

The phrase is American and dates from at least the late nineteenth century. It obviously originates in an occupation of some sort, but which one is obscure. The most respected suggestion is that the wooden countertop in a country or draper's store would have brass-headed tacks hammered into it at carefully measured intervals. The customer who had got to the point of having her cloth measured out against the tacks was about to make a purchase and was really getting down to business.

The expression, however, seems to suggest a removal of layers in order to reveal the tacks. Two suggestions from different American authorities cover this implication.

The first is that the brass tacks may refer to those used by upholsterers to fix the wadding and fabric in place. Any re-upholstery job meant first stripping a chair down to the original brass tacks.

The second suggestion is that the expression originated in the shipyard and referred to the cleaning of a ship's hull, a process which involved scrubbing off all the barnacles to reveal the bolts which held the structure together. The exponent of this theory admits that such bolts would be of copper and not brass and that a tack is rather a flimsy fastening with which to secure a ship, but puts this down to American understatement for humorous effect.

The two leaders **got straight down to brass tacks** *when they talked away from the ears of their own advisers over pre-dinner drinks.*
THE INDEPENDENT, 22 SEPTEMBER 2001

brave new world
a sinister future world that promises much but may well not deliver

Aldous Huxley published *Brave New World* in 1932. It was a telling and prophetic book, and merits its place in the tradition of Wells' *The Time Machine* (1895) and Orwell's *Nineteen Eighty-Four* (1949). A world, apparently moving on to better things, in fact produces nightmare results. Huxley's tale, sadly, shows all too many signs of coming true, as the author himself came to see. His *Brave New World Revisited* of 1958 explores his own concerns at the far too imminent fulfilment of the prophecies and prescience he had shown decades earlier in his exploration of a technological and totalitarian utopia. Modern usage of the phrase has the same bitter edge of irony – what is promised to make our world better is in fact offered for self-seeking purposes, or will not in fact produce the results.

The negative tone of the current expression is a far cry from that of its origin. In Shakespeare's *The Tempest* (1611), Miranda is cast adrift with her father, Prospero, and lands on a lonely island. After many vicissitudes and adventures, the island weaves its enchantment (not least by allowing the magical mending of a ship that allows them to return to Italy), and it draws from Miranda the awestruck and heartfelt:

> *O wonder!*
> *How many goodly creatures there are here!*
> *How beauteous mankind is!*
> *O brave new world*
> *That has such people in't!*

All this becomes even more important as we look to the **brave new world** *of broadband. As has been noted, it is content that is going to persuade people to hand over their £30 a month for a faster web connection.*
THE GUARDIAN, 25 MARCH 2002

In New Labour's **brave new world***, soft drugs are fine. Experimental sex is natural. Absolute standards are worthless.*
DAILY MAIL, 28 JUNE 2002

For other idioms from Shakespeare, see WILLIAM SHAKESPEARE, page 152.

bread: the best thing since sliced bread
the best innovation for some time

Rees (1990) mentions a clever advertisement of Sainsbury's from 1981: *Sainsbury's brings you the greatest thing since sliced bread. Unsliced bread.* These days we pour scorn on the tastelessness and spongy texture of the product which we take so much for granted, but when it first appeared in 1928 it caused quite a stir.

The bread-slicing machine was the brainwave of Iowa-born salesman and inventor Otto Rohwedder. Rohwedder began work in 1912 but, when he tried to interest bakeries in his idea, he was told that sliced bread would soon go stale. Long pins to hold the loaves together were among the devices he subsequently thought up to address this problem. By 1928 Rohwedder had designed a machine that sliced bread and wrapped it to keep it fresh. Success. By 1933 around eighty per cent of bread consumed in America was sliced, while people in Britain had been enjoying pre-cut bread brand-named Wonderbread since 1930.

It may have been at this time that the phrase *the best thing since sliced bread* was coined to express enthusiasm, or it may have been after 1950 when pre-cut loaves were reintroduced after prohibition during the war years, and supermarket chains were developing. Certainly records seem to indicate that the phrase belongs to the 1960s, in Britain at least.

*It's that fine line, between winning and losing. Win, and you're the **best thing since sliced bread**, lose – it's an absolute disaster. Then you receive the sort of press Dick Advocaat's had this year...*
THE SCOTSMAN, 5 MAY 2001

*Its creator, Gerry Hinton, can barely contain his excitement at his own product. 'I'm telling you, it is the **best thing since sliced bread**,' he says enthusiastically.*
THE SCOTSMAN, 9 MAY 2001

breadline: on/below the breadline

very poor, living at/below subsistence level

Breadline is an Americanism dating back to the nineteenth century when it literally described a queue of poor people waiting for handouts of free or cheap bread (*line* is the American term for 'queue'). The original *breadline* is now thought to be that which gathered nightly outside Fleischmann's Model Vienna Bakery in the late 1870s, where any bread left over from the day's trading was handed out to the poor and destitute. In an account penned in 1905 former Congressman Henry George Jr described how the Fleischmanns' philanthropy caught on in New York:

Each night for twenty-seven years a line has formed in front of Fleischmann's Vienna Bakery at Broadway and Tenth Street, New York. Each man in that line has received half a loaf of bread and a steaming cup of coffee. The line has not shortened with years. If anything it has lengthened. Other free bread and coffee lines have been established, and one of the most popular of the daily newspapers gave night food to thousands last winter (The Menace of Privilege, 1905).

The term *breadline* was first recorded in 1900 in a story published in *Lippincott's Magazine,* but before 1910 it had already gained the more general sense of 'subsistence level'.

*But while Shaw is no doubt suffering, he is hardly **on the breadline**. The television in the sitting room is a state-of-the-art one, the kitchen is littered with expensive German electrical equipment, and a newish BMW X5 stands outside.*
EVENING STANDARD, 12 AUGUST 2002

breath: to save one's breath

to keep silent, not to waste one's time talking because no one will take any notice

This is a shortened form of the phrase *save your breath (wind) to cool your pottage* which, though subject to minor variants, has been in frequent use since the sixteenth century. The expression dates in its current form from the 1920s.

*He can **save his breath** because no one in the Arab world will believe him.*
THE GUARDIAN, 14 APRIL 2003

If you want a lame excuse for not investing for your future, you've come to the right place. Take your pick of the ones I most frequently hear:
'I don't have any extra money to invest.'
'I've got decades until retirement.'
'Stop harassing me, Dayana, or I'm telling on you to Mom and Dad.'

Save your breath: I've heard them all.
THE MOTLEY FOOL, 26 APRIL 2005

brownie points
notional credits for things done to gain another's regard and favour

Brownie point, which originated in America in the 1960s, most likely refers to the system of award points earned by the Brownies, the junior branch of the Girl Guide and Girl Scout movement. The term was then humorously applied to good deeds in general, sometimes sarcastically if toadying were suspected. It is possible, therefore, that the phrase was also influenced by the rather less wholesome American slang term *to brown-nose* meaning 'to curry favour', the insinuation being that ingratiating behaviour amounts to much the same as kissing the bottom of the person whose favour is solicited. (*Brown* has been an American slang term for 'anus' since the mid-nineteenth century.)

The left-wing Liberal Democrats gain **brownie points** *for an explicit promise to raise tax to fund even more public spending.*
THE SCOTSMAN, 21 MAY 2001

On Sunday evening I'd deliver an hour's comedy at the Tivoli Theatre in aid of the said hospice – and on Monday morning fly home replete with Guinness and **Brownie Points***.*
GOOD HOUSEKEEPING, JULY 2002

If people do not understand what you are saying they cannot prove it to be nonsense. It is all of a piece with those cartels that are said to exist in academia. The 'members' agree to quote each other's work so that they can all gain **Brownie points** *– whether anyone understands them or not.*
JOHN HUMPHRYS,
LOST FOR WORDS, 2004

buck: to pass the buck
to sidestep responsibility by passing it on to someone else

This is a poker term which originated in America in the second half of the nineteenth century. The *buck* was a marker, perhaps a piece of buckshot or a knife with a buckhorn handle, which was passed from player to player to indicate the next dealer. When the buck was passed on, the responsibility for dealing went with it. The phrase began to be used figuratively in the early twentieth century: *'Do you get the idea?' 'Sure I get the idea. It's the old army game: first, pass the buck; second, never give a sucker an even break....'* (Theodore Fredenburgh, *Soldiers March!*, 1930).

A well-known variation was used by President Harry Truman who had a sign on his desk at the White House which read *The buck stops here*. The phrase, which indicates acceptance of responsibility, was not coined by the President, however; the plaque was given to him by a friend who had seen a similar one at the Federal Reformatory at El Reno, Oklahoma. Nevertheless, Truman often referred to it in his speeches: *You know, it's easy for the Monday morning quarterback to say what the coach should have done, after the game is over. But when the decision is up before you – and on my desk I have a motto which says 'The Buck Stops Here' – the decision has to be made* (National War College Address, 19 December 1952).

Later presidents have stood by the phrase, among them Jimmy Carter and Gerald Ford, who famously used it in his pardon of Richard Nixon on 8 September 1974: *I do believe that the buck stops here, that I cannot rely upon public opinion polls to tell me what is right.*

Mr Straw is handing the sentencing of the toddler's killers to the Lord Chief Justice, Lord Bingham – who is expected to confirm the ten years set by his predecessor, Lord Taylor, rather than the 15 years later decreed by the then Tory Home Secretary Michael Howard. With this decision Mr Straw appears to be **passing the buck**. But the unpalatable truth is that he had no option...
DAILY MAIL, 14 MARCH 2000

Phil Willis MP, Liberal Democrat education spokesman, said the report demanded improvements from the Government as well as schools. He said: 'When results were improving, ministers took the credit. Now the results are not so good, they **pass the buck** to teachers and local education authorities.'
THE TIMES EDUCATIONAL SUPPLEMENT, 7 DECEMBER 2001

I've actually tried to visit my impotent rage on those I hold responsible – only to find myself trapped in the cruellest of all modern oxymorons, the telephone help-line. What followed was an excruciating game of **pass-the-buck**, since the hardware supplier knows full well that you have no way of proving that the fault doesn't lie in the software and ditto everyone else involved.
THE INDEPENDENT, 13 MARCH 2002

See also the BUCK stops here and, for other idioms derived from poker, see page 320.

buck: the buck stops here
this is where ultimate responsibility lies

See to pass the BUCK.

But **the buck must stop somewhere**. If consultants are the experts, they should know where the weak links commonly exist. They should signal these weak points in the reports that give their recommendations in the first place.
IT WEEK, 24 SEPTEMBER 2001

We can't make excuses and hide behind the manager – it's down to the players. The teams we have put out recently have been good enough to win matches and we haven't done it. The **buck stops with** the players when they go out on the pitch.
THE DAILY TELEGRAPH, 17 MARCH 2004

buck: to buck up
to cheer up; to get a move on

In eighteenth-century London there were apparently societies run along the same lines as the Freemasons, whose young male members called themselves bucks and whose president was known as the Grand Buck. A buck was 'a rake, a spirited young man, a dashing fellow' and, according to Francis Grose in the 1811 edition of his Dictionary of the Vulgar Tongue, a buck of the first head was one who in debauchery surpasses the rest of his companions. The allusion, of course, was to the condition and skittishness of a fine male deer, a buck.

During the Regency period of the early nineteenth century the word buck came to describe one who was elegantly and fashionably attired; one who, like Beau Brummell, polished his boots with champagne and took five hours to dress:

If the morning be fine, the pavement of the Strand and Fleet Street looks quite radiant with the spruce clerks walking down to their offices, governmental, financial, and commercial. Marvellous young bucks some of them are. These are the customers, you see at a glance, whom the resplendent wares in the hosiers' shops attract, and in whom those wary industrials find avid customers. These are the dashing young parties who purchase the pea-green, the orange, and the rose-pink gloves; the crimson braces, the kaleidoscopic shirt-studs, the shirts embroidered with dahlias, death's heads, racehorses, sun-flowers, and ballet-girls; the horseshoe, fox-head, pewterpot-and-crossed-

pipes, willow-pattern-plate, and knife-and-fork pins (George Augustus Sala, *Twice Round the Clock, or The Hours of the Day and Night in London*, 1859).

Consequently *to buck up* meant 'to get dressed up'.

There's nothing like a wash and brush up and some glad rags to lift the spirits, and so gradually the phrase came to mean 'to cheer up, to be glad'. Schoolboys at Winchester College also used the exhortation *buck up* to mean 'rouse yourself, get a move on' and thus the expression gained the sense 'make an effort' or 'move along'. Nowadays *buck your ideas up* is also often heard.

You poms are merely going through a bit of a slump. It will pass. Why are you losing confidence so? Cricket is a wonderful, voluptuous thing. Be heroic! Lose graciously while you have to. Save your intellect and learning for demonstrations on that field of endeavour. **Do buck up**. *Really. You are so much more than cricket.*
THE SPECTATOR, 25 AUGUST 2001

Sophie…has lived in a children's home for the past four years. 'I was having problems at home that made me get behind with my school work,' she says. 'The teachers begged me to **buck up***, so I did lots of work one week and I handed it in, but it was all thrown back in my face and I was told it was awful. I was so upset I just blew.'*
THE GUARDIAN, 24 JULY 2002

bull: to take the bull by the horns
to face up to difficulty with boldness

Some authorities propose an origin in Spanish bull fighting where the *banderilleros* pierce the bull's neck muscles with darts until its head begins to droop, then play him with capes, seizing his horns to keep his head low. American rodeos and the now-obsolete English sport of bull-running have also been suggested.

A much earlier practice which certainly involved taking the bull by the horns quite literally was that instigated by King Minos of Crete, some 3,500 years ago. He was a worshipper of the sacred bull, and insisted that Athens should send every seven years seven men and seven women to act as 'bull dancers' in his palace. Few survived long.

However, the idiom is clarity itself and probably does not need a story to explain its existence. It may just come from the farmyard. An early example occurs in Swift's political pamphlet *The Conduct of Allies* (1711) where the author argues that *to engage with France was to take the bull by the horns*, and Sir Walter Scott uses the phrase in *Old Mortality* (1816) in a context that confirms it as a familiar expression.

Houllier revealed Gerrard's groin problems have become more frequent this year, leaving Liverpool with no choice but to 'take the bull by the horns' and consider surgery.
LIVERPOOL ECHO, 14 MAY 2002

burn: to burn one's boats/bridges (behind one)
to be so committed to a course of action that it is impossible to withdraw

This phrase refers to the practice Roman generals sometimes employed of setting fire to their own boats after mounting an invasion. This was to remove any notion of retreat from the minds of their soldiers. There are few instances in history of such dramatic practices. One such case is that of the praetorian prefect Asclepiodotus. He led an army to Britain in about AD 296, to bring to heel a ten-year breakaway from Rome by Carausius and then Allectus. Spurred on, apparently, by the loss of their ships, the invading force defeated and killed Allectus near present-day Farnham, and brought the errant province back under Caesar's control. Still earlier, the tyrant Agathocles (361–289 BC) is reputed to have used the same motivational tactic in his lifetime of battles at the head of armies of mercenaries.

The first metaphorical use seems to date from the second half of the nineteenth century:

But Edgar, not wishing to go too far in the way of provocation, nor to burn his boats behind him before he had decided on his settlement, skated off to Adelaide so soon as he had deposited Leam, and by a few judicious praises and well-administered tendernesses of voice and look succeeded in bringing her back to her normal condition of quiescent resolve and satisfaction (E Lynn Linton, *The Atonement of Leam Dundas*, in *Lippincott's Magazine*, March 1876).

A similarly decisive synonymous expression is *to burn one's bridges behind one*. Metaphorical use goes back to the end of the nineteenth century:

The young Lord Berkeley, with the fresh air of freedom in his nostrils, was feeling invincibly strong for his new career; and yet—and yet—if the fight should prove a very hard one at first, very discouraging, very taxing on untoughened moral sinews, he might in some weak moment want to retreat. Not likely, of course, but possibly that might happen. And so on the whole it might be pardonable caution to burn his bridges behind him. Oh, without doubt. (Mark Twain, *The American Claimant*, 1892).

*He…was tested when the TV script-writers decided they wanted to kill off Ellie Pascoe, Peter's left-wing lecturer wife. Fortunately the TV writers decided not to **burn their boats**, and have instead divorced the Pascoes.*
THE TIMES EDUCATIONAL
SUPPLEMENT, 21 SEPTEMBER 2001

*His relationship with the theatrical and operatic establishment in Britain has long been a tense one. Now Jonathan Miller, giant of the stage and respected man of letters, has fallen out in dramatic style with one of the most prestigious opera houses in the world, the Metropolitan in New York… A less confident man might be worried about **burning his bridges**, but Miller has been outspoken before.*
THE GUARDIAN, 20 MAY 2002

For other fatalistic expressions, see *the* DIE *is cast and the* POINT *of no return*. For other idioms drawn from ancient life and history, see page 317.

burn: to burn the midnight oil

to stay up late to study, read or work

The idea of burning away oil in the pursuit of learning and creativity is not uncommon in classical literature. In his *Life of Demosthenes*, Plutarch speaks of the orator's meticulous care in composition, then writes: *For this many of the orators ridiculed him, and Pytheas in particular told him, 'That all his arguments smelled of the lamp.' Demosthenes retorted sharply upon him: 'Yes, indeed, but your lamp and mine, my friend, are not conscious to the same labours.'*

The phrase *midnight oil* has been around since at least the 1630s. It was used by the poet Francis Quarles in *Emblems* (1635), a book of short devotional poems that found favour with the Puritans:

Wee spend our mid-day sweat, or
mid-night oyle;
Wee tyre the night in thought; the day in
toyle.

In the following century, the poet John Gay, developed a fondness for the expression. Here he uses it in the introduction to his *Fables* (1727):

Whence is thy learning? Hath thy toil
O'er books consumed the midnight oil?

and here in a passage from *Trivia*
(1716) which describes bookstalls in
London streets:

Walkers at leisure leaning's flowers
may spoil,
Nor watch the wasting of the midnight oil.

Although, these days, we enjoy the
benefits of electric lights, the phrase
has remained current to describe those,
especially students, who write or study
far into the night.

The chancellor spent much of last week
burning the midnight oil *working on the*
speech with close aides.
THE GUARDIAN, 1 OCTOBER 2001

Kidder shadowed Farmer as he toiled at
his hospital in Haiti from dawn to dusk,
as he hiked vast distances to follow up on
patients and then **burned the midnight**
oil *writing grant applications and*
preparing speeches.
NEW YORK TIMES, 14 SEPTEMBER 2003

burton: to go for a burton

to be killed; to fail, to be completely
spoiled

During the Second World War the
RAF used this euphemism to speak of
colleagues who were killed or missing
in action. What, then, is a *burton*?
Where there is doubt, folk etymology
proliferates. The most commonly held
theory claims that *burton* refers to a
brew of strong beer made in Burton-
on-Trent. Some even say that the
slogan *Gone for a Burton* featured in
advertisements of the immediately pre-
war period. Friends were not said to
have gone to their deaths, they had
just gone out for a beer.

An alternative story, equally lacking in evidence, states that records of
RAF casualties were kept in offices by

the Blackpool branch of Burton
Menswear.

Nowadays the phrase has lost its
association with death. Instead it is
commonly used to refer to objects
which are broken beyond mending
(vases, lawn-mowers, cars) or to hopes,
dreams and plans that are shattered.

This seemed the wrong orchestra, the
wrong hall and the wrong repertory…
Is it the killer Royal Albert Hall acoustic,
which robs any live audience of precision?
Is it that the performers cannot hear each
other, so intonation and ensemble **go for**
a burton*?*
THE INDEPENDENT, 19 AUGUST 2002

For other idioms derived from the
army and warfare, see page 317.

bury: to bury the hatchet

to restore a relationship after a long
quarrel, to make up with someone

When American Indians negotiated
the cessation of hostilities, each party
would ceremonially bury a tomahawk
to seal the pact. In the *New England*
Historical Register of 1680 Samuel
Sewall writes of one such ceremony,
this between Indians and white men:
Meeting with the Sachem they came to an
agreement and buried two Axes in the
Ground;…which ceremony to them is more
significant and binding than all Articles of
Peace, the Hatchet being a principal
weapon. Of course the tomahawks
could always be dug up again, and this
meant renewed aggression.

A pair of Devon families warred for seven
years over a strip of boundary land just
4in wide – spending £10,000 on legal fees,
before reluctantly **burying the hatchet**
after 11 weeks of mediation.
THE SUNDAY TELEGRAPH,
16 SEPTEMBER 2001

KENTUCKY'S MOST FAMOUS FEUDING FAMILIES BURY THE HATCHET

The Hatfields and the McCoys were facing each other in the mountains of eastern Kentucky yesterday, armed with baseball bats. But no one was ducking for cover, waiting for the shotgun blasts which would surely have followed 100 years ago.

The two clans, whose legendary rivalry once epitomised the rural violence of the region for many outsiders, were holding a family reunion this weekend, bringing thousands back to the region they once called home.
THE TIMES, 11 JUNE 2002

*Sir Paul McCartney's attempts at brokering a truce between his children by Linda and his new, young Linda-lookalike wife have fallen on deaf ears. Instead of trying to **bury the hatchet** in the ground, designer daughter Stella seems more intent on burying it in Heather.*
DAILY MAIL, 13 JUNE 2002

bush telegraph

rapid spreading of news or rumour; an informal network of contacts

The phrase comes from Australia, probably in the 1860s, where it originally referred to the network of informers who fed escaped convicts and dangerous criminals living in the bush information about the activities of the police. It may be modelled on the earlier American idiom *grapevine telegraph*.

*An ingrown toenail would set the Renwick **bush telegraph** working.*
ANN WIDDECOMBE,
THE CLEMATIS TREE, 2000

*Jewish hawkers were Istanbul's **bush telegraph**.*
THE GUARDIAN, 17 NOVEMBER 2003

See also *(on/through) the* GRAPEVINE.

bushel: to hide one's light under a bushel

to keep quiet about one's abilities, knowledge and achievements

The phrase is a biblical one. Jesus has been teaching his followers that they are the light of the world. He then goes on to say in Matthew 5:14–15: *Ye are the light of the world. A city that is set on an hill, cannot be hid, neither do men light a candle and put it under a bushel, but on a candlestick, and it lighteth all them which are in the house* (Tyndale's translation, 1526) and he urges them to go out and bring glory to God by the way they lead their lives. The *bushel* in the text is a bowl that would have held a bushel volume or weight of ground meal or flour.

Figurative reference to hiding various qualities under bushels, the very opposite of Christ's command, has occurred since at least the mid-sixteenth century. The idiom as we know it dates from the second half of the nineteenth century.

*Once summer is over, pupils will return to school to face the same destructive criticism. Unless children's attitudes can be changed, those for whom Leonardo means da Vinci rather than DiCaprio will continue **to hide their light under a bushel**.*
THE TIMES EDUCATIONAL
SUPPLEMENT, 11 AUGUST 2000

*He's especially anonymous when it comes to his favorite activity, making charitable contributions. 'Many with his wealth want to buy a Picasso,' says Yeminidjian, 'he prefers to give to charity – and I'm talking about hundreds of millions of dollars.' Unlike many donors, Kerkorian **hides his light under a bushel**, refusing to receive any acknowledgement.*
VARIETY, 19 APRIL 2004

For other idioms from the Bible, see page 317.

busman's holiday, a

a holiday spent doing the same thing
one would be doing at work

The earliest record found to date of
this phrase comes in an edition of the
English Illustrated Magazine of 1893. At
that time buses were horse-drawn,
giving rise to the common theory that
any bus driver who became greatly
attached to his horses would spend his
days off riding on his own vehicle to
ensure that the relief driver was treat-
ing them properly.

An intriguing alternative is
advanced by Evan Morris (*Word
Detective*). Although he is mistaken in
his assertion that the word *busman* does
not even exist (there are references
from the mid-nineteenth century
through to at least the late 1930s), it is
quite feasible that it appears in this
expression as a corruption of *buzman*.
This word was a piece of nineteenth-
century thieves' cant denoting 'a
pickpocket'. Farmer (*Slang and its
Analogues*, 1890) says it was probably
derived from *buzz* in the sense of 'to
talk busily', one thief engaging the
victim in conversation while another
picked his pocket. Since pickpockets
never take a break but are always on
the lookout for an opportunity to lift a
purse or wallet, the corrupted expression *busman's holiday* began to be
applied to the leisure activities of
workaholics in general. What a shame
there is no evidence of *buzman's holiday*
to secure the theory.

*Then…the conversation turned to politics.
Sally, not wanting a **busman's holiday**,
left most of the conversation to Claire, who
inveighed heavily against the unions and
environmental lobbies.*
ANN WIDDECOMBE,
THE CLEMATIS TREE, 2000

*Eugenius Birch was a prolific Victorian
engineer who liked to be beside the seaside.
Born in London in 1818, he designed and
built no fewer than 14 piers off the coasts
of England and Wales… These robust but
whimsical structures, stoutly fixed to the
sea bed by Birch's patent cast-iron screw-
piles, were a **busman's holiday** of sorts for
the engineer of the Calcutta–Delhi railway,
Exmouth docks, Ilfracombe harbour and the
West Surrey waterworks.*
THE GUARDIAN, 11 MARCH 2002

· C ·

cake: to take the cake

to deserve honour or merit; to be outrageous

Many people believe that the phrase has its origins in the cakewalk, an amusement devised by black slaves in Southern US plantations in the nineteenth century. Participating couples would promenade about the room arm in arm and the pair judged as walking and turning most gracefully were given a cake as a prize, the admiring cry 'That takes the cake' giving rise to the idiom.

However, the expression and the awarding of a cake as a prize are really centuries older. As far back as the fifth century BC Aristophanes wrote in *The Knights*: *If you surpass him in impudence, we take the cake*. A cake, a confection of toasted cereal sweetened and bound together with honey, was a reward given to the most vigilant man on a night watch or to one who remained most alert during a drinking party. The phrase became idiomatic to the Greeks and was then used to refer to any prize for any event. Nevertheless, it is much more probable that nineteenth-century American authors had the cakewalk in mind when using the phrase.

To take the biscuit is a variant that may have been introduced by Irish journalist and dramatist George Bernard Shaw in *John Bull's Other Island* (1904). It is, if anything, now more commonly heard than the phrase from which it sprang and is often spoken in a tone of exasperation or disbelief at events.

*The romancing is done at a series of social gatherings (it's all they ever do); and for amusing social gaffing, **it takes the cake**.*
THE GUARDIAN, 15 FEBRUARY 2002

*We've visited some extraordinary ruins together – Pompeii, Knossos, Volubilis – but **this takes the cake**!*
THE GUARDIAN, 22 FEBRUARY 2003

See also *to take the* BISCUIT.

can: (to open) a can of worms

(to broach/expose) a complex problem involving much unpleasantness

This phrase is probably of American origin and dates from the mid-twentieth century. It alludes to the angler's live bait, a container of slippery, squirming worms, all entwined round one another, a vivid metaphor for an unpleasant and complex problem.

One of the prisoners, Mac, wrote a graphic short story about a day in the life of a heroin addict, based on real events. Others told their life stories straight to camera…

*However, most of the prisoners had not spoken to their families about their crimes – let alone bared their souls in public. 'It was **a can of worms**,' admits Spike.*
THE GUARDIAN, 7 AUGUST 2002

Brian White, a Labour MP on the Commons public administration committee examining the scope of the royal prerogative, forecast that the prince's habit of lobbying ministers will continue to be controversial… 'There will be some times

when it will be advantageous for him to speak but other times when it won't .
A whole can of worms will be opened up,' *he said.*
THE SUNDAY TIMES, 3 JUNE 2003

candle: not to hold a candle to

to be inferior to, not do as well as

In the sixteenth century, when every task done after dark was accomplished by candlelight, *to hold a candle to another* meant quite literally 'to help someone out by holding a candle close to his work'. Candle-holding was not the most demanding of tasks and therefore usually fell to an assistant, subordinate or servant, hence the contemporary proverb: *Who that worst maie, shall holde the candell* (John Heywood, *Proverbs*, 1546). In the following century John Ray (*English Proverbs*, 1670) recorded the same proverb with its French counterpart:

He that worst may, still holds the candle.
Au plus débile la chandelle à la main.

It follows, then, that if someone were deemed *not fit to hold a candle to* his master or superior, he was judged incapable of carrying out the simplest chore and so, over time, this phrase became one of comparison between the best and the very worst:

> *Others aver that he to Handel*
> *Is scarcely fit to hold the candle*
> (John Byrom, *On the Feude Between Handel and Bononcini*, 1773)

Everyone in television knew that during his 20 years in commercial television Mr Dyke had never produced a single distinguished programme. (I partly exclude Roland Rat, for whom I had a slight fondness, though he could never **hold a candle to** *Basil Brush.)*
THE SPECTATOR, 16 FEBRUARY 2002

candle: (the game is) not worth the candle

(the activity is) not worth the effort or expense

This began as a French idiom *le jeu ne vaut pas la chandelle,* 'the game is not worth the candle', which appeared in Randle Cotgrave's famous French–English dictionary of 1611. The allusion is obviously to some sort of gambling activity – dice, perhaps, or cards – where the stakes were so low that it was not worth the expense of a candle to light the game. The shortened phrase, *not worth the candle*, began to appear in English usage towards the end of the seventeenth century.

Given that from next year the cost of a three-year degree will be abotu £75,000 in tuition fees, living expenses and missed earnings, there is bound to come a point when, for many graduates, **the game is no longer worth the candle**.
THE DAILY TELEGRAPH, 11 JUNE 2001

candle: to burn the candle at both ends

to work or play until late into the night and then get up early next morning; to invest energy and resources in more than one project at once, to one's own detriment

The appearance of *brusler la chandelle par les deux bouts* in Randle Cotgrave's French–English dictionary (1611) reveals that this was originally a French expression. He defines it thus: *To wast, or spend, things disorderedly; to squander hee cares not how, nor what.* It had caught on in English by the 1650s when one of Richard Flecknoe's *Enigmaticall Characters* (1658) did just that: *He consuming just like a candle on both ends, betwixt wine and women.* And it still meant much the same some seventy-two years later when it was quoted in Bailey's popular *Dictionarium Britannicum*

(1730): *The Candle burns at both Ends. Said when Husband and Wife are both Spendthrifts.*

Not until the middle of the nineteenth century did the notion of staying up late and rising early also attach itself to the expression: *Far too many of our girls go to wreck nowadays. They burn the candle at both ends; and when they break down they blame the books, not the balls* (Louisa M Alcott, *Little Men,* 1871).

Naughtie, who is 50, usually does Today *four times a week, presents opera broadcasts and has a monthly book programme, as well as making lucrative appearances on the conference circuit. 'It's been quite tough,' he admits, 'and I've been guilty of burning the candle at both ends.'*
THE GUARDIAN, 28 SEPTEMBER 2001

The Italian nobleman was born in 1467 and was quite a lad in his youth. Merrily burning the candle at both ends, he led a life fuelled by sensual pleasures, overindulgence and extremes. By middle age, he was crippled...
EVENING NEWS, 26 NOVEMBER 2001

But she thinks it was stress. She was burning the candle at both ends, working hard and playing hard.
THE SCOTSMAN, 21 JULY 2002

cards: to be on the cards
to be possible, to be likely to happen

The expression, which dates from the early nineteenth century, probably refers to the practice of using Tarot cards to predict future events, a practice that has been current in Europe since the fourteenth century.

...the report reinforced the feeling in the market that a rate reduction may be on the cards...
EVENING STANDARD, 8 AUGUST 2002

carpet: (blood) on the carpet
a stern rebuke, strong action; widespread job loss

Centuries ago carpets were imported from Turkey and were precious items. They often covered tables, chests and beds in the homes and offices of the well-to-do. During the early eighteenth century if a matter of importance was *on the carpet* it meant that it was on the council table and, therefore, 'under consideration'. This sense was obsolete by the turn of the nineteenth century, but the phrase lived on with the meaning 'receiving a reprimand', an expression that originated in America and is recorded in *Scribner's Magazine* in the 1880s. In the nineteenth century any worker in need of correction would be summoned to his employer's office. Since only the affluent could afford the warmth of carpet underfoot, the worker would have the rare experience of standing on a carpet while being rebuked.

Other phrases from the first half of the nineteenth century share this origin: the verb *to carpet* meant 'to rebuke' while a sloppy or dishonest maid would be made to *walk the carpet,* to receive a scolding from the lady of the household.

Nowadays houses and offices have wall-to-wall carpeting and so the modern idiom has developed a graphic new form to compensate. An apprehensive employee can now expect *blood on the carpet.* Sometimes the wound can be self-inflicted, as in this curious anecdote of power in high places:

It is against the tradition of the Foreign Office to show emotion in any emergency. Private secretaries are almost unapproachable persons. One of these was Henry Foley, who on one occasion received the visit of a desperate consul, monomaniacally bent on obtaining a particular post. When Foley was obliged to tell him that he could not have it, the poor fellow there and then drew a revolver from his pocket and blew his brains out. Foley at once rang the bell, whereupon the office keeper appeared and, maintaining an impassive silence, mopped up the blood on the carpet with official blotting paper (J D Gregory, *On the Edge of Diplomacy,* 1928).

*There was blue **blood on the carpet** at investment bank Lazard yesterday, with seven managing directors being shown the door – about a quarter of the firm's corporate finance team.*
THE GUARDIAN, 13 JULY 2002

carrot and/or stick
reward and/or punishment to induce compliance

Donkeys and mules have a fabled reputation for stubbornness. There are but two methods to make an unwilling donkey move: entice it forward with a carrot, a promise of reward, or, if that fails, beat it with a stick, the use of force. Metaphorical *carrots* have been dangled since the late nineteenth century: *carrot and stick* dates from the mid-twentieth.

*Even donkeys need **the carrot as well as the stick**. During Labour's time in office, despite receiving regular performance bonuses, Railtrack has publicly had nothing but stick…but the donkey needs incentives if it is not to turn mulish, and this is what Mr Winsor is now offering.*
EVENING STANDARD, 19 APRIL 2000

*The '**carrot**' of your desired goal is being demonstrated to you in mouthwatering detail by the person who's just achieved it. The '**stick**' of bad feeling about your lack of success is being applied to you in painful detail by yourself. In a neat twist, envy takes this **carrot-and-stick** strategy and provides you with a role model to turn your untapped energy into action.*
GOOD HOUSEKEEPING, MAY 2001

cart: to put the cart before the horse
to reverse the sensible order, to do something back to front

This phrase is an example of what the Greeks called *hysteron proteron,* that is, putting last that which should come first. There are various such figures in classical literature. Theocritus had *the hind hunts the dogs,* Cicero *the cart before the horse* and Lucian *the cart often draws the ox.* The earliest use of a similar phrase in English comes in Dan Michel's *Ayenbite of Inwyt* (c. 1340), a translation of a thirteenth-century French devotional manual into Kentish dialect, where it appears as *setting the oxen before the yoke.* The French expression is *Folie est mettre la charrue devant les boefs* (it is folly to set the plough before the oxen).

So what exactly does it mean to put the cart before the horse? American playwright George Kaufman provides a fine example. *She put the heart before the course,* he quipped, upon hearing of a college girl who had eloped.

*More pedestrian areas, progressively less parking space, higher penalties will eventually lead to a situation where it is simpler to hop on a bus rather than take the car. At the moment we **put the cart before the horse**, which is sometimes the fastest method of transport anyway.*
THE GUARDIAN, 4 JULY 2001

For other idioms drawn from Greek and Roman writers, see page 318.

castle in the air/in Spain
a fanciful theory or scheme, a daydream

One first hears of *castles in Spain* in *The Romaunt of the Rose* (c. 1365), a translation, possibly by Chaucer, of *Roman de la Rose,* a thirteenth-century French allegorical romance:

Thou shalt make xastels thanne in Spayne,
And dreme of joye, all but in vayne.

The phrase, then, is a borrowing of the French *faire des châteaux en Espagne* (to build castles in Spain). The nineteenth-century French scholar Émile Littré claims that there was no particular significance in the choice of Spain: variants speak of imaginary castle building in Asia and Albania, suggesting that any culturally diverse country would do. Spain certainly qualified at that period as it was largely Moorish. The English variant *castles in the air* arose in the second half of the sixteenth century, perhaps influenced by St Augustine's writings: *By taking away the foundation to build in the air* (*Sermons* c. 386–430 AD).

*And, to be fair, who can believe it? We have heard so many earnest statements of intent from the despatch box, so many aggressive promises, seen the scaffolding raised for so many **castles in Spain**.*
THE GUARDIAN, 28 JULY 2000

*Now, many [corporations] have been revealed as **castles in the air** built on fantasy profits and fiddled accounts. Even the financial apparatus that had helped to prop them up was rotten.*
THE SPECTATOR, 5 OCTOBER 2002

For other idioms drawn from literature, see page 319.

cat: no room to swing a cat
very cramped

An early record of the idiom dating from 1665 refers to it as a *vulgar saying*, suggesting that it was already well established. But what is its origin?

The picture which springs to mind is that of a cat being whirled round by its tail, and this literal interpretation is certainly valid. Another suggested etymology is scarcely less horrific. It

seems that it was not uncommon in the sixteenth century to put a cat inside a sack of some sort and then string it up as a moving target for archery practice. Shakespeare refers to the activity in *Much Ado About Nothing* (1598). According to Funk (1950) *no room to swing a cat means* that there was insufficient space for target practice.

A more common theory is that the *cat* is the *cat o' nine tails*, a whip with nine knotted thongs which was used as a punishment in the navy. The name apparently alludes to the long marks left on the victim's back, like the scratch marks of a cat. *No room to swing a cat* is said to refer to the cramped conditions below deck, the punishment being necessarily administered in the open air on the deck above. However, as *no room to swing a cat* has never been recorded as a naval phrase, animal torture of some kind seems more likely.

*A couple of the bedrooms are on the small side – you could probably **swing a cat** in number 6, but never a lion.*
THE SUNDAY TIMES, 1 JUNE 2003

cat: to grin like a Cheshire cat
to have a broad grin on one's face

The mysterious Cheshire cat makes an unforgettable appearance and disappearance in Lewis Carroll's *Alice's Adventures in Wonderland* (1865). In the story, the Cheshire cat is seen completely but then gradually fades away until all that remains is its broad grin. Carroll's book is so well-known that it is inevitable that the invention of the remarkable animal should be attributed to him. However, the Cheshire cat existed long before Carroll wrote about it and there are several stories to explain its origin.

Cheshire is famous for its cheeses, and some say that long ago the cheeses were either made in the shape of a cat or had the head of a cat stamped on them Alternatively the Cheshire cat might refer to the unsuccessful efforts of a Cheshire sign painter to represent the lion rampant on the coat of arms of an influential county family. The results looked more like a grinning cat than a roaring lion and became the subject of much hilarity.

The final story tells of one of Richard III's Cheshire gamekeepers named Caterling, a burly monster of a man who would grin unpleasantly while poachers were hanged. Originally the simile was *to grin like a Cheshire Caterling* but, as time went by, economy of effort reduced *Caterling* to *cat*.

Whatever the origin, the actual phrase is first found towards the end of the eighteenth century, a hundred years before Carroll's powerful image ensured its popularity.

*Wes Clark was more brazen still, the old general **grinning like a Cheshire cat** as he endorsed the Massachusetts Senator within 48 hours of folding his own campaign.*
THE INDEPENDENT, 16 FEBRUARY 2004

*Bush was **grinning like a Cheshire cat** at yesterday's meeting with NATO to hand power back to the Iraqi people. Why? Because he can start bringing his boys home to be replaced with NATO troops.*
DAILY EXPRESS, 30 JUNE 2004

cat: to let the cat out of the bag

to divulge a secret inadvertently

The idiom is widely thought to originate in a trick played by wily country folk who would substitute a stray cat for a piglet, then bring it to market in a canvas bag. The wary customer who opened the bag to check his purchase would discover the deception and *let the cat out of the bag*. The secret would be out. The earliest written records of

the phrase date from around the mid-eighteenth century but the practice, and probably the idiom, is much older as the related expression *to buy a pig in a* POKE shows.

*McCartney is the stuff of which myth is made. That much was clear from the air of expectation in the foyer of the Everyman Theatre last night... No-one was expecting McCartney, until the Liverpool Echo **let the cat out of the bag** a few days ago.*
THE INDEPENDENT, 22 MARCH 2001

cat: to play cat and mouse with

to tease a victim

In the early years of the twentieth century those demanding the vote for women began to adopt increasingly aggressive tactics to publicise their cause and so earned themselves prison sentences. In 1909 Marion Dunlop, an imprisoned suffragette, went on hunger strike but was released soon after for fear she should become a martyr. Needless to say, other suffragettes followed her example. At first the authorities, resistant to releasing all the prisoners, force-fed them but the problem became so pressing that, in 1913, the government was obliged to introduce the Prisoner's Temporary Discharge of Ill Health Act. This allowed women on hunger strike to be released as soon as their health began to deteriorate, but required their return to prison to complete their sentences as soon as they were fit again. This successful piece of legislation became known as the Cat and Mouse Act, the allusion being to a cat toying with its helpless victim.

Annie Kenney was a leading member of the Women's Social and Political Union. In her memoirs, *Memories of a Militant* (1924), she narrated her own experience under the Act:

I had as my visitors the matron, the Governor, the doctor, the clergyman, and the visiting magistrate. They all asked me to eat and drink, but nothing would tempt me. The matron, the doctor and I became good friends. The doctor was ever so kind and did his best to persuade me to have fruit, but fruit was no use to me. 'I must be out in three days, doctor, or I'll die on your hands!' And the good doctor did not want a death. In three days the gates were opened… Mrs. Brackenbury lent us her house at 2 Camden Hill Square. We called it 'Mouse Castle'. All the mice went there from prison and were nursed back to health and prepared for further danger work… When I recovered I was re-arrested.

Even if the phrase *to play cat and mouse* did not originate with the bill, it was certainly popularised by it.

*Sigmar Polke, who is almost 60 years old now and is Germany's best-known post-Pop Art prankster, seldom says he wants to be interviewed, and even when he's agreed to be interviewed, he tends to **play cat and mouse games with** the unfortunate interviewer. Glance through the cuttings files on him and you'll find acres and acres of wearisome and self-important exegesis, and almost nothing about the man himself.*
THE INDEPENDENT, 19 DECEMBER 2000

*Saddam has **played cat and mouse with** the West over weapons inspectors too often for Washington and London to greet this latest ploy with anything more than a cynical shrug.*
EVENING STANDARD, 6 AUGUST 2002

For another idiom influenced by the suffragette movement, see SHIPS *(that pass) in the night*.

cat's pyjamas/cat's whiskers, the
the best

See the BEE'S knees.

*Handsome model Calum, 22, who has had more than his fair share of beautiful women and has dated supermodel Caprice, confirmed that Catalina is definitely **the cat's whiskers** when it comes to loving.*
THE PEOPLE, 4 MAY 2003

*Whoopi Goldberg wrote: 'I think you're **the cat's pyjamas**'; Mr Clinton replied: 'From the moment I met you I felt I had found a friend.'*
THE GUARDIAN, 18 NOVEMBER 2004

catch-22: a catch-22 situation
a troublesome situation from which there is no apparent escape since the solution leads back to the original difficulty

Catch-22, a novel by American novelist and dramatist Joseph Heller, was published in 1961 and is a darkly humorous satire on the evils of war. *Catch-22* itself is an apparently humane Air Force regulation which traps the airmen by its cyclical logic. The book describes it as follows:

There was only one catch and that was Catch-22, which specified that a concern for one's own safety in the face of dangers that were real and immediate was the process of a rational mind. Orr was crazy and could be grounded. All he had to do was ask; and as soon as he did he would no longer be crazy and would have to fly more missions. Orr would be crazy to fly more missions and sane if he didn't, but if he was sane he had to fly them. If he flew them he was crazy and didn't have to; but if he didn't want to he was sane and had to. Yossarian was moved very deeply by the absolute simplicity of this clause of Catch-22 and let out a respectful whistle.

Heller's novel was a great success and, following its release as a film in 1970, *Catch-22* entered the popular idiom to describe any circular or nonsensical problem.

*The particular **Catch 22** that afflicted
LBH Radio was that they couldn't
persuade advertisers to peddle their wares
on their station without first knowing how
many listeners were tuning in; but Riley-
Smith couldn't afford the £10,000-a-
month cost of audience research that would
provide the answer.*
DAILY MAIL, 19 DECEMBER 2001

*'At 32 I feel I should really be able to
afford to buy my own place,' says Sarah.
'At the very least I'd like to be able to rent
somewhere bigger. At present, our rent is
£250 a week and I'm in **a catch-22
situation**. Because my rent is so high I
can't build up my savings, but if I move
further out of town I'll spend more money
on commuting each day.'*
THE GUARDIAN, 20 FEBRUARY 2002

See also VICIOUS *circle*. For other
idioms drawn from literature, see
page 319.

chase: to cut to the chase
to come straight to the point

This American phrase originated in the
late 1920s as a film director's order to
leave the slower preliminary scenes and
move straight on to the *chase*, a generic
term to describe any fast, action-packed,
attention-grabbing sequences. These
were often central to the appeal of the
film. The action and the importance of
these scenes in films explain the
idiomatic senses that have evolved since
the 1950s in America. Nowadays the
expression is found on both sides of the
Atlantic, usually among high-powered
executives and professionals under
pressure to get down to essentials.

*Phil McGraw…doesn't have time to beat
around the bush during his brief, televised
sessions with patients, so he **cuts to the
chase** and goes for the jugular. That's led
to an almost cult-like following as the TV*

*psychologist graduates from weekly
appearances on 'Oprah' to a syndicated
show of his own.*
INDIANAPOLIS STAR, 13 SEPTEMBER 2002

*Gay men are incredibly easy to be around.
No one makes me laugh as much as they do
– they will shamelessly discuss anything, **cut
to the chase** on the most difficult subjects
and are always, always totally honest.*
THE DAILY TELEGRAPH, 20 MAY 2004

cheek by jowl
in close intimacy, close together

At the beginning of the fourteenth century the idea of being nice and close to
someone was expressed as *cheke by cheke*.
It was not until the second half of the
sixteenth century that *cheek by iowl* put
in an appearance. *Jowl* means 'jaw' or
'cheek', so the phrase changed only in
form, not meaning. The implication of
the phrase is 'crammed together'. *Cheek
to cheek* sounds like a modern-day variant of the original phrase but was, in
fact, coined in the 1920s to describe the
permissive romantic intimacy of dancing with the cheek of one partner
touching that of another.

*The Exhibition was a cross between a trade
fair and a freak show… Wonders of the
world like the Hope diamond and the
Koh-i-Noor were on display **cheek by jowl**
with Colt revolvers, steam-powered
machines and the first waterproof coats
made by Mackintosh.*
THE SPECTATOR, 7 APRIL 2001

*Prison officials were a close-knit
community; they lived **cheek by jowl** with
one another in the prison lines and their
families often intermarried.*
ALEXANDER MCCALL SMITH,
THE KALAHARI TYPING SCHOOL
FOR MEN, 2002

cheek: to have the cheek
to have the audacity, effrontery (to do something)

The word *cheek* began to be used with the sense of 'impudence' around the middle of the nineteenth century. It occurs, for instance, in Dickens's *Bleak House* (1852). It literally means to have the 'face' to do something: to be able to look someone squarely and calmly in the eye while making known an outrageous request, statement or intention.

*'The interviewer even **had the cheek** to suggest that I couldn't recognise a line of Greek, saying that he was sure I thought the line was "funny squiggles".'*
THE GUARDIAN, 10 JULY 2001

cheek: to turn the other cheek
to have an attitude of patience or forgiveness when one is wrongly or unkindly treated

This phrase, which dates from the nineteenth century, alludes to the teaching of Jesus in Matthew 5:39: *But I say unto you, that ye resist not evil but whosoever shall smite thee on thy right cheek, turn to him the other also*. In his poem 'Astraea' (1850), American poet Oliver Wendell Holmes points out the difficulty in having but two cheeks to offer:

> *Wisdom has taught us to be calm and meek,*
> *To take one blow, and turn the other cheek;*
> *It is not written what a man shall do*
> *If the rude caitiff smite the other too!*

*Since it's not in my nature to **turn the other cheek**, I sent a postcard to express my dismay at such needlessly destructive cynicism.*
THE INDEPENDENT, 27 JUNE 2000

For other idioms from the Bible, see page 270.

chestnut: an old chestnut
a tired old joke; an overly familiar topic

Although the origins of the idiom are in an English melodrama, it was allegedly an American actor who brought it to particular attention. According to an 1888 edition of the *Philadelphia Press*, the actor William Warren once found occasion to quote from *The Broken Sword* (1816), a rather mediocre play by William Diamond. One of the characters has the irritating habit of telling and retelling the same stories and jokes. He is embarking upon one such tale about a cork tree when his companion, Pablo, interrupts crying: *A Chestnut, I should know as well as you, having heard you tell the tale these twenty-seven times, and I'm sure it was a chestnut.*

Warren, who had played the part of Pablo in the melodrama, was at a dinner one evening when a fellow guest started to recount a well-worn and rather elderly anecdote, whereupon Warren was heard to say: *A chestnut. I have heard you tell the tale these twenty-seven times*. The rest of the company was delighted with Warren's very appropriate quoting from the play and it was not long before news of the incident had spread amongst their acquaintances and beyond.

Whether or not the story about Warren is true, Diamond's play was certainly the inspiration behind the phrase which, according to the *Detroit Free Press* for 25 September 1886, had become *one of the latest slang terms*.

*Schools always encourage children to write about their heroes… I hadn't even realised that her English teacher had set this **old chestnut**, but last night Ginny suddenly asked me about Emily Davison. I wonder how many of you know that name? Ginny didn't.*
THE TIMES EDUCATIONAL SUPPLEMENT, 7 JULY 2000

Now I adore Homer and Jim et al, *but maybe it's time for a new template. Because in the wrong hands, what it throws up is the hoary* **old chestnut** *that boys will be boys. And the best wives are feisty and witty but also long suffering.*
THE INDEPENDENT, 31 MAY 2002

For other idioms drawn from literature, see page 319.

child's play

an easily accomplished task, an insignificant matter

The figurative use of *child's play* or *child's game* to describe 'an insignificant matter' or 'an easy task' dates back to at least the first quarter of the fourteenth century. Chaucer in his *Merchant's Tale* (c. 1386), which tells of the marriage between old man January and his young bride May, warns that it is no trifling matter, *no childes pley To take a wyf with-outen avysement*. The old variants *ball play* and *boys' play* are now obsolete.

Claiming tax credits is just **child's play**
EVENING STANDARD,
18 NOVEMBER 2002

chip: a chip off the old block

a child who is very like its father in character or appearance, or both

The reference here is to a small chip hacked from a block of wood. The chip is from the same wood as the block, as the child is of the same stock as the parent. The concept is an old one, Theocritus preferring *chip-of-the-old-flint* (*Idyls*, c. 270 BC.)

The idiom has been in use in English from at least the early seventeenth century in the form *a chip of the old block*. Edmund Burke, present when William Pitt the Younger delivered his maiden speech to Parliament on 26

February 1781, commented that he was *not merely a chip of the old block, but the old block itself*. Pitt was just twenty-two years old. Some two years later he was to become Prime Minister, like his father before him.

The standard form for the last hundred years or more has been *a chip* off *the old block*.

When the man who has gone before you is a racing legend, following in father's footsteps can't be easy, but Alan Berry is fast proving how much of a **chip off the old block** *he really is.*
THE SCOTSMAN, 31 MARCH 2000

chip: to chip in

to contribute

The allusion is to poker where players place their *chips* (money tokens) in the pot, thus contributing to the sum to be won. The idiom is of American origin and has been in use since the second half of the nineteenth century.

In exchange for board and lodging, everyone is expected to **chip in** *with the weeding, digging, trimming, and the growing and harvesting of vegetables.*
THE GUARDIAN, 26 OCTOBER 2002

For other idioms derived from poker, see page 320.

chip: to have a chip on one's shoulder

to display anger or resentment because of feelings of inferiority or grievance

The phrase is of American origin and, surprisingly, refers back to a literal chip of wood on the shoulder. An article in the *Long Island Telegraph* from May 1830 states that *when two churlish boys were determined to fight, a chip would be placed on the shoulder of one and the other demanded to knock it off at his peril*. The phrase *a chip on one's shoulder* was coming into figurative use by the 1850s, while the practice itself continued well into the twentieth century. British social anthropologist Geoffrey Gorer had this to say in *The Americans* (1948), his study of that nation's character: *Boys in the country and small towns who are validating their manhood sometimes walk around with a literal chip of wood balanced on their shoulder, the sign of a readiness to fight anyone who will take the initiative of knocking the chip off.*

Few people are more surly or resentful than teenage boys unless, of course, it's top athletes. British Olympic champion Linford Christie, who had a reputation for being prickly, was once described by fellow athletes as being *the most balanced runner in Britain because he's got a chip on both shoulders* (*Daily Telegraph*, 18 May 1992).

Donald was having two intensive coaching sessions to determine why, at 50, he was constantly job-hopping and dissatisfied, and whether he should change career completely. At the first session he's recognised that a chip on his shoulder was blocking him from going for what he wanted at work.
THE TIMES, 29 APRIL 2000

Paxman told The Sunday Times *it was 'extremely bizarre' that certain Scots had a 'chip on their shoulder' about their nationality. While it was left unsaid to whom he was referring, the most high profile Scottish members of the Cabinet are Gordon Brown and Alistair Darling.*
THE DAILY TELEGRAPH, 14 MARCH 2005

chock-a-block (with)
crowded, crammed full

This is a nautical term since the nineteenth century. It is used when two pulleys (*blocks*) in the running rigging of a ship are hard together (*chock*) so that they cannot be tightened any further. It came into colloquial English

with the sense 'crammed full' or 'crowded' in the 1880s. A colloquial contemporary derivative, from the mid-twentieth century, is *chocker(s)*, for 'very crowded'.

The phrase *chock-full* to mean 'over-full, full to bursting', which is of uncertain origin, has been in English since around the turn of the fifteenth century.

Choc-A-Block with Low Prices
ASDA PRICE NEWS, EASTER 2003

*At night, the area is **chocker** with blonde-highlighted bohos; in the day, things are quieter.*
EVENING STANDARD, 21 MAY 2004

*If there was once a green peppercorn mountain in the west of Scotland, it must be in serious danger of becoming an anthill. Norm's ribeye steak came with a green peppercorn sauce that was absolutely **choc-a-bloc** with the things...*
SCOTLAND ON SUNDAY,
28 NOVEMBER 2004

For other nautical idioms, see A LIFE ON THE OCEAN WAVES, page 24.

chop: to chop and change
to keep changing one's mind or tactics

This phrase, pleasing in its alliteration, originated amongst merchants in the Middle Ages where it meant 'to barter, to exchange goods'. The roots of *chop* are uncertain but it is possible that the word is a variant of *chap*, also meaning 'to barter'. As this use of *chop* declined, the meaning of the phrase *chop and change* gradually altered so that, by the mid-sixteenth century, it was already beginning to acquire the modern sense of 'to alter, to make frequent changes'.

The problem is that, while older people still stick to their word and do what they say they are going to do, the young (i.e. anyone

under 45 years old) now like to be able to **chop and change** *their plans right up until the last minute.*
THE SPECTATOR, 1 DECEMBER 2001

See also COUPLINGS, page 294.

cleft: in a cleft stick
in a predicament, in a difficulty that has no easy solution

The idiom was in general use in the second half of the eighteenth century. *We are squeezed to death, between the two sides of that sort of alternative which is commonly called a cleft stick,* wrote William Cowper in 1782. The allusion is probably to the trapping of snakes and the like by pinning them down behind the head with a forked stick.

The war against terrorism has left corporate America **in a cleft stick***. On the one hand, the kneejerk reaction of business is to retrench – rapidly – after the terrorist attacks...*
On the other hand, there is an unease about laying off staff after September 11, a feeling that to do so is unpatriotic.
THE GUARDIAN, 15 NOVEMBER 2001

cloak-and-dagger
involving clandestine intrigue

Spanish playwrights Lope de Vega (1562–1635) and Pedro Calderón de la Barca (1600–81) had a genius for writing entertaining dramas with intricate and varied plots. These often told of secret love affairs complicated by misunderstandings and points of honour. The principal characters were gentlemen of minor rank who, at that time, wore a cloak and carried a dagger or sword. Thus the genre became known as *comedia de capa y espada*, which translates into English as 'comedy of cloak and sword'. The phrase *cloak and sword* or *cloak and dagger* was originally used by English writers from the early nine-

teenth century strictly to refer to the works of Lope and Calderón. By the 1840s, however, it was beginning to be used for any fictional work of intrigue and melodrama and from there the phrase also came to describe any real-life secretive plot or conspiracy.

So why the **cloak-and-dagger** *approach at the High Commission? John still doesn't know for certain. '...the possibility can't be excluded that a known individual high up in the Kenyan hierarchy had something to do with the murder and that very senior figures were protecting him...'*
EVENING STANDARD, 10 JANUARY 2003

For other idioms drawn from literature, see page 319.

close: at close quarters
in immediate contact, adjacent

Ships intended for war in previous centuries were fitted with a number of stout wooden barriers which spanned the width of the vessel. If the enemy managed to board the ship, the crew would shelter behind these barricades and fire at them through loopholes. The barriers were known as *close-fights* in the sixteenth and seventeenth centuries and as *close quarters* from the eighteenth onwards. By the early nineteenth century the expression *to* or *at close quarters* had come to mean 'in direct contact with the enemy', whether on sea or land. The term was put to wider use, outside the context of war and with the sense 'in immediate contact, in close proximity', in the mid-twentieth century.

Some of the dwellings were built of concrete, but they were huddled together in an ancient configuration, the families **at close quarters** *with mules and donkeys.*
THE SPECTATOR, 8 SEPTEMBER 2001

For other nautical idioms, see A LIFE ON THE OCEAN WAVES, page 24.

close: to close your eyes and think of England

to endure unwanted sexual intercourse; to put up with any unpleasant action

According to Eric Partridge's *Dictionary of Catch Phrases* (1977), this phrase originated around the turn of the twentieth century amongst Britons living in difficult or depressing conditions in various parts of the Empire and beyond. *Remind yourself of your service to the mother country*, is the advice. The phrase is still used with the sense of stoically putting up with unpleasantness today, although it has lost its original patriotic tone and has become rather jocular. This shift may be due, at least in part, to its association with unwelcome sexual intercourse, which seems to have sprung from a much quoted passage in the 1912 journal of Lady Hillingdon, who allegedly wrote: *I am happy now that Charles calls on my bedchamber less frequently than of old. As it is, I endure but two calls a week and when I hear his steps outside my door I lie down on my bed, close my eyes, open my legs and think of England*. In making this appropriate use of a common phrase, the lady had inadvertently added a whole new layer of meaning.

There are, however, alternative earlier suggestions which could have both patriotic and sexual interpretations. The least likely is that it was advice given to Queen Victoria on the eve of her marriage to the German Albert in 1840 – advice that was not needed since she was known to be eagerly looking forward to her wedding night. More possible is that it was encouragement given to Lucy Risdale on her marriage to the future Prime Minister Stanley Baldwin in 1892. In any event, if it is true, she must have ended her life a very patriotic woman – she gave birth to four daughters and three sons.

WHEN CELEBRITIES STRIP
'Close your eyes and think of the ratings,' said one ITV producer.
THE GUARDIAN, 20 JUNE 2000

The tranquil, hopeless sex life cherished by the British male will remain that. And those many selfless women, on whose willingness occasionally **to lie back and think of England** *the continuation of our island race depends, won't need to memorise the second verse of Jerusalem just yet.*
THE DAILY TELEGRAPH, 4 AUGUST 2004

cloud: (living) in cloud cuckoo land

divorced from the reality of ordinary life

This evocative phrase is a translation of the Greek *Nephelokokkugia* (*nephele*, 'cloud', and *kokkux*, 'cuckoo') from Aristophanes's comedy *The Birds* (414 BC). *Nephelokokkugia* was the name of a city built by the birds which separated the gods from mankind:

LEADER OF THE CHORUS: *Let's see. What shall our city be called?…*
EUELPIDES: *Some name borrowed from the clouds, from these lofty regions in which we dwell – in short, some well-known name.*
PITHETAERUS: *Do you like Nephelokokkugia?*
LEADER OF THE CHORUS: *Oh! capital! truly that's a brilliant thought!*

The phrase is first found outside translations in the later part of the nineteenth century. Its unreal, fanciful meaning may have been reinforced by the American slang expression *cuckoo*, meaning 'crazy', from the early years of the twentieth century.

Sir Stephen Lander, the MI5 director general, said last week: 'Anyone who believes terrorist plots can always be foiled is **living in Cloud-cuckoo-land.***'*
THE INDEPENDENT, 12 JULY 2002

For other idioms drawn from Greek and Roman writers, see page 318.

cloud: on cloud nine
on a high, in a state of elation, supremely happy

There is a good deal of uncertainty about the date and origin of this phrase. *On cloud eight* first appeared in the 1930s, with reference to drunkenness. Then there was in the 1950s *on cloud seven* and *on cloud thirty-nine*, as well as the now established *on cloud nine*. It first became popular among jazz musicians who might simply have been looking for a suggestive phrase for a high – often alcohol or drug induced – and a release from the harsh realities of life.

An alternative explanation is that it comes from a classification of clouds used by the US Weather Bureau – the highest level of cumulonimbus clouds was level nine, an apt metaphor for being on top of the world, with hints of being in a dream-like, floating state. There was also in the 1950s the *Johnny Dollar* radio show in America, in which the hero was regularly knocked unconscious and transported to *cloud nine*, where he recovered his speech. This popular show doubtless served to fix the number nine as the definitive numeral for the idiom.

*Howard Petty of Homosassa last flew when he was 19. For his 87th birthday, his family treated him to his second flight, in a single-engine Cessna thousands of feet above Citrus County. 'He's **on cloud nine**!' exclaimed his daughter Barbara Whitney. Petty agreed. 'It was really wonderful up there,' he said afterward. 'I told them that it made my day.'*
ST PETERSBURG TIMES,
2 SEPTEMBER 2004

clue: not to have a clue
to have no idea; to lack inspiration; to be ignorant

For this phrase we need to look to the ancient Greek story of Theseus and the Minotaur.

The Minotaur was a terrible beast, half-man and half-bull, which lived in a huge and complicated Labyrinth on the island of Crete. The king wished to be rid of the monster but no opponent ever came out of the Labyrinth alive: they were either killed by the Minotaur or lost in the maze of corridors. Theseus determined to slay the Minotaur. When he entered the maze he took with him a ball of thread which he unwound and let out as he groped his way down the dark corridors. After a mighty struggle Theseus killed the monster and was able to find his way safely out of the Labyrinth by rewinding the ball of thread.

Originally *clue*, a variant of Old English *clew*, meant 'a ball of thread'. From Chaucer's time this word was also used to denote 'a ball of thread by which characters of myth or legend found their way through a labyrinth, in particular Theseus in Crete'. From here *clue* came to mean 'a key to the solution of any puzzle, investigation or difficulty'. According to lexicographer Eric Partridge *He hasn't a clue,* meaning 'he is incompetent, he doesn't know what's going on', was World War II forces' slang . *Not to have a clue* with the sense 'not to know, to be ignorant' took hold around the mid-1900s, perhaps evolving from the forces' expression.

*It was a bewildering time and **I didn't have a clue** what I was doing. But you learn with experience...*
GOOD HOUSEKEEPING,
SEPTEMBER 2001

*He had envisaged us growing old together, continuing to lead our separate lives. I realise it must have come as a big shock to him – I'd been thinking about leaving for a while, but he **didn't have a clue**.*
GOOD HOUSEKEEPING,
SEPTEMBER 2001

*I promise you, sir, she did not leave through the front door. **I haven't a clue** how the hell she got out.*
KEN WHARFE & ROBERT JOBSON,
DIANA: A CLOSELY GUARDED
SECRET, 2002

For other idioms derived from ancient legends, see page 317.

coals: to carry coals to Newcastle
to take something to a place where there is already an abundance; to engage in a superfluous activity

Newcastle-upon-Tyne owes its prosperity to its vast coal fields and to the fact that it is conveniently situated on a tidal river. In 1239 King Henry III is said to have granted a charter to the freemen of the town to dig coal. Much of the coal was shipped to London but the resulting smog was so hazardous to the citizens' health that, in 1306, Parliament made a complaint to Edward I who forbade its use in the city. Gradually, however, as the supplies of wood needed for shipbuilding dwindled, the use of coal for both domestic and industrial purposes became increasingly common until, by the seventeenth century, it was an important source of fuel. Newcastle, being the first field to be worked, was the most prolific. Thus, by the early seventeenth century metaphorical references were being made to Newcastle coal and, by the middle of that century, the idiom *to carry coals to Newcastle* was known: *So far from being needless*

pains it may bring considerable profit to carry Char-coals to New-castle (Thomas Fuller, *A Pisgah-Sight of Palestine*, 1650).

It is a very old concept indeed to take something vainly to a place where it is not necessary. Aristophanes in *The Birds* (414 BC) uses the Greek idiom *to carry owls to Athens* – a completely useless task, since the patron goddess of that city was Pallas Athene. Her emblem was the owl, and it was embossed on the local currency. Today, a North American version is *to sell refrigerators to Eskimos*. We are still subject to the same vain compulsion.

*I know there are good salesmen who really can sell **coals to Newcastle**. I read just the other day about a car dealer who invited two Jehovah's Witnesses into his house; they left 20 minutes later with a P-reg Ford Mondeo.*
THE SUNDAY TIMES, 4 MAY 2003

*You've heard of **coals to Newcastle**. Now here's bagpipes to Edinburgh… A cheeky businessman from Pakistan is opening a shop on the Royal Mile in Edinburgh selling his Asian-made bagpipes and kilts.*
SUNDAY MIRROR, 25 APRIL 2004

coals: to haul (someone) over the coals
to give (someone) a severe reprimand

This is a reference to the ordeal by fire suffered by heretics. In past centuries heresy was regarded as a crime, a threat to social stability that had to be stamped out. One way of deciding the guilt of a heretic was to haul the suspect over a bed of glowing coals. A person who survived the ordeal was declared innocent. Death meant the person had been guilty of the charge. *Augustin*, declared the zealous sixteenth-century Catholic churchman William Allen, *knewe best how to fetche an heretick ouer the coles* (in William Fulke, *Confutation*, 1565).

The modern variant *to haul someone over the coals* dates from the late eighteenth century, when it was figuratively applied in the sense 'to administer a severe reprimand, to call to account'. Nelson, in a remark of 1795, complains of an admiral who deprived him of ships to fight a battle and who will be *hauled over the coals* in consequence.

*Our head was given £1.5 million to spend on new technology and spent it with largesse. Four years later the auditors caught up with him and **hauled him over the coals**.*
THE TIMES EDUCATIONAL SUPPLEMENT, 14 JUNE 2002

*Mr Bush deserves **hauling over the coals** for his stewardship of the government's finances, and his failure to reform America's creaking entitlement programmes. However, as a senator in the Congress that has indulged Mr Bush's spending habit, Mr Kerry is not particularly well placed to sponsor cutbacks.*
THE ECONOMIST, 29 JANUARY 2004

cobblers: a load of old cobblers
rubbish

This is a piece of Cockney rhyming slang. The full term is *cobbler's awls*. An *awl* is a pointed tool used for making holes, particularly by cobblers and other leatherworkers, although this fact is totally irrelevant to the expression. *Cobbler's awls* was devised to rhyme with *balls*, 'testicles', and in the 1930s became a crude way of dismissing something as rubbish. The shortened version, *cobblers*, is however quite acceptable, probably because most people are unaware of its origins.

*'I want to dispel the folklore legend that the East End was a safer place when they [the Kray twins] were around. That's **a load of old cobblers**.'*
DAILY MAIL, 8 AUGUST 2003

For other idioms with a similar meaning, see *a load of old* CODSWALLOP and MUMBO JUMBO. For more examples of expressions from rhyming slang, see HAVE A BUTCHER'S AT THIS, page 80).

cock and bull story, a
an unbelievable story, a fabricated tale intended to mislead

The two pubs The Cock and The Bull, close together on Stony Stratford main street, are very proud of their claimed connection to the phrase, as locals are at pains to tell visitors. After all, the pleasure of sitting in a pub, talking of this and that, is an old one. *Some men's whole delight*, wrote Robert Burton in the seventeenth century, *is to talk of a Cock and Bull over a pot* (*The Anatomy of Melancholy*, 1621).

At the risk of offending the inhabitants of Stony Stratford, it is very unlikely that the origin of the expression lies in the Buckinghamshire town. The phrase may simply be a reference to a now forgotten fable about a cock and a bull. Certainly the French had an equivalent phrase *coq-à-l'âne* ('cock to the donkey'), which was known in England in the seventeenth century and was corrupted to *cockalane* in English. Rambling tales and disconnected chit-chat often contain exaggeration and so, by the second half of the eighteenth century, *a story of a cock and a bull* had come to mean 'an unbelievable yarn; a story made-up as an excuse or with the intention to mislead'. By the end of that century the form that we know today was in circulation.

*'I don't like to be late, it's disrespectful. But I don't ever lie about why I was late, some **cock-and-bull story**. I just say I'm late.'*
NAOMI CAMPBELL, QUOTED IN THE GUARDIAN, 5 JULY 2004

Have a butcher's at this

Have a butcher's? Yes, a *butcher's hook*, in other words 'a look'. *Butcher's hook* is an example of rhyming slang, originally a means of secretive communication in which a key word was replaced by a rhyming phrase. Sometimes, as a further challenge to eavesdroppers, the rhyming word would be dropped, as in the example above. According to Henry Mayhew, by the middle of the nineteenth century London street traders of dubious reputation had begun to communicate with each other in rhyming phrases (*London Labour and the London Poor*, 1851). Mayhew's observation was confirmed eight years later by John Camden Hotten in *The Slang Dictionary*: *The cant, which has nothing to do with that spoken by the costermongers, is known in Seven Dials [a shady district in central London] and elsewhere as the Rhyming Slang... I learn that the rhyming slang was introduced about twelve or fifteen years ago.*

Rhyming slang grew apace until the early twentieth century, sometimes appearing in novels, so that, even today, most speakers of British English have a passive vocabulary of common terms: *mince pies* 'eyes', *trouble and strife* 'wife', *plates of meat* 'feet', etc. Some of the terms have become embedded into current idiom and are no longer thought of or recognisable as rhyming slang. *Not a dicky bird*, for instance, means 'not a word', while *Use your loaf* means 'Think', 'Work it out', *loaf* being short for *loaf of bread*, 'head'.

Other phrases have an underlying crudity of which most speakers are ignorant. *A load of old* COBBLERS is one such. The expression *to get on someone's wick*, current since the 1940s, is another, the phrase coming from the late nineteenth-century term *Hampton Wick*, a euphemism for 'prick', slang for 'penis'. And then there is the phrase *to blow a raspberry*, current since the late nineteenth century, which means 'to make a rasping noise with one's tongue thrust between one's pursed lips, usually in disdain'. *Raspberry* is short for *raspberry tart*, 'fart', which describes the sound admirably. Even the mild phrase *to take the mickey*, meaning 'to deride', 'to tease', originates in bodily functions. *Mike* or *Mickey Bliss*, 'piss', was coined in the early twentieth century to denote 'urinating'. *To take the Mike/Mickey Bliss*, 'to take the piss', meaning 'to mock or tease', dates from the 1930s. *Take the Mickey* dates from the 1950s, as does the self-consciously polite variant *to extract the Michael*.

It is not known who Mickey Bliss was, if indeed he ever existed, and the identity of Nelly Duff is also unknown, and probably invented. Nelly Duff makes an appearance in *not on your Nelly*, meaning 'not on your life'. Her name rhymes with an earlier phrase *not on your puff*, where puff signified 'breath of life', hence 'not on your life'.

Other rhyming slang characters were real personalities, even though their claim to fame is unknown to modern speakers of British English (see under *how's your* FATHER). The idiom *on one's tod*, 'on one's own', 'alone', refers to Tod Sloan, a famous American jockey who came to Britain in the late nineteenth century and rode horses for the Prince of Wales (later King Edward VII).

And, indeed, contrary to expectation, rhyming slang has recently had a new lease of life, many of the new expressions being based on the names of celebrities and pop stars: a barman might be asked for a couple of *britneys* (Britney Spears, 'beers') while broadcaster and clubland DJ Pete Tong's name is used to mean 'wrong' – *everything's gone Pete Tong*. Whether the longevity of these twenty-first century pop star phrases will equal the Victorian street traders' coinings remains to be seen.

cock of the walk, the

the undisputed leader of a group

The pen where a gamecock was kept was known as a *walk*. Here he reigned supreme since he would permit no other cock into the same enclosure. The term *cock of the walk* to denote 'the undisputed leader in any circle' was recorded by Francis Grose in his *Classical Dictionary of the Vulgar Tongue* (1785). Grose's definition adds that the term also applied to *the best boxer in a village or district*. The fact that *cock of the walk* was included in the dictionary at all indicates that it was originally a low term that has gradually attained respectability. The noun *cock*, however, had already been used figuratively by genteel authors since at least the mid-sixteenth century to denote 'any greatly superior person', and had been used in phrases such as *cock of the club* and *cock of the school*.

Mr Davis' manner suggested that he saw himself as the real **cock of the walk***. Just weeks after becoming party chairman he joined the press in cracking jokes about the man he was supposed to help make prime minister.*
THE GUARDIAN, 23 JULY 2002

cock: to cock a snook at someone

to show defiance, contempt or opposition

A *snook* is an offensive gesture made by putting the end of the thumb of one hand on the tip of the nose and spreading out the fingers. The word, whose origins are obscure, is generally found in the phrase *to cock a snook*, meaning 'to make a gesture of contempt'. *Snooks* were first *cocked* at the end of the eighteenth century.

From the first half of the twentieth century, however, the idiom no longer simply described the offensive gesture but was often applied more widely to any demonstration of contempt or disrespect.

Why do we do it? It is the old problem. British drinking, like the British infatuation with sex, is mostly puritanism inverted. The smiles and laughter of the women at the bar are part genuine fun, part **snook-cocking***. We are not just knocking back our whisky cokes with the best of them or making a point with our pints, we are giving society the finger, subverting the moral law.*
EVENING STANDARD, 19 APRIL 2000

The Commonwealth Games provide a mouth-watering opportunity for the citizens of Manchester to **cock a snook** *at their countrymen in the capital. Look, they will say, see how the athletes of the world enjoy our brand new facilities, our efficient transport infrastructure, our welcoming hostelries.*
THE DAILY TELEGRAPH,
24 JULY 2002

But he is also a member of the revolutionary generation. Part of him wants to provoke, to **cock a snook** *at the Establishment. The other part is flattered by power.*
THE TIMES, 19 SEPTEMBER 2002

cock-a-hoop

delighted, jubilant

In medieval drinking bouts, the *cock* (tap or spigot) was removed from the barrel of beer and set on the top, the *hoop*. This led to heavy drinking, drunkenness and jubilation – for a while at least. The phrase was originally *to set the cock on the hoop* and its first use was appropriately in Thomas More's *Dialoge of Comforts against Trybulacion* in 1534: *They...set them downe and dryncke well for our sauiours sake, sette cocke a hoope, and fyll in all the cuppes at ones, and then lette Chrystes passion paye for all the scotte.* More had every reason to write the dialogue, as he had just been committed to the Tower of London by Henry VIII for refusing to back the king in his divorce and remarriage. He lost his head the following year.

The verbal phrase rapidly developed a wider metaphorical use, 'to give way to wild excitement, abandonment'. The adjectival usage of today dates back to the second half of the seventeenth century, when the quotations of the period show an association with the cock bird, rather than the cock of the barrel.

One alternative that is certainly wrong is the idea that the phrase comes from the French *coq à huppe*, a cock with its comb raised in pride and boasting. The phrase occurs in no major French dictionary. The similarity of form provides the basis for a fanciful piece of folk etymology.

Barnaby Thompson…insists that when People *magazine listed him as one of the '50 Most Beautiful People' last year, Col was* **cock-a-hoop**.
THE SUNDAY TIMES, 25 AUGUST 2002

cocked: to knock/beat into a cocked hat

to defeat roundly, to show someone/ something to be inferior to the opposition

The phrase alludes to the bowling game of *cocked hat* in which three pins are set thirty-six inches apart in a triangular shape, reminiscent of the three-cornered cocked hat worn in the late eighteenth and early nineteenth centuries. The allusion is to the scattering of the pins when they are all bowled over. The idiom is American in origin and dates from the first half of the nineteenth century.

It beats Southfork into a cocked hat. It makes Graceland look like a shoebox… It is now officially the most expensive house ever put on the property market in the United Kingdom – possibly in the world.
THE INDEPENDENT, 21 JULY 2001

Russia's Yelena Isinbayeva has vaulted a new world record of 4.91m, **beating her compatriot Svetlana Feofanova's 4.75m into a cocked hat**.
THE GUARDIAN, 24 AUGUST 2004

For a similar expression, see *to* KNOCK *the spots off*.

codswallop: a load of old codswallop

a lot of nonsense, something of no value, rubbish

The story goes that Victorian businessman Hiram C Codd made his living by selling fizzy drinks. In 1872 he patented a bottle made of green glass with a marble as a stopper. The container was designed to cope with the pressure that built up in the soft drink. The gas inside pushed the glass ball against a rubber ring in the bottle neck, thus providing an effective seal. Before long Mr Codd's products were well known but were no substitute for an honest pint. Drinking men laughingly dubbed it *Codd's wallop*, *wallop* being a slang term for 'beer'. The word caught on and was later applied to anything regarded as substandard or rubbish.

Although Hiram Codd and his soft drinks company certainly existed, it is doubtful that *codswallop* was coined with reference to his products, for the word does not appear in English until the early 1960s. It must thus be labelled 'origin unknown'.

What makes Spooks *so watchable is that, although one knows perfectly well that most of what they get up to is* **a load of old codswallop**, *the stories are played out with*

such gusto and the characters deliver their lines…with such conviction that you can't help being caught up in it all.
DAILY MAIL, 3 JUNE 2003

*Not only do heels set off any outfit, they make your legs look fantastic. So all this talk about them being bad for you is madness, **absolute codswallop** and complete blasphemy to a shoe-lover like me.*
DAILY MIRROR, 8 JANUARY 2004

For another idiom with a similar meaning, see *a load of old* COBBLERS.

cold: to get/have cold feet

to feel anxious and uncertain about an undertaking, to the point of wanting to withdraw

According to an old Lombard proverb, known in England in the seventeenth century through Ben Jonson's play *Volpone* (1605), *to have cold feet* signified 'to be without means or resources', a reference, perhaps, to the fact that the destitute cannot afford shoes. If this is the source of our modern idiom, it is not evident how the expression came to mean 'nervous and uncertain', nor why there is scant literary record of it until centuries later. It has been proposed that a novel by Fritz Reuter (1862, translated from German into English in 1870), in which a card player pleads cold feet as his excuse for backing out of a game, might have influenced this shift in meaning and popularised the phrase. The expression might have been picked up from the word-for-word translation of the German, or from the usage of the many immigrant Germans who arrived in America in the latter part of the nineteenth century.

The first modern use is at the very end of the nineteenth century in America. The reference may possibly be to an unwillingness to continue a journey once the going gets uncomfortable.

All three of the following quotations tell the story, from a different perspective, of a Georgia bride who *got cold feet.*

*A Georgia bride-to-be who vanished just days before her wedding turned up in New Mexico and fabricated a tale of abduction before admitting Saturday that she had **gotten cold feet** and 'needed some time alone,' police said… The wedding was going to be a huge bash. The couple had mailed 600 invitations, and the ceremony was to feature 14 bridesmaids and 14 groomsmen.*
ASSOCIATED PRESS, 30 APRIL 2005

COLD FEET COMMON IN WEDDING BIZ
For florists, wedding planners, bridal shop operators and others in the wedding industry, last-second cancellations and jittery grooms and brides come with the territory.

They say there is no concrete proof more people are being left at the altar. But it sure seems more likely to happen nowadays, said Cindy Cote, a Charlotte wedding consultant.

As the wedding approaches, 'reality starts to set in,' and people sometimes fear the commitment of marriage, said Heather Casselberry, an ordained minister who performs weddings.
KANSAS CITY STAR, 1 MAY 2005

*Initially there were speculations that Wilbanks simply **got cold feet**. Some mental health professionals say the issues are more complex than that. 'There's more going on here than just **cold feet**,' said Robert Carlson, Ph.D. 'My sense of it is that we are probably dealing with a personality disorder, minimally. And perhaps something even more severe. But there is clearly more pathology here than someone who just couldn't go through with it.'*
LEDGER-ENQUIRER, 3 MAY 2005

cold: to give someone the cold shoulder

to treat someone with intentional coldness, to snub someone

Earliest references to this idiom appear in the works of Scottish author Sir Walter Scott in the early nineteenth century. The phrase could, of course, simply allude to a deliberate turning away and coldness of manner when a person one dislikes approaches. However, it is generally considered to refer to the custom of serving a tasty hot dinner to welcome guests while presenting unwelcome visitors, or those who had stayed rather too long, with slices from a cold shoulder of beef or mutton, probably leftovers from dinner the night before.

As temperatures in Manchester plunged well below freezing last night, nobody was feeling the chill more than David Beckham. Omitted from Sir Alex Ferguson's starting line-up for the seventh time in eight matches…the England captain was left to ponder at what point rotation becomes demotion. No mystery back injury was cited this time: it was definitely the cold shoulder.
THE TIMES, 3 JANUARY 2002

First she wanted town and I wanted country, then she wanted old and I wanted very old. We have had nights of the long cold shoulder.
THE SUNDAY TIMES, 10 FEBRUARY 2002

cold: to go cold turkey

to come off (hard) drugs abruptly, rather than gradually and more easily

This phrase, which is of American origin, has been drug-world terminology since at least the first quarter of the twentieth century. A favourite explanation for the use of *cold turkey* in this context is that it is a plain dish requiring no preparation and served up without frills or ceremony: by analogy,

the withdrawal method is the most basic and straightforward. Other commentators claim that the phrase is descriptive of an addict's clammy mottled skin which looks like that of a plucked turkey once this drastic treatment is underway.

There is, however, a third explanation. When the expression *cold turkey* was coined another American idiom *to talk cold turkey*, meaning 'to be frank, to talk in plain terms', was current (this was a twist on the earlier phrase *to talk* TURKEY, which had the same meaning) and it is possible that the drug-related term derived from this.

Amrhein's bartender Lisa Kelly said she's worried about the effect of the [smoking] ban on business but is 'thrilled' at the prospect of working in a smoke-free environment. Some customers have told her they kicked the habit in recent weeks rather than face the ban cold turkey at the bar.
BOSTON HERALD, 5 MAY 2003

cold: to pour/throw cold water on something

to discourage, to quench enthusiasm for something

Plautus used this expression in 200 BC in the sense of 'to slander', but it is only since the beginning of the nineteenth century that it has been current in English and with the changed sense of 'to discourage'. The origin of the term is unknown, but it brings to mind the dousing in cold water of brawling cats, mating dogs or even ardent suitors, thus bringing their intentions to an abrupt end.

Mr Wanless was expected to pour cold water on Downing Street plans for a 'fat tax' on unhealthy foods.
THE SCOTSMAN, 25 FEBRUARY 2004

colours: to nail one's colours to the mast

to be resolute, unwavering in one's opinions or principles; to declare one's allegiance publicly

Battleships always fly their colours, that is, their ensign or standard. If the flag were taken down in battle it was a sign of surrender. In the days of wooden ships and masts, and close-range barrages of cannon, it was all too easy to lose the tops of masts in the fire. So, a flag literally nailed to the mast would show the determination of the crew to fight on, come what may.

Today the phrase is used to show a person's determination to stand by his opinion or principles, a stand which is not always easy to maintain. Sir Robert Peel mocked an opponent who found it difficult: *I never heard him make a speech in the course of which he did not nail, unnail, renail and unnail again his colours* (quoted in *The Croker Papers*, 1844). The familiar fuller form, including *to the mast*, dates from the same period.

Time is on his side and I bet he will not **nail his colours to the mast** *until he has had a good look around.*
THE GUARDIAN, 14 JANUARY 2004

See also *to show one's true* COLOURS.

colours: to show one's true colours

to make one's true opinion known, to show one's real self (after being deliberately misleading)

As in the expression *to nail one's* COLOURS *to the mast*, 'colours' are a ship's ensign which every vessel is obliged to fly. In the days when piracy was rife on the high seas it was a common deception of pirates to *sail under false colours*, that is, to fly a friendly flag. In this way the pirate vessel was able to approach a likely treasure ship

without exciting suspicion. Only when sailing at close quarters would the pirate ship unfurl its *true colours*.

A similar subterfuge was occasionally carried out to gain advantage in war. Ships sometimes broke the rule that each vessel should display its national flag, and revealed their true colours only when within easy firing range of the enemy. In his *Sailor's Word-Book* (1867), Admiral William Smyth called this an allowable stratagem of war. Figurative use of *to show one's true colours* dates from the first half of the nineteenth century.

Comedian Gervais wrote, directed and stars in the cinema commercial, in which he plays a factory worker who claims he would have no problem employing a disabled person. But in a typically cringeworthy Brent-like way, the character **shows his true colours** *by listing a series of ridiculous reasons why candidates with disabilities would not fit into the workplace, such as restricted growth, blindness or deafness.*
THE GUARDIAN, 27 NOVEMBER 2002

See also *to nail one's* COLOURS *to the mast*.

coot: as bald as a coot

having very little hair

The coot is a fiercely territorial bird which lives at the edge of still water. It is remarkable for having what the sixteenth-century poet John Skelton described as *a balde face*, that is, the base of its beak extends and broadens onto its forehead giving the appearance of receding hair. As early as 1430 those with receding hairlines were described as being *as balde as is a coote*.

Blokes try to hide their 40-ness with wigs and ponytails. But no 20-year-olds send off for tonics that promise to make you **as bald as a coot** *in 21 days or your money back.*
THE INDEPENDENT, 29 JUNE 2000

Bald as a coot and with the look of a permanently startled snake, Moby is an unlikely pop star.
DAILY MIRROR, 25 MARCH 2005

copper-bottomed
absolutely guaranteed, first rate

Wooden sailing ships were very prone to attacks by marine parasites and became encrusted with barnacles. They were also vulnerable to damage from rocks. In the eighteenth century those companies that could afford it began to sheath the bottoms of their vessels in copper to reduce the problems. The investment probably paid for itself as copper-bottomed ships, clear of barnacles, slipped more smoothly through the water, thus making the voyage time shorter. During the nineteenth century *copper-bottomed* became a mercantile expression for 'of good quality', 'first rate' and passed into general usage towards the end of that century. Nowadays it is often found in the phrase *copper-bottomed guarantee*.

*This match comes with a **copper-bottomed guarantee** that it will finish in a draw.*
DAILY MIRROR, 8 MAY 2004

*Reliable, honest, **copper-bottomed**, good journalism is guaranteed, in the wake of the Hutton enquiry.*
EXPRESS ON SUNDAY, 4 JULY 2004

For other nautical idioms, see A LIFE ON THE OCEAN WAVES, page 24.

cosh: under the cosh
at someone's mercy; at risk, under threat; under pressure, severe examination

Cosh is an underworld slang term for 'a heavy stick' or 'policeman's truncheon' that arose in the nineteenth century. The word was also taken up by school-

boys to mean 'a cane'. The phrase *under the cosh* is recorded from around the middle of the twentieth century as a prisoners' term denoting 'to be at the mercy of warders'. More generally it means 'to be threatened', 'at risk', and is increasingly common with the sense 'under pressure from an opponent'. Incidentally a new prison term, *liquid cosh*, has recently arisen to refer to another method of keeping inmates under control – tranquillisers administered by forcible injection: *From his cell in 1982 he recounted numerous incidents of beatings and enforced sedation (the infamous liquid cosh) that he had been subjected to by mob-handed prison officers (The Guardian, 30 October 2003).*

*Sixth form numbers have fallen so far as to threaten the continued existence of languages as a major option. Languages, one specialist told me, are '**under the cosh**'.*
THE GUARDIAN, 10 JUNE 2003

*Laura Davies opts for Sorenstam's 'calmness **under the cosh**'…she must feel pressure but she never shows it.*
THE DAILY TELEGRAPH, 25 MARCH 2004

couch potato, a
someone living a mindless life with minimum effort; an inactive TV addict

To Brits a *boob tube* is an elasticated bodice young girls wear as a top. Across the Atlantic it is a slang expression for 'television' from which American Tom Iacino derived the term *boob tuber* to describe someone who generally vegetates in front of the small screen. In 1976 Iacino's coinage caught the attention of cartoonist Robert Armstrong who, musing on the word *tuber*, came up with *potato* by association. He imagined the lumpy vegetable slouched on the sofa watching hour after hour of television and the term *couch potato* was born. The television magazine *TV Guide* ran a major article featuring the *couch potato* and the term entered the language. Armstrong had the foresight to register *couch potato* as a trademark in 1982, thus making healthy profits on a variety of merchandise, such as his illustrations for Jack Mingo's *The Official Couch Potato Handbook* (1982). He also founded an organisation, Couch Potatoes, for male TV addicts in his home state of Pasadena.

With television rights deals so crucial, and match day receipts waning in importance, where does the traditional fan now come in the pecking order? 'The most important policy question for European soccer,' says Szymanski, 'is, "What is the exchange rate of a couch potato for a diehard fan?"'
TIME, 5 JUNE 2000

Did they ask for a pay rise where you held back? Did they sign up for the gym to get healthy while you stayed a couch potato?
GOOD HOUSEKEEPING, MAY 2001

Today's children risk diabetes, heart disease and cancers because of what they eat and the damage is compounded by a 'couch potato' lifestyle.
DAILY MAIL, 31 MAY 2002

Coventry: to send to Coventry
to ostracise, to refuse to speak to someone

There are two suggestions as to why this Midland town lends its name to the idiom.

The first claims that during the English Civil War (1642–49) supporters of Parliament in Birmingham rose against small groups of their fellow citizens who were known to have pledged allegiance to the Crown. Some they killed, others were sent as prisoners to neighbouring Coventry, a town which was staunchly pro-Parliamentarian. This story comes from a passage in the

Earl of Clarendon's *True Historical Narrative of the Rebellion and Civil Wars in England* (begun in 1647), where the author's description of events even includes the words *and sent them to Coventry*. The literal sense of Clarendon's phrase has since become a figurative expression of ostracism.

The second theory is that the townspeople of Coventry took a dislike to having soldiers garrisoned in their town and forbade their young women to talk to them. Any maid caught disobeying was shunned by her neighbours. The soldiers, of course, had no desire to be sent to Coventry where social contact was so difficult.

Whatever the origin of the phrase, it was well known by the middle of the eighteenth century.

Week after week she shuffled through the school, head hung to the ground, handing out magazines murmuring, 'Only Jehovah saves'; in a school where an overexcitable pustule could send you to Coventry…
ZADIE SMITH, WHITE TEETH, 2000

Unpleasant terms such as 'scab', 'blackleg' or 'send him to Coventry' are from the vocabulary of factory worker judgmentalism.
DAILY MIRROR, 9 FEBRUARY 2004

cows: until the cows come home
for a long time, for ever

The phrase refers to the leisurely pace of cows making their way from the field to the milking parlour and has been in use since the late sixteenth century.

As far as he was concerned, you could analyse it until the cows came home…
ZADIE SMITH, WHITE TEETH, 2000

'I say if he wants to sit in that chair and sleep his life away, that's just fine. I love that idea. I'm one-thousand-percent a fan of that idea. But first let's yank that

*chair out a three-floor house that's falling apart and losing value. Let's get Mom some kind of quality of life. Just do that, and he can sit in his chair and feel sorry for himself **till the cows come home**.'*
JONATHAN FRANZEN,
THE CORRECTIONS, 2001

*You can do market research and analysis **until the cows come home**, and still end up with no idea how to sell effectively to the customers in those target markets.*
LAWRENCE FRIEDMAN,
GO TO MARKET STRATEGY, 2002

For another idiom with a similar meaning, see KINGDOM *come*.

crocodile tears
a show of hypocritical sorrow; insincere tears

According to ancient belief the cunning crocodile arouses the curiosity of its unsuspecting victims with pitiful sighs and groans. Once its prey is within reach of its powerful jaws, the crocodile snaps it up and devours it, shedding insincere tears of sorrow all the while. Pliny and Seneca both give rather fanciful accounts of the crocodile's wiles and *crocodile's tears* is used figuratively in both Greek and Latin to refer to a show of false emotion.

It is not surprising that, before travel and exploration became commonplace, people were prepared to accept the ancient belief. Around 1356 *The Voiage and Travaile of Sir John Maundeville, knight* appeared. This account of things strange and fantastic mentions *in a certain countree… cokadrilles*, adding, *Theise Serpentes slen men, and thei eten hem wepynge*. Two centuries later, in 1565, Sir John Hawkins wrote of a voyage he had undertaken and repeated the information. Small wonder, then, that Shakespeare and his audiences were well aware of the creature's supposed deceit and that, by that time, *crocodile tears* were idiomatic for 'counterfeit sorrow'.

*My husband plays Sir Galahad to other women, frequently putting them before me. The worst thing was at a party when he kissed and cuddled a woman in front of me and he knows she dislikes me. Then he comforted her when she turned on **crocodile tears** as though I was not important to him at all.*
DAILY MAIL, 12 AUGUST 2002

*'The schmaltzy, false sorrow is the most revolting thing to me,' Erikson said. 'It's **crocodile tears** when you hear him crying over the dead when he is the one who caused their deaths.'*
SAN DIEGO UNION-TRIBUNE,
14 APRIL 2004

For other myths derived from fabled animal behaviour, see page 318.

Croesus: as rich as Croesus
extremely wealthy

Croesus was a king of celebrated wealth who reigned over Lydia from 561 to 546 BC. The source of his riches was the significant deposits of gold found in the River Pactolus, resources attributed by legend to King Midas, who was said to have washed there. The English simile *as rich as Croesus* dates back to the sixteenth century: *As riche as Cresus Affric is* (Timothy Kendall, *Flowers of Epigrams*, 1577).

Incidentally, according to the Greek historian Herodotus, the brilliant court of Croesus was visited by all the wise men of Greece including Solon, the lawmaker of Athens, who despised the king's wealth. Asked by Croesus if he had ever come across a happier man than he, Solon gave examples of contented men of more modest means, adding that wealth is useless unless fortune also decrees a trouble-free life:

He who unites the greatest number of
advantages, and retaining them to the day
of his death, then dies peaceably, that man
alone, sire, is, in my judgment, entitled to
bear the name of 'happy'. But in every
matter it behoves us to mark well the end:
for oftentimes God gives men a gleam of
happiness, and then plunges them into ruin
(Herodotus, *Histories*, Book I, 440 BC).

Indeed, Croesus faced a very turbulent
future, losing Lydia to the Persians
under Cyrus in 546 BC.

*Where mediaeval alchemists failed,
J K Rowling has succeeded. Her* Harry
Potter and the Philosopher's Stone, *now a film, and her subsequent Potter
books have certainly turned her words into
gold, and she is now* **as rich as Croesus**.
THE SPECTATOR, 29 DECEMBER 2001

To find out more about King Midas,
see *the* MIDAS *touch*, and for other
idioms derived from ancient legends,
see page 317.

crow: as the crow flies
in a straight line; the shortest distance
between two places without the need
to follow a winding road

Modern-day research seems to suggest
that bees do indeed go in a straight
line from and to their hives (see *to
make a* BEELINE *for*). But it may be
that crows aren't quite as direct,
despite their proverbial reputation.
According to a report in the *Daily
Telegraph* of 5 February 2004:

*Zoologists now believe the phrase 'as the
crow flies' no longer means the shortest, most
direct route between two points. Animal
behaviouralists at Oxford University are
stunned by their findings, which follow 10
years of research into homing pigeons.*
*'It really has knocked our research team
sideways to find that after a decade-long
international study, pigeons appear to ignore*
*their inbuilt directional instincts and follow
the road system,' said Prof Tim Guilford,
reader in animal behaviour at Oxford
University's Department of Zoology. 'Up
until now, we have always thought about
the way that birds go in terms of the
energetics of the flight efficiency, which is
the most direct route home…as in the phrase
"as the crow flies". But the answer is, they
don't go as the crow flies, and neither, it is
my hunch, do crows. As they get familiar
with the environment, they just follow the
obvious features which often don't take them
directly home.'*

*A free shuttlebus service is being launched
to ferry shoppers from the underground car
park in Park Lane to the Marks & Spencer
Marble Arch store in Oxford Street – a
distance of around 600 metres* **as the
crow flies**.
EVENING STANDARD, 18 APRIL 2001

*The distance between St. Louis and
Minneapolis* **as the crow flies** *is 464
miles; the distance between Milwaukee
and Minneapolis* **as the crow flies** *is
295 miles.*
STAR TRIBUNE, 27 NOVEMBER 2001

cuff: off the cuff
unrehearsed, extempore

The idiom is of American origin, dating back to the 1930s, and refers to the
practice after-dinner speakers had of
making last-minute notes on their
starched shirt-cuffs.

*…Fidel Castro rambled on in the hot
sunshine (his* **off-the-cuff** *doorstep
interviews last as long as everyone else's
full-scale sit-down ones).*
EXPRESS ON SUNDAY, 4 JULY 2004

cup: not/just one's cup of tea
not/just to one's taste

Tea is traditionally the national beverage of the British and has been enjoyed

by them since it was brought into the country in the seventeenth century. This rapturous tribute from Colley Cibber's *The Lady's Last Stake* (1708) gives us a glimpse of the tea drinker's heaven: *Tea! thou soft, thou sober, sage and venerable liquid, thou female tongue-running, smile-soothing, heart-opening, wink-tipping cordial, to whose glorious insipidity I owe the happiest moments of my life.*

By the middle of the eighteenth century, tea had replaced ale and gin as the drink of the masses, and become the most popular national beverage. Later that century, Cowper (in *The Task*, 1785) gave expression to the British affection for and dependence upon tea when he wrote:

> *...the cups*
> *That cheer but not inebriate...*

A misquotation of this is still frequently and contentedly murmured over the nation's tea cups. Over 163 million cups of tea per day are drunk in twenty-first-century UK households, so for a British citizen to declare that something is *not my cup of tea* is a damning statement showing distaste. On the other hand the comment *That's just my cup of tea* brings with it an aura of approval.

Comparisons with the beverage began in the early twentieth century when *a cup of tea* simply referred to 'a person', initially quite favourably: '*It's simply impossible to help liking him.*' To which Sally replied, borrowing an expression from Ann the housemaid, that Fenwick *was a cup of tea. It was metaphorical and descriptive of invigoration* (William Frend de Morgan, *Somehow Good*, 1908).

Describing something that was to one's taste or in one's interest as *one's cup of tea* dates back to around the 1930s.

And while blue pots, purple concrete screens or acres of decking **may not be everyone's cup of tea**, *let's face it, doesn't every gardener wish at some point in their lives*

that the experts would come and give their tired plot a facelift?
THE DAILY TELEGRAPH, 6 MARCH 2003

curate's egg, a
something of varying quality, part good and part bad

The edition of the English humorous magazine *Punch* dated 9 November 1895 carried a cartoon by George du Maurier, appropriately titled 'True Humility', showing a timid curate eating a bad egg at the home of his bishop and bravely assuring his host that *parts of it are excellent*. The cartoon so appealed to the public that phrases such as *good in parts* and *parts of it are excellent* were soon in common use and *curate's egg* came to denote something that is poor but has its good points. Logically, of course, a bad egg is bad through and through and so a *curate's egg* ought to be a diplomatic way of saying that something is dreadful. But logic is not always the way with idiomatic phrases (see NONSENSICAL IDIOMS, page 124).

The latest in Weidenfeld's series of short biographies is a bit of a **curate's egg**. *At its best it is a thoughtful and incisive essay, but at its worst it is a prosecution brief, with all the distortion and special pleading that implies.*
THE INDEPENDENT, 5 AUGUST 2002

curry: to curry favour
to seek someone's approval through flattery, to ingratiate oneself with someone

The phrase is a corruption of Middle English *to curry favel*, itself from the Old French *estriller fauvel*, meaning 'to rub down or groom a chestnut horse'. (*Fauvel* derives from the French *fauve*, meaning 'fallow-coloured'.) In *Le Roman de Fauvel*, a French allegory dating back to the early fourteenth century, a chestnut horse representing hypocrisy and deceit is carefully combed down by other characters in order to win his favour and assistance. (In equestrian circles, *to curry* still means to groom or rub down an animal.) The popularity of the work led people to accuse those intent upon furthering their own ends by flattery of *currying favel*. This form persisted in English from around the beginning of the fifteenth century until the early seventeenth, but the closeness in pronunciation between *favel* and *favour* and an association between sycophancy and favour-seeking led to the form *to curry favour* being used from the early sixteenth century, and this finally won out.

Gail and I and the other minor misfits **curried favour** *with the pack in our separate ways.*
LORNA SAGE, BAD BLOOD, 2000

However, Worthington knows that he needs **to curry favour** *with the stars if his name is to be known in the States.*
THE SUNDAY TIMES, 3 FEBRUARY 2002

For other idioms drawn from literature, see page 319.

cut: to cut and run
to make a quick get-away, to quit

According to David Steel's *The Elements and Practice of Rigging and Seamanship* (1794), the sailors' bible for those aboard warships of the period, *to cut and run* meant *to cut the cable and make sail instantly without waiting to weigh anchor*. The phrase therefore refers to sailors at war making a speedy departure by *cutting* the anchor cable, easily done if it were of rope and not a chain, and allowing the vessel to *run* before the wind. The nautical phrase had become idiomatic by 1861 when Dickens used it in *Great Expectations: I*

treasonably whispered to Joe, 'I hope, Joe, that we shan't find them,' and Joe whispered to me, 'I'd give a shilling if they had **cut and run***, Pip.'*

For the foreseeable future his main preoccupation will be Iraq. White House officials insist that he is committed to not **cutting and running***. 'I don't see it in Bush's personality to go through this and then* **cut and run***,' said one.*
THE DAILY TELEGRAPH,
4 NOVEMBER 2004

For other nautical idioms, see A LIFE ON THE OCEAN WAVES, page 24.

cut: to cut no ice with someone
to make no impression, to be powerless to influence

This idiom originated in America towards the end of the nineteenth century and was in British usage by 1917 when Arthur Conan Doyle used it in *His Last Bow, An Epilogue of Sherlock Holmes*: *It cuts no ice with a British copper to tell him you're an American citizen.* The phrase probably refers to ice skating. One can move about with ease on skates only if the blades are keen and cut into the ice. Blunt blades make no impression. And so, metaphorically speaking, a plan or argument that is less than sharp will *cut no ice*.

But such arguments **cut no ice** *with my informant.*
THE TIMES, 10 MARCH 2004

As he rids himself of the reputation as a party-loving playboy, the actor spends one day a week handing out cups of tea to hospital staff and patients at Manchester's Christie cancer hospital. But last night this **cut no ice** *with Sara, who said: 'I just want Tina to know what Ryan is like.'*
THE SUNDAY PEOPLE, 27 JUNE 2004

D

damn: to damn with faint praise

to praise someone or something with so little feeling that it implies censure

The sentiment behind the idiom is an old one. An apophthegm of the Roman philosopher and rhetorician Favorinus, written around AD 110, recognised that *it is more shameful to be praised faintly and coldly than to be censured violently*. From the seventeenth century onwards writers and collectors of proverbs and maxims have drawn on the truth, notably William Wycherley who, in the prologue to his play *The Plain-Dealer* (1677), has the line: *With faint praises one another damn.* During the early eighteenth century Wycherley struck up a friendship with the poet Alexander Pope, who revised much of his work. It seems that Pope also borrowed bits of it for, in his *Epistle to Dr Arbuthnot* (1735), he satirises the politician and writer Joseph Addison, whom he calls Atticus, with the following lines:

> *Damn with faint praise, assent with civil leer,*
>
> *And, without sneering, teach the rest to sneer.*

*The cursory reference to Sorenstam and her achievements seemed unfair to a woman who won two major championships, became the sixth woman to win the career grand slam and competed with considerable élan against men in a tournament in the US last May as well as finishing second in a skin's game in which the other three competitors were men. Talk about **damning with faint praise**!*
THE TIMES, 18 DECEMBER 2003

For other idioms drawn from Greek and Roman writers, see page 318

dark horse, a

an unknown quantity, a person whose abilities are not yet known and tested

Benjamin Disraeli is credited with bringing this piece of racing slang to wider attention. His novel *The Young Duke* (1831) contains a description of a horse race in which the two favourites cannot make the running while *a dark horse which never had been thought of, and which the careless St James had never even observed in the list, rushed past the grandstand in a sweeping triumph*. In the world of horseracing *a dark horse* is one whose form is unknown to the public.

Such was Disraeli's popularity that before long the phrase began to be used figuratively in America, initially in political contexts, to describe a candidate about whom little is known but who unexpectedly takes the lead. In 1845 James K Polk became the first *dark horse* President. More likely candidates for the Democratic nomination could not muster the required number of votes so the compromise candidate, the relatively unknown Polk, came through. A few years later, in 1860, Abraham Lincoln was a similar *dark horse* compromise candidate of the Republican Party.

Nowadays the idiom is no longer restricted to candidates or competitors but can also be applied to someone who has not yet had the opportunity to show what he can do or whose hidden talents come unexpectedly to light.

*The favourite? Jimmy McGeough, the former boss of Waterford. **The dark horse?** Don O'Riordan, sacked by Sligo last week, and ready to return to management.*
DAILY MIRROR, 28 JUNE 2004

*As Washington waits expectantly for an announcement as early as Tuesday, the Veepstakes are headed by three front-runners, with a larger following field of **dark horses** and surprise packages.*
THE TIMES, 5 JULY 2004

For other horsey idioms see page 319.

darken: to darken someone's door

to appear on someone's doorstep (as a visitor)

The allusion here is to the figure of an unwelcome visitor casting a shadow over the threshold and blocking out the light. The idiom, in use since at least the first half of the eighteenth century, is almost always used negatively and in modern English is often found in the imperative *Don't ever darken my door again,* meaning 'Go away and don't come back'.

*With some firms, the attitude if you leave is '**don't ever darken my door again**'.*
THE INDEPENDENT ON SUNDAY,
20 JANUARY 2002

'CHILDREN MUST BE WELL BEHAVED.'
*This is actually code for: '**Never Darken Our Doors** With Brats Of Any Age.' For even angels have off days. But then so do adults and no one bans them from pubs.*
DAILY EXPRESS, 24 FEBRUARY 2003

day: as plain as day

totally obvious

See under *as plain as a* PIKESTAFF.

*The rest of us can see the real reason **as plain as day**. The Hindujas got special treatment because they are rich.*
THE GUARDIAN, 13 MARCH 2001

*The broad outlines of a Social Security fix are **plain as day**: a modest combination of higher payroll taxes and changed benefits phased in over time.*
CHICAGO TRIBUNE, 22 APRIL 2005

day of reckoning

a time of giving a (final) account for one's actions; a time when one's success or failure in an endeavour will be made known

The phrase refers to the day when, according to the Bible, Jesus Christ will return and pronounce the final judgement on both the living and the dead. It has been in use since the nineteenth century to signify 'a calling to account' for one's behaviour or in one's endeavours, in much more general contexts.

*Tony Blair will face a '**day of reckoning**' at the next election as voters desert him for attempting to 'destroy the education system', it was claimed yesterday.*
DAILY MAIL, 14 APRIL 2004

*Arts Council England has already advocated the dismantling of the company. Its forthcoming gimmicks of open-air performances in the mud of Glastonbury and the traffic noise of Trafalgar Square cannot long defer the **day of reckoning**.*
EVENING STANDARD, 23 JUNE 2004

daylights: to beat/scare the (living) daylights out of someone

to beat or frighten someone excessively

Back in the mid-eighteenth century *daylights* was a slang term for 'eyes'. The word may have originated in boxing circles for, according to Francis Grose in his *Classical Dictionary of the Vulgar Tongue* (1785), the phrase *to darken his daylights* meant 'to punch a man's eyes closed during a bout'. By the middle of the nineteenth century *daylights* referred not just to the eyes but to any vital organ, and was invariably found coupled with a verb of violence, such as *beat*, *belt*, *thrash* or *scare*, with *living* often used as an intensifier from the middle of the twentieth century.

Ditto Straw, whose countenance has **scared the living daylights** *out of more children than the monster of Victor Frankenstein ever did.*
THE SPECTATOR, 30 DECEMBER 2000

In the past few days, Stevens and the press have egged each other on like bullies preparing themselves **to thrash the living daylights** *out of their target.*
THE OBSERVER, 29 APRIL 2001

For other boxing idioms, see PACKING A PUNCH, page 45; for other idioms with intensifiers see GIVING IT TO THEM HOT AND STRONG, page 176, and the list on page 319.

deaf as a post

totally deaf, inattentive

Similes about deafness abound. *Deaf as an adder*, referred to by Shakespeare in *Troilus and Cressida* (1602), was rooted in an old belief that snakes could not hear. The folklore of several English counties has proverbs, jingles and superstitions to that effect. The belief had its origin in a Bible passage, Psalm 58:4–5, which reads: *They are like the deaf adder that stoppeth her ear; which will not harken to the voice of charmers...*

More understandably, many of the similes compare deafness to inanimate objects: *deaf as a door*, *deaf as a doornail*, *deaf as a doorpost* are all mentioned in sixteenth-century literature, as is *deaf as a post*. The qualities of stupidity and ignorance had already been attributed to posts from the fifteenth century. Add to these their proverbial inability to hear, and confidences were quite safe, as the nineteenth-century idiom of secrets *between you, me and the* GATEPOST/*bedpost*/*doorpost* shows.

Lillian's sister, Meredith, could sometimes be a bit grumpy and was **as deaf as a post**...
MICK JACKSON, FIVE BOYS, 2001

deep: in at/off the deep end

having to learn rapidly something difficult with little preparation/ overreacting, flying into a rage

The deep end is, of course, the deep end of a swimming-pool and the phrase alludes to jumping in and letting oneself go. The expression dates from around 1921 when an article in *The Times Literary Supplement* refers to it as *the slang of the moment*. There are two main senses today. One is an obvious metaphorical extension of the literal act of jumping in the deep end of the swimming pool and refers to undertaking any task that requires quick action with minimal preparation:

'There wasn't any formal induction at all – no time was set aside, so it all had to be done on an ad-hoc basis.'
'I didn't really receive any induction, everyone seemed so very busy.'
One word is used above any other to describe their initial experiences –
'Traumatic!'...

These and other research findings are reported in full in the SCRE Project Report 'In at the Deep End?' (Peter Gartside and Julie Allan, *SCRE, Research in Education*, No 42, 1989)

The second involves a shift of sense, to express indignation or rage:

The Paris city council agreed last week to give a EUR 2,300 subsidy to the Paris naturist association to hold nude swimming and aqua-gym sessions in municipal swimming pools after hours. The decision sent right-wing town councillors off the deep end. 'Why should the 370 Parisian nudists need a subsidy to get undressed?' councillor Pierre Charon wanted to know. 'Why should swimming-pool attendants have to stay late at work to watch "nude cardio-vascular training"?' (*The Independent*, 13 July 2004)

*Ken Simpson revealed how the other day he was angry at his wife for something, but rather than confront her, decided to think it over for a while and see if it really was an issue. Turned out, he says, that it wasn't really a problem. 'I had manufactured the whole thing in my mind. It worked out because I did not go **off the deep end** over something that wasn't an issue.'*
SEATTLE TIMES, 2 MARCH 2005

*A self-described minister of spirituality, the 60-year-old Busey was prone to such philosophical tangents during the hourlong press conference. But every time you thought he would go **off the deep end**, he would return to Earth with an interjection of humor.*
ST PETERSBURG TIMES, 14 MARCH 2005

'I always thought about coming back into the game and what the situation would be and my ideal thought was to come back with an experienced manager.

*I had been thrown **in the deep end** at just 34 years of age and I was taught some wonderful lessons and got a good education of management but my next step, I felt, was to work alongside an experienced guy.'*
THE SCOTSMAN, 15 MAY 2005

devil: between the devil and the deep blue sea

trapped between two equally difficult sets of circumstances

Despite first appearances, there is no satanic influence behind this phrase. Rather, it is a nautical idiom. *The devil* was a seam on the hull of a wooden sailing ship that was close to the water level. It was an awkward place to reach and a precarious place to be, hence its name. Pity the poor sailor, then, to whom it fell *to caulk the devil*. Perched *between the devil and the deep sea* he ran grave risk of plunging, unnoticed, into the waters below.

An early use of the idiom occurs in an account (1637) given by Colonel Robert Munroe of his expedition with the Scots regiment. The regiment was serving under a Swedish commander. During one engagement Munroe found himself exposed not only to the fire of the enemy in front of him, but also to Swedish guns at his back. These guns weren't sufficiently elevated so the cannonballs were falling short, killing Scottish soldiers instead of the enemy. No wonder Colonel Munroe wrote afterwards *I with my party did lie on our post as betwixt the devil and the deep sea.*

Nowadays the form *between the devil and the deep blue sea* is more familiar but the addition of *blue*, which makes the phrase more rhythmical and emphatic, dates only from around the mid-twentieth century.

*Schools are **between the devil and the deep blue sea**, often accused of not being hard enough on the bully and of not doing enough to help the bully overcome his or her tendencies.*
THE TIMES EDUCATIONAL SUPPLEMENT, 14 JANUARY 2000

The Department for Transport's consultation paper on the development of air transport in the United Kingdom had an explosive impact across the West

Midlands. Attention was understandably focused on what turned out to be a choice **between the devil and the deep blue sea** *– either opt for a second runway at Birmingham International Airport, or we'll make you have a new airport in the Warwickshire green belt.*
BIRMINGHAM POST, 18 APRIL 2003

See also *the* DEVIL *to pay*. For other idioms with a similar meaning see *between a* ROCK *and a hard place* and CATCH-*22*. For other nautical idioms, see A LIFE ON THE OCEAN WAVES, page 24.

devil: talk/speak of the devil

said when a person one has been talking about suddenly appears

The devil needs no encouragement to get up to his evil tricks. The mere mention of his name will summon him to one's side. There is an abundance of proverbs to this effect in English. John Ray records both *The Devil is never nearer than when we are talking of him* and *Talk of the Devil, and he'll come or send* in his collection of *English Proverbs* (1670). And according to Giovanni Torriano *The English say, Talk of the Devil, and he's presently at your elbow* (*Piazza Universale di Proverbi Italiani*, 1666). A seventeenth-century variant is *Talk of the Devil, and see his horns*. Over the border James Kelly records *Speak of the Dee'l, and he'll appear*, in his collection of Scottish proverbs (1721) adding, *Spoken when they, of whom we are speaking, come in by chance.*

These proverbs are rarely heard today but still, when someone just mentioned unexpectedly comes along, the phrase *talk of the devil* is the natural comment. The word *devil* is not, perhaps, appropriate for everyone. Dickens was kinder. *Talk of the angels*, he wrote, *here she is* (*Bleak House*, 1852).

Poulter…is the maverick of the group. 'Poulter is Poulter,' Casey laughs. 'He's a great player – at times.'…Casey, sitting on a trailer step at Loch Lomond, stops in mid-flow. **'Speak of the devil,'** *he eventually says, before he and a passing Poulter swap ritual insults…*
THE GUARDIAN, 14 JULY 2003

devil: the devil to pay

terrible consequences following a course of action

Many have tried to make a Faustian bargain with the devil (hence *to sell one's soul to the devil*), but for the favours or powers received he always exacts a price. The earliest instance of the proverbial expression comes from a manuscript dating back to around the beginning of the fifteenth century:

> *Beit wer he at tome for ay,*
> *Than her to serve the devil to pay.*
> (in *Reliquiæ Antiquæ*, ed. Wright and Halliwell, 1845)

By the eighteenth century the expression meant no more than reaping the consequences of a course of action; neglecting one's wife, for instance: *I must be with my wife on Tuesday, or there will be the devil and all to pay* (Swift, *Polite Conversation*, 1738).

During the early nineteenth century an amplified version of the phrase began to appear, *the devil to pay and no pitch hot*. This possibly originated in a humorous play on words, for *the devil* was a seam on a wooden sailing vessel (see *between the* DEVIL *and the deep blue sea*) while another sense of *to pay* was 'to caulk' (from Old French *peier*, from Latin *picare*, 'to smear with pitch'). The extended idiom makes good sense, however. If the vessel began to leak and there were no pitch ready the consequences would be severe – just the sense of the earlier idiom.

*There's always **the devil to pay**. The Faust myth has a dark fascination that has endured for centuries.*
THE INDEPENDENT, 16 MARCH 2002

DEVIL TO PAY OVER FILM OF BULGAKOV'S NOVEL
Russia's Orthodox church has reacted with dismay to a film of the seminal novel The Master and Margarita, *saying it offers a version of the Gospel that is 'nothing but negative' and fearing it will offend or confuse many believers.*
THE GUARDIAN, 3 NOVEMBER 2004

devil: to play devil's advocate
to argue against something to which one is not necessarily opposed in order to test its validity or to provoke; to advocate an unpopular view

Devil's advocate is a translation of the Latin *advocatus diaboli*. This was the popular title given to the official appointed by the Roman Catholic Church to argue against the proposed canonisation of a saint by bringing up all that was unfavourable to the claim. (His proper title is Promoter of the Faith, *promotor fidei*.) The post seems to have been established by Pope Leo X early in the fifteenth century. Since those proposed for sainthood generally enjoyed the goodwill of the church, the official was presenting a view with which he probably did not himself agree, hence the coinage in the second half of the eighteenth century of the phrase *to play devil's advocate*. In 1959 the Catholic novelist Morris West published an intriguing mystery, *The Devil's Advocate*, in which a papal investigator is dispatched to investigate Giacomo Nerone's claim to sainthood.

The devil

Speak of the DEVIL *and he will appear* goes the old proverb. Those not wishing to test out this wisdom, or those fearful of the censure of others, use euphemisms instead. Some terms for the devil make him sound like the man down the road, doubtless so that he will not realise he is being referred to. *Old Harry* has been in use since the second half of the eighteenth century. The phrase *to play Old Harry with* meaning 'to make mischief or indulge in devilment with' dates from the nineteenth century. During the twentieth century, it also meant 'to give someone a good telling off'. *Old Nick* is of seventeenth-century origin. Attempts have been made to link the name with *nicker*, an Old English term for a water monster, but conclusive evidence is wanting.

Dickens has been used in exclamations of surprise or irritation (*where, what, why, how the Dickens*) since the sixteenth century:

So we caught up with Ms Mills, 33, at the Jubilee Concert to ask her what the dickens was going on. And the former model did nothing to dispel the hot gossip that she had already become Mrs McCartney (*Daily Mirror*, 5 June 2002).

Suggestions are that *Dickens* is a corruption of *devilkins*, or even of *Nick*, but it more likely comes from *Dickon* or *Dickin*, diminutive forms of *Dick* in the sixteenth century when the euphemism was first coined. Indeed, Shakespeare makes a play on this fact in *The Merry Wives of Windsor* (1597):

FORD: *Where had you this pretty weathercock?*
MISTRESS PAGE: *I cannot tell what the dickens his name is my husband had him of.*

*When a Vaughan rant is in full flow, you sense he wants you **to play devil's advocate**. He seems to enjoy verbal sparring and might sulk if it stopped.*
THE GUARDIAN, 3 SEPTEMBER 2001

dice: to dice with death
to take risks

The verb *to dice* has been in use since the fifteenth century with the meaning 'to gamble with dice'. In the twentieth century the verb developed the more general extended sense of 'to take great risks', evident in the phrase *to dice with death*. Towards the middle of the century this expression was used to dramatic effect by motor-racing journalists amongst whom it became such a cliché that the motor-racing fraternity derived from it the term *dicing* to mean 'driving in a race'. When the general public picked up on the word in the 1960s, it was used to describe the kind of perilous driving that mimicked that of a race track: *On the M1 or the M4 a lot of them try to dice with us… You'll get the bod who will come up behind you, an Aston Martin, a Sprite, a Mini Cooper, and they'll be flashing their lights to get by you* (The Observer, 23 March 1969).

*Blast off to Mars in a spacecraft, **dice with death** in a tank full of sharks, or watch a fairy story unfold in fireworks across the night sky. Florida, the fantasy capital of the universe, always has a few rabbits to pull out of its hat.*
THE TIMES, 1 NOVEMBER 2003

*Kids in Co Down are **dicing with death**. It is feared children who are using a viaduct in Dromore to skateboard on could seriously injure themselves.*
THE PEOPLE, 2 MAY 2004

die is cast, the
an irrevocable step has been taken

The phrase is a translation of the Latin *jacta alea est*, words attributed by the Roman biographer Suetonius to Julius Caesar as he crossed the river Rubicon in 49 BC, thus committing himself to war against Pompey. Although it is his momentous use of the expression which we recognise, Caesar was in fact alluding to a Greek metaphor to be found in the writings of Herodotus (c. 445 BC) and Meander (c. 300 BC). Plutarch even suggests that Caesar uttered the phrase, already a proverb, in Greek.

The meaning of the expression speaks for itself. *Die* is the singular of *dice*, though it is rarely used nowadays. All dice games carry an element of chance and, once the die has been thrown, the player must reconcile himself to the outcome, whether favourable or not. The phrase was first taken up by English writers in the first half of the seventeenth century.

*But Joanne Kathleen Rowling…had already written her first story at the age of six. It was about a rabbit, called Rabbit. And she had always dreamed of being an author right from the start. **The die was cast**.*
GOOD HOUSEKEEPING, APRIL 2001

*OK, that's it. **The die is cast**. The votes must be nearly all in by now. You want to know how I voted in the Tory leadership election? It was the same as last time and the time before that. I voted for the fat guy.*
BORIS JOHNSON IN THE DAILY TELEGRAPH, 6 SEPTEMBER 2001

For an idiom of similar meaning arising from the same incident see *to cross the* RUBICON. For more fatalistic expressions, see *to* BURN *one's boats/bridges* and *the* POINT *of no return*. For other idioms drawn from ancient life and history, see page 317, and for more idioms from Greek and Roman writers, see page 318.

die-hard, a
a person fanatically committed to a
minority, usually political, view point

It seems that this term may have been
coined at the gallows. According to an
issue of *The Gentleman's Magazine* dated
1784, *to die hard* is a *Tyburn phrase*,
Tyburn being a place of execution in
London from 1571 to 1783. (The
gallows stood at the junction of
present-day Oxford Street, Bayswater
Road and Edgware Road.) A convict
who *died hard* died reluctantly, resisting
to the end.

This was just the sort of attitude
that William Inglis, wounded commander of the 57th Regiment of Foot in
the British Army, demanded of his men
at Albuhera (16 May 1811), the blood-
iest battle in the Peninsular War. The
men responded to his courageous lead
with such boldness that they became
known as *the Die-hards*, a description
that, in the second half of the nineteenth century, was also applied to
other men of valour or of principle who
refused to admit defeat.

By the early twentieth century *die-
hard* had come to describe a member of
a political faction that stubbornly
resisted change: that opposed to the
Home Rule Bill of 1912, for instance.
The term is still used, in mainly political contexts, for someone who makes
known an opinion and then refuses
against all the odds to back down.

*Now the 30-year-old, who used to work in a
fabric shop, is a **die-hard** fighter in the
Mahdi Army, the militia of a Shiite Muslim
cleric who has vowed to take on the Americans.*
PHILADELPHIA INQUIRER, 3 MAY 2004

dilly-dally, to
to loiter

In the Middle Ages *to dally* meant 'to
converse idly'. Since young couples do a
great deal of this, the sense 'to flirt' soon
emerged. By the mid-sixteenth century,
all that hanging about billing and cooing
had given rise to a new, additional
meaning, 'to pass one's time frivolously,
to loiter'. The English have a fondness
for alliterative phrases, and so *to dilly-
dally*, meaning 'to loiter' or 'to be
indecisive', was coined, the element *dilly*
invented just for effect. Written references to the verb date from around
1740, but it had probably been in spoken English for some time, since
dilly-dally as a noun, meaning 'hesi-
tancy' is recorded nearly 150 years
earlier, and written records of similar-
sounding phrases, WILLY-NILLY and
SHILLY-SHALLY for instance, date from
the seventeenth century.

The phrase is familiar through a
music-hall song, popularised by Marie
Lloyd at the end of the nineteenth
century, about a couple doing a moonlight flit:

> *My old man said, 'Follow the van,
> don't dilly dally on the way!'*
> *Off went the cart with the home packed in it,
> I walked behind with me old cock linnet.
> But I dillied and dallied, dallied and dillied,
> Lost the van and don't know where to roam.
> You can't trust the specials like the
> old-time coppers
> When you can't find your way home.*

*The little mulatto girl didn't **dilly-dally**;
she came to see me and it all came pouring
out almost by itself; she told me everything
she knew.*
JOSÉ MARMOL, AMALIA, 2001

*But the then Prime Minister, Harold
Wilson, did not **dilly-dally** about the
timing of his resignation.*
THE OBSERVER, 13 SEPTEMBER 2004

See COUPLINGS, page 294.

dodo: as dead as a/the dodo
dead, extinct, obsolete, out of date

The dodo, a peculiar, comical-looking bird with a large, hooked, bulbous bill and short, curly tail-feathers, was a native of Mauritius. Heavy and clumsy, the dodo was flightless, its small wings being out of proportion to its bulky body. The bird's name comes from the Portuguese *doudo*, meaning 'silly, stupid'. Sadly the increase in exploration and trade in the sixteenth and seventeenth centuries brought about the extinction of the dodo. Seamen and colonists found the cumbersome creatures an easy and substantial meal to catch. In his *Natural History* (1774) Oliver Goldsmith wrote that *three or four dodos are enough to dine a hundred men*. The settlers also brought rats to Mauritius on board their ships, and these fed upon the large eggs the unwary dodos laid in exposed places. By the close of the seventeenth century the luckless bird was extinct.

But the creature did leave a legacy. The Victorians became fascinated by it. One gentleman even reconstructed a specimen from a pile of old bones. Unsurprisingly, then, during the late nineteenth century *dodo* began to be used to describe someone who was rather stupid or behind the times (a sense that is now obsolete) and, by the beginning of the twentieth century, the phrase *as dead as a dodo*, with its pleasing alliterative ring, had been coined.

Incidentally, there is a curious after-effect of the extinction of the dodo. The tambalacoque tree flourished in Mauritius up to the time of the bird's demise but subsequently no new trees took root. By the 1970s only thirteen tambalacoque trees remained on the island. It is known that many seeds will only germinate if they pass through the digestive system of a certain creature. It seems the tambalacoque needed the dodo! In an attempt to preserve the endangered tree American ecology expert Stanley Temple used turkeys as a replacement, with some success. So perhaps the tambalacoque tree will not in its turn become *as dead as a dodo*.

*Then there was the pashmina, that glorified comfort blanket. Supermodels snuggled under it on first-class flights across the Atlantic. Designers such as Matthew Williamson wrapped it around the shoulders of their denim jackets. It was the ideal accessory of any self-respecting It Girl. But, suddenly, the pashmina was **as dead as a dodo**.*
THE DAILY TELEGRAPH,
27 AUGUST 2001

For a similar idiom see *as dead as a* DOORNAIL. See also ALLITERATIVE SIMILES, page 23.

dog days
the hottest days of the year; an unwholesome season

In the northern hemisphere *dog days*, or *dies caniculares* as the Romans called them, last from about the beginning of July until the middle of August. During this period the dog star, Sirius, rises and sets with the sun. The star shines so brightly that the Romans believed it gave off a heat which, together with that of the sun, made this the hottest time of the year. In reality, of course, the sultry days of summer are caused by the earth's tilt. The oppressive heat of this season was generally regarded as unwholesome. During the sixteenth century, *dog days* was used figuratively to describe a corrupt or destructive time, in a political administration for instance, a use which is still current.

*Who on earth would be interested in reading stale anecdotes about the **dog days** of the last Thatcher administration...*
THE SPECTATOR, 5 OCTOBER 2002

*At the end, possibly in the **dog days** of summer when the heat is trained elsewhere, David Beckham will become a Real Madrid player.*
THE OBSERVER, 27 APRIL 2003

*It's rare indeed that I am present at chambers meetings, held under the chairmanship of Soapy Sam Ballard... But these were the **dog days** in the cold, wet and bleak start of the year, the criminals of England seemed to have all gone off for a winter break to Marbella or the Seychelles, and I had wandered into Ballard's room as an alternative to yet another struggle with the crossword puzzle.*
JOHN MORTIMER, RUMPOLE AND THE PENGE BUNGALOW MURDERS, 2004

For other idioms drawn from ancient life and history, see page 317.

dog eat dog
ruthlessly ambitious, at the expense of others

Dog does not eat dog is quoted as a proverb by the Roman writer Varro in the first century BC, and about a century later one of Juvenal's *Satires* has: *Wild beasts do not injure beasts spotted like themselves.* The same idea, that two of a kind should not harm each other, is variously expressed in English literature from the late sixteenth century. The nineteenth-century clergyman Charles Spurgeon saw mankind as an exception to the animal kingdom, however. *Dog won't eat dog*, he wrote, *but men will eat each other up like cannibals (John Ploughman*, 1869). He was apparently right, for the first half of the twentieth century saw the appearance of *dog eat dog* to describe the more ruthless side of human character, often in business and political contexts.

*It's **dog eat dog** in Waterstone's these days. Book shops are no longer sweet, sedate, cerebral places in the calm,*

It's a dog's life

A dog's life is really not so bad: a warm house, plenty of food and fun, and an affectionate scratch behind the ears every now and then. Dogs have it pretty cushy these days; better than humans, really. In past centuries, of course, this was not the case. Dogs were kept as working animals, often mistreated, fed on scraps. Others were scavengers and carriers of disease. In the sixteenth century *to lead a dog's life* was to lead a miserable existence and the derived nineteenth-century phrase *to lead someone a dog's life* was to inflict similar misery on another. *To die like a dog* was to die a disgraceful or wretched death, while in the early seventeenth century a person or thing that was *going to the dogs* was sliding into ruin. Something considered *not fit for a dog* was shabby or unappetising indeed.

In spite of the improvement in a dog's general standard of living as the centuries passed, idioms coined in the twentieth century also dwell on this notion of the unloved cur. *A dogsbody* is a junior who is expected to perform menial tasks no one else wants to do. Someone who is *in the* DOGHOUSE is in disgrace. Something described as *a dog's breakfast* is a 'mess', the analogy being to the bowlful of unappetising scraps and leftovers thrown together for the dog, while someone dressed *like a dog's dinner* has perhaps gone a bit over the top in dressing up for an occasion.

But when a dog is happy, he's very happy. Since the mid-twentieth century, anyone who is delighted with life has been described as being *like a dog with two tails*.

See also DOG *eat dog*.

measured business of selling knowledge.
They're battlegrounds for publishers,
piled high battalions of their products
coming after you. Their weapon is the
book cover.
THE GUARDIAN, 15 SEPTEMBER 2001

See IT'S A DOG'S LIFE, page 101,
and for other idioms drawn from
Greek and Roman writers, see
page 318.

dog: (to be) a dog in the manger

(to be) unwilling to let others benefit
from things one cannot use oneself;
spoiling

One of Aesop's fables tells of a dog
which sat in a manger full of hay and
snapped at a hungry ox to prevent it
from eating. The dog had no use for
the hay but begrudged the ox its
fodder. The idiomatic application to
someone who holds on to things he
cannot use in order to deprive someone else of having them has been in
use since the sixteenth century.

Now the European airlines…are
surreptitiously discounting prices without
*officially saying so. And, **like dogs in the***
***manger**, they are refusing to release the slots*
they no longer need at big airports, such as
Gatwick, to low-cost carriers such as Go.
THE TIMES, 6 OCTOBER 2001

For other idioms derived from fables,
see page 318.

dog: to see a man about a dog

a phrase used to disguise the purpose of
one's business

The idiom is notably used in a play,
Flying Scud, by Irish-born actor and
playwright Dion Boucicault, which was
written and produced in 1866.
Although now long forgotten, *Flying*

Scud, a melodrama, was popular in
America in its day. The phrase *to see a*
man about a dog was used by one of the
characters as a ploy to get away from a
tricky situation. Subsequently it was
used euphemistically with the sense 'to
go and buy alcohol', this particularly
during Prohibition, or 'to visit the
bathroom/loo'. From these circum-
locutions has arisen the present day
sense, that of making an excuse to
leave without disclosing the reason for
one's departure. It is now often used in
a jocular way.

I am waiting for a call to tell me that I
*have to go **to see a man about a dog**.*
THE DAILY TELEGRAPH, 16 MARCH 2002

doghouse: in the doghouse

in disgrace

The figure here is that of a bad dog put
out of the house and sent to its kennel
as a punishment. The earliest written
examples date back to the 1930s and
'40s and are chiefly American. Indeed,
the word *doghouse* has a long history
dating back to the beginning of the
seventeenth century, but although it is
retained in American English it has
faded from use in Britain.

The sense of the idiom is illustrated by the literary example of Mr
Darling in J M Barrie's *Peter Pan*
(1904). The Darling children are
cared for by Nana, a Newfoundland
dog. Mr Darling, who is jealous of
his children's affection for Nana, ties
her up in the yard. That night the
children are visited by Peter Pan who
teaches them to fly and takes them to
visit 'the Never Land'. The children
are away for some time and Mr.
Darling, who *felt in his bones that all the*
blame was his for having chained Nana
up, goes to live in her kennel as a
penance, *swearing in the bitterness of his*
remorse…that he would never leave the

*kennel until his children came back.
He was now firmly **in the diplomatic
doghouse** as international pariah.*
EVENING STANDARD, 6 OCTOBER 2000

*Durkin should have sent Le Saux off and
for failing to do so was condemned to a
spell **in the doghouse** at the weekend,
if refereeing a Third Division match
between Luton and Swansea can be so
described.*
THE GUARDIAN, 30 OCTOBER 2001

See also IT'S A DOG'S LIFE,
page 101.

doldrums: (in) the doldrums
depressed, low in spirits; calm seas

In a letter to his son dated 22 October,
1824, Sir Walter Scott expresses the
earnest hope that *he will make his way to
the clever fellows and not put up with
Doldrums, that is with dolts and dullards.*
Indeed, the slang word *doldrum*, which
dates back to before 1811, is thought
to derive from Old English *dol*, 'dull',
and to be influenced in form by
tantrum. Used normally in the plural,
the doldrums denoted 'a state of listless-
ness and depression' or 'a period of
dullness and inactivity'. This last is
seen, from the mid-1820s, in a particular maritime application of *the doldrums*
to denote 'any region of calm seas and
light winds'.

Still more specifically from the
1850s, the calms near the equator where
the south-east and north-east trade
winds meet and cancel each other out
were notorious among sailors and were
referred to as *the Doldrums* (often with an
initial capital for this geographical reference). Here the progress of sailing ships
would be greatly delayed, their frustrated crews finding themselves *in the
doldrums* in all senses of the expression.
From the end of the nineteenth century,
the figure of a ship becalmed *in the dol-*

drums has frequently been applied to
political and commercial inactivity: *True,
economic policymakers in Japan seem to be
bereft of ideas for shocking the country **out**
of the doldrums, but then they have been for
a decade* (*Time*, 30 April 2001).

*We are officially **in the Doldrums** now,
but we're lucky enough to have a little bit
of breeze. There's a soft eight knots at the
moment...*
THE DAILY TELEGRAPH,
8 OCTOBER 2001

*The days are dark. The wind is cold. At
this most dreary time of year, British
consumers usually cheer themselves up by
booking two weeks in the sun for August
and UK package holiday industry chiefs
drag their spirits **out of the winter
doldrums** by listening to the sound of
shillings pouring into the tills.*
THE GUARDIAN, 13 JANUARY 2002

donkey: not for donkey's years
not for a very long time

The long characteristic of a donkey is
not his life, as this phrase might lead
one to believe, but his ears. There
existed formerly an uneducated pronunciation of *ears* as *years* and the
expression is therefore a punning allusion to a pair of very long ears. The
idiom is recorded in the early twentieth century but must date back at least
to the nineteenth: *Years ago – years and
years and donkey's ears, as the saying is*
(E M Wright, *Rustic Speech*, 1913). The
variant *donkey's years* was established
by the 1920s.

*We're supposed to be a rich country but
we're very mean when it comes to
pensioners – I worked **for donkey's years**
but I've not got much to show for it.*
EXPRESS ON SUNDAY, 16 MARCH 2003

doornail: as dead as a doornail
unquestionably dead

It is to be expected that preoccupation with death will give rise to a number of euphemisms and similes. Over recent centuries people have been *as dead as mutton, a mackerel, a herring, a nit* and even *Queen Anne (the day after she dy'd)*. But the oldest expression of them all, *as dead as a doornail*, used in the poem *William of Palerne* (c. 1350), has best survived into modern usage.

Medieval doors were studded with large-headed nails to strengthen and protect them, but it is not easy to understand why the comparison with a doornail should have arisen, unless the nail in question were that which was struck by the knocker. Anything repeatedly pounded in this fashion would definitely be dead. That said, *dead as a doornail* is pleasingly alliterative (as are the other doornail similes *as deaf as a doornail* and *as dumb as a doornail*, both now obsolete), so probably the origin of the phrase can be attributed, at least in part, to this.

The fight must have lasted for several hours, with man and lion trading blow for blow, but when the dust finally settled the lion lay flat on its back, **as dead as a doornail***, which was a lesson to bullies of all shapes and sizes about biting off more than they could chew.*
MICK JACKSON, FIVE BOYS, 2001

For a similar idiom see *as dead as a/the* DODO. See also ALLITERATIVE SIMILES, page 237.

dose: like a dose of salts
swiftly, efficiently

The *salts* here are laxative salts, making the phrase slightly cruder than casual use by the unwary speaker might have intended. The expression dates back to the first half of the nineteenth century when it appears in Davy Crockett's 1837 *Almanac of Wild Sports in the West*.

Several careers are needed in a lifetime, and several husbands or wives. We travel through life **like a dose of salts***.*
THE DAILY TELEGRAPH,
14 SEPTEMBER 2002

Galway won by eight points, running through Donegal **like a dose of salts***.*
THE SUNDAY TIMES,
31 AUGUST 2003

down in the dumps
depressed, low, dejected

Such a very evocative phrase seems to call for a pleasing etymology. Instead *dump* is no more than a borrowing from Northern European languages. Swedish has *dumpin*, 'melancholy'; Dutch has *domp*, 'damp' or 'hazy'; and German has *dumpf*, meaning 'gloomy, damp' – all depressing stuff.

Nevertheless, the usage is old. People have certainly been *in the dumps* since the early sixteenth century: a version of 'The Ballad of Chevy Chace', composed by, or part of the repertoire of, sixteenth-century minstrel Richard Sheale, has the line: *I wail as one in doleful dumps*. Singing the blues is not exclusively a twentieth-century malady.

[Hamlet]…broods and spits his way through the play for a couple of hours and only cheers up for a bit when his plan to expose his father's murderer comes off. But – thank God, for all us misery fans – he's soon right back **down in the dumps***.*
THE DAILY TELEGRAPH, 31 MAY 2004

drive: to drive a coach and horses through (something)
to reveal the inadequacies of an argument or proposal, to rebut; to breach

Sir Stephen Rice, Chief Baron of the Irish Exchequer, is credited with coining this phrase around 1670 in his vigorous opposition to the Act of Settlement. According to Archbishop King it was a term he employed often in this context:

He was (to give him his due) a man of the best sense among them, well enough versed in the law, but most signal for his inveteracy against the Protestant interest and settlement of Ireland, having been often heard to say, before he was a judge, that he would 'drive a coach and six horses through the act of settlement,' upon which both depended (State of the Protestants in Ireland under the late King James's Government, 1691).

The phrase as we know it today was a reworking of the original by Daniel O'Connel, an Irish barrister who pressed for Catholic Emancipation in the early nineteenth century.

*The mobs have been thriving because of an anomaly in the law, a loophole **through which they have driven not so much a coach and horses** as most of the neighbourhood's missing cars.*
THE GUARDIAN, 27 JANUARY 2003

*The bill **drives a coach and horses through** a ruling by Italy's highest court that Mr Berlusconi's Mediaset group should transfer one of its channels to satellite.*
THE ECONOMIST, 26 JULY 2003

duck: a lame duck
an ineffectual person, a failing business

This idiom makes its earliest appearance in the Stock Exchange in the eighteenth century when the slang of that institution began to fill with animal references: *a bull,* for instance, was 'a speculator for a rise in the price of shares', *a bear* 'a speculator for a fall in prices' and *a lame duck* 'a jobber, or broker, who cannot honour his financial commitments'. Indeed the latter was responsible for

another, now obsolete, slang expression, *to waddle* or *to waddle out* which meant 'to default': *He's been neither bull nor bear for these three years. He was obliged to waddle* (Captain Marryat, *Peter Simple*, 1834).

From one ineffectual person to another, *lame duck* was next also applied in America, after the Civil War, to politicians whose term of office was nearly over and whose power, therefore, was waning.

Back in 1970s Britain the expression came to describe industries which, failing to generate enough business, were reliant on government subsidies for their survival.

From all these specific, and still current, applications of the term there evolved a more general sense of 'a helpless person' or 'a failing undertaking'.

*The Giants have lost seven consecutive games and have obviously quit on **lame duck** coach Jim Fassel.*
BOSTON HERALD, 26 DECEMBER 2003

*Research by Investec Private Bank shows that companies are continually adjusting their rates for savers with big deposits, turning 'best buy' deals one week into **lame-duck** offerings the next.*
THE MAIL ON SUNDAY, 27 JUNE 2004

Dutch courage
courage found by drinking alcohol

Dutch courage arose from the belief that the Dutch were heavy drinkers, a commonly held opinion amongst the English since at least the time of the Dutch Wars in the seventeenth and early eighteenth centuries. A magnificent, though short-lived, victory over the Dutch at the battle of Lowestoft during the Second Dutch War brought the following lines from the pen of Edmund Waller, and show what the English thought of the courage their adversaries displayed:

The Dutch their wine and all their brandy lose,
Disarm'd of that from which their courage grows.
(Instructions to a Painter for a Picture of the Victory over the Dutch, 1665)

Nevertheless, written records of the phrase *Dutch courage* date back only to the late eighteenth century, showing that British hostility towards the Dutch was an enduring sentiment. Sir Walter Scott was fond of the expression, using it first in *Redgauntlet* (1824). It replaced *pot valour,* a term in use since the seventeenth century, which meant exactly the same.

[Eamon was] thinking about taking his act on the road…and I wondered if he could really still do it…without the **Dutch courage** *of cocaine.*
TONY PARSONS, MAN AND WIFE, 2002

I was surprised to find I was quite nervous before meeting Joy – I don't normally go on formal dates. Went for a couple of drinks first, just to give myself some **Dutch courage***.*
DAILY MIRROR, 28 MAY 2004

Acting is a very self-conscious profession and a lot of people use drugs as a kind of **Dutch courage** *and then it gets out of hand.*
DAILY EXPRESS, 9 JUNE 2004

For other anti-Dutch expressions see NATIONAL RIVALRIES, page 108. See also *double* DUTCH and *to go* DUTCH.

Dutch: double Dutch

gibberish, incomprehensible speech, a language that one does not understand

If you want to insult someone, insult his language. English contempt of the Dutch, their powerful economic rivals, is evident in this phrase. It implies that the Dutch language is ridiculous, nothing more than gibberish. Insults

began with speaking *Dutch fustian* (Christopher Marlowe, *The Tragical History of Dr Faustus*, 1592), then *High Dutch* in the eighteenth century and *double Dutch* in the nineteenth.

By the way, can anyone tell me the genesis of Mike Myers's accent? Is it Welsh or just **double Dutch***?*
EVENING STANDARD, 29 JUNE 2004

For other anti-Dutch expressions see NATIONAL RIVALRIES, page 108. See also DUTCH *courage* and *to go* DUTCH.

Dutch: to go Dutch

to share the costs of an outing instead of allowing one's companion to pay (especially if a man has invited a woman out)

This phrase, just like the slightly earlier *Dutch treat* which has the same meaning, is American in origin and dates back only to the early twentieth century. It has been suggested that it arose from the careful money management that characterised Dutch immigrant households of the period. In fact any hint of meanness amongst the Dutch population would have sufficed, since *Dutch* is recognised as derogatory when affixed to another noun and a long list of such couplings has existed and been added to since the seventeenth century.

However, as half of all women believe that a man should pay for everything on a first date…it's safe to assume that men thinking of **going dutch** *should think again.*
THE OBSERVER, 27 JUNE 2004

For other anti-Dutch expressions see NATIONAL RIVALRIES, page 108. See also DUTCH *courage* and *double* DUTCH.

dyed in the wool

having ingrained characteristics, habits or opinions, usually political ones

The idiom refers to the practice of adding dye to raw wool rather than to the spun yarn or finished cloth. By this method the dye permeated all the fibres so the colour of the finished cloth was more even and longer lasting. Used figuratively the phrase suggests someone who is imbued with a certain characteristic or set of beliefs. More than one sixteenth-century author made use of the figure. Richard Hooker, for instance, writing at the end of the sixteenth century, considered that *Children as it were in the Wooll of their infancie died with hardnesse may never afterwards change colour* (*Of the Lawes of Ecclesiastical Politie*, 1597). But the idiom as we know it was a product of the American political scene during the presidency of Andrew Jackson (1829–37). *In half an hour [he can] come out an original democrat, dyed in the wool*, said Federalist politician Daniel Webster in a speech given on 10 February 1830.

*Being a **dyed-in-the-wool** republican, the latest contortions of the monarchy only induce in myself a sense of ennui.*
THE SCOTSMAN, 4 NOVEMBER 2002

*Clad in a sports coat (and matching skirt) of almost awesome tweediness, the figure staring from its cover looks the stolid embodiment of **dyed-in-the-wool** conservatism.*
THE SUNDAY TIMES, 23 MAY 2004

*My North Oxford friend is a lifelong Labour voter. She has never not voted Labour, ever. She's so **dyed in the wool** that we haven't been able to have a political conversation for years without rancour.*
THE DAILY TELEGRAPH,
22 MARCH 2005

For an idiom with a similar sense, see DIE-HARD.

National rivalries

A nation is a society united by a delusion about its ancestry and by a common hatred of its neighbours (Dean William R Inge, 1860–1954).

International politics being what they are, one country or another is inevitably out of favour. During the seventeenth century, it was the Dutch who stirred up English animosity. The Dutch were hated commercial and military rivals. The extensive trading empire they had built up, and the control they had over the European carrying trade, were prejudicing the development of the British economy. A literary example of the relations between the two countries comes from John Dryden, who set out to fan the flames of chauvinism with his tragedy *Amboyna* (1673). Amboyna was the name of a clove island in the Moluccas. In 1623 the Dutch had tortured and massacred some Englishmen on trumped-up charges in an attempt to drive their rivals out of the spice islands altogether.

One way of nursing a grudge is to insult one's enemy in everyday language, and the British became adept at crafting unflattering references to the Dutch character, as they perceived it.

Initially, the phrases sneered at Dutch trading practices. Coined in the seventeenth century, a *Dutch bargain* was a one-sided bargain; a *Dutch reckoning* was either a bill stating the total sum owed with no breakdown of individual items, or a bill that went up if it was challenged; a *Flanders fortune* was but a very small one; and a *Flemish account* did not balance. More personally, a *Dutch widow* was 'a whore', while a *Dutch palate* was unrefined.

By now the ball was well and truly rolling and antipathy towards the Dutch so strong that, for the next two and a half centuries, the English language continued to admit new anti-Dutch coinages. In America this dislike may well have been fuelled by a popular confusion between 'Dutch' and 'deutsch', both applied negatively to German immigrants. The Dutch were famously fuelled by DUTCH *courage* (18C), but an invitation to a bar or restaurant would inevitably mean a miserly *Dutch treat* (19C) or *going* DUTCH (20C). Or one might be invited to a *Dutch feast* (18C), one where the host hogged most of the alcohol and got drunk before his guests, or even to a *Dutch concert* (18C), an excruciating performance since each musician was playing a different tune.

The Dutch were portrayed as solid, unattractive people. *Dutch built* (19C) described a thickset person and a *Dutch cheese* (19C) was a bald one, after the round, wax-covered Edam and Gouda cheeses. They were also stern in character, *talking like Dutch uncles* (19C), given to unsympathetic criticism and an abundance of *Dutch comfort* (18C), the kind of consolation that cries *Thank God it is no worse* (Grose, *Dictionary of the Vulgar Tongue*, 1785). And all this in unintelligible *double* DUTCH (19C).

Anyone who *beat the Dutch* (18C) had achieved something remarkable, while the phrase *that beats the Dutch* (19C) was one of incredulity. To finish any statement with *or I'm a Dutchman* (19C) implied the strongest possible confidence in the truth of the remark, since the acceptance of the name *Dutchman* would be the ultimate disgrace: *Come and stay here for a night or two…and you'll change your mind. Or I'm a Dutchman* (*The Observer*, 24 February 2002).

During the eighteenth century, however, the Netherlands began to decline as a major power, eclipsed on the European stage by the French under the ambitious leadership of Napoleon. *Frenchmen*, wrote the English poet Coleridge, *are like gunpowder, each by itself smutty and contemptible; but mass them together, they are terrible indeed.* France was Britain's new enemy and, as such, had to suffer similar linguistic indignities to the Dutch, although the volume of negative vocabulary resulting from this new enmity is somewhat smaller.

There is the mock apology *Excuse* or *Pardon my French* (late 19C). Colloquially it is used after some swearing or offensive language: the bad language isn't English, it's French you can hear. Another example is *to take* FRENCH *leave* (18C), meaning 'to absent oneself without leave or permission'.

However, the majority of fixed phrases relating to the French are sexual. The French have traditionally had a reputation as fine lovers, but the abundance of crude sexual phrases coined in English at their expense simply portrays them as 'dirty'. A *French kiss* (20C) is a kiss with the tongue in the partner's mouth. A *French letter* (19C) is a condom, and so is a *French tickler* (early 20C) and the punning *French safe* (19C). These are recommended for those who visited a prostitute or *French article* (mid 19C). *To French* (late 19C) meant 'to have oral sex', this being seen as a particularly French perversion, hence the expression *the French way* (20C) for oral sex, along with a variety of other phrases to express the finer points of performance. Equally censorious is *the French disease* (late 16C–late 18C), 'venereal disease', together with an impressive number of related terms. And from around the mid-twentieth century, in an age before Gay Liberation, comes an extensive range of camp homosexual phraseology.

But the English should not be accused of being unfair. They are prepared to offer every nation an appropriate share of prejudice:

There have been many definitions of hell, but for the English the best definition is that it is a place where the Germans are the police, the Swedish are the comedians, the Italians are the defence force, Frenchmen dig the roads, the Belgians are the pop singers, the Spanish run the railways, the Turks cook the food, the Irish are the waiters, the Greeks run the government, and the common language is Dutch (David Frost and Antony Jay, *To England with Love*, 1967).

However, no one reading this article should be under the misapprehension that the British bear anyone ill will. What all this national prejudice really boils down to is the simple fact that the poor foreigners had the misfortune to be born in the wrong place:

> *Oh, how I love Humanity,*
> *With love so pure and pringlish,*
> *And how I hate the horrid French,*
> *Who never will be English!*

(G K Chesterton, 'The World State', in *Collected Poems*, 1933)

· E ·

eager beaver, an

an overly zealous person, one who tries to impress others with enthusiasm and hard work

This is an American phrase which came into vogue about the time of the Second World War. Some authorities say it originated amongst the armed forces and described those keen recruits who volunteered for absolutely everything. Beavers have long been known for their industry, as the eighteenth-century American phrase *to work like a beaver* shows, and 'eager' conveys enthusiasm. Put together, these two words make a catchy little rhyming phrase but one which carries the critical overtones of trying rather too hard to please.

The laptop is the essential working tool – airport lounges are filled with **eager beavers** *(or maybe just late filers) tapping away.*
THE TIMES, 19 SEPTEMBER 2003

ear: to go in one ear and out the other

to be heard but disregarded or easily forgotten

The concept of information passing through the head without engaging the brain is an ancient one. *The things he says*, wrote Roman rhetorician Quintilian, *flow right through the ears* (*Institutiones Oratoriae*, c. AD 80). The idiom is commonly found in most European languages. It occurs in *The Romaunt of the Rose* (c. 1365), a translation of a French poem into Middle English, and Chaucer used it in *Troilus and Criseyde* (c. 1380).

In the sixteenth century the phrase was included in collections of English and Scottish proverbs, and Arthur Golding employed it in his translations of John Calvin's *Sermons on Deuteronomy* (1583), where it was noted that a sermon *goes in at the one eare and out at the other*. It has been in regular use ever since.

Even where American kids are taught who Winston Churchill really was, for instance, it often **goes in one ear and out the other**.
THE GUARDIAN, 17 DECEMBER 2002

I find recipes a little like jokes; **in one ear and out the other**, *and this is just about the only recipe I can ever remember.*
THE INDEPENDENT, 8 NOVEMBER 2003

For other idioms drawn from Greek and Roman writers, see page 318.

ear: to have/keep one's ear(s) to the ground

to listen carefully to current rumours and concerns, or to trends in public opinion

A scene made familiar by old 'cowboys and Indians' movies is of a Native American scout with his ear to the ground, listening for the sound of approaching horses. The idiom is American in origin and dates from the late nineteenth century.

The idiom is now usually used in the political, showbiz and fashion worlds, where it is deemed important to be at the forefront of the very latest events. American commentator

H L Mencken took a critical view in his *Dictionary of Quotations* (1942): *A politician is an animal which can sit on a fence and yet keep both ears to the ground.* Winston Churchill was equally uncharitable: *The nation will find it very hard to look up to the leaders who are keeping their ears to the ground.*

*He **keeps his ear to the ground** in his native Holland for bargains and recommended Paul Bosvelt, a player from the same combative mould as himself...*
THE SUNDAY TIMES, 27 JULY 2003

ears: my ears are burning
a remark made by those who think they are being talked about

A tingling or burning sensation in the ears supposedly means that a person is being discussed by others. The origin of this belief goes back to Roman times. Pliny, for instance, wrote: *It is acknowledged that the absent feel a presentiment of remarks about themselves by the ringing of their ears* (*Naturalis Historia*, AD 77). The ancient belief that the left signified 'evil' and the right 'good' (see *to put one's best* FOOT *forward*) applies here also. Both Plautus and Pliny hold that if a person's right ear burns then he is being praised but a burning left ear indicates that he is the subject of evil intent.

English literature, from Chaucer to Dickens, abounds with references to burning ears:

One Ere tingles; some there be,
That are snarling now at me.
(Robert Herrick, 'On Himself', 1648)

According to ancient belief, other unexpected bodily twitches and sensations also serve as warnings, among them those in the eye and the thumb. A flickering right eye, for instance, indicates that a friend will visit or that something longed for will soon be seen, and a pricking in one's left thumb warns of an evil event.

*And indeed, under the surface there is, apparently, a simmering undercurrent of rivalry. As one would expect, it is Victoria Beckham, wife of the England captain, **whose ears are burning** the most.*
DAILY MAIL, 29 MAY 2004

For other idioms drawn from Greek and Roman writers, see page 318.

eat: to eat someone out of house and home
to consume a great deal and use up a person's resources

The idiom we recognise was used by Mistress Quickly as a complaint against Falstaff's greed in Shakespeare's *Henry IV, Part II* (1597), but it had been in common use in English since at least the turn of the fifteenth century in the form *eat out of house and harbour*, which amounts to the same. In 1469 one vindictive fellow wrote to the Paston family *I eete lyek an horse, of purpose to eete yow owte at the dorys*. The phrase, however, goes back even further. It was used by Philo of Alexandria in *De Agricultura* (c. AD 40).

*[Grey squirrels] are literally **eating our birds out of house and home**. The squirrels eat the same seeds the birds need for food, take over their nest sites and eat chicks and eggs in the nest.*
DAILY EXPRESS, 13 MARCH 2004

For other idioms from Shakespeare, see WILLIAM SHAKESPEARE, page 152, and the list on page 320. For other idioms from Greek and Roman writers, see page 318.

egg: a bad/good egg

an untrustworthy/dependable person

It is impossible to tell from simply look-ing at the shell whether an egg is fresh or not. Once an egg is broken it may reveal an unpleasant surprise, but a good egg will be sound to its very cen-tre. So it is with people; the outward appearance will not reveal the content of the character. This is only discovered when time is taken to get to know them better. A *bad egg* is someone to avoid but a *good egg* is totally dependable. And, as the nineteenth-century American news-paper editor Charles A Dana put it, *all the goodness of a good egg cannot make up for the badness of a bad one*.

The term *bad egg* was the first to appear, around the mid-nineteenth century, perhaps as public school slang. An 1864 edition of the political and literary magazine *Athenaeum* defined *a bad egg* as *a fellow who had not proved to be as good as his promise*. The correspon-ding *good egg* did not come into use until the early twentieth century. There is a suggestion in Compton Mackenzie's novel *Sinister Street* (1913) that it may have been coined amongst students at Oxford: *Oxford was divided into Bad Men and Good Eggs*.

Given the likely public school and Oxbridge origins of the phrases, it is not too surprising that they find their most natural home in the upper-class world of P G Wodehouse – in 1940 he even published a collection of stories entitled *Eggs, Beans and Crumpets*. Nowadays, the expressions have something of a self-conscious, antiquated ring.

'I think Peter's tactics are sometimes wrong, but I thought what he did against Mugabe was incredibly brave. And he's doing good work in a world where most people are too timid. So, yes, I think Peter Tatchell is a good egg.'
ELTON JOHN, QUOTED IN THE SUNDAY TELEGRAPH, 9 SEPTEMBER 2001

The former Taliban leader is undoubtedly a bad egg but the fact that he rides a motorbike is for me a point in his favour.
DAILY MAIL, 7 JANUARY 2002

For another idiom on the freshness of eggs, see CURATE'S *egg*.

eggs: as sure as eggs is eggs

certainly, beyond doubt

It has been suggested that this idiom has nothing to do with eggs but is a corruption of the mathematical state-ment 'x is x'. The expression is recorded from the second half of the seventeenth century and, certainly, algebraic equations were being written in the way with which we are now familiar by the close of the sixteenth. However, one of the early references to the phrase, in the form *as sure as eggs be eggs*, occurs in BE's *Dictionary of the Canting Crew* (c. 1698), a record of slang terms used by the lowlife of Tudor and Stuart England, whose grasp of such learning would be non-existent.

The expression makes a later appearance in *Vade Mecum for Malt-worms* (1720), a sort of literary eighteenth-century pub-crawler's man-ual by an unknown author, this time in the form *Certainly, as eggs are eggs*. If the phrase did have a mathematical origin this writer, in using the plural verb, was unaware of it. By the time Oliver Goldsmith made use of the idiom in the 1760s the phrasing was *as sure as eggs is eggs*, and it has continued thus to the present day. The use of the singular verb, which may have prompted the algebraic theory, could simply have been an attempt at humour.

Everywhere George goes, trouble follows, as sure as eggs is eggs.
THE INDEPENDENT, 5 APRIL 2004

eggs: to teach one's grandmother to suck eggs

to offer unnecessary advice to someone who is older and more experienced

This phrase has been in use since at least the early eighteenth century to reprimand someone who, although young in years and green in experience, thinks it necessary to lecture an older and wiser person. It has, of course, been pointed out that a toothless grandmother would naturally be more successful in sucking the meat from an egg than a grandchild with a complete set of teeth. The phrase is the sole survivor of a number of earlier expressions which were coined along the same lines. In the mid-sixteenth century the young were exhorted *not to teach our dame to spinne* and from the beginning of the seventeenth century they were advised *not to teach our granddame to gropen her ducks* (that is, to feel her ducks and see whether they will lay or not).

To teach your grandmother to suck eggs is open to a certain amount of humorous embroidery. R D Blackmore alluded to it thus: *A...twinkle, which might have been interpreted – 'instruct your grandfather in the suction of gallinaceous products'* (*Christowell*, 1882). And there is a little Victorian ditty of unknown origin:

Teach not a parent's mother to extract
The embryo juices of an egg by suction:
The good old lady can the feat enact
Quite irrespective of your kind instruction.

According to Partridge (1950), in later years *egg* became an underworld slang term for a confidence trickster's victim, in other words for a *sucker*, a reference to the expression under discussion.

*Delia could **teach your grandmother to suck eggs**...three programmes maximum.*
THE GUARDIAN, 21 OCTOBER 2000

*At the risk of **teaching all you grandmothers to suck eggs**, it will be no news to you that, in common with the rest of the world, racing is not short of chancers and conmen.*
SUNDAY MIRROR, 27 JUNE 2004

element: in/out of one's element

at ease, in one's natural environment/ ill at ease, awkward

Earth, water, air and fire are the four primary elements which were once believed to be in the make-up of all things, as well as the environments in which any living thing existed. People themselves were classified according to their humorous dispositions, each associated with a corresponding element: the introspective, yet creative melancholic man, whose ruling element was the earth (cold and dry); the wiry, red-haired, ambitious choleric man, dominated by fire (hot and dry); the sluggish, corpulent phlegmatic man, influenced by water (cold and moist); and the fortunate sanguine man, a red-cheeked optimist who enjoyed the healthful benefits of air (hot and moist).

The trick for a happy existence was to keep these humours, and one's environment, in balance. The phlegmatic man, for instance, was advised against eating fish, while the melancholic individual would avoid eating root vegetables.

The characters in the plays of Shakespeare and his contemporaries reveal this understanding of medicine and psychology. References to being *in one's element*, that is in the surroundings in which one feels most at ease, or employed at the occupation one feels most comfortable with, date from the late sixteenth century.

It's all in the blood

For over a thousand years, right up to the renaissance, European medicine subscribed to the views of the ancient Greek physician Galen. It was he who was responsible for the complex theories derived from Hippocrates' system of the four bodily humours (see *to be in one's* ELEMENT), one of the foundations of medical practice. According to Galen, the four humours, together with natural spirits, originated in the liver, an organ which made blood and from which the veins of the body spread. The heart was the centre of emotional life. The arteries were connected to the heart and were channels carrying blood permeated by substances known as vital spirits around the body. Thus the state of the blood controlled a person's emotional life.

There is, in English, a number of idioms arising from this ancient theory. For instance, a person receiving bad news might say *It makes my blood run cold*, a reference to the perceived chill one experiences at such a moment. The observation *His blood is up* describes someone agitated and angry while *It makes my blood boil* is a similar expression of fury. Someone who commits murder *in cold blood*, however, performs the action with no feeling whatsoever – his blood has not been warmed by passion.

As the seat of the emotions, the heart has been referred to figuratively for centuries. A person may be *light at heart*, without a care in the world, or have *a heavy heart* full of sorrow. A lover may seek to *win the heart* of a sweetheart, and possess all the romantic affection in it. A snub may *break his heart*.

But if the heart was the emotional centre of the body, Galen understood the brain to be the seat of memory, of reason and of imagination, giving rise to this conundrum:

> *Tell me where is fancie bred,*
> *Or in the heart, or in the head?*
> (Shakespeare, *The Merchant of Venice*, c. 1596)

We are instructed to *keep* or *bear* instructions or advice *in mind*. Things we have been told might later *come to mind* or be *brought to mind* from the recesses of our memories. When we think things through we might *have a mind* to take a certain course of action or decide to *speak our mind* and make our thoughts known. We might be *of Catherine's mind*, that is 'share her view' on a matter. If we are in agreement with several others, then we are *all of one mind*, but if we can't decide and *make our mind up*, we are *in two minds* about something. Of course, if our reason is in our mind, that is our brain, we need to be *in our right mind* to remain healthy mentally. It would not do to be *out of our mind* or to *lose our mind*.

So with all this activity in the liver, heart and brain, which organ dominates? Is the relatively modern notion of mind over matter even a possibility? Shakespeare, knowledgeable about Galen's medical theories, thinks not:

> *The braine may deuise lawes for the blood, but a hot temper leapes ore a colde decree.*
> (*The Merchant of Venice*, c. 1596).

It's all in the blood.

For a list of idioms drawn from ancient life and history, see page 317.

Shakespeare himself was obviously *in his element* in the theatre and writing plays. Had he been totally unsuited to this way of life, he would have been *as much out of his Element, as an Eel in a Sand-bag* (Thomas Fuller, *Gnomologia*, 1732). One can, of course, be too much at ease in different circumstances, as the songwriter Charles Dibdin mockingly suggested in *Jack in his Element* (1793):

> *I sails the seas from end to end,*
> *And leads a joyous life,*
> *In every mess I finds a friend,*
> *In every port a wife.*
> *I've heard them talk of constancy,*
> *Of grief and such like fun,*
> *I've constant been to ten, cried I,*
> *But never grieved for one.*

Women are born for gossip and grooming, the social glue, while men are **in their element** *out there on their own tracking bison, fixing the boiler or calculating the properties of the universe before Big Bang.*
THE DAILY TELEGRAPH, 4 MAY 2003

See also IT'S ALL IN THE BLOOD, opposite.

eye: to give one's eye teeth for
(to be willing) to make a great sacrifice to obtain something

The *eye teeth* are the canine teeth, so called because they are under the eye. The pain of having them drawn and the subsequent permanent gappy smile are indeed a high price to pay for anything at all. The idiom dates from the first half of the twentieth century.

But for all the positive aspects of single parenting that I tell myself there are, I would still **give my eye teeth** *for a bit of 'time out'.*
DAILY MAIL, 17 OCTOBER 2002

· F ·

face: the face that launched a thousand ships

a very beautiful woman

In Christopher Marlowe's play *The Tragical History of Doctor Faustus* (1592), Mephistopheles, in accordance with Faustus's wishes, summons Helen of Troy, the beautiful wife of King Menelaus of Greece, whose abduction by Paris provoked the Trojan War. Faustus greets Helen with a speech beginning

> *Was this the face that launched*
> *a thousand ships*
> *And burnt the topless towers of Ilium?*
> *Sweet Helen, make me immortal*
> *with a kiss...*

The opening line has since been flatteringly applied to a stunning beauty or, sarcastically, to a plain Jane.

*For many people last year the one word 'Helen' conjured up, not the owner of **the face that launched a thousand ships**, but a ditzy Welsh blonde, possessed of that appalling thing, a 'sense of fun'. Helen of Troy was a woman of mystery, Helen of Swansea was a woman of no mystery at all.*
THE INDEPENDENT, 4 JUNE 2002

For other idioms drawn from literature, see page 319.

face: to lose/save face

to lose/maintain one's reputation, good name, honour

The Chinese expression *tiu lien*, meaning 'to lose one's good name', 'to suffer public disgrace', was translated into English as *to lose face* in the late nineteenth century. In 1876 Sir Robert Hart, an Irish financier who worked as an economic mediator between Western nations and China, wrote an essay entitled 'Arrangements by which China has lost face' (in *These from the Land of Sinim*). Of course, if one can *lose face* one can also *save* it, and maintain one's dignity and reputation. *To save face* does not exist in Chinese, however; it seems to be an English coinage, although Chinese does have *for the sake of his face*, which means much the same. The phrase is found from the end of the nineteenth century.

*The macho culture prevalent in building means that men are afraid they will **lose face** if they admit that they have poor literacy and numeracy skills.*
THE INDEPENDENT, 2 OCTOBER 2003

*But while it may be justifiable to lie to save lives, it is not all right to lie merely **to save face**.*
EXPRESS ON SUNDAY, 4 APRIL 2004

fair and square

straightforwardly, in an honest manner

The idiom is tautological since *fair* and *square* have meant the same thing since the sixteenth century (a *fair deal* is a *square deal*). They have been coupled in this rhyming phrase since the early seventeenth century. *Square* in the sense of 'honest' probably alludes to a square's perfectly equal angles and sides, the opposite of anything twisted or crooked.

*He is the fourth person to win the millionaire jackpot **fair and square**, and the first since Major Charles Ingram was caught cheating in 2001.*
DAILY MAIL, 26 APRIL 2004

See COUPLINGS, page 294.

fair to middling
passable, average

From the sixteenth century on, goods of any kind graded for market were described as *middling* if they were 'in the middle', of average quality, neither the best nor inferior. According to etymologist Michael Quinion, the expression *fair to middling* originated in the United States in the early nineteenth century and referred specifically to the quality of cotton. *Fair* and *middling* were grades at the centre of the scale, the phrase *fair to middling* sometimes occurring to describe an intermediate quality. In England, the phrase dates to the second half of the nineteenth century.

*The latest in a steadily lengthening line of **fair-to-middling** McCartney albums...*
THE INDEPENDENT, 9 NOVEMBER 2001

*Strikingly deficient up front, near watertight in defence, Middlesbrough are **fair to middling** in the Premiership...*
THE INDEPENDENT, 30 DECEMBER 2003

fall: to fall on one's sword
to take full responsibility for a grave error

The phrase refers to the practice Roman generals had of committing suicide by falling on their swords if they had acted dishonourably or suffered a defeat in a strategic battle. One such was Poenius Postumius. When Queen Boudicca of the Iceni tribe wrought havoc in rebellion against Roman rule in AD 60, Suetonius Paulinus, the governor of Britain, asked for help. Poenius Postumius, acting commander

of the second legion, ignored the request and other Roman forces went on to victory without him. According to the Roman author Tacitus, as soon as news of the brave exploits of the fourteenth and twentieth legions reached him, Poenius Postumius *felt the disgrace of having, in disobedience to the orders of his general, robbed the soldiers under his command of their share in so complete a victory. Stung with remorse, he fell upon his sword, and expired on the spot* (from Arthur Murphy, *Works of Tacitus*, 1794).

In the modern world disgraced politicians do not take such drastic action: a resignation is usually sufficient.

*In the end, Jim Singleton did the honorable thing. An old political soldier, he **fell on his sword** for the good of the cause by pulling himself out of the hunt for a cushy, $114,000-a-year job in Mayor Ray Nagin's administration.*
GAMBIT WEEKLY, 16 JULY 2002

For other idioms drawn from ancient life and history, see page 317.

fast: to play fast and loose
to say one thing but do another, to be inconsistent with one's affections

In the sixteenth century *fast and loose* was a cheating game, often played at fairs. A belt or cord would be wound up in such a way as to leave an apparent loop in the middle. A punter would then be invited to make the belt *fast* by catching it through the loop with a stick while it was being unwound. It all looked simple enough but a tricky way of folding the belt ensured that the hapless dupe was at the mercy of the showman. Invariably the belt was not *fast* but *loose*. The phrase *fast and loose* began to be used figuratively around the middle of the sixteenth century. It is now found in a range of contexts: exploitation by salesmen and inconstancy by lovers, for instance.

*But some critics have begun to question whether some of the judges have run amok, either abusing their powers or **playing fast and loose** with the rules in their quest for indictments and media attention.*
INTERNATIONAL HERALD TRIBUNE,
8 NOVEMBER 2001

fat cat, a

a very wealthy person, a highly rewarded executive

This derogatory rhyming term, which alludes to a sleek, overfed, self-satisfied cat, is American in origin. It was current in political circles in the 1920s where it specifically referred to capitalists who contributed to the funding of political parties. By the middle of the century the term was being applied more widely to any rich individual. An issue of *Flying* magazine for April 1971 commented on *Those who view the business jet as a smoke-belching, profit-eating chariot of the fat cat.* In current British usage there is sometimes an implication of unfair practice and exploitation.

*The head of BP has been given a 58 per cent pay rise that takes his earnings to £60,000 a week... The package made the workaholic bachelor one of Britain's most highly paid businessmen, and prompted renewed complaints about '**fat cat**' pay. Bill Morris of the Transport and General Workers Union, said: 'Some **fat cats** are bigger than others, but this one is clearly the biggest...'*
THE DAILY TELEGRAPH, 14 MARCH 2002

*If the people who suffered from these financial disasters were **fat cats**, few of us would worry. But it isn't. Ordinary people are the big losers, with huge cuts in their savings and pensions.*
DAILY MIRROR, 27 JUNE 2002

father: a bit of how's your father

sex, intercourse

Harry Tate (1872–1940) was a music hall performer. (He is honoured in Cockney rhyming slang where *in a bit of a Harry Tate* meant 'in a bit of a state'.) One of his sketches had him on a couch trying to take advantage of his girlfriend but, whenever the young lady was about to yield to his advances, her father would appear and Tate would nonchalantly lean back and inquire 'Tell me, how is your father?' Tate also used the phrase in other contexts where the subject needed to be changed suddenly. And the slight variant *That 'how's your father' over there* meant any item whose name temporarily escaped the memory, a synonym for 'thingummy', 'what's its name', etc. Today, the main remaining sense of the phrase is as a comical euphemism for · sexual activity. Showing its informal use, the spelling is often 'yer' for 'your'.

*The Naked Chef has admitted that he's often too tired after a day slaving over his accent to indulge in any **how's yer father** with his missus...*
EVENING STANDARD, 6 MARCH 2001

*According to French writer Agnes Catherine Poirier, 'On matters of sex, the British learn only how to laugh.' What does she mean? Is she saying we don't know how to indulge in a bit of **how's your father** in an adult, sophisticated, continental way?*
HUDDERSFIELD DAILY EXAMINER,
19 APRIL 2005

For more rhyming slang, see HAVE A BUTCHER'S AT THIS, page 80.

fatted: to kill the fatted calf

to celebrate (someone's return) with feasting

A *fatted calf* is one that has been fattened up for a feast. The phrase *to kill the fatted calf* comes from the story of the prodigal son, one of the parables that Jesus told (Luke 15:11–32). A man had two sons. One day the younger son came to him and demanded his inheritance. He then went away and spent it on riotous living. When it was all gone and he was reduced to making a living tending pigs, the boy came to his senses. He decided to return home, apologise to his father and ask if he could serve in his father's household. But while the young man was still a long way off the father saw him, ran to greet him and embraced him, calling on his servants to kill *the fatted calf* in celebration that the boy who was once lost was now found.

To kill the fatted calf has been idiomatic for 'to hold a celebratory feast' since at least the middle of the seventeenth century. The archaic form *fatted* goes back to William Tyndale's translation of 1526: *Then said the father to his servants: bring forth that best garment, and put it on him, and put a ring on his hand, and shoes on his feet. And bring hither that fatted calf, and kill him, and let us eat and be merry: for this my son was dead, and is alive again. He was lost, and is now found. And they began to make good chear* (Luke 15:22–24).

*They did not exactly **kill the fatted calf** yesterday to celebrate the return of the prodigal retailer: its share price actually finished the day marginally down.*
THE TIMES, 17 JANUARY 2002

*Jonny Wilkinson is back. The long-awaited return will not be heralded by **a fatted calf**, however, but there will be a virtually full house to greet their England hero when he trots out for Newcastle Falcons…*
THE INDEPENDENT, 27 DECEMBER 2003

For other idioms from the Bible, see page 317. See also WILLIAM TYNDALE, page 270.

feather: a feather in one's cap

credit, acknowledgement for one's work, achievement

It has been the custom amongst the people of very different cultures to wear a feather on the head for every enemy killed. The American Indians with their head-dresses are perhaps best known for this but the custom existed in other cultures, too. Richard Hansard in *A Description of Hungary* (1599) wrote: *It hath been an ancient custom among them [the Hungarians] that none should wear a feather but he who had killed a Turk, to whom only it was lawful to show the number of his slain enemies by the number of feathers in his cap.* The phrase dates from the early seventeenth century.

*Apart from hoping to boost his waning popularity by being seen on television hobnobbing with other world leaders, Mr Obuchi viewed the Okinawa summit as **a feather in his cap**.*
THE ECONOMIST, 8 APRIL 2000

*Going on an expedition with a well-respected mountaineer would be another **feather in his cap** and would no doubt increase his already huge fan base.*
DAILY EXPRESS, 29 JULY 2002

feet of clay

a weakness perceived in someone held in high regard

This is a biblical expression and comes from a story in the Book of Daniel. Daniel, after spending the night in prayer, was the only person in Nebuchadnezzar's kingdom able to interpret the king's troublesome dream. Nebuchadnezzar had seen a huge statue of a man, dazzling in appearance. The statue was made of several different metals, starting with gold at the head down to iron on the legs. The statue's feet were part iron and part clay. In the interpretation Daniel tells the king that, by God's will, he is the golden head but that other inferior kingdoms will succeed him, ending with a divided kingdom represented by feet of iron and clay: *As the toes were partly iron and partly clay, so this kingdom will be partly strong and partly brittle. And just as you saw the iron mixed with baked clay, so the people will be a mixture and will not remain united, any more than iron mixes with clay* (Daniel 2:42, New International Version). The mighty statue was not as strong as it appeared, its greatest weakness being its feet of clay. Even the greatest – and superficially perfect – may have hidden flaws.

*He is, however, only mortal and now he has the mantle of herodom thrust upon him it can only be a matter of time until he ends up putting at least one of his **feet of clay** in it.*
DAILY EXPRESS, 25 NOVEMBER 2003

*He was a dream come true for most women: a faithful, loving, hard-working man. Suzi Godson laments an idol with **feet of clay**.*
THE TIMES, 29 JUNE 2004

For other idioms from the Bible, see page 317.

feet: to fall/land on one's feet
to experience a fortunate outcome from difficult circumstances, to be lucky

The phrase dates from around the middle of the nineteenth century. Trollope uses and explains the allusion in *Barchester Towers* (1857): *It is well known that the family of the Slopes never starve: they always fall on their feet, like cats.*

*A former court jester was responsible for the founding of one of London's best hidden churches as well as its oldest hospital. Not much is known of Rahere, though it is widely accepted that he **landed on his feet** in the court of Henry I and became his jester.*
THE TIMES, 4 OCTOBER 2003

fiddle: as fit as a fiddle
on top form, in excellent health

The earliest known reference to this alliterative simile has been traced to William Haughton's play *Englishmen for My Money* (1598): *This is excellent, i'faith; as fit as 'a fiddle*. In the sixteenth century the word *fiddle* was applicable not only to the instrument but also to the fiddler and, by extension, to an entertainer or mirth-maker. It is possible, therefore, that the phrase describes the fiddler, a vivacious character who made the company merry and played his instrument with vigour.

More likely, however, is the theory that the phrase is really about the instrument, not its player. Its supporters hold that *fit* is used in the sense of 'suitable for a purpose'. So the phrase meant 'as suitable for its purpose as a fiddle is for music-making'. They argue that the phrase changed in meaning, and subsequently became nonsensical, when *fit* gradually came to be synonymous with bodily well-being. An alternative phrase *fine as a fiddle* was also found in the same period. Indeed, it appears in the same Haughton play.

Possibly people were excited by the appearance of this new instrument, for it was not until that century that the fiddle in the form we know it today came over from Italy. Certainly it was admired, for an expression *a face made of a fiddle* was in use, from the seventeenth to the nineteenth centuries, to describe someone with fine features. By contrast, the only comparison that survives nowadays between the face and the fiddle is a relatively recent one from the beginning of the twentieth century, *to have a face as long as a fiddle*, and that means 'to look miserable'.

*Three weeks later Lesley rang to say she'd got a letter stating that the clinic needed to see me urgently. I was sure there couldn't be anything wrong. I felt **as fit as a fiddle**.*
DAILY EXPRESS, 25 MAY 2004

See ALLITERATIVE SIMILES, page 237.

fiddle: to fiddle while Rome burns

to be occupied with trivialities while a crisis is taking place

In AD 64 the Emperor Nero, under the pretence of detesting the dark, narrow lanes of the city and in order to clear ground for the erection of an opulent palace, had Rome set ablaze. According to the gossipy Roman biographer Suetonius, Nero was so delighted at the sight of the flames, which brought to mind the burning of Troy, that he sang and played his lyre as he watched the city burn (not a fiddle, which was invented centuries later). The Roman historian Tacitus tells us that Nero himself denied the act, blaming the fire on the small Christian community whom he then persecuted ruthlessly. Allusions to Nero's *fiddling* began in the seventeenth century but the idiom itself dates from around the mid-nineteenth century.

*I don't imagine that the committee's findings will change the thinking of committed anti-environmentalists for as much as a millisecond. After all, it is so much easier **to fiddle while Rome burns** than rush hither and thither with buckets of water.*
EVENING STANDARD, 10 JANUARY 2003

For other idioms drawn from ancient life and history, see page 317.

fig: not to care/give/be worth a fig

to be completely indifferent/worth nothing

Although the ancients used *fig* to refer to anything of little value or unworthy of notice, it is likely that its idiomatic use in English, which dates back to at least the fifteenth century, alludes to an obscene gesture of contempt made by clenching the fist and thrusting the thumb between the middle and index fingers. Although the gesture is Italian in origin, Shakespeare and his contemporaries referred to it as *the fig of Spain*.

French lexicographer Maximilien Littré (1801–81) cites the following story to explain the gesture. In 1159 the Milanese revolted against the Holy Roman Emperor, Frederick Barbarossa. As a mark of contempt, they placed his Empress back to front upon a mule and led her thus out of the city. In 1162, when Frederick returned to retake the city, he humiliated his prisoners by forcing them to extract a fig from the backside of a mule with their teeth before declaring *Ecco la fica* ('Here is the fig').

Subsequently *giving someone the fig* became a scornful sign of disrespect which spread throughout Europe. Italian *far le fiche* became *dar la higa* in Spanish, *faire la figue* in French and *die Feigen weisen* in German. In English, from at least the fifteenth century, *fig* also appeared in expressions of sheer contempt for the worthlessness of something: *a fig for your money*; *I don't care a fig for her*; *that boy isn't worth a fig*.

*...Pet was almost a golden retriever but not quite, standing two inches shorter than the regulation male dog, when only a single inch was the permitted tolerance for the breed, not that Lois **cared one fig about that**.*
CAROL SHIELDS, UNLESS, 2002

filthy lucre
money, dishonourable profit

The Middle English word *lucre* comes from Latin *lucrum*, 'gain, profit'. The word is a neutral one but, in his translation of the New Testament (1534), William Tyndale coupled it with the adjective *filthy* to denote 'dishonourable gain'. Tyndale's phrase has survived into idiomatic English through the Authorised Version of the Bible, where it appears three times in the New Testament (Titus 1:7 and I Timothy 3:3 and 3:8). However, because of its archaic ring, *filthy lucre* is now more likely to be found in satirical contexts.

*They will reasonably wonder why, 14 years after the end of the affair, she has chosen, having kissed, to tell us all about it. They will conclude it is either for **filthy lucre**...or revenge for not being brought back into government by her lover when he became Prime Minister in 1990.*
DAILY MIRROR, 30 SEPTEMBER 2002

*So opposed is he to getting his hands dirty with **filthy lucre** that Kawakami waives the interview fees many professional authors charge in Japan and gives the money he makes from his books and articles to his favourite causes.*
THE INDEPENDENT, 18 MAY 2004

For other idioms from Tyndale's translations, see WILLIAM TYNDALE, page 270; for other idioms from the Bible, see page 317.

finger: to have a finger in every pie
to play a part in many activities; to be meddlesome, interfering

When the pie looks so tempting it's difficult to resist having a quick taste. The greater the number of pies, the greater the temptation. The idiom nearly always carries an implication of meddling in other people's business, a universal human tendency that has been reflected in the phrase for at least four hundred years, as in the comment Shakespeare's Duke of Buckingham makes on Cardinal Wolsey in the opening scene of *Henry VIII* (1613):

> *No man's pie is freed*
> *From his ambitious finger*

In 1656, Bartholomew Harris published a translation of Jean Nicolas de Parival's *History of this Iron Age*, which includes what was evidently a well-known phrase, still current today: *Lusatia...must needs, forsooth, have her Finger in the Pye.*

*The communications director **has a finger in every pie**, advising the Prime Minister on everything from speeches to diplomacy to strategy.*
THE TIMES, 26 JULY 2003

*He was not a man readily subject to influence. He made up his own mind... He did not think a prime minister needed **to have a finger in every pie**.*
THE TIMES, 25 AUGUST 2003

*I have a lot of ideas for different things. All sorts. I want **to have my finger in every pie**. You only live once.*
BOSTON SUNDAY HERALD,
13 MARCH 2005

fingers: to be all fingers and thumbs
to be very clumsy

The modern idiom is rather nonsensical since everyone has fingers and thumbs. It is derived from the earlier, more comprehensible expressions *eche finger is a thumbe*, recorded by John Heywood in his collection of *Proverbs* (1546), and the variant *all his fingers are thumbs*, which dates from around the middle of the seventeenth century. To complete fine manual tasks with ten thumbs and no fingers would be awkward indeed.

*Scooping up the warm rice and hot pickle by hand feels natural enough till it gets to my mouth; then I am **all fingers and thumbs**, bits of curry-stained rice dropping into my lap, and still so obviously, embarrassingly, a tourist.*
THE OBSERVER, 13 MAY 2001

See also NONSENSICAL IDIOMS, page 152.

fingers: to have/keep one's fingers crossed
to hope for a happy outcome

Crossing one's fingers is a quick and easy way of making the sign of the cross to shield oneself from diabolic power. It is also easy to *keep* them crossed, thus ensuring lasting protection from the devil's tricks. Funk (1950) suggests that the practice probably originated among America's black slave population. Written records of the phrase date from the 1920s. Of course, these days there is no necessity actually to cross one's fingers – speaking the words is deemed sufficient.

A less likely alternative is put forward by Charles Panati in his *Extraordinary Origins of Everyday Things* (1989). In pre-Christian times, the cross was a symbol of unity, and benign spirits made their home at the intersection. The original gesture involved two people making a wish by each placing a finger as one axis of the cross, for the spirits to guard until the wish was fulfilled. Subsequent simplification allowed for one person only to be involved in the wish-making.

Another use has grown up, particularly among children, of crossing one's fingers behind one's back when making a promise, with the sense of 'I

don't intend to do what I am now promising'. But it can reach adults as well. Tony Banks MP was recorded on camera and reported in *The Times* of 14 May 1997 as having his fingers crossed as he took the oath of allegiance to the Queen. Republican Banks could have been showing his anti-monarchist feelings; he might have been playing out a part in a prominent debate about the appropriacy of the oath of allegiance in Parliament. He claimed subsequently that he did it to bring himself luck in his new job as Sports Minister. Whatever his motives, adults do childish things.

*However, it could be bad news on Saturday as heavy rain is expected in the morning with temperatures struggling to top 13°C... A source said: 'Everyone is **keeping their fingers crossed** for good weather.'*
DAILY MIRROR, 1 JULY 2004

fish: to drink like a fish
to drink alcohol in excess

Fish appear to be doing nothing else but drink as they open and close their mouths all the time in the water. Those who overindulge in alcohol have been compared with fish since the first half of the seventeenth century.

*For years **he drank like a fish**, but now he has traded in alcohol, which had claimed the lives of an aunt and his younger brother Piers, for Diet Coke and fruit juice.*
THE SUNDAY TIMES, 18 APRIL 2004

flash in the pan, a
something which, after a promising start, amounts to nothing

The expression comes from a malfunction in the old flintlock gun. When the weapon was fired, a hammer striking against a flint produced a spark which lit the priming, a small quantity of

Nonsensical idioms

Some people believe football is a matter of life and death, said Bill Shankly, acclaimed manager of Liverpool Football Club, in 1973. *I'm very disappointed with that attitude*, he continued, *I can assure you it is much, much more important than that*. The dramatic nineteenth-century phrase *a matter of life or death* has the all-important *or* instead of *and*, thus making perfect sense, both literally in a life-threatening situation and figuratively with respect to a matter of vital importance. However, *a matter of life and death* has been a common but nonsensical variant since the second half of the nineteenth century. Both are still current and it remains to be seen whether the illogical will triumph in the end. Bill Shankly was obviously in the *and* camp.

There are other phrases like this one, which began straightforwardly enough, but went astray. *Head over heels*, like *to be all* FINGERS *and thumbs*, makes no logical sense but was inexplicably derived from a much more sensible turn of phrase. It is an eighteenth-century variant on the now obsolete *heels over head*, which had been in use for four hundred years before that. The phrase can either refer literally to a somersault or fall (the original sense), or it can be used as an intensive as in *head over heels in love*, the allusion being to the giddy feeling of spinning out of control: *My guts ached and I felt dizzy, as if I was head over heels in love* (*The Spectator*, 18 August 2001).

Yet another common idiom in this category is *to have one's cake and eat it*, meaning 'to benefit from both of two mutually exclusive alternatives' or 'to have it both ways'. Back in the sixteenth century people talked of not being able to *eat their cake and have it*, a phrase that makes perfect sense. Why, then, in the early twentieth century, was it felt necessary to tamper with the idiom and reverse the order of the verbs?

All this just goes to show how little we think about what we are actually saying when the words that tumble out of our mouths are familiar to us. Take, for instance, the phrase *no love lost*, meaning 'animosity'. There has been considerable confusion about this phrase since its beginnings in the seventeenth century, when it could express either 'mutual affection' or 'mutual dislike'. Logic seems to be on the side of the former sense, that all the love between two individuals remains intact. The more

gunpowder held in the *pan*. This small explosion ignited the main charge, forcing the ball to fly from the barrel. Sometimes the priming caught but failed to ignite the main charge, resulting in nothing more than *a flash in the pan*, a hint of promise but no result.

The phrase, in common use amongst soldiers and huntsmen from the seventeenth-century invention of the weapon, began to be used figuratively in the eighteenth century, particularly in the now obsolescent *to flash in the pan*, 'to fall flat'. By the late eighteenth century, it had become a form closer to the one we are more acquainted with today. Benjamin Malkin's 1809 translation of Le Sage's *Adventures of Gil Blas of Santillane* includes: *I was not remiss in composing a fine compliment...with which I meant to launch out on her part; but it was just so much flash in the pan.*

*These facts would not be so disturbing if the recent discrepancies in economic growth rates were a mere **flash in the pan** produced by the vagaries of the economic cycle. But they are not. They are the established trends.*
THE SUNDAY TELEGRAPH,
15 FEBRUARY 2004

*We need a Modern Gardens Day. It will open eyes to new gardens, and show that they are an intrinsic part of our tradition and not some trendy **flash in the pan**.*
THE TIMES, 12 JUNE 2004

convoluted reasoning behind the latter can only be that no love existed in the first place, so none could be lost. Nevertheless, it is the second, apparently nonsensical and somewhat ironic, meaning that has won out.

Sometimes seemingly nonsensical idioms have sound etymological explanations to them. The common exclamation *cheap at half the price*, used nowadays to make an item sound like a bargain, is one such. Surely if the item is described thus, then the asking price is either fair or too much? It is probable that the original phrase commonly shouted out by market vendors was *cheap at twice the price*. The customer's substitution of *half* makes a witty comment on tacky, over-priced goods, the original intention behind the phrase. Only more recently has the expression *cheap at half the price* been erroneously and nonsensically used to signify 'good value': *Oscar returned home a hero… Before long he had signed a $1m dollar contract to turn pro – the richest ever for an amateur. It was cheap at half the price; everyone knew that the 'Golden Boy', as he was now called, was a licence to print greenbacks* (*The Guardian*, 5 November 2001).

In individual cases, such as those above, it is often not clear why the apparently illogical forms have taken precedence over the more obvious alternative. But in general terms, language itself, and language users, do seem attracted to the absurd and the nonsensical. Nursery rhymes (the classic *The cow jumped over the moon*, for instance) are often whimsical; writers such as Lewis Carroll and Ogden Nash demonstrate the same tendency. Idioms share this common characteristic of language, and it is part of their appeal to the ordinary user. As the French etymologist Guiraud put it: *oddity, nonsense indeed, are a source of success and survival for many idioms*. Another expert summarises the attraction: *There is a certain irrelevance in the human mind, a certain love for the illogical and absurd, a reluctance to submit itself to reason, which breaks loose now and then and finds expression for itself in idiomatic speech* (Logan Pearsall Smith, *Words and Idioms*, 1925).

See also *a* CURATE'S *egg*.

For another idiom arising from the use of the flintlock gun see *to* HANG *fire*. For other idioms derived from the army and warfare, see page 317.

flavour of the month, the

something temporarily in fashion, a fad

In the 1940s American ice cream manufacturers tempted their customers to eat more of their products by offering a *flavour of the month* on special promotion. The excitingly entitled periodical *Ice Cream Review* for September 1946 reported that the Illinois Association of Ice Cream Manufacturers had set up a committee to look into organising a *flavour-of-the-month programme* for the following year, while an advertisement in the *Ice Cream Field* for March 1955 encouraged its readers to *Run any ripple flavor as your flavor of the month – every month of the year*. The phrase was in general use in America by the 1970s and had crossed the Atlantic by the 1980s.

*Another trend harks back to the Sixties and Seventies: lounge bars decorated in orange, brown or pink are the **flavour of the month**.*
THE TIMES, 27 MARCH 2004

flog: to flog a dead horse

to attempt to arouse fresh interest in a matter that is either hopeless or already settled

A dead horse is a useless horse and past reviving. From the seventeenth century onwards the phrase was related to the earning of money from which there was no profit: the repayment of debts, for instance, or working off an advance. Nineteenth-century sailors were usually paid an advance on signing up with a vessel, money which was usually spent on debts and living expenses until the ship set sail. They spent their first months on board *working their dead horses*, that is their advances, and would parade a straw effigy of a horse around the deck before setting fire to it and casting it overboard to celebrate becoming solvent again.

The same sense of uselessness and unremitting effort for little reward is conveyed by the metaphor *to flog a dead horse*. It is attributed to John Bright MP, who used it to castigate the apathy of his fellow parliamentarians towards a reform bill of 1867 introduced by Lord John Russell. It was such an arresting phrase that he used it again when a measure proposed by Richard Cobden similarly found little parliamentary support.

'Maybe I was trying to bully the Conservative Party into changing. After a while you give up trying **to flog a dead horse.**'
THE INDEPENDENT, 5 AUGUST 2000

It is no longer enough **to flog a dead horse**: *brands must be constantly reinvented if they are to survive.*
EVENING STANDARD,
12 NOVEMBER 2001

For other horsey idioms see page 319.

fly: a fly in the ointment

something trifling that spoils or mars the whole

The idiom comes from the Old Testament. Ecclesiastes 10:1 reads: *Dead flies cause the ointment of the apothecary to send forth a stinking savour; so doth a little folly in him that is in reputation for wisdom and honour.*

The biblical metaphor vividly speaks of a sound reputation ruined; modern usage is generally more flippant, *the fly in the ointment* usually being some trifling matter that takes the edge off perfection. For Charles Lamb, it was the presence of a poor relation that spoiled an otherwise contented life: *A poor relation – is the most irrelevant thing in nature, – a lion in your path, – a frog in your chamber, – a fly in your ointment* (*Essays of Elia*, 1833).

The phrase has become increasingly popular since the early twentieth century.

Squeals of delight at Queens Ice Rink and bowling alley in Bayswater yesterday afternoon as modelturnedactress Elle Macpherson, 39, hosted a sixth birthday party for her son. The only **fly in the ointment** *was the moans from other skaters who complained that the management had cordoned off part of the rinkside coffee shop for the bowling party.*
DAILY MAIL, 12 FEBRUARY 2004

fly: a fly on the wall

an unperceived eavesdropper

The idiom is alluded to in Nancy Mitford's *Love in a Cold Climate* (1949) and, indeed, this may have been its source: *I had been throwing an occasional glance in their direction, wondering what it could all be about and wishing I could be a fly on the wall to hear them.*

By the 1970s the phrase *fly-on-the-wall* had been adopted by film makers to describe an approach in which a slice of real life is presented to the viewer without the interference of direction or commentary. However, participants still had to get used to being followed around by a camera crew – hardly as inconspicuous as a fly on the wall.

LORD OF THE FLY-ON-THE-WALLS
Paul Watson, revered and reviled documentary maker, is…the man who arguably invented the docusoap in 1974 with his then astonishing series The Family…

'*I have, over my career, been lucky enough to invent three or four things that have been borrowed by other people, a certain type of* **fly-on-the-wall**, *a way of doing a political film, documentary soaps if you like. And I have just invented something that I think is my last throw of the dice and I'm tremendously excited by it.*'
THE OBSERVER, 27 JANUARY 2002

Hickey had no real urge to be **a fly on the wall** *at yesterday's meeting between Mr Jack McConnell and London's very own despotic tyrant, Mr Ken Livingstone.*
DAILY EXPRESS, 7 JULY 2004

This new **fly-on-the-wall** *series follows a group of medical students through their critical third year at Southampton University as they graduate from lab-based dummies and dissections and get to grips with hospital patients.*
DAILY EXPRESS, 12 JULY 2004

fly: he wouldn't harm/hurt a fly

he is incapable of hurting anyone

There is nothing quite so annoying as a fly. The creatures sometimes provoke strong reactions and are generally despised, and thought to be so insignificant that few people baulk at swatting them. A French innkeeper during the First World War was heard to comment: *The Americans are good soldiers, but they are all mad. Whenever a fly enters the* *dining-room you'd think it was a Boche, for they go into a rage and chase it around until it is killed.*

On the other hand, those who resist the temptation to swat the annoying fly are traditionally considered to have the mildest of temperaments. The phrase *wouldn't hurt a fly* first occurs in *Ludus de Morte Claudii* (c. AD 50), a work attributed to the Roman philosopher Seneca. The general idea was expressed much later by Laurence Sterne in *Tristram Shandy* (1759–67), where the narrator, Tristram, illustrates the kindliness of his uncle Toby with the following tale:

He was of a peaceful, placid nature, no jarring element in it, all was mixed up so kindly within him; my uncle Toby had scarce a heart to retaliate upon a fly. Go, says he, one day at dinner, to an over-grown one which had buzzed about his nose, and tormented him cruelly all dinner-time, and which after infinite attempts he had caught at last, as it flew by him; I'll not hurt thee, says my uncle Toby, rising from his chair, and going across the room, with the fly in his hand, I'll not hurt a hair of thy head; – Go says he, lifting up the sash, and opening his hand as he spoke, to let it escape; go, poor devil, get thee gone, why should I hurt thee? – This world surely is wide enough to hold both thee and me.

The expression *wouldn't hurt a fly* was subsequently taken up by twentieth-century writers, possibly influenced by Sterne's work.

Ken **wouldn't hurt a fly**. *He was a peaceful man of letters and always promoted non-violent demonstrating.*
THE OBSERVER, 20 OCTOBER 2002

For other idioms drawn from Greek and Roman writers, see page 318. For other idioms drawn from literature, see page 319.

fly: to fly off the handle
to lose one's temper

This expression was current amongst American frontiersmen in the first half of the nineteenth century. The reference is to an axe-head which, having worked loose on its handle, finally flies off at the next hefty blow. For an axe to break in this way was not only dangerous but also meant that work had to stop until a new handle had been made. It was not surprising, therefore, that the event was invariably accompanied by an outburst of temper, so that angry behaviour came to be associated with the loss of an axe-head and a person was said to have *flown off the handle*. Canadian author Thomas Chandler Haliburton popularised the phrase in *The Attaché or Sam Slick in England* (1843–4): *You never see such a crotchital old critter as he is. He flies right off the handle for nothing.*

She reckons I hardly do anything in the house and moans all the time about picky little things...I must admit I fly off the handle when she asks me to do boring chores like go to the local shop.
DAILY MAIL, 24 JUNE 2004

foot: to get/set off on the right/wrong foot
to begin something well/badly

Which is the *right foot* and which the *wrong*? This phrase, in use since the early twentieth century, may have originated in some sort of superstitious belief (see *to have got out of the* WRONG *side of the bed*). Alternatively, since the idiom alludes to beginning a journey, *right* and *wrong* may have no deep significance but simply describe the nature of that journey – whether, in its initial stages, it passed without incident or ran into difficulties.

In recent use, the phrase is often applied to new relationships.

Eric managed to win a place at the famous London drama school RADA but got off on the wrong foot when he ignored his father's advice to lodge at the YMCA and instead checked into the Dorchester Hotel... It appeared to confirm his old schoolmates' decision to dub him Rich Brat.
DAILY EXPRESS, 8 JULY 2004

The next thing you noticed during the performance on Friday, soon into the first movement of the Haydn, was a sense of faltering, when things came out of alignment. It felt as if the musicians had got off on the wrong foot, and there were similar moments throughout.
NEW YORK TIMES, 14 DECEMBER 2004

foot: to put one's best foot forward
to begin a project with determination and hard work, in order to make a good impression

The phrase has been recorded in English literature since the moor Aaron bade his companions *Come on, my lords, the better foot before* in Shakespeare's *Titus Andronicus* (1594). Which the *better* or *best* foot is, however, is hard to say. It might be one's strongest foot, or one's right foot (since, traditionally, the left is unlucky and the right lucky).

With the caution of an invalid only recently recovered from a battering, English National Opera is slowly putting its best foot forward again... ENO is beginning to reinvent itself...with a new managerial team led by artistic director and chief executive Sean Doran.
THE DAILY TELEGRAPH,
10 OCTOBER 2003

See also *my* EARS *are burning*.

foot: to put one's foot in it/in one's mouth

to get into a mess, to make a blunder; to make a verbal gaffe

Some authorities suggest that the present-day idiom, which dates from the second half of the eighteenth century, may be derived from a much earlier phrase, *the bishop hath set his foot in it.* Apparently, this was a common cry when broth or milk was burnt. Milton referred to it in his *Animadversions* (1641): *It will be the bishop's foot in the broth.* And Swift employed it almost a century later in *Polite Conversation* (1738): *This cream is burnt too – Why madam, the bishop hath set his foot in it.*

William Tyndale, however, suggests that the phrase has a rather darker origin than that of a minor ecclesiastical faux pas: *If the podech [soup] be burned to, or the meat over-roasted, we say the Bishop hath put his foot in the pot, or the Bishop hath played the cook. Because the Bishops burn who they lust and whosoever displeases them (Works,* 1528). Tyndale's conflict with the established church may account for his more sinister interpretation.

In any event, the roots of many idiomatic phrases fade from memory with the passage of time and this one is no exception; all connection with dislike of the clergy has long since been forgotten. Interestingly, French has a similar phrase with an explicit link to the origin: *pas de clerc* ('priest's footstep') is used when someone has committed an indiscretion through ignorance or lack of good sense.

Of course, intriguing though all this is, the expression may have a much more straightforward origin and simply refer to the embarrassment of putting one's foot in some mess on the pavement, or allude to inadvertently trespassing in forbidden territory.

The idiom has evolved further over the years: *to put one's foot in one's mouth* means 'to make a verbal gaffe'. Some commentators say that it was first used of Sir Boyle Roche, an Irish politician in the 1770s who had a knack of making verbal blunders and malapropisms: *Half the lies our opponents tell about me are not true,* for instance, or *The country is overflowing with absentee landlords.* However, since the phrase has been in use only since the early twentieth century, this origin would seem unlikely. The expression has been condensed more recently into the much-used adjective *foot-in-mouth,* a pun on the cattle disease foot and mouth.

MINNIE DRIVER IS SUFFERING **FOOT-IN-MOUTH DISEASE** AGAIN *The winner of the Little Miss Unpopular prize this week? Why, Minnie Driver, of course. Her crime was to describe Dame Judi Dench, the world's most respected actress, as 'very small, round and middle-aged'… Driver's comments are of the sort that breach Hollywood's complicated etiquette and can make you enemies for life.*
THE DAILY TELEGRAPH, 24 JANUARY 2002

Prince Philip **put his foot in it** *on a tour of the* Queen Mary II *– by joking that terminally ill passengers could book a place in the ship's mortuary. The prince made the gaffe on a visit to the ship's hospital.*
DAILY MIRROR, 10 JANUARY 2004

She also seems to be pitching to become the next health secretary… Particularly as the current post-holder, John Reid, **has just put his foot in his mouth** *with remarks about the working classes' smoking habits.*
THE SUNDAY TIMES, 13 JUNE 2004

footloose and fancy free
free from care and responsibility;
romantically unattached

Footloose, an American coinage from
the late seventeenth century,
describes someone who, without
responsibilities to restrain him, is free
to do or wander as he pleases. If that
person is also *fancy free* he has a free
heart, with no sweetheart to tie him
down. The word *fancy* originally
meant 'fantasy' or 'imagination'
before coming to mean 'whim' and
finally, in the mid-sixteenth century,
'love'. The phrase, which dates from
around the 1970s, is appealing
because of the alliteration and the
balance of the words.

*At the time owning property was the last
thing on my mind and I enjoyed being
footloose and fancy free.*
THE INDEPENDENT, 15 JULY 2000

*Both players in this blossoming relationship
are footloose and fancy free.*
DAILY MIRROR, 22 JANUARY 2002

See COUPLINGS, page 294.

forlorn hope, a
a hopeless or desperate undertaking

The Dutch term *verloren hoop*, which
translates as 'lost troop', referred to a
small band of soldiers picked out for
the extremely dangerous task of heading up an attack, or for some other
equally perilous undertaking. When
the term was taken into English in the
first half of the sixteenth century, it
retained its meaning but the soldiers
exchanged the foreign words for similar
sounding English ones, a process
known as folk etymology. Thus the
term *forlorn hope* was coined. By the
early 1640s, with all understanding of
the origin lost, the phrase had come to
mean 'a faint hope' and described a

plan or enterprise that would almost
inevitably fail.

Some read their Evening Standards,
*turning back to the beginning when they
had finished in the forlorn hope of finding
something vaguely interesting which they
had missed the first time.*
ANN WIDDECOMBE,
THE CLEMATIS TREE, 2000

*There is certainly nothing okay about the
BBC, as you will discover if you sit on in
the forlorn hope that something decent
will come on.*
THE DAILY TELEGRAPH, 14 MARCH 2002

For other idioms derived from the
army and warfare, see page 317.

French: to take French leave
To leave one's duties without
permission, to leave without notice

Although the expression was current
amongst the armed forces during the
First World War (see NATIONAL
RIVALRIES, page 108) in the sense of
'to desert', it is, in fact, considerably
older and originated not in the
trenches but in polite French society
in the eighteenth century. In these circles it was not considered impolite to
leave a social gathering without first
making a formal farewell to one's host
and hostess. English society was
stricter and was not amused by the lax
ways of its French counterparts, so it
seized upon the custom to express the
idea of 'sneaking off without permission or notice'. The phrase was current
by the 1770s.

The French, however, have coined a
phrase of their own which carries the
same meaning. *Filer à l'anglaise* translates as 'to leave in the English
fashion', i.e. to slip away without
authorisation.

SCOTS TOURISM MANDARIN TAKES **FRENCH LEAVE**

The civil servant in charge of attracting tourists to Scotland in spite of foot-and-mouth disease has decided to spend his Easter holiday at Disneyland Paris... The Scottish National Party said yesterday that neither Scotland's ministers nor its civil servants would be taken seriously if they ignored their own advice.
THE TIMES, 13 APRIL 2001

In France they call it 'filer à l'anglaise', *while in England the phrase is* '**French leave**'. *Whatever the language, the irony is palpable, as the manager of the French national team, Jacques Santini, is slipping away from his current duties after the European Championship to become head coach at Tottenham Hotspur.*
THE INDEPENDENT ON SUNDAY,
6 JUNE 2004

· G ·

gallery: to play to the gallery

to perform/speak in a way intended to appeal to the less sophisticated members of an audience; to seek approval by excessively dramatic actions

In a theatre the cheap seats are those in the gallery. In the second half of the nineteenth century, when this expression was coined, it was assumed that members of the public who occupied them were less well off and therefore less refined. Any actor who *played to the gallery* and sought the approval of the common crowd was looked down upon.

*Mr Forth and Cabinet Office spokesman David Davis **played to the gallery** all the while, deepening their leader's discomfort. Watched by roaring MPs, Mr Forth pretended to put a gun to his own head and shoot after Mr Blair said Mr Forth pioneered AS-levels.*
DAILY MAIL, 17 OCTOBER 2002

*It is rare to see him make more than the most perfunctory of gestures after scoring. Dagnall is not one to **play to the gallery**. He explains: 'I see goal scoring as my job. It's something I am supposed to do, so unless it's a really big important goal. I don't make much of a fuss.'*
LIVERPOOL DAILY POST, 28 APRIL 2004

garden: to lead someone up the garden path

to lead someone on, to deceive

Away from prying eyes and straining ears, the end of the garden is the spot for flirtation and courtship. Some girls promise a lot and give away nothing, while others get more than they bargained for: *They're cheats, that's wot women are! Lead you up the garden and then go snivellin' around 'cos wot's natcheral 'as 'appened to 'em* (Ethel Mannin, *Sounding Brass*, 1925).

*Don't fall for unscrupulous crooks who claim they will get your idea patented and marketed as long as you pay them an up-front fee. These people will never turn anybody away and will **lead you up the garden path** in letting you believe you have just invented the best thing since sliced bread.*
DAILY MIRROR, 3 DECEMBER 2001

*Environmental groups are angry with BP and Shell for supposedly **leading them up the garden path** on their commitment to renewable energy and the fight against global warming.*
THE GUARDIAN, 23 OCTOBER 2003

gatepost: between you, me and the gatepost/bedpost/doorpost

spoken when a secret or confidence is about to be shared

The phrase has had, and still has, a number of forms. In the 1830s, the final element was *bedpost* or simply *post*; there are later instances of *doorpost*, and *gatepost* appears in 1875. *Gatepost* is nowadays perhaps the preferred word, largely because Browning's poetry is widely read, and that was his choice in *The Inn Album* (1875), a psychological study of crime. A relatively uncouth young man who has just inherited a million pounds makes friends with a sophisticated older man, whose brother is a duke. Needless to say, he is relatively poor. Not realising what he is letting himself in for, the young man sits with his new friend on a convenient gate, and urges him:

Make a clean breast! Recount!
A secret's safe
'Twixt you, me, and the gate-post!

*Exempted from the Republican-initiated term limit for presidents established by the 22nd Amendment, Truman could have run in 1952. His inclination had been to run. The presidency, Truman declared to a Florida audience, 'was an all-day-and-night job...but just **between you, me, and the gatepost**, I like it.'*
BERGEN COUNTY RECORD, 13 MAY 2004

*By 2pm, some 6,000 people had been informed that she had suspected pancreatitis and by 4pm an astonishing 12,000 people had been advised that '**between you, me and the gatepost**', the minister's wife was being fitted with a colostomy bag.*

THE SUNDAY TIMES, 23 MAY 2004

See also DEAF *as a post.*

gauntlet: to pick up the gauntlet
to accept a challenge

See *to throw down the* GAUNTLET.

*Maybe, if she'd been a better person, she would have left Robin alone. Maybe she wanted to make Robin like her to deny her the satisfaction of disliking her – to win that contest of esteem. Maybe she was just **picking up the gauntlet**. But the desire to be liked was real.*
JONATHAN FRANZEN,
THE CORRECTIONS, 2001

If the challenge seems beyond your resources – due to lack of confidence, or an inability to *talk in public or to confront, for example – it gets shelved as impossible. The rewards, though, of **picking up the gauntlet** are not only that you get what you want, but also, that you automatically improve a whole raft of skills that will make it easier to make changes in the future.*
GOOD HOUSEKEEPING, OCTOBER 2001

gauntlet: to run the gauntlet
to suffer or risk abuse, criticism or danger

The idiom has its origins in a military punishment of Swedish invention in which the offender, stripped to his waist, was forced to run between two lines of soldiers who beat him with clubs, knotted ropes or other weapons. The Swedish term for this torture was *gatlopp* (from Old Swedish *gatulop*, 'passageway'), a word made up of *gata*, 'lane', and *lopp*, 'course'. The Germans observed the punishment during the Swedish phase (1630–35) of the Thirty Years War (1618–48), when the well-disciplined forces of King Gustavus Adolphus won a number of resounding victories. The English got it from them later in the war.

The Swedish term was borrowed into English as the corruption *gantelope* by the mid-1640s, with the phrase *to run the gantelope* being put to figurative use just a few years later. But the Swedish word was to undergo a further shift in English. A similarity between *gantelope* and the existing word *gauntlet* (see *to throw down the* GAUNTLET) was perceived and, from the early 1660s, the latter became increasingly common, winning out in the first half of the nineteenth century.

In Britain *running the gauntlet* seems to have been particularly common on board ship; it was certainly a method of discipline on Cook's voyages. Even after it had been abolished in military circles, the punishment was still a part of schoolboy justice in public schools. The author Hammond Innes recalls an experience of his from the 1920s: *When the dormitory leader came back I poured out the whole incident. The leader then told the school prefect – he didn't go to the masters – and together they lined up the whole school so that the bully had to run the gauntlet, being hit with a sockful of earth* (*Daily Telegraph*, 7 September 1991).

This 'educational' practice seems to have persisted into the twenty-first century. The following extract describes Wesley College in New Zealand, the old school of the celebrated All Black, Jonah Lomu: *The school is not a place for the faint-hearted. In recent years there was still a punishment known as 'two lines', whereby a younger boy would have to run through a severe beating by his older peers* (*The Daily Telegraph*, 2 June 2005).

Nowadays the phrase *to run the gauntlet* is restricted to figurative use when someone is subjected to a barrage of criticism, for instance, or has a run of difficult or dangerous circumstances to contend with.

In Britain, money has also helped to transform the game [soccer] from decline to boom. This was precipitated, oddly, by the fallout from the 1989 Hillsborough tragedy in Sheffield when 95 fans were crushed to death against wire cages designed to contain spectators. Afterwards clubs were forced by law to convert their stadiums into all-seat venues, which drew new fans – including women and families – who no longer had **to run the gauntlet** *of the sometimes unruly standing-room areas.*
TIME, 5 JUNE 2000

Nowadays, to get to Ibrox, Rangers supporters must **run the gauntlet** *of scores of lads and lasses, all trying to ply them with plastic.*
THE PEOPLE, 10 MARCH 2004

For other idioms derived from the army and warfare, see page 317.

gauntlet: to throw down the gauntlet
to issue a challenge

The word *gauntlet* is a borrowing of *gantelet*, the medieval French diminutive of *gant*, 'glove'. In the Middle Ages a knight challenging another to combat would throw his gauntlet, his protective glove, on the ground. If his opponent picked it up, then the challenge had been accepted.

There is one challenge that has never been accepted, however. From the fourteenth century to George IV's coronation in 1821, it was the practice for the King's Champion to ride in full armour into each coronation banquet. Three times he would *throw down the gauntlet*, daring any opponent to the king's rule to mortal combat. Over nearly five hundred years, none accepted.

When the days of knights in shining armour were finally over, the gauntlet was replaced by a gentleman's glove when a challenge to a duel of honour was issued. *To cast down the gauntlet* was put to figurative use in the first half of the seventeenth century.

Greater Europe's prospects haven't looked this bright for a long time. Unfortunately, most European business leaders are still so preoccupied with playing catch-up in a new, euro-dominated single market that, rather than **throw down the gauntlet** *to their U.S. and global competitors, they look more likely to absentmindedly hand over the European market on a plate.*
TIME, 5 JUNE 2000

MPs **threw down the gauntlet** *to the banks and cash machine operators as the Treasury Select Committee warned there would be important public policy concerns if free access to cash withdrawal declined.*
MIDDLESBROUGH EVENING GAZETTE, 31 MARCH 2005

gift: the gift of the gab
the ability to talk fluently about
trivial matters

Gob is a slang term for 'mouth', possibly of Scottish and Irish Gaelic origin.
It has been in use since the mid-fifteenth century and was ultimately
derived from an unattested Celtic
term *gobbo-*, meaning 'mouth' or
'beak'. Its variant *gab* has been around
since the second half of the eighteenth century, with the additional
sense of 'idle prattle'. The phrase *gift
of the gab*, to denote 'a facility for talking twaddle', was originally *gift of the
gob* and dates from the late seventeenth century.

*He deals mainly with children and
teenagers who might be damaging things
or simply hanging around.*
   *'I can approach anybody,' says Loftus.
'I've got **the gift of the gab**. We get
on with them, you always get those
that are cocky, but if you confront them
they're okay.'*
THE BIG ISSUE, 25 JUNE 2004

*To an outside observer, Mr Ahern
personifies the Irish politician. He is a
cheerful, ruddy-cheeked man with **the
gift of the gab**, a ready handshake for
potential voters and a big smile.*
THE ECONOMIST, 14 OCTOBER 2004

gild: to gild the lily
to over-embellish, to add unnecessary
ornamentation

Here once again we sit, once again crown'd,
states Shakespeare's King John with
satisfaction (*King John*, c. 1591). But,
according to his barons, this was one
coronation too many. Pembroke calls it
superfluous, telling the king that he was
crowned before, and that *high royalty
was ne'er pluck'd off*, while Salisbury is
poetically outspoken:

*Therefore, to be possess'd with double
    pomp,
To gild refined gold, to paint the lily,
To throw a perfume on the violet,
To smooth the ice, or add another hue
    Unto the rainbow...
Is wasteful and ridiculous excess.*

Not until the early twentieth century,
however, was the phrase *to paint the lily*
picked out as an idiom with the sense
'to apply unnecessary ornamentation,
to over-embellish'. But familiar texts
are usually only half-remembered and
before long Shakespeare's figure was
being misquoted as *to gild the lily*, an
error that has now been completely
absorbed into the language.

*The players of the LSO Chamber
Ensemble are so good that you wonder
why they feel the need **to gild the lily**
by inviting the violinist Sarah Chang to
join them.*
THE TIMES, 29 JUNE 2002

For other idioms from Shakespeare,
see WILLIAM SHAKESPEARE,
page 152.

gingerbread: to take the gilt
off the gingerbread
to strip something of its appeal

Cakes made with treacle and flavoured
with ginger and other spices were introduced to England from Europe in the
fifteenth century. Often a carved board
would be pressed into stiff dough to
mark the shape of a saint or animal in
the surface, or the cakes would be highly
coloured or even gilded – painted over
with egg white and then covered with
gold leaf. A recipe from Robert Mays'
The Accomplished Cook (1600) instructs
the reader to mould the gingerbread
dough *and roul it thin, then print it and dry
it in a stove, and guild it if you please*. The
cost of exotic ingredients meant that
such confections were originally enjoyed

only by the rich but, as these became more affordable, gaudy gingerbreads became a favourite treat at fairs: *Buy any gingerbread, gilt gingerbread*, cries Joan Trash, the gingerbread woman in Ben Jonson's play *Bartholomew Fayre* (1614).

The popularity of gingerbread lasted through the centuries, with the practice of gilding the sweetmeats profusely with gold leaf being particularly prevalent in the nineteenth century. Already, since the early seventeenth century, *gingerbread* had been used to denote 'something showy and superficial', probably because of its gaudy appearance, while to describe someone as *a knight or lord of gingerbread* was no more than ironic praise. The idiom *to take the gilt off the gingerbread* is rather more modern, dating from the early nineteenth century.

*She's not just an A-list celebrity. She's on a list all by herself…whatever the event, even if it's already stuffed with very famous people, Madonna is the one who turns heads. Madonna is the one who **puts the gilt on the gingerbread**.*
EVENING STANDARD,
21 MARCH 2000

*If the worst thing that can happen to the Government is some tactical voting **taking a sliver of gilt off its gingerbread**, something has gone very right in the past four years.*
THE INDEPENDENT, 6 JUNE 2001

gird: to gird (up) one's loins
to prepare oneself for action

Robes and loose clothing can be in the way when one needs to get down to hard physical work or exercise. The sensible thing to do is to tie them up out of the way with a belt. The phrase *to gird up one's loins* is a biblical one, occurring frequently in both the Old and New Testaments. God instructing the people of Israel about the preparations they

were to make for their deliverance from Egypt, for instance, told them to eat their Passover meal *with your loins girded, and shoes on your feet, and your staves in your hands* (Exodus 12:11, Tyndale's Old Testament translation, 1526) in complete readiness for the journey. In his letter to the Ephesians (6:14) St Paul urges his readers to be alert and ready to fight against worldly rulers of the darkness of this world *clothed in the whole armour of God, with your loins gird about with verity*.

*He will do more TV chat shows…and corporate gigs before **girding his loins** to begin taping another 100 editions of his day-time quiz show* Wipeout *next March.*
THE SUNDAY PEOPLE, 1 DECEMBER 2001

*Those who believed the intoxicating drama of the 2003 title run-in would never be repeated may have to eat their words as the Old Firm **gird their loins** for a scintillating climax to the 2004/05 campaign.*
DAILY MAIL, 4 MARCH 2005

For other idioms from the Bible, see page 317.

gloves: to handle/treat with kid gloves
to handle with utmost care

Stout gloves are often used to protect the hands while doing rough work, whereas gloves of the very best quality come from kidskin, the treated hide of a young goat. The leather is very fine and supple, hence the application to gentle handling. The idiom has been in use since the second half of the nineteenth century. An implication of the phrase today is that there is need for extra care because the person in question may be particularly prickly and unpredictable to deal with.

The logical stance now for his nearest rival…would be to open up a ferocious attack on him… But he has not hitherto

done so. Instead, he has **treated the front
runner with kid gloves***.*
THE DAILY TELEGRAPH,
6 FEBRUARY 2004

*While the United Nations, Western
Europe and the Israeli left* **treated him
with kid gloves***, their inability to confront
Mr. Arafat's evil is a sad moral lesson and
an exercise in hypocrisy.*
WASHINGTON TIMES,
10 NOVEMBER 2004

glutton for punishment, a
a person who takes on challenging or
unpleasant tasks no one else wants to
do, a person who overworks

The word *glutton* has been used figuratively since the early eighteenth century
to denote a person who is overly partial
to a particular object or activity. A *glutton of books* was common, a translation of
the Latin phrase *helluo librorum*, and,
from the end of the nineteenth century,
a *glutton for work* was also frequent.

In eighteenth-century boxing circles
a *glutton* was a fighter who could take a
lot of punishment. In *Tom Crib's
Memorial to Congress* (1819), a book
about boxing, Irish author Thomas
Moore tells his readers that *glutton...is
well known to be the classical phrase at
Moulsey-Hurst for one who, like Amycus,
takes a deal of punishment before he is satisfied.* (From the 1770s through to about
1810 Moulsey-Hurst was the location
of many bare-knuckle prize fights.)

A late-nineteenth century article in,
of all things, *The Licensed Victualler's
Mirror* (30 January 1891) tells of a
fighter who was known to be *an awfully
heavy hitter with both hands, a perfect
glutton at taking punishment.* It was not
until the second half of the twentieth
century that the phrase in its
contemporary form became the established choice.

Gluttons for punishment*, they even
walked on rest days, whereas we took the
train to Padua.*
EVENING STANDARD, 5 JUNE 2002

*Within half an hour they will be making
us lie on our ample stomachs in the mud
and wet of this South London park,
wrestling against one another. Never has
the phrase* '**gluttons for punishment**'
seemed so apt.
THE TIMES, 1 MAY 2004

*'The objective is to close the bridge between
the IRS and taxpayers,' Vivona said. 'We
are a sounding board for issues to work
back to the IRS.'*

*Given the way many taxpayers feel
about paying taxes, Vivona may sound like
a* **glutton for punishment***. But he says
taxpayers have good ideas on how to
improve the system.*
SARASOTA HERALD TRIBUNE,
24 MARCH 2005

For other boxing idioms, see
PACKING A PUNCH, page 45.

goat: to get someone's goat
to irritate, annoy someone

The phrase came into use in America
in the early years of the twentieth
century. Some say it originated in the
racing stable where it was common for
a highly strung racehorse to have a
goat as a stable companion. Goats were
considered to have a calming influence
on nervy thoroughbreds. Naturally
attempts would be made to sabotage a
horse's chance of success by stealing
the goat the night before a big race,
thus reducing the would-be champion
to a state of agitation. A more down-
to-earth explanation rests on the goat's
tendency to butt when provoked.

*There are many irritating things about the
BBC. But the thing that really* **gets my
goat** *at the moment is the way in which*

*Michael Buerk winds up the BBC's
10 o'clock news.*
THE DAILY TELEGRAPH,
14 MARCH 2002

*Another theatre myth that irritates her is
the idea that acting ability is genetically
transmitted. 'Nothing **gets my goat** more
than people saying it's in the blood. I won't
name all the children of great actors who
disprove it. What happens is that actors
have a more than averagely fun home life.
Different and interesting people come, so the
children think that's a good thing to do.'*
BIRMINGHAM POST, 9 MARCH 2005

going: heavy going
slow progress

See *to go while the* GOING *is good.*

*I am fussy about what I read and find that
some books are more **heavy going** than others.*
DAILY EXPRESS, 8 DECEMBER 2003

*If you find brown rice a bit **heavy going** at
first, cook half brown and half white until
you get used to it.*
DAILY MIRROR, 29 APRIL 2004

For other horsey idioms see page 319.

going: to go while the going is good
to leave or to begin a course of action
while the conditions are favourable

Televised horse racing often begins with
the commentator giving an assessment
of the course. *The going*, the condition of
the ground, may be *heavy* or *good*,
depending on how much rain there has
been. Similarly in the days before roads
had hard surfaces, the *going*, the ease of
travelling, would be commented upon.
Figuratively, therefore, *heavy going* means
'slow progress', while *to go while the going
is good* means 'to make a start while the
conditions for success are favourable'.
There is often the implication that

something unpleasant is about to happen, and so urgent action is needed.

*It might be thought that the shareholders
were getting out as quickly as was possible,
while the going was good.*
THE TIMES, 12 FEBRUARY 2004

*So goodbye, Tony Blair! Someone will clear
up your mess. Someone always does. Off you
go to the Lords – **while the going is good**!*
DAILY EXPRESS, 11 MAY 2004

For other horsey idioms, see page 319.

(little) goody-two-shoes
a smug, self-righteous person

A moralistic nursery tale, *The History of
Little Goody Two-Shoes* (1765), probably
written by Irish-born author Oliver
Goldsmith, is the source of the idiom.
It tells of a little girl, Goody, who had
only one shoe. When she was given a
pair of them one day, she was so
delighted that she went around showing them off to everybody and saying,
'Two shoes.'

*We can indulge, even celebrate the thuggish
activities of a Vinnie Jones on the football
field – and even pay him to write sneering
references to a '**goody two-shoes**' like
Gary Lineker, a world-class performer of
unblemished disciplinary record.*
THE INDEPENDENT, 26 JULY 2000

*Based on the novel by Gregory Maguire,
which re-imagines 'The Wizard of Oz',
it proves the old adage that it's not easy
being young, misunderstood and green –
especially with a **goody-two-shoes** such
as Glinda running around.*
TAMPA TRIBUNE, 19 MARCH 2005

For other idioms inspired by literary
characters, see MAN/*Girl Friday* and *to
grow like* TOPSY. For idioms drawn
from literature in general, see page 319.

goose: to cook someone's goose

to ruin someone's plans or chances of success

A favourite story connected with this phrase attributes it to King Eric XIV of Sweden whose reign began in 1560. According to an old chronicle: *The Kyng of Swedland coming to a towne of his ene-myes with very little company, his enemyes, to slyghte his forces, did hang out a goose for him to shoote, but perceiving before nyghte that these fewe soldiers had invaded and sette their chiefe houlds on fire, they demanded of him what his intent was, to whom he replyed, 'To cook your goose!'*

Unfortunately, no copy remains of the old chronicle to testify to the antiquity of the legend and the expression does not seem to have been current before the middle of the nineteenth century, when it was used in a street ballad objecting to the attempts of Pope Pius IX to revive the influence of the Catholic church in England by the appointment of Cardinal Wiseman:

> If they come here we'll cook their goose
> The Pope and Cardinal Wiseman.

Funk (1950) is not convinced by this explanation. He prefers the story recorded under *to kill the* GOOSE *that lays the golden eggs*, where the aspirations of the greedy peasant are frustrated: all he has left is a dead goose to cook. But perhaps the most straightforward theory is that proposed by Brewer (15th ed., 1995) who claims that the phrase is a reference to the early slaughter and consumption of a goose that was intended for a special occasion.

*Babbage finally **cooked his goose** when he visited Sir Robert Peel to plead for more help, and instead of adopting the modest tone of a supplicant, chose to lecture the Prime Minister about what the Government owed him.*
THE TIMES, 31 MAY 2000

goose: (to kill) the goose which lays the golden eggs

(to destroy) a source of profit (through greed)

In 1484 the printer William Caxton translated into English a fable by Aesop which tells the tale of a peasant who had the good fortune to own a goose that laid golden eggs. In his hurry to become rich he cut the goose open to have all the eggs at once, thus butchering his source of future wealth. The moral Aesop intended was that of being content with one's fortune and guarding against greed. It entered English as the expression *to kill the goose which lays the golden eggs*, meaning 'to make excessive demands on a source of profit, such that it is ruined'. An altered form, *the goose which lays the golden egg*, is also sometimes found and refers to 'a valuable source of income'.

Students are particularly at risk from religious cults, whose typical member is young, well educated and idealistic, says Ian Haworth. In its 1990 publication, Shining Like Stars, *the London Church of Christ describes campus ministry as '**the goose that laid the golden egg**'. In the first two weeks of the academic year, adherents recruiting for the group are advised to 'set personal goals of between 10 and 20 new acquaintances each day…' There is an openness to new relationships at university that will fade dramatically within the first two weeks, the book explains.*
THE TIMES EDUCATIONAL SUPPLEMENT, 14 APRIL 2000

*The danger is that the country will stifle him with the extent of its obsession with the new prince of sport. The answer is that it is up to all of us to give our phenomenon some space. To let him breathe. Not **to kill the goose that laid the golden egg**.*
DAILY MIRROR, 24 NOVEMBER 2003

For other idioms derived from fables, see page 318.

Gordian: to cut the Gordian knot

to solve an extremely complicated problem with prompt, decisive action

Though born a peasant, Gordius, through miraculous means, rose to become king of Phrygia in Asia Minor. Out of gratitude he built a shrine and dedicated his ox cart to Zeus, binding it to a pole with a huge knot of great complexity. An oracle foretold that whoever succeeded in untying the knot would become ruler over all Asia. Many years passed and the knotty puzzle remained unsolved until Alexander the Great came by and, hearing of the oracle's promise, severed the knot with his sword. Interest in the tale arose in the second half of the sixteenth century when *to cut, loose* or *untie the Gordian knot* was used figuratively to mean 'to solve a great difficulty with bold, decisive action'. The term *Gordian knot* also exists to denote 'a complex problem'.

When he became prime minister, Koizumi was supposed to be the clean-up kid who would ***cut through Japan's Gordian knot*** *of bureaucratic inertia and political torpor to bring about reform.*
THE GUARDIAN, 11 FEBRUARY 2002

Frustratingly, ***the Gordian knot*** *at the centre of Chinese society – the tension between the leadership's desire to create ever greater levels of economic growth without allowing the equally rapid development of personal freedoms – is never mentioned.*
SCOTLAND ON SUNDAY,
5 JANUARY 2003

Gordius, having no heir, adopted Midas as his son. For information on Midas, see *the* MIDAS *touch*, and for other idioms derived from ancient legends, see page 317.

grace: to fall from grace

to lose favour

This is a biblical reference, dating back to William Tyndale's translation of Galatians 5:4 in 1526. The apostle Paul is explaining that the only way to earn God's approval is to live by his grace. To attempt to do so by living under the Law, struggling to please God by one's own efforts, is impossible and results in placing oneself outside divine favour in a state of falling away from grace. More widely, Adam and Eve, the devil and sinning humanity have all removed themselves from favour by wilful disobedience. In recent times the phrase has been used in general contexts to describe those who have disgraced themselves and ruined their reputation.

But even in the BBC as it is currently run, is it appropriate that a man whose stock-in-trade on Have I Got News For You *is the belittlement of other famous names who have* ***fallen from grace*** *should seek the protection of the courts to shield his own behaviour from the public eye?*
DAILY MAIL, 10 JUNE 2002

For other idioms inspired by Tyndale's translations, see WILLIAM TYNDALE, page 270. For other idioms from the Bible, see page 317.

grapevine: (on/through) the grapevine

gossip, rumour; information spread through an informal network of contacts

What God hath wrought was the first ever telegraph message, sent from Washington to Baltimore by Samuel Morse on 24 May 1844 as a demonstration of his new invention to Congress. The telegraph was welcomed with great excitement and companies rushed to erect lines. Swift communication between far-flung communities was now possible. But rumour and gossip also have a way of spreading at speed, even if more circuitously. So, just a few years after Morse's demonstration, the term *grapevine telegraph* was coined, the comparison being between the direct telegraph wire and the twisted branches of the vine. During the American Civil War rumour abounded and the phrase was frequently used, ensuring its place in the language.

*I had the excitement of college to keep me occupied and although I still thought about Jason, I have to admit I recovered pretty quickly. I used to hear about him **through the grapevine**, but I was so wrapped up in my own world of new friends and college life that I didn't have the time to mope.*
GOOD HOUSEKEEPING, AUGUST 2001

See also BUSH *telegraph*.

gravy: the gravy train
a job that commands a good profit for little effort, a sinecure

Gravy is the sauce, the little 'something extra' that is poured over a meal. In American slang from the beginning of the twentieth century, *gravy* came to denote 'an unearned bonus', 'a tip', 'money easily come by'. By the 1920s the term *gravy train* was in use to mean 'an occupation that brings in generous remuneration for little effort'. This was possibly a coinage from the railway yard for an easy route that brought in the same pay for less work. One can *board* or *ride the gravy train*.

*The **gravy train** is over for Chris DiMarco, who realized Friday at the Sony Open he was going to have to play hard to earn his money.*
SOUTHERN ILLINOISAN,
18 JANUARY 2003

*MEPs have been accused of 'milking' the taxpayer-funded European '**gravy train**'. Last month an Austrian MEP exposed colleagues said to net thousands a year from allowances for parliamentary sessions they did not attend.*
DAILY MAIL, 6 MAY 2004

grease: to grease someone's palm
to offer a bribe

The Romans had a slippery term for a bribe. Pliny the Younger refers to such a sum as *unguentarium*, which translates as 'ointment-money'. The English idiom, however, refers to the application of grease to make something run smoothly. The notion of sliding a bribe unnoticed into someone's hand occurs in John Skelton's *Magnyfycence* (c. 1529), a morality play about the downfall and restoration of a generous prince, which has the following lines:

*Wyth golde and grotes they grese my hande
In stede of ryght that wronge may stande.*

Later writers speak of *greasing in the fist*, while the early nineteenth century sees the first references to the *greased palms* of the modern idiom.

*One of the letters Zucker translated deals with the need to buy Metternich an expensive present to **grease his palm**.*
THE TIMES, 21 MAY 2002

*'I still can't get one of those funky ringside seats near the dance floor.' The table he craves is on the inner ring of seats next to the mass of gyrating bodies, where there is a minimum spend of £1,000. As well as the astronomical bar bill, hopefuls must **grease the palm** of the management with another £3,000 to secure such a highly visible billet. Even then, they may be refused if there are more influential names in town.*
DAILY MAIL, 30 AUGUST 2004

Greek: it's (all) Greek to me

I don't understand what is being said, it's all nonsense (said when confronted with language, or ideas or concepts, that one cannot understand)

The idiom comes from Shakespeare's play *Julius Caesar* (1599). There are, in Rome, those who want to see ambitious Caesar crowned and those who love freedom and oppose the crowning. Cassius and Brutus, who are amongst the latter, ask Casca the reason for Caesar's crestfallen appearance. Casca tells how Caesar was offered a crown three times but three times refused because the common crowd was hostile to it. Cassius presses Casca for every detail and Casca answers to the best of his ability:

CASSIUS: *Did Cicero say anything?*
CASCA: *Ay, he spoke Greek.*
CASSIUS: *To what effect?*
CASCA: *Nay, an I tell you that, I'll ne'er look you i' th' face again. But those that understood him smil'd at one another, and shook their heads; but for mine own part, it was Greek to me.*

The remark *it was Greek to me* is both a statement of fact and a comment on the unintelligibility of what has been said. Not understanding Greek was a familiar problem in medieval times, when European scholars coming across Greek script would comment in Latin *Graecum est, non potest legi* ('It is Greek, it cannot be read'). There was a renewed study of Greek in the Renaissance, though a continuing unease with that language surfaced in English in a prose comedy which predated *Julius Caesar* by some thirty-three years. George Gascoigne's *Supposes* (1566) was a translation of *I Suppositi* (1509) by Italian poet and playwright Ludovico Ariosto and contained the comment, *The gear is Greek to me*.

Shakespeare certainly knew Gascoigne's play, for it was the inspiration for his own *Taming of the Shrew* (c. 1592). He was probably also aware that the Greeks themselves had run into linguistic difficulties. They had found Hebrew a bit of a challenge and had the idiom *It's Hebrew to me* to denote 'unintelligible speech'. Thus there is probably more to Casca's witty remark than is at first apparent.

In modern English *it's Greek to me* is used not only to denote 'unintelligible speech' or 'twaddle' but also 'incomprehensible concepts or ideas'.

Not being a fluent German speaker, Maw did an internet search to find out exactly what the phrase meant. The German–English translation website was not much help, coming up with a long list of possibilities. Right at the end is the translation that Maw has decided is most appropriate: 'It's all Greek to me.'
THE DAILY TELEGRAPH, 5 JULY 2001

Don't you know any Latin?
  It's all Greek to me.
  Aramaic?
  No thank you. I don't want to ruin my lunch.
  Alas, the entire film will be in Latin and Aramaic, with no subtitles.
THE GUARDIAN, 25 SEPTEMBER 2002

For other idioms from Shakespeare, see WILLIAM SHAKESPEARE, page 152.

green: the green-eyed monster

jealousy, envy

As early as the turn of the fourteenth century the pallor of a sickly or emotionally distressed person was identified as being *green*, this inspiring Shakespeare to describe jealousy as *green-eyed* in *The Merchant of Venice* (c. 1596) and as *the green-eyed monster* in *Othello* (1604). Jealousy is an emotion arising from rivalry: Othello believed that Cassio had stolen the affections of his wife, Desdemona, and was jealous. Recently *the green-eyed monster* has also come to denote 'envy', a related emotion, where a person resents the good fortune or possessions of another.

*Envy. **The green-eyed monster** is an ugly creature that can eat away at the soul of a person. Envying others for their ambition, character, recent promotion, company car or looks is pointless.*
THE GUARDIAN, 23 JULY 2001

*The doctor's hunch was confirmed: I was in premature ovarian failure. I remember walking out of his office and standing on a street corner, my head swimming. All of my dreams have just been stolen from me, I thought... A lot of my friends are having kids now, and dealing with **the green-eyed monster** is rough. I do everything I can to get out of baby showers.*
COSMOPOLITAN, 1 MARCH 2005

*Julia Roberts plays a woman who only realises she loves her best friend when he announces he is to marry someone else. **The green-eyed monster** strikes and she then does everything in her power to stop the big day from going ahead.*
DAILY RECORD, 4 MARCH 2005

See also *with a* JAUNDICED *eye*. For other idioms from Shakespeare, see WILLIAM SHAKESPEARE, page 152.

grin: to grin and bear it
to endure one's pain or difficulties without complaint

Sometimes there are problems for which there is no solution, where the only thing that can be done is to *grin and bear it*. This may sound like an exhortation to cheerfulness under pressure but, when the phrase was coined, a *grin* was understood to be not so much a smile as a grimace. Old English *grennian*, from which the verb *to grin* was

derived, meant 'to pull back the lips and show the teeth in pain or rage'.

The idiom evolved from an earlier eighteenth-century proverb *to grin and abide*, which Erasmus Darwin tells us was for those situations *where no help could be had in pain* (*Zoönomia*, 1794). Its current form dates from the beginning of the nineteenth century. The phrase lends itself to plays on words, as here:

T-shirts bearing cheesy wisecracks have always been a component of middle-class American fashion, but the messages are snarkier these days and the irreverent tops are selling fast among hip teens...shirts like 'Fast Girls Finish First,' and 'Grin and Bare It in St. Tropez' (Los Angeles Daily News, 15 September 2004).

*We don't **grin and bear** hard times like our parents did. We want answers.*
THE SUNDAY TIMES, 31 AUGUST 2003

*Muscle movement or twitching may also take place during the REM phase of sleep when dreams occur... This problem may be one that you'll just have **to grin and bear**.*
DAILY MIRROR, 8 JULY 2004

gum: up a gum tree
stuck in a difficult or embarrassing situation

The phrase is American in origin and dates from the early nineteenth century. It refers to an animal, such as a possum, that has been trapped in a gum tree by hunters. Even worse, it may find itself sticking to the tree, possibly at a vertiginous height, since many eucalyptus (the genus to which gum trees belong) grow to an immense height, one or two species exceeding even that of the Californian sequoia.

This phrase is common in Australian English, probably because gum trees are native there and account for more than two-thirds of the country's vegetation.

So it is hardly surprising that Australians can find themselves literally and idiomatically *up a gum tree*, as this parachutist did:

WOMAN UP A GUM TREE AFTER PARACHUTING FROM PLANE

A woman has parachuted out of a plane flying in Victoria's north-east and landed in a gum tree. Police say details of the incident are still sketchy, but the woman jumped from the plane flying over Euroa, 150 kilometres north-east of Melbourne, shortly before midday. She landed in a gum tree, where she was stuck about 12 metres from the ground. A police spokeswoman says a police helicopter has gone to the rescue (AAP General News, 25 July 2000).

At Heathrow last week thousands of Brits found themselves **up a gum tree**, *as British Airways, plagued by staff shortages and technical hitches, scrapped more than 100 flights to and from the airport.*
SCOTLAND ON SUNDAY,
29 AUGUST 2004

guns: going great guns

acting with great energy, achieving great success

The *great guns* of the idiom are, of course, cannons, which inspired a number of idiomatic phrases in the nineteenth century. Comparison between these large, mounted pieces and small portable firearms led to *great gun* being used to denote 'a distinguished person'. The roar of cannon was also likened to the sound of a violent gale so that the phrase *to blow great guns* became current as a weather idiom while, in America, *Great guns!* was an exclamation of astonishment. The phrase *going great guns* dates from the early twentieth century and alludes to the repeated firing of mighty cannon in battle.

Fleming came from Auchterarder House, where the restaurant had been **going great guns** *under Willie Deans.*
THE SUNDAY TIMES, 19 MAY 2002

Princess Michael's alleged recent remarks in a New York restaurant don't seem to have had any adverse effect on her daughter's relationship with her Indian boyfriend... 'Ella and Aatish are **going great guns**,' *says one friend.*
THE DAILY TELEGRAPH, 17 JUNE 2004

For other idioms drawn from the army and warfare, see page 317.

· H ·

hair: a/the hair of the dog
a tot of alcohol as a remedy for a
hangover

An ancient remedy recommended that,
whenever someone suffered a dog bite, a
hair from the offending animal should
be bound to the wound to help it to
heal and to offer protection against disease. A recipe book of 1670 repeats the
centuries-old advice: *Take a hair from the
dog that bit you, dry it, put it into the
wound, and it will heal it, be it never so sore.*
The cure was still deemed good in the
second half of the eighteenth century.
Robert Jones recommends it in *The
Treatment of Canine Madness* (1760): *The
hair of the dog that gave the wound is advised
as an application to the part injured.*
Procuring the important hair must have
been a tricky business at times.

During the sixteenth century this
same logic was applied to the hangover,
the sufferer being urged to drink the
next morning some of the same liquor
he had binged upon the previous night.
John Heywood quotes the advice in
Proverbs (1546). And it worked! Well, if
Samuel Pepys is to be believed, it did:
*Up among my workmen, my head akeing all
day from last night's debauch... At noon
dined with Sir W Batten and Pen, who
would needs have me drink two good drafts
of sack to-day, to cure me of my last night's
disease, which I thought strange but think I
find it true* (*Diary*, 3 April 1661). And a
contemporary of Pepys, William Lilly
(1602–81), famous for his astrological
predictions and yearly almanacs, put
the remedy into rhyme:

*If any so wise is that sack he despises,
Let him drink his small beer and be sober,
And while we drink and sing,
As if it were spring,
He shall droop like the trees in October.
But be sure, over night, if this dog you do
bite,
You take it henceforth for a warning,
Soon as out of your bed, to settle your
head,
With a hair of his tail in the morning.*

*I was just driving along looking for
somewhere, you know, somewhere to have
another drink, New Year's Day, **hair of
the dog** and all that...*
ZADIE SMITH, WHITE TEETH, 2000

*The last thing you may feel like on New
Year's Day is hauling yourself on to the
streets of London for a crazy carnival
atmosphere but the kids will probably be
desperate to witness an event that's dubbed
'the world's greatest parade'... It kicks off
at noon from Parliament Square via
Whitehall through to Piccadilly and takes
110 minutes, by which time you'll be ready
for **a hair of the dog**.*
EVENING STANDARD,
19 DECEMBER 2002

hair: not to turn a hair
to remain calm and unperturbed

Jane Austen had obviously listened to
many young men boasting about their
horses, for the earliest written record of
not to turn a hair is hers. In *Northanger
Abbey* (1798) John Thorpe is trying to
impress the heroine, Catherine, by

bragging about the speed at which his gig has covered the distance between Tetbury and Bath. Catherine's remark that the horse does indeed look very hot is swiftly brushed aside by Mr Thorpe: *Hot! he had not turned a hair till we came to Walcot church.* Even Catherine's untutored eye had noticed a roughening of the animal's coat, which happens when a horse perspires through agitation or exertion. A horse that shows no sign of discomfort does not *turn a hair* but remains sleek. The expression stayed within the horse world until the twentieth century when it began to be used to describe people who remain calm in times of stress.

The unexpected humidity of a sodden, Yorkshire July put paid to one of Lars-Ulrik Mortensen's harpsichord strings, which exploded with an almighty crack during a furious passage from the A major harpsichord concerto. **He didn't turn a hair**.
THE GUARDIAN, 14 JULY 2000

*...some people can get up at 6am, see their children off to school, commute to work, come home at 6pm and fix supper, supervise homework, organise the school fête and attempt intelligent conversation with their partner **without turning a hair**, while others are left on their knees.*
GOOD HOUSEKEEPING,
SEPTEMBER 2002

For other horsey idioms see page 319.

hair: to let one's hair down
to lose one's inhibitions

In the mid-nineteenth century, when this expression was coined, ladies appeared in public with their long hair dressed. Not until they retired to their bedrooms did they unpin it and allow it to fall free. Indeed, the original phrase was *to let one's back hair down*. Of course, only those on intimate terms with a

lady entered her private chamber and so the idiom meant 'to put reserve aside' or even 'to exchange confidentialities': *Helen and I have just had a grand heart-to-heart talk; we've undone our back hair* (Noel Coward, *The Vortex*, 1925).

Since the second half of the twentieth century the phrase has lost its 'confiding' sense and has come to mean 'to lose one's inhibitions', 'to relax and enjoy oneself', possibly to the extent of behaving outrageously.

They wear their party hats all night – to the bitter end. And they say, 'It's nice **to let your hair down***, isn't it?', forgetting that they have no hair.*
DAILY MAIL, 9 JANUARY 2002

Everyone knows that you have **to let your hair down** *at frequent intervals, and that if you do not, you will harm your health and emotional well-being most terribly.*
THE DAILY TELEGRAPH, 16 MARCH 2004

halcyon days
idyllic times of happiness and tranquillity

Greek *alkuōn* was a fabled bird identified as the kingfisher. The word is said to be a compound of *háls*, 'sea', and *kúōn*, 'conceiving' and reflects the ancient Greek belief that kingfishers built nests for rearing their young on the sea. Greek mythology tells of the goddess Alcyone who, beside herself with grief when her husband was drowned in a shipwreck, cast herself into the sea. The gods, moved by her devotion, brought him back to life, changing both Alcyone and her husband into kingfishers. Alcyone yearly built her nest on the sea where her father, Aeolus, the god of the winds, restrained the gales and ensured that, whenever Alcyone was brooding on her nest, the sea would be calm and no storm would arise. According to legend, kingfishers bred on the seven days before and the seven days after the winter solstice. These were *alkuonídes emérai*, 'halcyon' or 'kingfisher days', guaranteed to be calm and fair. The phrase has alluded to 'times of peace and tranquillity' since the first half of the sixteenth century. Given its rather literary character, it has been a favourite with poets. As an example, this extract is taken from Walt Whitman's *Leaves of Grass* (1891 version):

As the days take on a mellower light,
And the apple at last hangs really finish'd
and indolent-ripe on the tree,
Then for the teeming quietest, happiest
days of all!
The brooding and blissful halcyon days.

*Holidays depress me… This was not always the case. For a **halcyon period** between infancy and the age of 25, say, the idea of lounging around without a purpose was my idea of bliss.*
THE DAILY TELEGRAPH, 23 AUGUST 2003

*In those **halcyon days** of unbridled optimism when I dared to dream, I imagined myself as a cricket commentator on the radio.*
SOUTH WALES ECHO, 2 JUNE 2005

For other idioms derived from ancient legends, see page 317.

hammer: to go at/for it
hammer and tongs
to take part in an activity with great zeal, to fight or quarrel

The phrase dates from around the turn of the eighteenth century and alludes to the blacksmith who, having taken hot metal from his forge with tongs, proceeds to shape it vigorously with his hammer.

*At this point there is usually a fight or two. Last weekend's was terrific. I was there. Two married couples were **going at it hammer and tongs**.*
THE SPECTATOR, 2 JUNE 2002

*At first, Ayers **went for the rock 'n' roll lifestyle hammer and tongs**. 'I was completely drunk with the whole thing. Girls lining up outside the door, free drink everywhere.' But he soon tired of it.*
THE GUARDIAN, 4 JULY 2003

For another idiom from the forge, see *to have too many* IRONS *in the fire*.

hand over fist
rapidly, in large quantities

This idiom originated in the eighteenth century as the nautical phrase *hand over hand*. It described the vigorous action of sailors hauling in or climbing up a rope on board ship. During the first half of the nineteenth century *hand over hand* also began to denote 'rapid advancement' of one ship upon another. The variant *hand over fist*, which dates from the first half of the nineteenth century, is probably of American origin. Certainly its figurative application to 'rapid progress' in general and to the 'swift acquisition or loss of money' in particular is first found in American texts. Seba Smith in *Major Jack Downing* (1833) has: *They…clawed the money off his table, hand over fist*, while Mary Boykin Chesnut, wife of a senator from South Carolina, writes: *Fitzhugh Lee and Roony are being promoted hand over fist* (*A Diary from Dixie*, 1861, published 1949).

Since the mid-twentieth century the phrase has been used in progressively wider contexts, such as rapidly losing votes in an election, points in a sporting contest and market share in fashion designing.

*Because it's so hard to find a job that pays a decent wage, colleges that offer conversion courses for law are making money **hand over fist** from a surge in applications from graduates who think*

they'd better get a law qualification to see them through the dark days ahead...
THE DAILY TELEGRAPH,
6 DECEMBER 2003

*The good news for Sen. John Kerry is that many national polls have shown him gaining traction for the first time in months and narrowing the gap by which he trails President George W Bush. But the bad news for the senator from Massachusetts is that polls in key battleground states show him losing ground **hand over fist** to the president, and those are the polls that look like counting in the end.*
UNITED PRESS INTERNATIONAL,
28 SEPTEMBER 2004

For other nautical idioms, see A LIFE ON THE OCEAN WAVES, page 24.

hand: living (from) hand to mouth

an existence in which resources are used up out of necessity as soon as they are come by

The phrase dates from the sixteenth century when the problem of vagabondage and poverty became urgent following the collapse of the feudal system, the rise in population, the enclosure of agricultural land for raising sheep and the reduction in numbers of retainers after the long foreign and civil wars of the previous century. The poor were described as living *from hand to mouth*. This was a literal phrase as their hunger was such that they were forced to consume the alms put into their hands immediately, with no thought for the next day. The sense today is not of immediate hunger alleviation but of a lack of provision for the future, either from the necessity of a low income or from lack of foresight.

The Wordsworths had themselves invested £20,000 in the voyage of the Abergavenny, a staggering sum for a

*family still **living more or less from hand to mouth** in a tiny Cumbrian cottage with two bedrooms, stone floors, smoking chimneys and sheets of newspaper pasted on the walls.*
THE DAILY TELEGRAPH,
14 SEPTEMBER 2002

*It seems just yesterday that bars were filled with thirty somethings fantasising about spending the vast equity we suddenly had in bricks and mortar. This fantasy cash has vanished. It was never real anyway. It just hid the ugly truth that most of us **live from hand to mouth**. That 24 per cent of all British adults are sick with anxiety at not having saved for retirement.*
THE MAIL ON SUNDAY, 31 AUGUST 2003

hands: to win hands down

to win with great ease

Towards the end of a horse race a jockey certain of victory will drop his hands and relax his grip on the reins. *To win hands down* has been used in racing and then more generally to denote 'an easy victory' since at least the second half of the nineteenth century.

*In legal terms, Parkinson could sue against Sara's allegations and **win hands down**.*
THE SPECTATOR, 19 JANUARY 2002

If awards were being given, The Grapes of Wrath *would **win hands down** as the most spectacular production ever mounted at Syracuse Stage. And one of the finest-acted.*
SYRACUSE POST-STANDARD,
29 MARCH 2005

For other horsey idioms see page 319.

hang: to hang fire

to hesitate, to delay (usually over a matter of some urgency)

This is an expression from the use of firearms in the days when soldiers and sportsmen relied upon a charge of loose gunpowder. If the loaded powder were of inferior quality or had become damp, it might be slow to ignite and the gun was said *to hang fire*. Sorting out the problem was a hazardous business, given the volatility of gunpowder. The phrase has been in figurative use since around the turn of the nineteenth century and refers to a hesitation in taking decisive action, often on a matter of urgency.

The banks could in theory force [the company] into bankruptcy, but are likely **to hang fire** *in the hope of getting back more cash.*
DAILY MAIL, 28 JUNE 2002

The bargain holidays websites aren't showing any cut-price deals for July and August yet...so it might be best **to hang fire** *for a couple of months.*
THE MAIL ON SUNDAY, 7 MARCH 2004

For more details on flintlock guns see *a* FLASH *in the pan*. For other idioms derived from the army and warfare, see page 317.

happy hunting ground(s)
death, heaven; a place abounding in the things one treasures or is seeking

The early Native Americans believed that, after death, the souls of brave hunters and skilful warriors would inhabit the *happy hunting grounds*, a place teeming with game where they could enjoy plentiful hunting and feasting. This view of the afterlife, together with a belief in the Great Spirit, was probably influenced by Christian teaching on God and heaven.

First references to the *happy hunting grounds* are found in the work of American novelist James Fenimore Cooper who, in the first half of the nineteenth century, wrote about the frontier wilderness and advancing white civilisation. The idiom is apparently a translation of the native expression, though there is some doubt in general about the authenticity of Cooper's native phrases. By the late nineteenth century the phrase was being used euphemistically to mean 'death' and had also come to denote 'a place abundant in the things one is seeking' this side of the grave. In the present day the idiom, now usually in the singular, is a favourite of sports journalists who describe every venue where a player has enjoyed previous successes as *a happy hunting ground*.

Palm Springs is where corporate Californians come to die, **the happy hunting ground** *of the golden state.*
THE GUARDIAN, 8 APRIL 2001

The events of August 31 1997 have become **a happy hunting ground** *for conspiracy theorists.*
THE GUARDIAN, 24 OCTOBER 2003

Europe has proved **a happy hunting ground** *for Michael Owen. The Liverpool striker is hoping that his happy knack of scoring on foreign fields continues in Sofia tonight to help him come through a disturbing slump in form.*
THE DAILY TELEGRAPH, 3 MARCH 2004

hard and fast
said of an inflexible rule or requirement; rigorous, very clear

The phrase is tautological since both *hard* and *fast* mean 'firmly, securely'. According to Admiral William Smyth, *hard and fast* is said of a ship on shore (*Sailor's Word-Book: An alphabetical digest of nautical terms*, 1867). A vessel that has run aground or has been hauled clear of the water is immovable. In the second half of the nineteenth century the sailors' phrase was taken inland and applied to a rigidly inflexible rule that demanded strict adherence.

*There are no **hard-and-fast rules** about replacing the grip tape on racket handles, but if you feel your hand sliding as you swing, the time is probably right.*
THE TIMES, 26 JUNE 2004

*Candidate Art Goes says he had been leaning toward looking at the guide as a **hard-and-fast** document but since has learned from village officials that it legally cannot be looked upon that way.*
ARLINGTON HEIGHTS DAILY HERALD,
18 FEBRUARY 2005

For other nautical idioms, see A LIFE ON THE OCEAN WAVES, page 24.

hare: to run with the hare and hunt with the hounds

to try to keep in with both sides over an issue

This hunting metaphor has been current since the fifteenth century: *Thou hast a crokyd tunge .heldyng with hownd and with hare* (Unknown, *Jacob's Well*, c. 1440). John Heywood, in his book of proverbs (1546), has *holde with the hare and run with the hounde,* adding *fire in the tone hand, and water in the tother* to emphasise the notion of playing a double part. The current form of the idiom dates back to at least the second half of the nineteenth century.

*Ivan is a keen fox-hunter. Labour is the party that will ban fox-hunting... In choosing **to run with the hare**, Ivan is destined never **to run with his beloved hounds**.*
THE GUARDIAN, 3 AUGUST 2000

*Poor old Archbishop Williams, criticised on all sides; but if you will **try to run with the hare and hunt with the hounds** you always end up with a badly bitten bum!*
THE INDEPENDENT, 20 OCTOBER 2003

hat: at the drop of a hat

immediately, without hesitation or the need of persuasion

This is an American expression dating back to at least the 1850s. Its origin is obscure but a plausible suggestion is that it arose from the common custom in the West of dropping a hat to signal that a contest, in particular a fighting bout, should begin.

*'Doing well in my career had also been a factor. I've been the BBC's royal correspondent for 11 years and I know I can go on television **at the drop of a hat** and talk about almost anything to do with the royal family. It's a different level of assurance and it certainly gives me a boost.'*
JENNI BOND INTERVIEWED IN GOOD HOUSEKEEPING, SEPTEMBER 2001

*He lay so still that Aldred thought he must be praying. Either that or he was the kind of person who could fall asleep **at the drop of a hat**.*
MICK JACKSON, FIVE BOYS, 2001

hat: to throw one's hat in the ring

to issue a challenge; to proclaim one's candidacy

> *Throw in his hat, and with a spring*
> *Get gallantly within the ring.*
> (John Hamilton Reynolds,
>   *The Fancy*, 1820)

In the early nineteenth century anyone wanting to challenge a boxer to a bare knuckle fight would throw his hat into the ring. This would ensure he attracted attention amongst the ringside hubbub. The phrase was later generally applied to contests of a different kind and, more particularly, to political candidacy. In a newspaper interview at Cleveland, Ohio on 21 February 1912, Theodore Roosevelt was metaphorically stripped for action, declaring: *My hat's in the ring. The fight is on and I'm stripped to the buff.* The political application remains the most common today.

*The ruling Wednesday is likely to propel the smooth-talking, sharp-minded Mr. Strauss-Kahn back into the political arena at a time when he can help Mr. Jospin in his bid for the presidency, if Mr. Jospin should, as widely expected, **throw his hat in the ring**.*
INTERNATIONAL HERALD TRIBUNE,
8 NOVEMBER 20011

*If Alison Reed, formerly of Marks & Spencer, is seen as good enough for Standard Life, then Hughes could presumably **throw his hat in the ring** at William Morrison, Boots or Rentokil which are all on the lookout for bright new talent.*
DAILY MAIL, 7 APRIL 2005

For other boxing idioms, see
PACKING A PUNCH, page 45.

havoc: to play/wreak havoc
to devastate, destroy, spoil

Havoc was borrowed from the Old French *havot*, meaning 'plunder'. From medieval times the shout of *havoc* was an order, a war cry, a signal for pillage and the seizure of spoil to begin. There are several references to *havoc* in Shakespeare's plays. In *Henry IV Part I* we hear of *pellmell, havoc and confusion*, and in *Julius Caesar* come the lines:

> *Caesar's spirit, ranging for revenge,*
> *With Ate by his side come hot from hell,*
> *Shall in these confines with a monarch's*
> *voice*
> *Cry, 'Havoc!' And let slip the dogs of war.*

By the late fifteenth century the early sense of 'plunder' was gradually widening to mean 'devastation' and later 'disorder, disarray'. The phrase *to make havoc* became common and by the early twentieth century *to play havoc* was in

use, a variant that is still current. *To wreak havoc* also dates from the early twentieth century, *wreak* being an Old English verb meaning 'to give vent to, to carry out by way of punishment or revenge'. One can *wreak resentment, vengeance, punishment, wrath* or, more recently, *havoc*.

*Pouring with rain all day. Turn up for my last appointment – to put a very nice bungalow on the market – looking as though I have entered a wet T-shirt competition. Little old dear invites me in for sweet tea and biscuits in front of the fire to get dry... Must stop this additional eating, **playing havoc** with my waistline.*
THE SUNDAY TELEGRAPH,
9 SEPTEMBER 2001

*Living outside London not only affects work but can **wreak havoc** on any social life. Spontaneous socialising after work is often not an option and forward-planning is a necessary part of an evening's preparation.*
THE GUARDIAN, 24 SEPTEMBER 2001

*The state lost only $1.1 billion in taxes through this exemption in 2001... But if the exemption is eliminated, it will **wreak havoc** on the farm economy and on rural Texas.*
SOUTHWEST FARM PRESS,
16 JANUARY 2003

For other idioms derived from the army and warfare, see page 317.

haywire: to go haywire
to go wrong, to be out of order, to go completely out of control; (of a person) to become erratic, disturbed

The phrase originated in the early twentieth century in America where haywire, it seems, is used to mend anything from machines to fences. One American authority claims that the properties of lazy farmers who cannot be bothered with permanent repairs are

William Shakespeare (1564–1616)

The works of William Shakespeare have had an immense influence on English. During the sixteenth century there was a flowering of the language: the stock of English vocabulary was dramatically increased with borrowings from Latin and Greek, the revival of Old English words that had fallen into disuse and the adoption of new terms introduced from travel in the new world. Shakespeare's works are packed with words and phrases that had only recently come into modern English. What is more, Shakespeare himself played with the language; using the noun *petition* as a verb, for instance, or adding prefixes and suffixes to create *marketable*, *reword* and *misquote*. But Shakespeare is best recognised for his ability to create memorable phrases that have since been plucked from his plays to give English a store of vivid idiomatic expressions.

One authority lists ninety phrases coming from Shakespeare's work. That is, ninety *phrases*, not ninety quotations, of which we could all probably recognise hundreds. One such is Hamlet's *to shuffle off this mortal coil* (1604) meaning 'to die'. *Coil* at that time meant 'bustle' or 'turmoil'. The same speech also yields *there's the rub*, still used today with the sense 'there's the drawback'. *A rub* was a bowling term used for anything that impeded a bowl's intended progress on the green. Figuratively it had come to mean 'an obstacle or hindrance' by the late sixteenth century. By using it in Hamlet's soliloquy, Shakespeare ensured its survival.

Sport has always been a prolific source of idiom (see PACKING A PUNCH, page 45, and IT'S NOT CRICKET!, page 250). Besides bowling, Shakespeare also looked to falconry. The phrases *pride of place*, 'a pre-eminent position', and *at one fell swoop*, 'suddenly, at a stroke', are both from *Macbeth* (1606). *Place* was the falconer's term to describe the peak of a bird's ascent before it suddenly and dramatically swooped down upon its prey.

How often have we referred to something we are thinking about as being *in our mind's eye*? We are back to Hamlet again, who saw his dead father thus. He later encountered his father's ghost, this time *with bated breath*. This phrase, used earlier by Shakespeare in *The Merchant of Venice* (1596), now commonly expresses shock, terror or suspense.

BRAVE *new world*, *there is a* METHOD *in one's madness*, *to* LAY *it on with a trowel*, *a* SEA *change* were all coined by Shakespeare. But Shakespeare was writing for the people, in everyday language, and his plays are also full of existing colloquialisms. For instance, *out of joint*, meaning 'out of order', had been in use for at least two hundred years before Shakespeare used it in *Hamlet*. Sometimes, however, he took a current phrase and slightly reworked it to make it his own. *To* EAT *someone out of house and home*, *to wear one's heart on one's* SLEEVE and *thereby hangs a* TALE are examples of this, and there are many others. It is telling that Shakespeare's reworking of a phrase always supersedes the original version.

See also *to* GILD *the lily*, *it's all* GREEK *to me*, *the* GREEN-*eyed monster*, HOIST *with one's own petard*, *in the* PINK, *a* POUND *of flesh*, SALAD *days*, *to be made of* STERNER *stuff*, *the* WHEEL *has come full circle*.

---

virtually held together with the stuff. Haywire rusts quickly and the result is an untidy and chaotic mess. Such a place would be referred to as having *gone haywire* or as *a haywire outfit*.

Another American authority bases his interpretation on the real purpose of haywire, which is to bind up bales of hay. Haywire is thin and easily bendable but it is also very strong, requiring cutters to break it. Once the tight wires wound around a bale have been snipped, however, they spring apart and writhe wildly and dangerously in the air, totally out of control.

A third American source says the notion of general disorder and confusion alludes to the tangled mass of wire that is heaped in a corner of the yard once it has been cut off the bales.

*Under the Action Plan what had started as a process of simplification had **gone haywire**.*
THE TIMES EDUCATIONAL
SUPPLEMENT, 20 OCTOBER 2000

*That's the definition of a pro – how well you can do your job when all these other things in your life are **going haywire**.*
CINCINNATI POST, 14 FEBRUARY 2001

head: to hide/bury one's head in the sand
to ignore a difficulty, to pretend a problem does not exist

The allusion is to the ostrich, which is fabled to hide its head in the sand at the first sign of danger. The ostrich, in fact, does no such thing, but if the hen senses danger while she is sitting on her eggs she will stretch her long neck against the ground the better to blend in with her surroundings. Troubled folk in denial have been compared with the ostrich since the first half of the nineteenth century. Originally the ostrich featured somewhere in the comparison: *The ostrich-habit of burying their heads in the ground before anything they don't like* (F L Olmstead, *A Journey through the Seaboard Slave States*, 1856), but nowadays it rarely puts in an appearance.

Decommissioning is meaningless and Bruce Anderson well knows it. The IRA could re-arm tomorrow. All you really want is a surrender. You'll never get it. Face up to it, grasp the peace that exists today. Do it with both hands and do it with your eyes wide open. Gosh, we all get so sick and

*tired of you people **putting your head in the sand**! Wise up!*
THE SPECTATOR, 30 JUNE 2001

*A storm is brewing over Lancashire County Council plans to reduce the provision of care for elderly residents in the area…'This situation has not been arrived at overnight but has been the product of Labour's **head-in-the-sand** policies over the years which came in for severe criticism by the Social Services Inspectorate.'*
LIVERPOOL ECHO, 15 AUGUST 2002

For other myths derived from fabled animal behaviour, see page 318.

health: a clean bill of health
an assurance, after close scrutiny, that there are no irregularities – financial, moral, etc

In the seventeenth century, ships wishing to traffic in a port, particularly in southern Europe, needed *a bill of health* stating that the port of departure was clear of plague. The diarist John Evelyn, sailing to Italy from Cannes in October 1644, wrote: *…we agreed with a seaman to carry us to Genoa, and, having procured a bill of health (without which there is not admission at any town in Italy), we embarked on the 12th.*

By the late eighteenth century *a bill of health* was routinely required amongst a ship's papers. A 'foul' or 'unclean' bill confirmed the presence of contagious disease in port or on board the vessel at the time of its departure, a 'suspected' bill warned of a possible outbreak of infection and a 'clean' bill declared the port and vessel healthy. Figurative use of the phrase *clean bill of health* to mean that a person or institution has passed careful scrutiny dates from the mid-nineteenth century.

The BBC has finally given a broadcast slot for the much-touted Panorama *investigation entitled* The Corruption of

*Racing... It would seem a fair bet that with a title such as that the six-month investigation is not going to report **a clean bill of health** for the racing game!*
THE SCOTSMAN, 21 SEPTEMBER 2002

heaven: in seventh heaven
in ecstasy, in sheer delight

Early cosmography divided the skies up into seven spheres which corresponded to the orbits of the seven planets. The ancient Jews and Muslims believed these realms to be seven heavens (seven is widely believed to be symbolically the perfect number). The dead were judged according to how they had lived on earth and were sent to the appropriate level of reward. The highest was the *seventh heaven* where God himself dwelt surrounded by his most glorious angels. The soul entering the *seventh heaven* experienced unsurpassable bliss. The concept was turned into an idiomatic phrase in the first quarter of the nineteenth century.

*I am close to **seventh heaven**. I've done the beach holiday bit so necessary at this time of year, by visiting Langkawi in Malaysia but, lovely as that island is, there's nothing quite like the Swiss Alps.*
DAILY MIRROR, 27 MARCH 2004

*Rod Stewart seems **in seventh heaven** as fiancée Penny Lancaster whispers to him. Could it be the thought that Penny, 34, is set to make him a dad for the seventh time...*
DAILY MIRROR, 30 MAY 2005

heels: to cool one's heels
to be kept waiting

A brisk walk heats the feet; standing about cools them. The idiom has been in use since the early seventeenth century. Indeed, in George Chapman's acclaimed translations of the *Iliad* (1611), hard-ridden horses *lay down and cool'd their hoofs*.

*If there's something the director does not like, changes can be made on the spot – not in the recording studio with a swearing director chain-smoking in the background and a 60-piece orchestra expensively **cooling its heels** waiting for rewritten (probably handwritten) parts.*
THE GUARDIAN, 10 JUNE 2003

hell: until/till hell freezes over
a time in the unforeseeably distant future

The Christian view of hell is of a consuming fire for all eternity. There is no likelihood at all of its freezing over, so this phrase indicates graphically an impossibly long time in the future. It dates from the early twentieth century.

*Thompson seems intent on seeing **hell freeze over** before he ups sticks and moves his club to a new purpose-built shared stadium.*
THE SCOTSMAN, 11 APRIL 2004

*'For better or worse, I love this place and the people in it,' [Dan Rather] says in an interview. 'I am loyal to it, without apology. I like everybody here, and I mean everybody. Even the ones who don't think much of me... I'll stand with them **till hell freezes over**, then cut through the ice.'*
PHILADELPHIA INQUIRER,
5 MARCH 2005

high: to be left high and dry
to be stranded; to be left out of things, to be left in a difficult situation

This is a nautical phrase recorded from the early nineteenth century to describe a vessel that is left grounded when the tide goes out, or one that has been hauled into a dry-dock. Figurative application dates from the second half of the nineteenth century.

*However, the EOC is very concerned that, as more and more final salary pension schemes close to new entrants, a growing number of women will be **left high and dry** when their husbands die.*
THE DAILY TELEGRAPH, 10 MARCH 2004

*The disaster has left Mr Singh, a skilled painter…**high and dry** without a job and owed up to £1,700 wages. He said: 'I have been left with nothing.'*
BIRMINGHAM EVENING MAIL,
17 MARCH 2005

For other nautical idioms, see A LIFE ON THE OCEAN WAVES, page 24.

high jinks
high-spirited behaviour, boisterous fun and games, horseplay

The phrase, of Scottish origin, goes back to at least the seventeenth century. *High jinks* were assorted drinking games. One version consisted of throwing dice to see who among the assembled company should drink a large bowl of liquor and who should then pay for it. A passage from Sir Walter Scott suggests a game of forfeits:

The frolicsome company had begun to practise the ancient and now forgotten pastime of high jinks. This game was played in several different ways. Most frequently the dice were thrown by the company, and those upon whom the lot fell were obliged to assume and maintain for a certain time a certain fictitious character, or to repeat a certain number of fescennine verses in a particular order. If they departed from the characters assigned, or if their memory proved treacherous in the repetition, they incurred forfeits, which were compounded for by swallowing an additional bumper, or by paying a small sum toward the reckoning (Guy Mannering, 1815).

In the nineteenth century the phrase was popular amongst boarding-school and university students where it described high spirited behaviour and jolly japes, an era that has sadly quite recently drawn to a close: *One of the most unremarked social changes of the last 20 years has been the ending of the high jinks that have been an inevitable concomitant of English university life for the last several hundred years* (The Spectator, 8 March 2003).

Be that as it may, the idiom is alive and well and should remain so, at least as long as Britain's youth continues to indulge in binge drinking: *Foreign players who have spent time in the UK tell of their shock at British heavy drinking culture and the national celebration of 'laddishness'. Few overseas players are involved in any of their British counterparts' alcohol-fuelled high jinks* (The Guardian, 12 October 2003).

*Return to the London Oratory School will be a welcome relief for Euan Blair following his ignominious encounter with the law, and his nocturnal **high jinks** in an Italian hotel.*
THE TIMES EDUCATIONAL
SUPPLEMENT, 15 SEPTEMBER 2000

Hobson's choice
no alternative, no choice at all

Thomas Hobson (1544–1631) ran a livery stable in Cambridge. Customers were never permitted to choose their own mount but were obliged to take *Hobson's choice*, which was always the horse nearest the stable door. As Hobson moved his horses round in rotation, he was thus able to ensure that every horse was worked fairly and that no animal was ridden too often.

Hobson was also a carrier for Cambridge University, his regular coach service between London and the colleges carrying letters, students and guests for over sixty years. Indeed, it was rumoured that his death at the age of eighty-six was premature and that he would have lived much longer if his carrying activities had not been curtailed because of an outbreak of the plague in London. Inaction caused his death, as Milton points out in one of two humorous epitaphs:

Here lieth one who did most truly prove,
That he could never die while he could move,
So hung his destiny never to rot
While he might still jogg on, and keep
his trot…
His Letters are deliver'd all and gon,
Onely remains this superscription.

Milton was a student at Christ's College, Cambridge at the time of Hobson's death in 1631. Hobson's name survives not only in the expression *Hobson's choice* (first found in print some 130 years later) but in a street named after him in old Cambridge.

The iPaq's success means we could be left
*with a **Hobson's choice** of any device you*
want, so long as it runs Windows. This is
not attractive for users, who want
competition and innovation…
IT WEEK, 1 OCTOBER 2001

hog: to go the whole hog

to do something thoroughly, to go all the way

There is some uncertainty as to whether this phrase was coined in England or America, although the earliest examples so far discovered date from the late 1820s and Andrew Jackson's presidential campaign. Two nearly contemporary sources – Fanny Trollope in *The Domestic Manners of the Americans* (1832) and Frederick Marryat in *Japhet, in Search of a Father* (1836) – both refer to it as an American expression. There are also various speculative theories as to its origin.

The OED acknowledges this uncertainty but comes down in favour of a poem by William Cowper, who enjoyed popularity on both sides of the Atlantic. In *The Love of the World Reproved: or*

Hypocrisy Detected (1779) the poet discusses the strictures Muslims placed upon the eating of pork. Mohammed prohibited his followers from eating certain parts of a pig but was singularly unclear about what these were. Muslims were wont to interpret his decree according to their own personal taste so that, between them, the *whole hog* was devoured:

Had he the sinful part express'd,
They might with safety eat the rest;
But for one piece they thought it hard
From the whole hog to be debar'd;
And set their wit at work to find
What joint the prophet had in mind.
Much controversy straight arose,
These choose the back, the belly those;
By some 'tis confidently said
He meant not to forbid the head;
While others at that doctrine rail,
And piously prefer the tail.
Thus, conscience free from every clog,
Mahometans eat up the hog.
Each thinks his neighbour makes too free,
Yet likes a slice as well as he:
With sophistry their sauce they sweeten,
Till quite from tail to snout 'tis eaten.

On a totally different note, dictionaries of thieves' cant and street language from the late seventeenth century onwards record *hog* as meaning 'a shilling' and *half a hog* as 'sixpence'. Thus *to go the whole hog* might have indicated a willingness to spend the entire sum.

Finally, there is the home-spun domestic suggestion gleaned from information in Thomas Hamilton's *Men and Manners in America* (1833), and repeated in an issue of *Household Words* (July 1852), a weekly journal edited by Charles Dickens. This tells of butchers in Virginia who, when they slaughtered a pig, would ask their customers whether they wanted *to go the whole hog* at a lower price or buy only prime cuts more expensively.

Many Labour MPs will make clear they are not interested in a compromise plan and urge Mr Blair to **go the whole hog**.
THE TIMES, 28 FEBRUARY 2002

He then turned on pub chain JD Wetherspoon's, one of whose bar staff said they'd like smoking banned. 'For crying out loud, this is the pub chain that banned music. So now they want to ban smoking. Hey, why not **go the whole hog**, ban alcohol and then you can have tone deaf, teetotal, non-smoking dullards, drinking orange squash, chatting the livelong day about whatever such people care to talk about.'
'Accountancy, I should wager.' Ouch.
NEWCASTLE EVENING CHRONICLE,
25 NOVEMBER 2004

For other idioms drawn from literature, see page 319.

hoist with one's own petard
caught out by one's own device or scheme

A *petard* was a small bomb used from the late sixteenth century to blow up castle gates or to breach a fortification. It consisted of a heavy metal bell-shaped pot filled with gunpowder. A tunnel would be dug up to the gate and hardy (or foolhardy) soldiers would risk life and limb to clamp the device in place and light the fuse.

The word *petard* was borrowed from the French who derived it from the verb *péter* meaning 'to break wind' (from *pet*, 'a fart', from Latin *peditum*, from *pedere*, 'to break wind'). However, the etymological origins of *petard* belie the power of the bomb which, correctly fitted, was more than capable of tearing mighty walls asunder. Sadly these explosive devices were crudely made and sometimes went off prematurely, blowing up the retreating *petardiers* as well. Shakespeare described it thus in *Hamlet* (1604):

For 'tis sport, to have the engineer
Hoist with his own petar...

Hoist is the past participle of *hoise*, meaning 'to raise or lift up on high', like a flag or a sail. The obsolete verb *hoise* has been replaced by the derived form *hoist*.

Eminent Victorian writers such as Walter Scott (1826), Thomas De Quincey (1847) and George Eliot (1868) borrowed Shakespeare's words and gave them currency so that this archaic turn of phrase has become a modern idiom. Not surprisingly, its reference is not always understood; a statement from the New Zealand First party's Education Spokesperson, issued on 10 October 2001, stated that *secondary teachers are hanging the Minister of Education with a petard of his own making*.

Labour has been **hoist by its own petard** in the row over party funding. After the last election Tony Blair announced that even the perception of sleaze would be unacceptable in his brave new world. With huge sums of money heading for Labour's bank account from donors who in some cases may have benefited from the Government's policies, there is a whiff of sleaze around.
THE INDEPENDENT, 7 JANUARY 2001

The number of wind turbines required to replace just one power station may be 2700... There would eventually be such a proliferation of masts throughout the Scottish countryside that, given an extra strong north-westerly, Scotland could well disengage herself (preferable to taking off) from her southerly neighbour. As an island entity, an independent Scotland would be the logical outcome. Thus would Brian be well and truly **hoisted with his own unionist petard**!
GLASGOW HERALD, 19 FEBRUARY 2002

For other idioms from Shakespeare, see WILLIAM SHAKESPEARE, page 152. For other idioms derived from the army and warfare, see page 317.

hold: to hold the fort
to take care of things, take over briefly

Hold the fort, I am coming is popularly believed to be the message that General William Tecumseh Sherman signalled to fellow Union General John Murray Corse as he faced an overwhelming Confederate attack at Allatoona Pass on 5 October 1864, during the American Civil War. What the signal from the top of Kenesaw Mountain really read was *Sherman is coming. Hold out.* The misquote was perpetuated by Philip Paul Bliss, who wrote the words into the chorus of a well-loved gospel hymn:

> *Ho my comrades! See the signal,*
> *Waving in the sky!*
> *Reinforcements now appearing,*
> *Victory is nigh!*

> *'Hold the fort, for I am coming,'*
> *Jesus signals still.*
> *Wave the answer back to heaven,*
> *'By thy grace we will.'*

The hymn was widely sung in evangelistic meetings in England in the 1870s, brought over by American evangelists Dwight Moody and Ira Sankey.

It had been immensely stressful for Jonathan, with me suddenly going to pieces and him having to **hold the fort**.
DAILY MAIL, 21 AUGUST 2002

hold your horses
restrain yourself, be patient

This American phrase was once a literal command to restrain a team of horses impatient to be off. In the first half of the nineteenth century it began to be applied figuratively as a phrase to placate someone who was becoming overwrought, through anger, say, or frustration: *Oh, hold your hosses, Squire. There's no use gettin' riled, no how* (*The Daily Picayune*, 16 September 1844). Later the expression was extended to cover general situations where restraint was called for, with the meaning 'be patient' or simply 'wait'. It has been in British English since the first half of the twentieth century.

What about the inspectors? **Hold your horses**. *It takes two years to train as an inspector.*
THE GUARDIAN, 25 JANUARY 2000

For other horsey idioms, see page 319.

hook: by hook or by crook
using every possible means, honest or dishonest, to achieve something

The earliest written records for the idiom date from the late fourteenth century. A favourite theory for its origin suggests a law from feudal times which permitted the poor to gather firewood from nearby forests. In order to prevent the indiscriminate lopping of trees and branches, peasants were only allowed to take dead wood and what they could cut using their reaper's bill-hooks and shepherd's crooks. The Bodmin Register for 1525 says that *Dynmure Wood was open to the inhabitants of Bodmin...to bear away upon their backs a burden of lop, hook, crook, and hag wood.*

An alternative theory makes much of the rhyming of *hook* and *crook*, where *hook* means 'direct' (reachable with a long hook) and *crook* signifies 'indirect'. Against this on both counts is a quotation from John Gower who, in his *Confessio Amantis* (1390), has: *What with hepe and what with croke*, where hepe is 'a curved pruning knife'.

Two goals conceded, humiliation and embarrassment flooding through England's ranks and one man stepped forth to drag, **by hook or by crook**, *England back into this European Championship qualifier against Macedonia.*
THE DAILY TELEGRAPH,
17 OCTOBER 2002

*Mr Putin, it has become plain, is not the sort of politician who brooks either critics or rivals. He has shut down or stifled most of Russia's independent media. As the recent elections in Chechnya and St Petersburg illustrated so graphically, he has intimidated or bought his way towards ensuring that his preferred candidates emerge as winners of any vote. Few doubt that, **by hook or by crook**, he will retain majority support in the Duma after December's elections.*
THE ECONOMIST, 30 OCTOBER 2003

hook, line and sinker
completely, totally

This phrase is often, though not always, prefixed by *to swallow it* or *to fall for it*, and refers to a person's extreme gullibility. The allusion is to the fish who, not crafty enough to recognise the bait on the hook for what it is, swallows it trustingly, taking in the line and sinker (weight) at the same time. The idiom is American, dating back to around the middle of the nineteenth century.

*Real stars have agents who protect them and bang on about rights of privacy. Real stars do not give themselves **hook, line and sinker** to the red-top tabloids.*
THE SPECTATOR, 11 AUGUST 2001

*He swallows **hook, line and sinker** the notion that drug-addicts are driven to crime by their sheer desperation for drugs: but there is very much more to it than that.*
THE DAILY TELEGRAPH, 24 AUGUST 2003

For a similar phrase, see LOCK, *stock and barrel*.

hope: to hope against hope
to hope without reasonable grounds or justification

The phrase comes from the Bible. St Paul, in his letter to the Romans, makes reference to Abraham who, though elderly and childless, stead-fastly believed God's promise that he would have many offspring: *Who against hope believed in hope, that he might become the father of many nations* (Romans 4:18). Popular use of the idiom dates from the early twentieth century.

*...no single encounter has more riding on it than Mr Sharon's visit to the White House. On Mr Bush's ability to lean heavily on his guest depend America's credibility as a mediator and its standing in the Arab world – not to mention the **hope-against-hope** that a conference, assuming it is held, can advance the cause of peace.*
THE INDEPENDENT, 7 MAY 2002

*What keeps the reader turning the pages? Certainly not the secret, which would be old hat to any science fiction fan. Some of the book's appeal lies in Ishiguro's depiction of boarding-school life. But that's not enough. Readers will persevere because they will **hope against hope** that the students will finally show some gumption and take hold of their lives.*
BOSTON HERALD, 27 APRIL 2005

For other idioms from the Bible, see page 317.

horns: on the horns of a dilemma
faced with a choice between two evils

In Greek logic a *dilemma* was a skilfully crafted argument which presented an opponent with two alternatives, neither of which permitted him to win. The philosopher Zeno (c. 495–430 BC) was celebrated for his paradoxes, strongly influencing Aristotle. Latin coined a vivid phrase for the logistical impasse these two distinguished Greeks had highlighted, referring to it as an *argumentum cornutum*, 'horned argument', since one was figuratively impaled no matter which option was chosen. Nicholas Udall, in his translation of

Erasmus's *Paraphrase of Luke* (1548), a richly annotated text, puts it thus: *Thys forked question [Luke 20:3], which the sophisters call an horned question, because that to whether of both partyes a bodye shall make a direct aunswere, he shall renne on the sharpe poyncte of the horne.*

Subsequently Udall's *horned question* became *the horns of a dilemma*, which was used in very wide-ranging situations. A military commander might attack with cannon, forcing the defenders to open up their ranks, and at the same time co-ordinate an attack with cavalry, forcing the soldiers to close ranks. This puts the defenders *on the horns of a dilemma*. Nowadays the phrase is used not so much of a clever argument or military tactics as to describe a tricky situation presenting two undesirable alternatives.

[The BBC] is impaled on the horns of a dilemma. If it goes down the populist route and gives people what they want, it loses its claim to distinction and makes the licence fee indefensible: why should people have to pay for something that other channels will provide for free or at much lower cost? But if, on the other hand, it decides to give viewers not what they want, but what the BBC believes they ought to have, then it also makes the licence fee unsustainable: for what justification can there be for making people pay for programmes they do not watch?
THE DAILY TELEGRAPH,
27 AUGUST 2000

Like the South, Ohio is a strong banking region perched on the horns of a dilemma: remain independent or succumb to consolidation.
US BANKER, 1 MARCH 2005

For other idioms drawn from Greek and Roman writers, see page 318

horns: to draw/pull in one's horns

to withdraw, to retreat from a commitment

The allusion here is to a snail which draws in its horns, that is the soft tentacles bearing its eyes, when sensing danger. An unknown poet explains it thus:

> *They…gunne to drawen in her hornes,*
> *As a snayle among the thornes.*
> *Richard Coeur de Lion* (c. 1360)

This metaphor of self-protection and drawing back was also used by Chaucer in the same century.

After some tough talk by the unions, on Friday he pulled in his horns, saying there would be no compulsory redundancies.
SUNDAY EXPRESS, 16 DECEMBER 2001

Thirty years ago the actor developed stage fright, pulled in his horns, went into his shell and abandoned the theatre he had illumined with a Richard II, a Henry VI, a celebrated Hamlet.
THE TIMES, 19 FEBRUARY 2002

horse: (straight) from the horse's mouth

from an original and reputable source, on good authority

Before the 1920s, when it came to refer to any kind of evidence given on the best authority, this expression was a piece of racing slang. It alludes to the fact that a horse's age can be deduced just by inspecting its teeth. A dealer may twist the truth but the evidence *in the horse's mouth* is absolutely reliable.

Slang was originally seen as subversive, illicit. Partridge himself inherited this interest in criminal language… He was to hint that he had gleaned his information straight from the horse's mouth, so to speak. Characteristically, such authority is both undeniable and utterly unverifiable.
THE GUARDIAN, 7 SEPTEMBER 2002

Racing and fashion tips were traded between guests at last night's preview party for the Epsom Derby, held at jockey Frankie Dettori's eponymous Knightsbridge restaurant.... 'We wanted to sex up Epsom a little bit,' Jenks told me, as she discussed photographs of her recent creations, modelled by Francesca Cumani, daughter of Derby-winning trainer Luca. A tip straight from the horse's mouth: Cumani trains top filly Dash To The Top for the Oaks at Epsom.
EVENING STANDARD, 20 APRIL 2005

See also LONG *in the tooth* and, for other horsey idioms, see page 319.

horses for courses
different people enjoy/are gifted in different things

A phrase familiar on the turf, is horses for courses, writes A E T Watson in *Turf* (1898), his book on thoroughbreds. This expression encapsulates the theory that certain horses are better suited to particular courses. Watson elaborates: *...the Brighton Course is very like Epsom, and horses that win at one meeting often win at the other*. Extended uses beyond the horse-riding fraternity are found from some thirty years later. Nowadays, general sporting contexts abound: golfers preferring particular styles of courses, for instance. And quite unrelated ones are not uncommon: buying cars, or the right wood for a carpentry project, or lucky casinos.

But obviously it's an environment that doesn't suit everyone. It's horses for courses.
THE INDEPENDENT, 23 MAY 2002

Event organiser Euan Emslie said the display of pedigree beef bulls, heifers and cows with calves at foot was one of the most important aspects of Beef. He said: 'It is horses for courses and ensuring you have the right breed, or combination of breeds, to

suit your particular circumstances is one of the keys to profitable beef production.'
NEWCASTLE JOURNAL, 21 APRIL 2005

For other horsey idioms, see page 319.

horses: wild horses wouldn't drag something from someone (or someone to something)
very strong pressure would not elicit the required information or action

The phrase dates back to the second half of the nineteenth century and is thought to be a reference to medieval torture where a victim is dragged along or pulled apart by wild horses. Victorian novelist Walter Besant refers to such a scene in *The Demoniac* (1890): *To have his flesh wrenched off with red-hot pincers and to be torn to pieces by wild horses.*

'By all means, go, Lady Jones, go if you like,' said Alsana scornfully. 'But as for me, wild horses, wild horses could not do it.'
ZADIE SMITH, WHITE TEETH, 2000

One of my favourite games while listening to other Members [of Parliament] is identifying their equivalent in Wind in the Willows *– and, no, wild horses wouldn't drag the names out of me.*
ANN WIDDECOMBE IN GOOD HOUSEKEEPING, SEPTEMBER 2002

hostage to fortune, a
an impediment, action or comment that could lead to future difficulties

Francis Bacon coined the phrase in an essay *On Marriage* written in 1625. According to Bacon, the family is a potentially troublesome unit standing in the way of a man's ambition: *He that hath wife and children, hath given hostages to fortune; for they are impedimentes to great enterprises, either of vertue, or of mischief.* He was possibly influenced by a misreading of St Paul who, in his first letter to the Corinthians (7:32–3), wrote: *But I would have you without carefulness. He that is unmarried careth for the things that belong to the Lord, how he may please the Lord: But he that is married careth for the things that are of the world, how he may please his wife.* Bacon's opinion was later included in Thomas Fuller's *Gnomologia* (1732), a collection of adages and proverbs: *Wife and Children are Hostages given to Fortune.*

Although the phrase was used as the title of one of Mary Braddon's novels in 1875, it was not until the first half of the twentieth century that it began to be used freely across a wide variety of situations.

It would be a **hostage to fortune** *to say that full agreement has been reached over the euro between the Prime Minister and the Chancellor: the volatility of this debate and the personal tensions involved are such that the dialogue may flare up into rancorous disagreement at any time.*
THE DAILY TELEGRAPH, 25 MAY 2003

For other idioms drawn from literature, see page 319.

hour: at the eleventh hour
at the very last moment

The gospel of Matthew records the parable of the labourers (Matthew 20:1–16). It tells of a householder who went out one morning to hire men to work in his vineyard. He took men on at different times throughout the day right up until the eleventh hour. When the men were paid, however, the householder gave them all the same wage, even those hired right at the last minute. By this illustration Jesus was saying that God accepts everyone who comes to him on equal terms, whether they have spent a lifetime obeying him or approach him just before death, *at the eleventh hour*,

at the last possible moment. The phrase began to be used idiomatically in the first half of the nineteenth century.

India's doctors contacted The Anthony Nolan Bone Marrow Trust and gave them her details. They found a donor literally **at the eleventh hour** *– she was so ill there were grave concerns about her.*
GOOD HOUSEKEEPING, APRIL 2001

With several leavers, including opening bat Rizwan Haider and all-rounder Scott Dyson, it could be an uphill struggle for the Castle Hill side. And it could be a similar tale just down the road at Armitage Bridge, where they are still hoping to line up an **eleventh hour** *overseas man. Officials were desperately running an eye over a couple of likely candidates this week.*
HUDDERSFIELD DAILY EXAMINER, 14 APRIL 2005

For other idioms from the Bible, see page 317.

house: to put/get/set one's house in order
to sort out one's affairs

The biblical text in II Kings 20:1 has been well known since Matthew's Bible of 1537 (see WILLIAM TYNDALE, page 270) and recounts how the prophet Isaiah goes to King Hezekiah and tells him to prepare for death: *And the Prophet Isaiah son of Amoz came to him and said to him: Thus sayeth the LORD: put thine household in an order, for thou shalt die and not live.* Hezekiah, as king, needed to ensure a smooth succession to his throne. The phrase *to put one's house in order* was used idiomatically from the late nineteenth century. Incidentally, Hezekiah was granted a reprieve of fifteen years' more life because he was a righteous man.

*Over the 14 months since the food chain first published falling profits, McDonald's has worked hard **to get its house in order** – overhauling its menus, promoting healthier options, such as salads and fresh fruit, and cutting salt levels.*
THE INDEPENDENT, 20 APRIL 2004

*We boomers need to resist the narcissistic impulse to ladle out more resources for ourselves. Our top domestic priorities should be to ensure that all children get health care and **to get our fiscal house in order**. Otherwise, we boomers may earn a place in history as the worst generation.*
SEATTLE POST-INTELLIGENCER,
4 MAY 2005

For other idioms from the Bible, see page 317.

house of cards, a
an unsound plan, an insubstantial organisation

This idiom comes from the children's game of building a house from playing cards. References to playing cards in England date back to the turn of the fifteenth century but it is hard to imagine any but the most pampered of children being allowed to play with them as they were originally so expensive. Gradually, however, the cost came down and they became the playthings of the young. The likening of an insubstantial scheme or organisation to a fragile house constructed from cards that can be demolished with a breath dates from the first half of the seventeenth century.

*Harold Wilson's only claims upon the nation's respect were that, as Prime Minister, he kept Britain out of Vietnam and quit while he was ahead in 1976, leaving the **house of cards** to collapse in Jim Callaghan's hands three years later.*
DAILY MAIL, 15 JUNE 2004

*ICI hired Goldman Sachs to tell journalists that Hanson's accounts were a **house of cards**, and used corporate spooks to dig into his business dealings. They came up trumps, finding that Lord Hanson's partner, White, was running racehorses at shareholders' expense.*
THE ECONOMIST, 4 NOVEMBER 2004

hue and cry
a public outcry of protest or demand

Earliest references to *hue and cry* are in Anglo-French legal manuscripts dating back to the twelfth century. *Hue* comes from Old French *huer*, an imitative word meaning 'to shout out', which described a war or hunting cry. In the middle ages the community was partly responsible for the arrest of criminals, since there was no organised police force. If a criminal were observed committing a crime, those present were obliged *to raise hue and cry*, that is to shout and make whatever noise they could to warn others in the vicinity. They in turn were required to join in raising the alarm and pursuing the criminal to the neighbourhood boundary. Failure to raise or join in with *hue and cry* could result in fines for the community.

Although *hue and cry* was still a legal term in the second half of the sixteenth century, it was by then being used more generally to mean 'a shout of pursuit or alarm' and during the nineteenth century came to mean 'an outcry'.

*The **hue and cry** is up after the Lord Chief Justice's announcement that Robert Thompson and Jon Venables – the murderers of two-year-old James Bulger – are eligible for parole.*
THE INDEPENDENT, 29 OCTOBER 2000

*In the last few weeks, a great **hue and cry** has been raised among academics over the fate of the Villa dei Papyri in Herculaneum. Hundreds of scrolls,*

preserved underground in the great library of Lucius Calpernius Piso since the AD 79 eruption of Vesuvius, are in imminent danger of destruction from flooding caused by adjacent archaeological work.
THE SPECTATOR, 4 MAY 2002

See THE OLD CURIOSITY SHOP OF LINGUISTICS, page 198.

hum: to hum (hem) and haw
to hesitate (while speaking)

When asked a tricky question, British prime minister Harold Wilson (1916–95) would draw long and hard on his pipe before giving a carefully considered answer. Non-pipe-smokers taken off-guard or with something to hide usually resort to a fair amount of *humming and hawing*.

It was ever thus. John Palsgrave, tutor to the young Mary Tudor, was irritated by a fellow who *hummeth and haeth and wyll nat come out withal* (1530), and in Henry Fielding's *Tom Jones* (1749), a judge was similarly niggled by poor Frank as he stood in the witness stand, commanding him *not to stand humming and hawing, but speak out*.

Rather more recently the rebel Conservative MP Julian Critchley (1930–2000), who was himself a concise speaker, damned the level of debate in the House of Commons thus: *Humming, Hawing and Hesitation are the three Graces of contemporary parliamentary oratory* (*Westminster Blues*, 1985). There has surely been little improvement since then.

*The main customer for the Dickinson fake was the twee museum in her old home in Amherst, Massachusetts...but the curator had already smelled a rat. Sotheby's, after much **humming and hawing**, gave the money back.*
THE SPECTATOR, 14 SEPTEMBER 2002

*Court lawyers must be able to think on their feet. **Humming and hawing** at an unexpected interjection from the bench just does not look good.*
THE SCOTSMAN, 3 JUNE 2003

See COUPLINGS, page 294.

humble: to eat humble pie
to admit one's fault, to humiliate oneself while admitting wrong, to be submissive

The Accomplisht Lady's Delight in Preserving, Physick, Beautifying, and Cookery (1683) gives its readers *a Bill of Fayre upon an Extraordinary Occasion*. There follows a great list of dishes beginning with the magnificent and ending with no.18 – *an umble pie*. This pie would have been filled with *the umbles*, the offal and entrails of a deer, and was a dish to feed those of low estate at the second table, while the lord's family and guests enjoyed the venison. Because those who *ate umble pie* were of humble stock and because *umble* and *humble* are pronounced alike in common speech, confusion eventually arose between the two words, with the result that the phrase we know today means 'to be submissive' or 'to admit a wrong to the point of humiliation'. Yet even though lowly folk have been tucking into their umbles for centuries, the expression has only been in use since the first half of the nineteenth century.

The American version of this expression is *to eat crow* (found from about 1850).

*In a final act of contrition the NZRFU issued a 'formal apology to the rugby public of New Zealand...' Rarely has **humble pie** been more visibly consumed.*
THE DAILY TELEGRAPH, 24 JULY 2002

*And that is how it would have ended – with a boy coming back full of shame, **eating humble pie**, and a father saying,*

'I told you so – why didn't you listen to your mother and me?'
ROB PARSONS, BRINGING HOME THE PRODIGALS, 2003

*If he were **to eat humble pie**, withdraw his transfer request and plead mitigating circumstances, I am sure the Blues faithful would forgive him in time.*
SUNDAY MERCURY, 9 JANUARY 2005

See POSTER PROPAGANDA, page 208.

· I ·

ice: to break the ice
to break down social awkwardness and formality

This figurative phrase is found in Erasmus's *Adagia* (1500), a collection of Latin and Greek proverbs, and has also found its way into other European languages. It appeared in English in the second half of the sixteenth century, at first figuratively with the sense of starting out on an enterprise, and of forging a path for others to follow. From the second half of the seventeenth century there developed the extended meaning of 'to establish a relaxed relationship in socially awkward situations'.

Two centuries later still, after the acceptance of the idiom and the advent of a specially constructed vessel called an *icebreaker* to break up the hard ice that forms in rivers, channels and harbours, there appeared the first uses of *icebreaker*, 'an activity designed to help a group of people to get to know one another', as here: *That first day was designed, using icebreaker and trust-building games familiar to the organisers from their community education and youth work, to break down barriers and get everyone on the same wavelength fast* (*The Times Educational Supplement*, 2 August 2002).

I arrived at Warwick in October 1998 after weeks of interviews with journalists, radio presenters and Richard and Judy. Many students at Warwick had followed the story, which was a fantastic ice-breaker. People approached me, telling me that they had read my story...and a few tutors wanted to shake my hand for standing up for myself against Cambridge.
THE GUARDIAN, 10 JULY 2001

*Caroline Ashbolt...is profoundly deaf and has a hearing dog, Sable, that accompanies her throughout the day. 'My disability is not immediately apparent, so Sable increases people's awareness of the fact that I am deaf and can also **break the ice**.'*
THE INDEPENDENT, 26 JUNE 2003

iceberg: the tip of the iceberg
an unpleasant problem which is just the first phase of a much larger and even more difficult situation

An iceberg is a massive floating body of ice that has broken away from an ice sheet or glacier. Most of its mass floats beneath the surface of the sea; only a small portion is visible above the water. The iceberg has been used allusively since the mid-twentieth century. Michael Gilbert in his thriller *The Etruscan Net* (1969) calls it *a well-known metaphor*.

*When it comes to memory problems, forgetting is only **the tip of the iceberg**. The failings of memory run much deeper than an inability to recall your neighbor's name or the location of your keys.*
NEWSWEEK, 16 JULY 2001

*Last week, the information broker LexisNexis acknowledged that identity thieves...may have gotten information on as many as 310,000 individuals in the company's files. Yet '**this is only the tip***

of the iceberg,' says Gail Hillebrand, senior attorney with Consumers Union. In recent weeks, several financial, healthcare, and educational institutions have reported incidents of lost or stolen information on more than 2 million Americans.
US NEWS AND WORLD REPORT,
25 APRIL 2005

image: the spitting image of
the exact likeness of

An old phrase expressing the likeness of a son to his father which dates back to at least the early seventeenth century was *as like as if he was spit out of his mouth*:

> *Nay, I'm as like my dad, in sooth,*
> *As he had spit me out on's mouth.*
> (Charles Cotton, *Burlesque upon Burlesque*, 1675)

There is a similar phrase in French, *C'est son père tout craché*, 'It's his father spat out'. From here it seems that *the very spit* or *the dead spit* was coined, probably sometime in the early nineteenth century. One of the stories in the 1825 edition of *The Newgate Calendar*, a collection of tales about notorious criminals, mentions *a daughter...the very spit of the old captain*. Indeed, *dead spit* is still in use: *And as for show-off Bruce Forsyth. It's been driving me mad to work out who he reminds me of and I've finally got it. Basil Brush. He's the dead spit (Newcastle Journal,* 12 June 2004).

Also current in the nineteenth century, and well into the twentieth, was the dialectal *spitten image,* a form that was often misheard and subsequently variously reworked as *spit an' image, spit and image* and, finally, by the beginning of the twentieth century, *spitting image*. In 1984 *Spitting Image* was chosen as the title of a British TV show. Cruelly satirical, the programme featured puppets which were the *spitting image* of royalty, politicians and other well-

known figures in the news. The show became immensely popular and ran until 1996.

*Dubbed 'the clone' by party insiders, the square-jawed, green-eyed blonde with the gravelly voice is **the spitting** image of her pugnacious father and is increasingly powerful within the National Front.*
THE SCOTSMAN, 14 OCTOBER 2004

insult: to add insult to injury
to upset someone further with a second insensitive act or remark

The Roman writer Phaedrus published five books of fables. Although he is credited with translating Aesop into Latin verse, many of the fables were his own work. One of these, 'The Bald Man and the Fly' (c. 25 BC) tells of a man who attempts to squash an insect which has just bitten him on his bald patch by delivering a smart smack. The fly escapes the blow, as flies usually do, and mocks him for wanting to avenge the bite of a tiny insect with death: *What will you do to yourself who have added insult to injury?* To the injury of the sting he has only succeeded in adding the insult of the self-inflicted blow.

The phrase *to add insult to injury* has been current in English since the middle of the eighteenth century. It occurs in Edward Moore's *The Foundling* (1748). Belmont is threatening Sir Charles with his sword:

SIR CHARLES *Hold, sir. This is adding insult to injuries. Fidelia must be restored, sir.*
SIR ROBERT *Sir, Fidelia must be restored.*
FIDELIA *But not to him. Hear but my story...*

*To blame the spread of foot and mouth on farmers does not so much **add insult to injury** as calumny to catastrophe... Even*

*strong men are turning to despair. Yet
ministers would have us believe that these
same farmers, who now face the destruction
of their livelihoods, have deliberately
infected their herds as some kind of
compensation racket.*
THE DAILY TELEGRAPH, 28 MAY 2001

*It's at the delivery stage that most
customers tend to experience the most
dissatisfaction... half your perishables are
in dodgy nick and whole chunks of your
order are listed 'this product was not
available': quite inconvenient if, as on my
last Tesco order, those items included
nappies and toilet paper. **To add insult
to injury**, what often happens is that
something inappropriate is substituted.
A friend had her Christmas dinner ruined
when, instead of the premium free-range
turkey she'd ordered from Sainsbury's,
she was given a turkeyroast.*
THE DAILY TELEGRAPH,
13 OCTOBER 2001

For other idioms derived from fables,
see page 318.

iron: an iron hand in a velvet glove

firm and inflexible in leadership,
beneath a veneer of gentleness

Iron has been used metaphorically
since at least the fourteenth century
to denote 'hardness'. Over time it has
also come to mean 'unyielding' or
'inflexible'. Thomas Carlyle, while
telling of a visit he made to a prison,
attributes the extended phrase to
Napoleon (1769– 1821). In his
account, Carlyle describes the prison
governor as *one of the most perfect...;
professionally and by nature zealous for
cleanliness, punctuality, good order of
every kind; a humane heart and yet a
strong one; soft of speech and manner, yet
with an inflexible rigor of command, so far
as his limits went: 'iron hand in a velvet*

glove,' as Napoleon defined it (Latter-
Day Pamphlets, 1850).

If Carlyle's assertion is right, it
seems that Napoleon may only have
borrowed the phrase, for it has also
been attributed to Charles V, King of
Spain and Holy Roman Emperor from
1519 to 1558. It is quite likely that
there is some borrowing between languages, since the idiom is found in its
full form in French, German and
Spanish. The figure is often subject to
a fair amount of reworking in English,
as the examples below illustrate.

*She ruled the roost with **a velvet glove
covering a hand of razor wire**.*
MAVIS CHEEK, MRS FYTTON'S
COUNTRY LIFE, 2000

THE LOYAL HENCHMAN
*He's Alastair Campbell to your boss's
Tony Blair – the steel fist in the iron
glove... He won't chat. He'll just lurk and
glare and exude a terrifying air of menace.
He could snap you like that Twiglet, if he
wanted to.*
DAILY MAIL, 19 DECEMBER 2001

*Presumably he did not have to pretend to
be sincere because he actually was. As a
result, he did not look like the manipulative
actor that the country now assumes that he
is, or **like the velvet glove to Alastair
Campbell's iron fist**, but like the
statesman that he wishes to be.*
THE DAILY TELEGRAPH, 9 JULY 2003

*Her name was Yvonne... The minute I set
eyes on her, I realised she was going to be a
hard taskmaster... She **ruled with an
iron hand** and had complete control.*
THE GUARDIAN, 13 MARCH 2004

irons: to have (too) many irons in the fire

to have (too) many projects in hand, undertakings to be attended to

Someone with *irons in the fire* has a choice of projects to which he can turn his attention; if he has *too many irons in the fire* he has too many plans and cannot pay sufficient attention to any of them.

The phrase may be from the forge where the efficient smith had several irons gradually heating in the fire for when he needed them, since it took a while for them to become red-hot and malleable. Too many irons, and he would never get round to shaping them all.

Alternatively, it could have originated in the laundry, where the laundress would put several flatirons to warm on the coals and would use them in turn. Too many irons in the fire and they would become overheated through slow rotation and scorch the clothes. The idiom dates back to the mid-sixteenth century.

*We've got **some irons in the fire** for raising more money, but we are not going to go bust by spending money we haven't got.*
THE DAILY TELEGRAPH, 7 JUNE 2000

He has matured over the last years…
*Able and energetic organiser, tends to have **one too many irons in the fire**. On the whole, a bit risky but could, given a bit of luck and favourable circumstances, certainly become the leading paediatric pathologist in the UK.*
THE DAILY TELEGRAPH, 31 JANUARY 2001

For another idiom from the forge, see *to go at it* HAMMER *and tongs*.

ivory tower, an

a sheltered existence away from the problems and practicalities of life, an attitude of aloofness from the realities of life

The French Romantic poet, playwright and novelist Alfred de Vigny led a life of disappointment and frustration. In his later years he withdrew from society and became very solitary, although he continued to write. In a poem, 'Pensées d'Août' (1837), the critic Sainte-Beuve called Vigny's isolated existence his *tour d'ivoire*, 'ivory tower'. The idiom was used in an English translation of Henri Bergson's *Laughter – An Essay on the Meaning of the Comic* (1911), and thereafter is frequently found in English texts.

Sainte-Beuve was strongly influenced by the Christian faith, and may in his choice of phrase have drawn on the Song of Songs 7:4: *Your neck is like an ivory tower* (New International Version).

*'For too long scientists have been in some kind of **ivory tower**… Dysfunctional nerds…,' she snapped at one point in our interview.*
INTERVIEW WITH PROFESSOR SUSAN GREENFIELD, DIRECTOR OF THE ROYAL INSTITUTION OF GREAT BRITAIN, IN GOOD HOUSEKEEPING, APRIL 2000

For other idioms drawn from literature, see page 319.

· J ·

jack of all trades, a

a person who can turn his hand to anything

Jack has long been used in English as a general term for 'a man of the common people'. The earliest written reference to *Jack of all trades* is in Geffray Mynshul's *Essayes and Characters of a Prison* (1618). It was originally an unfavourable title, the inference being that a person who would dabble in every trade was incompetent at all of them, hence the proverb *Jack of all Trades is of no Trade* quoted by Thomas Fuller in *Gnomologia* (1732). The well-known variant *Jack of all trades and master of none* that reiterates this sentiment is not found until the turn of the nineteenth century: *'How comes it that I am so unlucky?' 'Jack of all trades, and master of none,' said Goodenough, with a sneer* (Maria Edgeworth, *Popular Tales: Will*, 1800).

Nowadays *a jack of all trades* is not necessarily regarded as lacking in skill: he is simply a person who can turn his hand to anything.

*There are 30 eight-year-olds in my class and I teach them all subjects – I'm **a jack of all trades**. It is challenging. Each day is different.*
THE GUARDIAN, 15 NOVEMBER 2003

Ms. Cohen calls the students who wake up late in their junior year and try to make up for lost time by joining a dozen groups 'serial joiners.'
*'They become **a jack of all trades and master of none**,' she says, 'but colleges are not looking for quantity, they're looking for quality.'*
WASHINGTON TIMES, 25 MARCH 2005

See WHAT'S IN A NAME?, opposite.

jackpot: to hit the jackpot

to win a large prize, to have an unexpected success or piece of good fortune

In the late nineteenth century, *jackpot* was coined as a poker term for a pot of money that gradually accumulates until one of the players is able to start the betting by laying down a pair of jacks or a higher ranking hand. The phrase *to hit the jackpot* dates from around the middle of the twentieth century. The term is now applied to any large accumulative prize, such as a large lottery win or, more generally, to a great success, usually of a financial nature.

*A man who queued all night in the rain for a chance to buy a postcard for £35 **hit the jackpot** today when it turned out the work was by artist Damien Hirst and could be worth thousands.*
EVENING STANDARD,
29 NOVEMBER 2002

*If you have a property with all five features and it happens to be near Oxford, Newbury, Winchester or some parts of Gloucestershire, you've **hit the jackpot**.*
THE DAILY TELEGRAPH, 30 MARCH 2003

For other idioms derived from poker, see page 320.

What's in a name?

> *When icicles hang by the wall,*
> *And Dick the shepherd blows his nail,*
> *And Tom bears logs into the hall,*
> *And milk comes frozen home in pail,*
> *When blood is nipped, and ways be foul,*
> *Then nightly sings the staring owl,*
> *Tu-who;*
> *Tu-whit, tu-who – a merry note,*
> *While greasy Joan doth keel the pot.*
> (William Shakespeare, *Love's Labour's Lost*, 1595)

This cameo of a sixteenth-century winter shows ordinary folk going about their daily tasks. The ordinary folk have ordinary names: Dick (short for Richard), Tom (Thomas) and Joan. In a number of idioms and proverbs the common working man or woman is represented by a name typical of that class. As the sixteenth-century proverb has it, *Jacke would be a gentleman if he could speake frenche* (Heywood, *Proverbs*, 1546).

That familiar pair *Jack and Jill* have been together since the fifteenth century: *For Iak nor for Gille wille I turne my face* (*Towneley Cycle of the Mystery Plays*, c. 1460). Proverbial wisdom has it that *Every Jack has his Jill* and *Good Jack makes good Jill*, while their exploits fetching water are made known in the nursery rhyme *Jack and Jill went up the hill*. Their fame has far outlived that of the sixteenth-century couple Tib and Tom.

Standing alone, *Jack* represents his gender and class in a number of phrases that have survived from past centuries. JACK *of all trades* goes back to the early seventeenth century at least, while the proverb *All work and no play makes Jack a dull boy* dates from around the middle of that century. *Every man Jack*, meaning 'every single fellow without exception', is quoted by Charles Dickens in *Barnaby Rudge* (1840). Common sailors have been known as *Jacks*, short for *Jack the Sailor*, since the mid-seventeenth century (*Jack Tar* does not appear till the latter part of the eighteenth). The early-twentieth-century phrase *I'm alright Jack*, to express smug self-satisfaction, originated on board ship but has been current amongst landlubbers since the middle of that century. Only the phrase *before you can say Jack Robinson*, meaning 'done swiftly', gives humble Jack a surname. The origins of this phrase are obscure; perhaps there was such a character. Or perhaps Robinson was regarded as a common enough surname to couple with Jack. Whatever the etymology, the phrase dates from the second half of the eighteenth century.

In the early seventeenth century, a statement by King James I, quoted by Thomas Fuller in his *Church-History of Britain* (1655), put Jack with a crowd of his common fellows: *Then Jack, and Tom, and Will, and Dick shall meet and censure me and my Council* (c. 1604). In those days a random selection of common names served to denote 'ordinary men or women'. Only a few years earlier, Shakespeare had similarly flung together *Tom, Dicke, and Francis* (*Henry IV Part I*, 1596). By the eighteenth century, however, one particular trio, *Tom, Dick and Harry*, had emerged:

> *Farewell, Tom, Dick, and Harry,*
> *Farewell, Moll, Nell, and Sue.*
> (Song, *Vocal Miscellany*, 1734)

and they are with us still, representatives of the rest of mankind:

You go around raking up the past and sharing it with every Tom, Dick and Harry you bump into. (Mark Haddon, *The Curious Incident of the Dog in the Night-Time*, 2003)

jam tomorrow

a promise of good things to come
which rarely appear

In Lewis Carroll's *Through the Looking
Glass* (1871), Alice helps the White
Queen to dress and is offered the
position of lady's maid at the salary
of twopence a week and jam every
other day. Alice comments that she
does not care for jam and does not
want any today, to which the Queen
retorts: *You couldn't have it if you did
want it... The rule is, jam tomorrow and
jam yesterday but never jam today.*
Jam tomorrow was taken up by other
writers around the middle of the
twentieth century and is now a
favourite expression amongst financial and political journalists, both of
whom frequently report on extravagant promises for a sunny future that
never seem to come to fruition.

*The Labour Party conference rejected Tony
Blair's promises of 'jam tomorrow' on
pensions and demanded last night that the
basic state pension be raised in line with
earnings rather than prices.*
THE INDEPENDENT, 28 SEPTEMBER 2000

*There is, of course, no denying that
companies have been raking it in lately.
But if they haven't been paying off debt or
investing, what has happened to that
money? According to the NIPA figures, an
astonishing 90% of it has been paid to
shareholders. In an era of low interest
rates, investors presumably want money
up front.*

*But in the absence of investment and
with balance sheets still heavy with debt,
jam today does not necessarily mean jam
tomorrow.*
THE ECONOMIST, 27 AUGUST 2004

For other idioms drawn from
literature, see page 319.

Janus-faced

hypocritical

Janus was a Roman deity, custodian of
the universe and Guardian of gates and
doors. As the god of beginnings and
endings he was represented as having
one face on the front of his head and
another on the back. Thus he was able
to look ahead and behind at the same
time. People who are hypocritical have
long been described as having two faces.
In his *Sermons* (1550), Thomas Lever
wrote: *These flatterers be wonders perilous
fellowes, hauynge two faces under one hoode.*
It is easy to see how the deity depicted
with two faces came to be linked with
the idea of hypocrisy: *This Janus-face of
writers, who with one countenance force a
smile, and with another show nothing beside
rage and fury* (Shaftesbury, *Characteristics
of Men, Manners, Opinions, Times,* 1711).

*...never has a government gone into a
literally life-and-death situation worse
prepared and more Janus-faced. Janus –
the Roman God with two faces – has come
to symbolise this Government.*
THE PEOPLE, 27 OCTOBER 2002

*A Janus-faced Prime Minister tries to sound
placatory in Europe and tough at home.*
THE OBSERVER, 20 JUNE 2004

See also TWO-FACED and, for other
idioms derived from ancient legends,
see page 317.

jaundiced: with a jaundiced eye

taking a cynical, resentful view

Jaundice is a medical condition caused
by obstruction of the bile duct or by
liver disease, in which the skin or the
whites of the eyes turn a yellowish
colour. Indeed, the word *jaundice* is a
borrowing from Old French *jaunice*,
from *jaune*, meaning 'yellow'. There
was once a belief that those suffering

from the disease also had yellow vision. Thomas Stanley subscribed to this notion: *To him that hath the yellow jaundies, all things seem yellow,* he wrote in his *History of Philosophy* (1656). Yellow vision does in fact occur, although only very rarely, but since a yellow-green hue was considered characteristic of envy, jealousy and resentment, figuratively to see the world *with a jaundiced eye* was, from the second half of the eighteenth century, to focus only on its faults.

*Unlike the male codfish, which, suddenly finding itself the parent of three million five hundred thousand little codfish, cheerfully resolves to love them all, the British aristocracy is apt to look **with a somewhat jaundiced eye** on its younger sons.*
THE INDEPENDENT, 18 JANUARY 2000

See also *the* GREEN-*eyed monster*.

jib: the cut of someone's jib
someone's personal appearance or manner

This is a piece of sailors' argot which came into more general use in the 1820s. The *jib* was a triangular sail stretching from the foretopmast head to the jib boom, and the nationality of a ship could often be recognised by the cut and number of these sails long before the vessel was close enough to be identified by its flag. Since the nose is a person's most prominent feature and, like a ship's jib, the first part to arrive at its destination, the phrase was applied figuratively to denote a first impression, whether favourable or unfavourable, of a person's general appearance or manner. Thus *the cut of one's jib* can be liked or disliked, although the latter is more frequently found these days.

*Was Mr Bolland a good thing? Many people I respect **do not like the cut of his jib**. They deplore his close association with tabloid editors such as Rebekah Wade of the* News of the World. *They do not approve of his methods.*
THE SPECTATOR, 9 FEBRUARY 2002

For other nautical idioms, see A LIFE ON THE OCEAN WAVES, page 24.

Job's comforter, a
a person who increases distress while professing to offer comfort

The story of the patriarch Job is found in the Old Testament. God permits Satan to bring distress into his innocent servant's life to test out his relationship with Him. Job loses his flocks, servants and family and is inflicted with painful sores but refuses to curse God. All the while Job is counselled by three friends who, in debating his situation with him, only increase his anguish. The three friends have been referred to as *Job's comforters* since the first half of the eighteenth century, and the term applied to anyone who, under the guise of compassion, aggravates distress.

*My nonconforming and wonderful daughter was married last week. It was a great day and we are delighted. However, again I found that some of my teaching colleagues felt obliged to make points about what they perceived to be my daughter's challenge to conformity... One **Job's comforter** – they are in every staffroom – told me that it was certain she would be divorced in a few years' time.*
THE TIMES EDUCATIONAL SUPPLEMENT, 7 SEPTEMBER 2001

For other idioms from the Bible, see page 317.

jockey: to jockey for position

to try to gain an advantageous position by adroit manoeuvring or unfair action

From the seventeenth century onwards *a jockey* was both a rider of horses and a horse-dealer. Dealers were unscrupulous fellows renowned for sharp practice, so that the verb *to jockey* meant 'to gain advantage over someone, to outwit', as this definition shows:

To Jockey a man, is to impose upon, to cheat, to overreach; to deal with any one, as Jockeys usually doe with all ye world. Nor is there any more deceitful race of Men than Jockeys, in their Sale of Horse flesh (Allen, *MS Dictionary,* c. 1740).

This sense of craftiness was carried over into the early twentieth-century phrase *to jockey for position* which literally meant 'to jostle for an advantageous position in a horse race' but which was used figuratively by the middle of the century to mean 'to cunningly outmanoeuvre someone', 'to promote one's own interests with scant regard for others'.

*Next year's primary calendar is unusually compressed. No one is sure what effect this compression will have. But several states hold contests on the same day. This should benefit candidates with names known nationwide (like Mr Lieberman) or with the best organisations (Mr Kerry, at the moment). Against that, a candidate able to build momentum could sweep all before him. The **jockeying for position** starts in South Carolina this weekend.*
THE ECONOMIST, 1 MAY 2003

*[Harold Pinter's play] Betrayal is really all about male bonhomie, the joking that covers **the jockeying for position**.*
THE INDEPENDENT, 12 OCTOBER 2003

For other horsey idioms, see page 319.

Joneses: to keep up with the Joneses

to endeavour to keep up financially and socially with one's friends and neighbours

In February 1913 the *New York Globe* began to run a comic strip by Arthur R 'Pop' Momand called *Keeping up with the Joneses*. It concerned the daily lives and struggles of the McGinis family. Their neighbours, the Joneses of the title, never actually appeared in the strip in the twenty-eight years of its life, but received numerous envious mentions. Momand based the storylines on his own family's struggles to manage on a limited income whilst maintaining a show of material affluence appropriate to the neighbourhood they lived in. Momand explains in a personal letter to C E Funk (quoted in Funk, 1955):

We had been living far beyond our means in our endeavour to keep up with the well-to-do class which then lived in Cedarhurst. I also noted that most of our friends were doing the same; the $10,000-a-year chap was trying to keep up with the $20,000-a-year man.

I decided it would make good comic-strip material, so sat down and drew up six strips. At first I thought of calling it Keeping up with the Smiths, *but finally decided on* Keeping up with the Joneses *as being more euphonious.*

By the mid-1920s the comic strip was being published in newspapers throughout America and, in a society increasingly aware of the link between material possessions and social status, *keeping up with the Joneses* became a telling idiom. In the 1950s the British *Daily Mirror* launched a new strip called *Keeping up with the Joneses*, some fifteen years after the original ceased publication. It had little in common with it except the title.

See the words 'luxury apartment' in a property brochure and you can never be quite sure what they signify. But you can be sure that you are being invited, in the nicest possible way, to keep up with the Joneses.
THE DAILY TELEGRAPH,
30 NOVEMBER 2002

jump the gun, to

to embark upon a course of action too hastily, at an inappropriate time; to take an unfair advantage

Running races are started by a pistol shot. An athlete who, in anticipation, moves off before the gun sounds has *jumped the gun*. The phrase *to beat the pistol* was in use on the running track from the turn of the twentieth century with the sense 'to make a false start'. The variant *to jump the gun* – the now dominant form – dates from around 1940.

Literary editors face a dilemma when one of their number jumps the gun. They have been 'scooped'. So what do they do? Wait till September 6, when the book will be dead as mutton? Or jump the gun as well?
THE GUARDIAN, 3 SEPTEMBER 2001

It would be easy to pounce on the Detroit police as being reckless for jumping the gun if it turns out they arrested the wrong person as the suspect in last week's tragic multiple shooting incident.
MICHIGAN CHRONICLE, 6 JULY 2004

· K ·

kettle: a (fine/pretty) kettle of fish

a mess, a problem, a predicament

The OED suggests that the origin of this idiom lies in a type of riverside picnic, common in the Scottish border country, in which the guests shared a feast of salmon cooked in a large metal pot known as a *kettle*. Thomas Newte, who made a tour of England and Scotland in 1785, wrote: *It is customary for the gentlemen who live near the Tweed to entertain their neighbours and friends with a Fete Champetre, which they call giving 'a kettle of fish'. Tents or marquees are pitched near the flowery banks of the river... a fire is kindled, and live salmon thrown into boiling kettles.*

In the earliest uses of the idiom, which date from the first half of the eighteenth century, a *kettle of fish* signifies 'a messy state of affairs', 'a predicament', and is described as *fine, pretty, nice* or *rare*, adjectives used for ironic emphasis. This suggests that the contents of the picnic kettle tasted better than they looked.

There is, however, a plausible alternative suggestion. *A kiddle* was a dam with an opening in it over which nets were stretched to catch fish. This venerable word was a legal term in the Magna Carta of 1215. *Kiddle* and *kettle* were easily confused: under the entry for *kiddle*, Blount's *Law Dictionary* of 1670 states that *Some fishermen corruptly call them kettles.* One assumes that the ironic exclamation *a*

Giving it to them hot and strong

Intensifying the force of one's words is a very common device of language. *It's nonsense* becomes It's *absolute/perfect/proper/pure/sheer/thorough/total/utter* nonsense. It is a characteristic that works with idioms, too, and there are a few favourite intensifiers. One of these is *blue*:

To the old DEVIL *and the deep sea* we add the adjective *blue* to produce the emphatic *between the* DEVIL *and the deep blue sea.* You can *get away with murder* or, if you do something outrageous and still aren't punished for it, you can *get away with blue murder.* If you *scream blue* MURDER you scream louder even than if you were being murdered. *To drive like blue murder* is to drive ridiculously fast. *In a funk* becomes *in a blue funk. To throw a fit* is, on occasion, *to throw a blue fit.* The sulphurous blue flames (blazes) of hell strengthen the euphemistic *What* or *where the blazes...?* to *What* or *where the blue blazes...?*

Other favourite intensifiers are *merry, fine* and *pretty*:
To play hell becomes *to play merry hell.*
In a PICKLE is often *in a pretty* PICKLE .
An alternative for *a fine* KETTLE *of fish* is *a pretty* KETTLE *of fish.*

pretty kettle of fish refers to a night's fruitless fishing.

Whatever the origin, the use of the related phrase *another* or *a different kettle of fish*, meaning 'a different matter altogether', dates from the first half of the twentieth century.

*'Going AWOL will get you into one sort of trouble,' the officer told him. 'Discharging a weapon is **a different kettle of fish**.'*
MICK JACKSON, FIVE BOYS, 2001

*She glanced over at the half-demolished outhouse that was to become the Woman House. **What a fine kettle of fish** – that was all Will had come up with. It would indeed be months before she could house the women.*
SYLVIA CHRISTIE,
THE WOMAN HOUSE, 2002

See GIVING IT TO THEM HOT AND STRONG, opposite.

kick: to kick against the pricks
to persist in useless resistance, to one's own cost

This phrase comes from the New Testament. Saul, who has been persecuting the young Christian church, is challenged by a voice from heaven as he journeys along the Damascus road: *And he seide, Who art thou, Lord? And he seide, Y am Jhesu of Nazareth, whom thou pursuest. It is hard to thee, to kike ayens the pricke* (Acts 9:5, Wyclif's translation, 1382). *Prick* is an old word for 'goad' and so the allusion is to an ox pointlessly kicking out and resisting his owner's goad.

The phrase has a long and venerable history, being found in proverbial form in Greek, Latin and Hebrew. It has been applied to those who are insubordinate, to their own detriment, since around the middle of the eighteenth century.

*Both were public men whose protagonists were passionate about their causes and shared what Osborne called a 'beholden duty **to kick against the pricks**'.*
THE GUARDIAN, 4 JUNE 2002

For other idioms from the Bible, see page 317.

kick: to kick over the traces
to become reckless, out of control; to rebel, throw off the usual constraints

The traces are two straps on a draft horse's harness connecting the collar to the crossbar of the vehicle. A frisky animal, resisting a day's hard labour pulling a heavy cart or carriage, may put a leg over the traces, thus becoming out of control. The phrase has been used figuratively since the second half of the nineteenth century to describe those who reject society's constraints upon them.

*Some people never feel the need for wildness. Some people don't **kick over the traces** until later (my generation waited until our 20s, as I recall, because then we had the money to make wildness fun).*
THE TIMES EDUCATIONAL
SUPPLEMENT, 26 NOVEMBER 2000

*Older brother William was the solid, dependable one: sensitive, wary of the media, without Harry's wild streak. Harry, on the other hand, was the one who had the greater fondness for nightlife and partying, who was always the most likely **to kick over the traces** of heritage and tradition.*
EVENING STANDARD, 21 OCTOBER 2004

For other horsey idioms, see page 319.

kick: to kick the bucket
to die

The origin of this phrase is open to conjecture. One explanation points to the common suicide method of tying oneself to a beam while standing upon an upturned bucket and then kicking the bucket away. It has even been suggested that the phrase was inspired by one suicide in particular. An article by Thomas De Quincey in an edition of the *London Magazine* (1823) talks of a tradition among the *slang fraternity* that *one Bolsover having hung himself to a beam while standing on the bottom of a pail, or bucket, kicked the vessel away in order to pry into futurity, and it was all up with him from that moment – finis*!

However, it seems that Bolsover topped himself after the phrase was coined, for it was already common in the eighteenth century, being listed in Francis Grose's *A Classical Dictionary of the Vulgar Tongue* (1785). Even so, this does not invalidate the general theory of suicide.

There is a preferred etymology, however, which suggests that pigs were suspended by their back legs from a beam known as a *bucket* (from Old French *buquet*, 'balance beam') in order to be slaughtered, and in their death throes would kick against it. Grim stuff.

*When musicians **kick the bucket**, it almost guarantees them mythical status.*
THE GUARDIAN, 24 APRIL 2000

*The film is about 'a lonely old man who is desperate to have a lady companion before he **kicks the bucket**'.*
DAILY EXPRESS, 21 NOVEMBER 2002

kill: to kill someone with kindness
to spoil or harm with well-intentioned but excessive kindness

Pity poor Draco the Athenian lawmaker who, according to Suidas, was so beloved by the population that, while attending the theatre at Aegina, he was smothered to death by the many cloaks flung into the air in tribute. The story may not be the origin of the phrase *to kill with kindness*, but it illustrates it well enough. Instead, during the sixteenth century there arose a notion that female apes often killed their young by wrapping them in a huge and loving embrace. *She killeth that which she loueth, by pressing it too hard*, wrote Edward Topsell in his *Historie of Foure-Footed Beastes* (1607). Could it have been this traveller's tale that inspired writers from the middle of the sixteenth century onwards to coin the phrase?

*He's a performer searching for love. Weird love. Warm love. Anything. He comes out of the closet as a bad guy, then tries **to kill us with kindness**.*
THE INDEPENDENT, 30 AUGUST 2002

*Too much nitrogen promotes leaf growth at the expense of flowers, making plants especially attractive to pests. Too much of everything else can make plants pale and sick-looking. You can actually **kill them with kindness**.*
THE DAILY TELEGRAPH, 13 MARCH 2004

For other myths derived from fabled animal behaviour, see page 318.

Kingdom come, (till)
the next life; forever, until death

He's gone to Kingdom come, he's dead is the rather blunt way the expression is defined in Francis Grose's *Dictionary of the Vulgar Tongue* (1785). *Kingdom come* is 'heaven' or 'the next life', and the words themselves are found in the Lord's Prayer as recorded in Matthew 6:10:

> *...your kingdom come,*
> *your will be done*
> *on earth as it is in heaven.*

Inclusion in Grose's dictionary means that the phrase was much used as a slang term in spoken language before it was considered suitable for the written word. An early written reference comes in John Wolcot's (Peter Pindar's) *Subjects for Painters* (1789):

And forty pounds be theirs, a pretty sum,
For sending such a rogue to Kingdom-come.

Nowadays *to blow someone/something to kingdom come*, referring to a gunshot or bomb blast, is more common.

The sense of *until* or *till kingdom come* is rather different. The notion here is that the second coming of Christ, when God's Kingdom will be established on earth, is a very long way off – so long that the activity under discussion can with impunity be continued almost for ever.

*…the stomach-turning moment when, girdled with a hidden bomb, she must place a garland round her victim's neck and then press a secret button **to blow them both to kingdom come**.*
THE GUARDIAN, 11 MAY 2001

*Martin Pipe, one of the targeted trainers, spoke of the harm done to racing by the much publicised [drug] raids… Pipe said he had never used EPO and never would. 'They can keep taking the blood samples for as long as they like, **until kingdom come**, and they will never find anything.'*
THE DAILY TELEGRAPH,
27 FEBRUARY 2002

For an idiom with a similar meaning see *until the* COWS *come home*; and for other idioms from the Bible, see page 317.

kiss: the kiss of death
an apparently helpful gesture that actually brings failure or ruin

The expression, coined around the middle of the twentieth century, is a reference to the kiss of betrayal that Judas bestowed upon Jesus in the garden of Gethsemane, to identify him to the soldiers (Matthew 26:48–50). Following the kiss, Jesus was arrested, tried and crucified. From the sixteenth century onwards the phrase *Judas kiss* has been used to signify 'an insincere action' or 'an embrace offered with an evil motive' but *the kiss of death* is used rather differently, in that motives are not usually in question, as the examples below show.

*Calling a city cool is a cultural **kiss of death**…*
THE INDEPENDENT, 5 FEBRUARY 2004

*The newly-commissioned paintings are billed as fresh evidence of a boom in religious imagery in art… But last year [Howden] complained bitterly that his work on religious themes had proved a **'kiss of death'** even with his regular clients.*
THE SCOTSMAN, 23 MARCH 2004

For other idioms from the Bible, see page 317.

kitchen: everything but the kitchen sink
absolutely everything

In his *Dictionary of Forces' Slang 1939–1945*, Eric Partridge says that *kitchen sink* was used to emphasise the severity of a heavy bombardment. Soldiers would comment that the enemy had thrown everything at them except, or including, the kitchen sink. Partridge adds that the variant *kitchen stove* was also current, though this did not survive for more than two decades after the war. No longer an expression of warfare, since the Second World War *kitchen sink* has been used in a wide range of contexts. The contents of a handbag, for instance.

*Although compact, this tan leather day bag is deceptively large. Will suit anyone who likes to carry around **everything but the**

kitchen sink on a daily basis, but still wants a bag that will fit neatly under their shoulder.
THE INDEPENDENT, 11 OCTOBER 2003

For other idioms derived from the army and warfare, see page 317.

knee-high to a grasshopper
very small (and young)

Young children are often described as being *knee-high to a grasshopper*. For a while in early nineteenth-century America, a youngster could be *knee-high to* virtually any tiny creature: *a toad, a frog* or *a mosquito*, for instance, or even *a bumbly-bee*. Comparisons to a *grasshopper* date from the middle of that century, and this version won out, in spite of a flurry of *ducks* and *woodchucks* that flew by in the first half of the twentieth century.

At 5ft 7ins tall, Lord of the Rings: The Two Towers *star Elijah Wood is just about* **knee-high to a grasshopper**. *But as a lover he is clearly a giant.*
DAILY MIRROR, 13 DECEMBER 2002

It's been a couple of years since we first heard the sound of Rothesay's very own little queen of song, Maria Tambini. She was **knee-high to a grasshopper** *then, and she's only a wee bit bigger now.*
THE DAILY TELEGRAPH, 22 MARCH 2003

knuckle: to knuckle under
to give in, to comply

From the fourteenth to the late seventeenth century the word *knuckle* denoted the end of a bone which, at a bent joint, makes a rounded protrusion. This occurs at the backbone, knee or elbow, for instance, as well as at the fingers when a fist is made. Dyche and Pardon's *New General English Dictionary* of 1740 defines the verb *knuckle* or *knuckle down*

as *to stoop, bend, yield, comply with, or submit to.* The literal sense obviously derives from the stooping posture when the joints are bent and the figurative from the fact that this is recognised as a sign of submission.

It was nearly a century and a half later before *knuckle under* was found with this sense, yet this form became dominant thereafter. *Knuckle down to*, dating from the second half of the nineteenth century, has the meaning 'to apply oneself conscientiously to a task', possibly from the hunched posture of someone hard at work.

Anyone who has ever worked for someone else will know the feeling. Your boss is sad, mad or bad; your talents are wasted; your pay is a joke; in fact, all things considered, you could do much, much better yourself. Most people settle for a good moan and then **knuckle under** *once more, but for some the voice telling them to strike out alone is irresistible. So they set themselves up in business. Which could be the worst mistake they ever made*
THE GUARDIAN, 24 APRIL 2001

Syria is the region's one country that still seems to resist American pressure. Yet this may simply reflect its bigger legacy of bad blood with the superpower, its isolated rulers may feel they have more to lose by **knuckling under***.*
THE ECONOMIST, 17 JANUARY 2004

· **L** ·

lap: in the lap of the gods

the unknown outcome will be revealed
in the future, Providence will decide

The *lap* is the place where gifts are
placed and objects held. The word has
been a favourite figure, used in any
number of expressions, since the
sixteenth century (*the greene lap of the
new-come Spring, pleasure's lap, nature's
lap*, etc), and there are references to the
Lap of Providence and *Fortune's Lap*
dating back to the first half of the eighteenth century. It is possible that *in the
lap of the gods* is simply an early
twentieth-century coinage along the
same lines. Perhaps the inspiration
came from the practice, common in
many cultures since ancient times, of
placing gifts on the knees of statues
depicting seated gods in the hope that,
in return, a prayer would be answered.

Alternatively the expression may be a
reworking of a phrase taken from the
works of Homer (eighth century BC).
Both the *Iliad* and the *Odyssey* contain
references to matters lying *on the knees of
the gods*. One such comes in the *Iliad*
when Patroclos, friend of Achilles, has
been killed and the Trojans, having first
stripped his corpse, are intending to
sever the head and march with it
through the city to help them gain the
upper hand in the battle. It is at this
point that Automedon, aware that the
outcome was in the balance, says, *These
things lie on the knees of the gods*. In fact, the
impending humiliation brought the
sulking Achilles back into the battle and
led to the rout of the Trojans and the

death of Hector. The gods, it seems,
were on the side of Achilles. (To find out
why Achilles was invincible, see
ACHILLES' *heel*.)

*Out there you're **in the lap of the gods**,
and if you've sailed an ocean for 50 days
and got out alive, you're certainly grateful.*
GOOD HOUSEKEEPING, DECEMBER 2002

*After Lily, I wasn't sure I'd ever get pregnant
again. We left it **in the lap of the gods**.*
DAILY MIRROR, 18 MARCH 2004

For other idioms drawn from ancient
life and history, see page 317.

last-ditch

used of a final, last-minute effort to
avoid defeat or disaster

The *last ditch* was the last line of an
entrenchment: an army defending this
position was making a final desperate
effort to avoid defeat. According to
Bishop Gilbert Burnet in his *History
of his Own Time* (c. 1710), William
Prince of Orange (the future King
William III of Great Britain and
Ireland, 1650–1702) once declared in
a speech that a sure way never to see
his country lost was *to die in the last
ditch*. The bishop had been a friend
and trusted adviser of William both
before he became king and after, and
was thus present on many auspicious
occasions. A similar sentiment of
resistance was voiced across the
Atlantic when in 1798, during the
American War of Independence, the
citizens of Westmoreland, Virginia,

declared *In War We know but one additional Obligation, To die in the Last Ditch or uphold our Nation*. Twenty-three years later Thomas Jefferson employed the phrase *driven to the last ditch* figuratively (in *The Writings of Thomas Jefferson*, published 1892), and from then on *last ditch* has been used to signify 'resisting to the very end'. From around the middle of the twentieth century, it has also gained the sense of a last-minute effort to avert disaster when coupled with words like *attempt, bid, appeal, compromise*. This is now the dominant sense.

*Five-times Tour de France champion Lance Armstrong and his wife are to divorce after a **last-ditch attempt** to save their marriage failed.*
DAILY MIRROR, 5 SEPTEMBER 2003

*A **last-ditch compromise** to avoid an outright ban on smacking has been hatched by Labour peers in the Lords, but campaigners last night said it was doomed to failure because it still left children vulnerable to abuse.*
THE GUARDIAN, 4 JULY 2004

For other idioms derived from the army and warfare, see page 317.

laurels: not to rest on one's laurels
to be careful to maintain one's high standards and success, to avoid complacency and inevitable failure

To the ancient Greeks the Pythian games were second in importance only to the Olympics. They were held at Delphi in honour of the god Apollo. Apollo himself always wore a laurel wreath because his love, Daphne, was changed into a laurel tree to save her from his advances: thus the prize for victorious athletes at the games was a laurel wreath cut from the valley of Tempe. The story and the custom are very old but the phrase *to rest on one's laurels* dates only from the second half of the nineteenth century. The expression is frequently found in the negative, as a warning; like victorious athletes, people who have known success should not *rest on their laurels* and rely on past achievements; they need to continue to work hard to ensure future successes. The phrase *to look to one's laurels* dates from slightly later in the nineteenth century. It is similarly used as a warning.

*Anyone thinking of selling their standard inner-city Victorian terrace with 30ft garden had better **look to their laurels**, too: a well-designed garden, even one without a famous name attached, can add thousands to the asking price.*
THE DAILY TELEGRAPH,
11 SEPTEMBER 2002

*'So if you said, why don't I **rest on my laurels** and remain chairman of Easyjet, that's not what I'm good at. I need a job and my job is to start companies.'*
THE SUNDAY TIMES, 13 OCTOBER 2002

*But Chaplin was successful not just because he had talent and drive – he was also teachable. He kept learning and perfecting his gift. Even when he was at the height of his popularity, the highest paid performer in the world **didn't rest on his laurels**.*
THE WORD FOR TODAY, 9 JUNE 2004

For other idioms drawn from ancient life and history, see page 317.

lay: to lay it on thick
to exaggerate in order to impress

The mid-eighteenth-century figurative phrase *to lay it on thick* has the same sense as to LAY *it on with a trowel* and is a variant on Shakespeare's phrase, *thick* referring to the mortar put on with the trowel. The slang comment

A transatlantic duo

In my office I have a little device for heating water in a cup so I can have a cup of coffee whenever I feel like it. It's not very robust, so I have a couple of elastic bands round it to hold it all together. It's very much a *Heath Robinson contraption*, a clumsy device for carrying out a simple task. The expression comes from William Heath Robinson who, in the first half of the twentieth century, was known for his cartoons of elaborate and ingenious machines designed to accomplish simple tasks.

Across the Atlantic the same sort of fantastic invention, a needlessly complicated gadget, is known as a *Rube Goldberg*, after the Pulitzer prize-winning cartoonist. He, too, worked in the first half of the twentieth century.

It's a bit thick, meaning 'It's too much to put up with', is probably derived from this.

*Tonight is as much about Dolly The Person as Dolly The Singer, with lengthy and well-rehearsed anecdotes between each number. She mercilessly **lays it on thick** with the story of her upbringing.*
THE INDEPENDENT ON SUNDAY,
24 NOVEMBER 2002

*'If [Ronnie Earle] wanted **to lay it on thick**, he could mention that he's been voted Texas Prosecutor of the Year and Public Administrator of the Year for Austin or that his office was listed among the country's ten model offices by the National District Attorneys Association or that the Harvard professor who wrote 'Broken Windows' – the influential study that helped Rudy Giuliani clean up New York – called his office 'one of the most thoroughly problem-oriented agencies in criminal justice today.'*
ESQUIRE, 1 MARCH 2005

lay: to lay it on with a trowel
to flatter excessively; to exaggerate grossly

A trowel and mortar are of the bricklayer's trade. It was Shakespeare who coined the phrase *to lay it on with a trowel* in *As You Like It* (1599). It means 'to exaggerate', 'to flatter excessively'. British Prime Minister Benjamin Disraeli, who became a great favourite

of Queen Victoria, is said to have offered the poet and critic Matthew Arnold the following advice: *Everyone likes flattery; and when it comes to Royalty you should lay it on with a trowel.* From the mid-eighteenth century reference to the trowel was sometimes omitted. The OED quotes Champion (1740) with the sense of doing something to excess: *You may lay on Honour and Beauty, and all Manner of Virtues as thick as you please.*

*I like **to lay it on with a trowel**, and add bourbon to the crème Chantilly that accompanies my pecan pie.*
THE INDEPENDENT, 17 NOVEMBER 2001

*Like many adults who were deserted by their fathers, she's very susceptible to flattery, which Carole.**lays on with a trowel**.*
DAILY MAIL, 11 DECEMBER 2002

See also *to* LAY *it on thick.* For other idioms from Shakespeare, see WILLIAM SHAKESPEARE, page 152.

leaf: to turn over a new leaf
to make a fresh start, to resolve to change one's ways for the better

The need *to turn over a new leaf* or embark upon a programme of self-improvement and character-building is common to everyone at one time or another. New leaves here have nothing to do with budding foliage on trees but rather the pages of a book. The expression originated in the first half of the sixteenth century. John Heywood has *Naie she will tourne the leafe* in his book of *Proverbs* (1546). It has been suggested that the book in question might be one of precepts to be learnt and mastered for self-edification. This fits with the improving tone of the expression, but does not satisfy the present-day notion of making a totally new beginning. The image is more likely to be that of turning over a page of blots and crossed out words and beginning again on clean, white paper.

You've got big ideas about how to improve your health and how to improve your job. In fact, you probably want to improve everything around you. You're on a Jedi Knight kick. Nothing less than perfection! (When you decide to turn over a new leaf – wow! – things happen.)
CHICAGO SUN-TIMES 25 APRIL 2004

The New Year is here and with it the chance to turn over a new leaf – and perk up a flagging sex life. So here are my alternative New Year resolutions...
SUNDAY MIRROR, 2 JANUARY 2005

leap: a leap in the dark
a step of faith, a venture whose outcome cannot be predicted

Now I am about to take my last voyage, a great leap in the dark. These are said to have been the words with which English philosopher Thomas Hobbes (1588–1679) quit this world. It was not long before Hobbes' striking words were being borrowed by others. In 1697, just eighteen years after Hobbes' death, Sir John Vanbrugh published his play *The Provok'd Wife* in which one of the characters, on the verge of matrimony, exclaims, *Now I am in for Hobbes's voyage – a great leap in the dark.* Marriage, it seems, is the other great unknown: *Make matrimony, like death, a leap in the dark*, wrote Daniel Defoe in *Moll*

Flanders (1722). Nowadays the term is loosely applied to any venture, particularly a risky one.

This five-year plan is a mixture of tried and tested schemes and a leap in the dark which could be at the children's expense.
SUNDAY EXPRESS, 11 JULY 2004

But if you think this all sounds risky, you're not alone. Groups including the Consumer Credit Counselling Service and National Consumer Council (NCC) urge caution – especially with consumer debt in the UK running at an all-time high.
Lenders and borrowers who get involved are taking 'a leap in the dark', according to an NCC spokeswoman. 'Don't go in in a big way until you've tested the water,' she says.
THE INDEPENDENT ON SUNDAY,
13 MARCH 2005

leg: to pull someone's leg
to make someone the target of a good-humoured joke or deception

There has long been a macabre suggestion that this idiom refers to the right of a criminal sentenced to hanging to have his relatives pull on his legs, so hastening death. Not only is it difficult to make the connection between this ghoulish action and the light, humorous sense of the expression but written records of the phrase date from the second half of the nineteenth century when hangings took place using the long drop and death was rapid. More likely is the proposal that pulling a person's leg meant pulling it from under him, so tripping him up in public and making him a subject of ridicule.

For grating smugness, self-aggrandisement, unprickable pomposity and perpetual namedropping, even the egotistical arena of sports television presenters can offer no one to rival Butch Harmon, the American golf coach. For those of us who watch hour upon hour of Sky's otherwise excellent golf

*coverage from the United States, the conundrum is that his co-presenters never laugh at him or even **pull his leg**.*
DAILY MAIL, 28 AUGUST 2002

*My father was a director of housing and I still **pull his leg** that when he arranged work experience for me, I wasn't sure if it was to put me off or to encourage me to follow in his footsteps.*
THE INDEPENDENT, 10 NOVEMBER 2002

leg: to show a leg
to get up, get moving

This mid-nineteenth century idiom is said go back to the days when women were permitted to stay on board ship to 'comfort' the sailors whilst it was in port and even, with permission, to remain for the voyage. (When the *Royal George* sank in Portsmouth Harbour in 1782, there were three hundred women aboard.) In the mornings, when the call came *to show a leg*, the crew were expected to get up and look lively. A woman who wished to sleep in had to dangle a leg over the edge of the hammock to prove that she, and not a rating, was the occupant. Evidence for the phrase in a naval context is wanting. There is a simpler explanation, of course: the fact that one first has to put one's legs out of bed in order to get up at all.

*There's no human alarm clock any more to rouse thousands of holidaymakers through dozens of blaring loudspeakers at 7.45am: 'Good morning campers, **show a leg** you lads and lasses, rub the sleep out of your eyes and prepare for another grand day of fun.'*
DAILY EXPRESS, 27 MARCH 2004

See also SON *of a gun* and, for other nautical idioms, A LIFE ON THE OCEAN WAVES, page 24.

level: to do one's level best
to do one's very best

On 24 January 1848 James Wilson Marshall discovered gold while building a sawmill on John Sutter's land in California. News of the find soon leaked out and people from all over the region and beyond raced to the area to seek their fortune. *Level best* dates from this period in the mid-nineteenth century when people panning for gold in the Californian goldfields would shake the grit and gravel in their pans until it was level and the precious yellow metal could be seen more easily.

The gravel was said to have *panned well* or *panned poorly*, depending on the gold yield. This became the source of the idiom *to* PAN *out (well/badly)*, meaning 'to work out'.

*Beckham has **done his level best** to disfigure himself beyond repair. Shaven-headed and frowning, with his beautiful body scribbled all over with bad art and worse lettering...*
THE DAILY TELEGRAPH, 12 JUNE 2004

*I feel sincerely sorry for Tim Henman. Year after year, he **does his level best**. But deep down, he knows that there will always be the equivalent of an unseeded Croat to trample on his dreams.*
THE MAIL ON SUNDAY, 4 JULY 2004

lick: to lick into shape
to give form to something, to make something or someone presentable

The ancients believed that bears gave birth to nothing more than formless lumps of flesh which they then literally licked into cub-shape. Pliny the Elder describes this in his *Naturalis Historia* (AD 77) and Plutarch takes up the theme in *Moralia: On Affection for Offspring* (c. AD 95): *And the she-bear brings forth her young formless and without joints, and with her tongue, as with a tool, she moulds into shape their skin*. This ancient belief, being first recorded in English in the early fifteenth century, seems to have prevailed until well into the sixteenth century, doubtless sustained by medieval bestiaries.

The belief took on a metaphorical dimension quite early. Around AD 150 Aulus Gellius described how Virgil, close to death, begged his friend to destroy the *Aeneid* because he had not had time to perfect it: *For he said that as the bear brought forth her young formless and misshapen, and afterwards by licking gave it form and shape, just so the fresh products of his mind were rude in form, but afterwards by working over them he gave them definite form and expression* (*Noctes Atticae*). Which is the exact meaning of our modern idiom: putting something in order and making it presentable, or getting someone to behave or work as expected.

Twelve unemployed young men volunteer for a three-week course designed to equip them to grab jobs, unaware of what awaits them: being **licked into shape** *by an American trio whose methods involve punishing exercise sessions, early-morning runs, lessons and homework.*
THE SUNDAY TIMES, 4 JANUARY 2004

In 2002, [Jamie Oliver] advertised for jobless applicants to become chefs in his restaurant venture. Watching the feckless, lazy, ungrateful crew being **licked into shape** *on the Channel 4 series* Jamie's Kitchen *made compulsive viewing and helped to win Jamie a new army of fans.*
EVENING STANDARD,
14 JANUARY 2005

For other myths derived from fabled animal behaviour, see page 318.

limelight: in the limelight
in the public eye, the centre of attention

In 1825 Thomas Drummond invented the Drummond light. This consisted of a cylinder of calcium oxide, or lime, heated in a hot hydrogen-oxygen flame and put either in front of a reflector or behind a lens. The result was a glaring white light that was visible from a great distance. Drummond, a Lieutenant in the Royal Engineers, was working with the Ordnance Survey in Ireland and used his invention to measure distances accurately. His invention was later used in lighthouses and also in the theatre, where it served as a spotlight to draw attention to the principal artiste on the stage. Someone standing *in the limelight* was very much the focus of public attention.

There are variants to the idiom. Someone who steps *out of the limelight* is avoiding scrutiny while a person who *steals the limelight* is pushing someone else aside to become the centre of attention.

Caroline, who's ingrained in the public comedy consciousness for her roles in Men Behaving Badly *and* Jonathan Creek, *is stepping* **out of the limelight** *to spend more time with her partner Sam Farmer and their two-and-a-half-year-old daughter Emily Rose.*
GOOD HOUSEKEEPING, MARCH 2002

As notoriety has grown for rapper Eminem, he has forced himself into a focused daily regimen, he says, laying low to avoid getting lost **in the limelight**.
CHICAGO SUN-TIMES,
30 DECEMBER 2002

lion: the lion's share
the larger part

In one of Aesop's fables, a lion and three other animals go hunting together and kill a stag which is then divided into equal pieces. Just as the animals are about to eat, the lion stops them. The first portion is his, he says, by right of his kingship over them. A second share is also his due because he is the strongest among them, while a third part must be made over to him because of his courage. The lion allows that the fourth portion belongs to the other creatures but warns them to touch it if they dare!

In a second fable by Aesop a lion, a fox and an ass make up the hunting party. The ass apportions the kill equally but is savaged to death by the lion. The fox then divides the spoil, a huge portion for the lion and a meagre one for himself.

In both fables might wins out over timidity and the lion gets the greatest share. The idiom has been current since the late eighteenth century.

*Recently, when my father was ill, my brothers made little effort to help out... They both have children and seem to think that, as I don't, it's only fair that I do **the lion's share**. How can I get the boys to pull their weight?*
GOOD HOUSEKEEPING, JUNE 2002

*Perhaps because he is more accustomed to the vast walk-in clothes closets more common in American homes, it is her husband who enjoys **the lion's share** of the wardrobe space.*
THE SUNDAY TIMES, 9 MARCH 2003

For other idioms derived from fables, see page 318.

lock, stock and barrel
completely, in its entirety

Although these sound like the contents of a hardware shop, the *lock, stock and barrel* referred to are the main parts of a musket. The *lock* is the firing mechanism, the *stock* the wooden handle that rests against the shoulder and the *barrel* the metal tube through which the shot is expelled. *Lock, stock and barrel* means the complete weapon. The earliest

recorded use is in a letter written by Sir Walter Scott in 1817: *Like the High-land-man's gun, she wants stock, lock, and barrel, to put her into repair*. This form of the expression was common for a hundred years but from the middle of the nineteenth century it gave ground before the word order we recognise today.

*Neither book does justice (or injustice) to Blair's domestic programme, inherited **lock, stock and barrel** from Thatcherism.*
THE SUNDAY TIMES, 4 JULY 2004

For a similar phrase, see HOOK, *line and sinker*.

loggerheads, at
involved in a bitter argument

The idiom dates from the first half of the nineteenth century but an earlier phrase *to go to loggerheads*, meaning 'to come to blows', dates from the second half of the seventeenth. The exact origin of these phrases is difficult to pin down. One theory hinges on the fact that, in the sixteenth century, a *logger-head* was 'a blockhead', 'a person with no sense' (a *logger* being a rough block of wood tied to a horse's leg to prevent it wandering off). Perhaps the idea was that only *loggerheads* would rush into a fight or argument instead of sensibly considering an alternative solution.

A second theory looks to a seventeenth-century definition of *logger-head*. The word was applied to a long-handled device with a great metal ball at one end, which was heated in the fire and then used to melt tar and pitch. The suggestion, tentatively advanced by the OED and for which evidence is wanting, is that such implements may also have been used as weapons on occasion, perhaps in naval battles if the enemy managed to get too close. In an exchange of this kind, the opposing forces would be truly *at loggerheads*.

*The feud between Nick Faldo and Mark James finally came to an end at the Lancome Trophy here yesterday. The two have been **at loggerheads** ever since the publication of James' controversial account of his Ryder Cup captaincy at Brookline last year.*
THE INDEPENDENT, 15 SEPTEMBER 2000

*As de Tocqueville pointed out almost 170 years ago, democracy and liberty are often **at loggerheads**, and Americans value the former above the latter.*
EVENING STANDARD,
4 OCTOBER 2001

*Earlier in the day, the Minister found himself **at loggerheads** with Railtrack chief executive Steve Marshall, who claimed Mr Byers's masterplan to save the railways, unveiled yesterday, would set their recovery back by up to two years.*
DAILY MAIL, 24 OCTOBER 2001

See THE OLD CURIOSITY SHOP OF LINGUISTICS, page 198.

long in the tooth
old

A glance in a horse's mouth will reveal the animal's age. One sign of advancing years is the state of its gums, which recede to reveal the roots of the teeth, making them look longer. Horses are not alone in this; the same applies to humans, and a mouthful of long teeth is a sure sign that the wearer of the smile is well past the first flush of youth. The French playwright Molière was well aware of the problem: *The teeth have time to grow long while we wait for the death of someone* (*Le Médecin Malgré Lui*, 1666). But it was not until around the middle of the nineteenth century that the phrase was used figuratively in English:

His cousin was now of more than middle age, and had nobody's word but her own

for the beauty which she said she once possessed. She was lean, and yellow, and long in the tooth; all the red and white in all the toy-shops in London could not make a beauty of her…in fine, a woman who might be easy of conquest, but whom only a very bold man would think of conquering (William Makepeace Thackeray, *The History of Henry Esmond*, 1852).

*If you're surprised that **long-in-the-tooth** rockers like The Rolling Stones and The Who are out on tour again, then perhaps you don't know this fact about the concert industry: It's fuelled by groups that were around long before Britney Spears could say 'Oops!' Slickly marketed teen idols may dominate the airwaves and MTV, but it's the veterans who bring in the big money on tour.*
CHRISTIAN SCIENCE MONITOR,
6 SEPTEMBER 2002

See also *(straight) from the* HORSE'S *mouth* and, for other horsey idioms, see page 319.

loose: a loose cannon
someone who behaves unpredictably, often with damaging results

Light guns had been used on board English warships since around the mid-fourteenth century, placed on the castles at stem and stern. In the sixteenth century great muzzle-loading cannon were developed. They were too heavy for the castles and were carried low in the ship, their muzzles protruding through gunports. They were mounted on gun carriages so that they could be wheeled out of the gunport for loading and pushed back for firing. When not being used the guns were secured to the deck. Sometimes, with the pitching of the vessel, a gun carriage would work loose and the huge cannon would roll back perilously and unpredictably, a danger to all and to the wooden fabric of the ship itself.

Surprisingly, given the long history of artillery at sea, the metaphorical use of the expression to describe an unpredictable person is recorded only in the latter part of the twentieth century.

Society still wishes to protect itself from the free woman, **the loose cannon,** *the wronged woman who will not lie down and take it.*
MAVIS CHEEK, MRS FYTTON'S
COUNTRY LIFE, 2000

Of course, Wells has been called **a loose cannon** *and loudmouth before. In these pages, Wells uses his colorful language to give the reader a locker-room view of baseball…in an era when big money and free agency have made the sport more peripatetic than ever.*
DENVER ROCKY MOUNTAIN NEWS,
4 APRIL 2003

She valued his skills as an editor, but regarded him as a '**loose cannon**' *liable to endanger the Trinity Mirror group.*
THE OBSERVER, 16 MAY 2004

loose: at a loose end
having nothing in particular to do

The reference is to a rope or piece of string that has been left unconnected and dangling loose. *Loose end* has described 'something unfinished or undecided' since the sixteenth century. Modern idiom has *to tie up loose ends*, meaning 'to finish things off properly'. The phrase *at a loose end*, meaning 'without regular employment', like a piece of string left hanging to no purpose, dates from around the middle of the nineteenth century. More recently, the sense has shifted to suggest having time on one's hands and nothing to do to fill it. Bored teenagers are often so described when, for example, their mates are all busy and they sit at home with time on their hands. In this sense, the connection with employment has been lost.

She had the kitchen to herself… There she half listened to the radio, read the paper, learned her lines, pottered and, as she said, was never **at a loose end**.
LORNA SAGE, BAD BLOOD, 2000

The mechanic, who denied that he was 'on the prowl' on the day Sarah vanished, said he had had no plans for that day. He claimed he spent the day drifting around, and added: 'I had a lot on my mind and no particular place to go. I was **at a loose end**.'
DAILY MIRROR, 5 DECEMBER 2001

loose: with/on a loose rein
without strict hands-on control;
indulgently

When a rider relaxes the reins of his mount and allows them to go slack, he is riding *with a loose rein*. One advocate of the loose rein was John Wesley, the itinerant eighteenth-century evangelist. Wesley travelled over a hundred thousand miles on horseback, much of it over difficult terrain. He would throw the reins over his horse's neck and then settle down to read poetry, history or philosophy along the way. He had very few falls and recommended the use of a loose rein to all his fellow travellers, convinced that it prevented horses from stumbling. The phrase *with a loose rein* was put to figurative use in the second half of the eighteenth century with the sense 'without strict control'. In 1775 the philosopher and politician Edmund Burke commented upon a sultan *who governs with a loose rein, that he may govern at all (Selected Works, 1775).*

Of course, the opposite, to keep someone *on a tight rein*, a metaphor which appeared rather later, means 'under strict control'. A more recent extension is found from the 1930s onwards: *to give someone free rein*, that is, to allow them complete freedom to act.

He rode his team from the different
*Whitehall departments **on a loose rein**,*
chain-smoking, intervening seldom but
always pertinently and to good effect.
THE DAILY TELEGRAPH,
17 SEPTEMBER 2000

*He relentlessly **keeps a tight rein** on*
spending, while she recklessly blows almost
a grand on window dressing.
THE GUARDIAN, 28 APRIL 2004

For other horsey idioms, see page 319.

lurch: to leave someone in the lurch

to abandon (a friend) to a difficult
situation

Lourche was a dicing game, supposedly
resembling backgammon, which was
played in sixteenth-century France.
The word, borrowed into English as
lurch, was used in a variety of games to
indicate one player being far ahead of
the other. In the game of cribbage, for
instance, *to lurch* was to leave one's
adversary trailing, having scored sixty-
one before he had reached thirty-one.
By the late sixteenth century a number
of idiomatic phrases centring on *lurch*
were being coined, among them *to leave*
in the lurch, meaning 'to leave someone
behind to face difficult circumstances':

> *There was I, waiting at the church,*
> *Waiting at the church,*
> *Waiting at the church;*
> *When I found he'd left me in the lurch,*
> *Lor', how it did upset me!*
> *All at once, he sent me round a note*
> *Here's the very note,*
> *This is what he wrote:*
> *'Can't get away to marry you today,*
> *My wife won't let me!'*
> (Henry Pether & Fred Leigh, 1906)

Midwives have volunteered to give up their
days off and work for free to keep an NHS
maternity unit open... An eight-strong
team of midwives at Harwich Maternity
Unit in Essex have pledged to work for
nothing to ensure that vulnerable women
*and babies are not **left in the lurch**.*
DAILY MAIL, 16 SEPTEMBER 2003

· M ·

McCoy: the real McCoy

the authentic, genuine article; the real thing

Theories about the origin of this expression abound on both sides of the Atlantic. Space does not permit a full list, so here are one or two to be going on with.

Many authorities subscribe to the theory that the phrase refers to Kid McCoy, an American boxer famous around the beginning of the twentieth century. On one occasion he was being provoked by a drunk who would not accept that this was really the lightweight champion. Eventually the boxer, goaded beyond endurance, punched the drunk and knocked him out. The man's first words as he came to were, 'You're the real McCoy.' The fighter is also said to have had so many imitators at showgrounds throughout the country that he was forced to bill himself as Kid 'The Real' McCoy. Could this be why the drunk disbelieved him?

A second American, Bill McCoy, was an infamous smuggler in the Prohibition period who brought hard liquor down the Atlantic coast of America from Canada. Hence, anything described as *the real McCoy* was the genuine article, not a home-brewed or distilled substitute.

Scotland provides two somewhat earlier derivations. One tells of a family feud where two branches of the MacKay clan were in dispute over which was the senior. Eventually it was established that the MacKays of Reay,

the Reay MacKays, held this honour. *Reay* could readily become *real*.

Most probable is the evidence that points to an advertising slogan used by Edinburgh whisky distillers Messrs G Mackay and Co. The Scottish National Dictionary, which records all Scottish words and phrases in use since 1700, says that *a drappie o' the real MacKay*, current in 1856, was taken as a company slogan in 1870. Robert Louis Stevenson referred to it in a letter written in 1883, and in 1906 another Scottish author, Robert Barr, used the phrase: *as we say in Scotland, a real MacKay – the genuine article* (*A Rock in the Baltic*). It is possible, then, that the Scottish whisky slogan *real MacKay* travelled to America, where it was transformed into the *real McCoy*, probably through the influence of a professional boxer and a liquor smuggler.

*Mason is **the real McCoy**, the comic as protester, the guy we love to say the unsayable.*
DAILY MAIL, 11 OCTOBER 2001

*We've no doubt that for most of you cleaning the oven and grill pan is the worst job in the kitchen and most cleaners just don't measure up to the task. We asked Michelle to take a bottle of Grillomat home to test, as we thought it would probably be just another run-of-the-mill cleaner that's all bark and no bite. But no, we've found **the real McCoy**! 'It's absolutely amazing,' she reported back.*
LAKELAND LIMITED HOME SHOPPING CATALOGUE, 2001

mad: as mad as a hatter
eccentric, crazy

Felt fabric for hat making was made from innumerable short animal hairs which bound together when treated. In order to coarsen the hair shafts and facilitate the felting process, the fur was first painted with nitrate of mercury. Work was carried out in rooms with little ventilation, and constant inhalation of the fumes slowly led to mercury poisoning amongst hatters. Some of their psychological symptoms included irritability, nervousness, fits of anger and memory loss. These, together with involuntary twitching and shaking, gave rise to the expression *mad as a hatter*, which originally meant not 'insane' but 'very angry'. (In North American usage, *mad* is also a slang term for 'angry'.)

The earliest known record of the phrase is in *The Clockmaker* (1837–8), by Canadian author Thomas Chandler Haliburton. Certainly North America had a thriving hat trade, so the phrase may well have originated across the Atlantic. In Britain the idiom was used by Thackeray in *Pendennis* (1849) and subsequently by Thomas Hughes in *Tom Brown's Schooldays* (1858). In the latter instance, *mad* was understood as 'eccentric'. Lewis Carroll's choice of the Hatter (a crazy, not an angry character) in *Alice's Adventures in Wonderland* (1865) doubtless confirmed this sense, which has predominated ever since.

He's *as mad as a hatter* and probably has one of the best jobs in the world. The wacky host of TG4's new series Amu le Hector *might not have the size of audience he deserves on the tiny Gaelic station – but that is bound to change.*
THE PEOPLE, 28 SEPTEMBER 2003

He's a brilliant bloke but *mad as a hatter*. He knows everything there is to know about racing, but ask him how to put on a kettle and he wouldn't have a clue.
THE RACING POST, 24 APRIL 2005

For more on Lewis Carroll's Mad Hatter, see *as* MAD *as a March hare*.

mad: as mad as a March hare
crazy

Hares have been considered mad since Chaucer's day. The reference is thought to be to their courtship behaviour in which the males pursue the females and then box with them before mating. It might be supposed from the idiom that this wild behaviour is confined to the month of March. In fact the breeding season is lengthy and the courtship ritual remains unchanged, so why *March* hare? There is some evidence that the original saying was *mad as a marsh hare*, which was then corrupted to *March hare*. The early-Tudor poet Colyn Blowbol has *as brainless as a Marshe hare* (*Testament*, c. 1500) and one of Erasmus's *Aphorisms* (1542) reads *Mad as a marsh hare*, with the comment *hares are wilder in marshes from the absence of hedges and cover.*

The earliest known instance of the idiom in its familiar form is in John Skelton's *A Replycacion* (1501). More familiar to the contemporary reader, in Lewis Carroll's *Alice's Adventures in Wonderland* (1865), the March Hare joins that other well-known eccentric, the Mad Hatter, at a tea party. Carroll comments: *In that direction..lives a Hatter; and in that direction…lives a March hare… They're both mad.* (See under *as* MAD *as a hatter* for more information on him.) Incidentally, Carroll does not describe his character as the Mad Hatter. This quotation is as close as he comes. The epithet is the invention of his enthusiastic readership.

One spin-off expression that dates from the mid-sixteenth century and which remains current is *hare-brained*. It refers to people who exhibit the same crazy characteristics as the mad hare, and is now often applied to schemes or plans that have little chance of success.

*My life has been awash with lunatics... My dear old grandad was **mad as a March hare**.*
THE OBSERVER, 22 OCTOBER 2000

Even Jimmy [Carr] was shocked when Brigitte Nielsen came on the Friday Night Project. *He says: 'She's **mad as a March hare**. She kept on getting naked and grabbing my packet and going, "Hey business is good." I've no idea why. She's mental.'*
DAILY MIRROR, 25 MARCH 2005

See ALLITERATIVE SIMILES, page 237.

make: to make (both) ends meet

to live within one's means

People have been lamenting their inability *to make ends meet* and live within their income since the seventeenth century; others are content with just enough to satisfy their needs: *Worldly wealth he cared not for, desiring onely to make both ends meet; and as for that little that lapped over he gave it to pious uses* (Thomas Fuller, *History of the Worthies of England*, 1662).

It is possible that the expression comes from accountancy and the need to balance both ends of the financial year. Tobias Smollett used the phrase in this way in *Roderick Random* (1748): *He made shift to make the two ends of the year meet*. Against this theory is the fact that Smollett's reference is the only known example of this more contextualised wording and it was written well after the phrase first came into use.

*Naturally, divorcées tell a different story: husbands running off with younger women while they downsize to a smaller home and work **to make ends meet** and watch their* *husbands swan about on endless holidays with their new girlfriends.*
GOOD HOUSEKEEPING, APRIL 2001

*One million pensioners are ready to sell their home to fund their old age, research revealed yesterday. Growing numbers are preparing to downsize to a smaller house simply **to make ends meet**.*
DAILY MAIL, 1 APRIL 2005

make: to make the grade

to achieve the required standard,
to be successful

The idiom is a North American one and springs from the use of *grade* for 'gradient' when describing the slope of a road or railway. *Making the grade* presumably alludes to getting to the top of a hill or, figuratively, climbing to the top of the ladder of success. An alternative explanation uses another sense of *grade*, that of reaching the 'academic standard' or 'pass mark'. Whatever the precise origin, the contemporary meaning is the same; the idiom has been current since the early twentieth century.

RURAL SCHOOLS STRUGGLE TO **MAKE THE GRADE** – MOST SUPPORT GOES TO URBAN SCHOOLS, ACCORDING TO REPORT
HEADLINE, PALM SPRINGS DESERT SUN, 22 FEBRUARY 2003

*An MBA from a top-ranking school such as Stanford would seem an obvious choice if you can **make the grade**. However, if your GMAT score is too low or the cost is prohibitive, it may be worth looking at some of the lesser-known American schools.*
THE INDEPENDENT, 12 MAY 2005

Man/Girl Friday

an efficient and valued personal assistant or helper, with a wide range of skills

The original Man Friday was the inspiration of Daniel Defoe, a character from his well-known novel *Robinson Crusoe* (1719). The shipwrecked Crusoe has lived alone on his desert island for many years when, to his amazement, he finds a human footprint in the sand. Later he comes across cannibalistic savages who have come to the island by canoe to eat their prisoners. When they next return, Crusoe frightens them away with his guns and saves their young victim, whom he teaches civilised ways. He calls his new companion *Man Friday*: *Man* meaning 'manservant' and *Friday* being the day they met. *Man Friday* came to signify an 'aide' or 'assistant' towards the beginning of the nineteenth century.

It could only be a matter of time before *Girl Friday* was coined to describe 'a female assistant'. This happened around 1940, the term being subsequently popularised by the 1940 comedy film *His Girl Friday*, in which a newspaper editor plots and schemes to prevent his top reporter, who is also his ex-wife, from remarrying. The term did not meet universal acclaim in the feminist era, but it remains in use in the twenty-first century.

*Ask a **Man Friday** to clean up the dog's muck odourising the main entrance and he'll go fetch a woman from somewhere.*
THE GUARDIAN, 13 FEBRUARY 2003

*But much to everyone's horror she changed her mind and ditched all thoughts of a degree in favour of a full-time job as **Girl Friday** for the deli in her hometown of Kirkcudbright, Scotland.*
DAILY MIRROR, 7 AUGUST 2003

For other idioms inspired by literary characters, see *(little)* GOODY-*two-shoes* and *to grow like* TOPSY. For idioms drawn from literature, see page 319.

man: a man of the world
a socially sophisticated person, one well versed in the ways of the world

What, historically, was a *man of the world*? Laurence Tomson, in his translation of Calvin's *Sermons* (1579), explains: *This man is of the worlde, that is to say, he is married: this man is of the Churche, that is to say, Spirituall.* This was at a time when the question of whether clergy should be permitted to marry or not was often debated. In England the 1549 law permitting clergy marriages was revoked soon after by Catholic Queen Mary. Thus, when in Shakespeare's *As You Like It* (1599) the court jester Touchstone speaks with joy of his forthcoming marriage to Audrey, the country lass, she replies: *I do desire it with all my heart; and I hope it is no dishonest desire, to desire to be a woman of the world*. Audrey meant that it was a respectable goal to want to be an ordinary lay person and not to aspire to holy orders.

This use of *a man of the world* to describe 'a secular person' persisted into the eighteenth century. In his novel *Tom Jones* (1749), Henry Fielding had this to say: *This gentleman whom Mr Jones now visited, was what they call a man of the world; that is to say, a man who directs his conduct in this world as one, who being fully persuaded there is no other, is resolved to make the most of this.* A person determined to make his way in the world inevitably becomes experienced in its ways, so that, by the mid-nineteenth century, *man of the world* had come to describe a sophisticated and worldly-wise individual.

*Soi-disant was brought to English in the 1750s by an urbane **man of the world**, the cynical, witty Earl of Chesterfield.*
THE GUARDIAN, 21 MARCH 2001

*Warren thought he was **a man of the world** before he became a cabbie. 'I was so naive it was untrue.'*
THE GUARDIAN, 25 MARCH 2004

man: the man in the street
the average, ordinary person

The term goes back to a time during the Industrial Revolution when town populations had swollen and there were rather more men in the street than formerly, all with their opinions. In 1831 the English political diarist Charles Greville used the phrase in his famous *Memoirs*, the context making it clear that the idiom was not yet in common use: *The other [side affirms] that the King will not consent to it, knowing, as 'the man in the street' (as we call him at Newmarket) always does, the greatest secrets of kings.* It swiftly gained currency, however, as the common view of the ordinary citizen became more important in a developing democracy.

International policy means far more than what politicians traditionally saw as foreign policy. To the man in the street, trade is of far more importance.
CHARLES KENNEDY, THEN LEADER OF THE LIBERAL DEMOCRATS, SPEECH, 25 JANUARY 2000

For another idiom with this meaning, see *the* MAN *on the Clapham omnibus*.

man: the man on the Clapham omnibus
the average man, the man in the street

In the nineteenth century, the legal profession was moving towards a concept of the ordinary, reasonable man. This idea needed a name, and Lord Bowen (1835–94) memorably and aptly coined the expression *the man on the Clapham omnibus* in the case of *McQuire v. Western Morning News*. It was rapidly accepted as a figure for the ordinary person of common sense, represented by members of the jury. According to an article in *The Listener* dated 30 July 1959, it had become a phrase *familiar to English lawyers*, though modern usage no longer restricts it to legal contexts.

A major simplification of the tax and benefits regime is long overdue. The man on the Clapham omnibus should be able to fill in his tax return without the assistance of a financial adviser or the Inland Revenue.
THE DAILY TELEGRAPH, 7 NOVEMBER 2000

For an idiom with the same meaning, see *the* MAN *in the street*.

marines: tell it to the marines
a remark expressing incredulity at a story

The phrase is not American, as is often supposed, but English. The *marines* referred to are the Duke of York and Albany's Maritime Regiment of Foot, a body of 1,200 soldiers first recruited in 1664 for military service on board ship.

Samuel Pepys' *Diary* for that year supposedly reports how Charles II was at a banquet with the diarist, who was entertaining him with anecdotes about the navy. The subject of flying fish came up in conversation and had the company laughing in disbelief, all except for an officer with the marines who claimed that he, too, had glimpsed these creatures. The king was convinced, saying that the marines had experience of the seas and customs in different lands and that should he ever again come across a strange tale he would check the truth of it by *telling it to the marines*.

Unfortunately, diligent searches of Pepys' *Diary* have come up with no such entry and the story has proved to be an ingenious twentieth-century hoax dreamed up by the novelist Major W P Drury, who spread it abroad in a book of naval stories he had written, *The Tadpole of an Archangel* (1904). Drury was obviously inspired by Pepys' position as clerk of the King's ships when the Duke of

York and Albany's Maritime Regiment of Foot was formed, and this gave the story its ring of credibility.

Instead, the expression probably has its origins in the contempt sailors in the navy had for the men of the marines. The sailors were jealous for their seafaring traditions and considered the marines to be gullible idiots with no understanding of the sea, a view encapsulated in the early-nineteenth-century expression *tell it to the marines, the sailors won't believe it*. The phrase as we know it today is found from the second half of the nineteenth century, a shortening of the older expression.

Despite the somewhat uncomplimentary reference to the marines, Paul Dickson in his *War Slang: American Fighting Words and Phrases Since the Civil War* (2003) says that *Tell that to the Marines* was used in recruiting posters in America.

A year on [the film] has been resurrected and now looks even more topical, for it tells how American confidence can fatally misjudge the foreign world and blunder into war. **Go tell it to the Marines**.
THE INDEPENDENT, 29 NOVEMBER 2002

*[Donald Rumsfeld] describes the situation in Iraq as 'untidy'. He should go and '***tell it to the marines***'!*
DAILY EXPRESS, 15 APRIL 2003

For other nautical idioms, see A LIFE ON THE OCEAN WAVES, page 24.

(you) mark my words

believe me, what I say is true; listen to my warning

Mark has been used with the sense 'give thought and attention to' since the fifteenth century. In his 1535 version of the Bible, Miles Coverdale rendered Isaiah 28:23 thus: *Take hede and heare my voyce, pondre and merck my wordes wel*. In addition to this sense of 'pay careful attention to what I am saying, and believe it', the phrase has been used ever since to draw attention to a reprimand or warning.

Mark my words, *Mr Snuffles means nothing good by this.*
THE DAILY TELEGRAPH,
4 FEBRUARY 2004

There are some advantages to growing old. For one thing, people stop trying to reform you. As children we were told things like: 'If you pull faces like that, one of these days you'll get stuck like it', and later on, 'If you carry on the way you're going, you'll die before your time, my girl, **you mark my words***.'*

By the time you're 84, they've given up on you. Whatever shape your face is going to get stuck in, it's done it already. And whatever terrible fates may await you, dying before your time isn't one of them.
WESTERN MAIL, 29 OCTOBER 2004

mend: to mend fences

to reconcile conflicting political views; to restore a broken relationship

In 1879 Senator John Sherman made a trip home to his Ohio farm, announcing that the purpose of his visit was *to look after my fences*. His statement was misunderstood, however. Instead of taking his remark at face value and regarding his visit as a domestic one, the people in his electoral district assumed a political motive, taking his words to mean that he was back in Ohio to shore up his political support through personal contact.

In America the phrase has meant just that ever since, first appearing in the Congressional Record to explain the summer whereabouts of politicians in August 1888. By the time it crossed to Britain the phrase also had the broader political sense of 'to reconcile conflicting views', and was then applied even more generally to the repair of professional or personal relationships. One thing is certain, however: the turbulent start to the twenty-first century has necessitated many attempts at repairing fences, so there is no danger of the phrase becoming obsolete on either side of the Atlantic: *Bush is looking at his upcoming trips to Europe and an international economic summit in Georgia as opportunities to mend fences with allies over Iraq and to promote the spread of democracy in the Middle East* (WJLA-TV report, 1 June 2004).

*Dr Boston…has some ground to make up before relations between him and heads and teachers can be described as cordial… He would be well advised to try **to mend fences** at today's annual conference of the QCA.*
THE INDEPENDENT, 9 OCTOBER 2002

*Don't you wonder what some people might have done differently if they'd known they wouldn't be around for the tomorrow we all take for granted? Hugged their loved ones more? Contacted estranged friends **to mend fences**?*
THE WORD FOR TODAY, 29 JUNE 2004

method: there is method in one's madness
there is a sound reason behind apparently illogical behaviour

The phrase is from Shakespeare's *Hamlet* (1604) and Polonius's comment on the prince's feigned madness: *Though this be madnesse, Yet there is Method in't*. The American short-story writer Edgar Allan Poe alluded to the line in *The Gold Bug* (1843), and other nineteenth-century writers subsequently began to use the idiom in the form known today.

*Their strategy is not to protect those targeted by organised racists, but to target them first: not eliminate racism, but to embrace it and enshrine it in law… **There is method in their madness**. They believe that by addressing anxieties about crime*

and immigration, they can 'neutralise' the threat of a surge by a populist right.
THE GUARDIAN, 25 APRIL 2002

For other idioms from Shakespeare, see WILLIAM SHAKESPEARE, page 152.

mettle: to be on one's mettle
to be ready to prove one's worth when faced with a difficulty

During the sixteenth century the word *metal* began to be used figuratively to denote 'the quality of a person's character and disposition'. It signified, in particular, 'a spirited or courageous temperament'. *Mettle* was originally a variant of the same word, which gradually, between the early eighteenth and nineteenth centuries, came to be the accepted spelling of its figurative uses. *To be on one's mettle*, meaning 'to be prepared to put one's energy and courage to the test' and *to put someone on his/her mettle*, meaning 'to test a person's courage or endurance', both date from the seventeenth century and are current favourites amongst sports journalists.

*Even Phineas Fogg would have been **put on his mettle** had he been required to get from end to end of Wales in a day with no help but that afforded by the National Rail Timetable.*
THE DAILY TELEGRAPH,
14 NOVEMBER 2001

*This theatre has established itself in less than a decade as an outpost for strong acting in classic and modern drama. You get the chance to see Hollywood actors treading the boards, trying to **prove their acting mettle** away from the sanitised studio system.*
THE ECONOMIST, 2 MAY 2005

See THE OLD CURIOSITY SHOP OF LINGUISTICS, page 198.

Midas touch, the

the ability to make money, to have continuous good fortune

Midas, the legendary king of Phrygia, was granted a wish by Bacchus in return for a helping hand extended to one of his followers. Midas wished that everything he touched should turn into gold. Problems arose, however, when he tried to eat. The wish was dissolved when Midas washed in the River Pactolus in Lydia.

Figurative uses of the phrase *Midas touch* go back to the mid-seventeenth century; by the late nineteenth there are references to knowledge and skills being turned into wealth. More recently the phrase's definition has broadened out still further. It is no longer applied uniquely to the ability to make money, but can also describe someone who is consistently fortunate and successful in any activity.

The Midas touch has not deserted the novelist Sebastian Faulks... Warner Bros has just decided to release the £15 million film of his wartime thriller Charlotte Gray *in time for a tilt at the Oscars and he has also sold his next novel* On Green Dolphin Street, *for an even bigger budget movie.*
THE DAILY TELEGRAPH,
29 SEPTEMBER 2001

*Jack McConnell's **Midas touch** seems to have well and truly disappeared. The First Minister used to be able to spin his way out of problems, dodge the blame and gain support from his colleagues at the same time. But now everything Mr McConnell touches appears to end in disaster.*
THE SCOTSMAN, 19 MAY 2004

The Old Curiosity Shop of Linguistics

Delving into the etymology of words, and particularly idioms, has been aptly described by the chairman of Harvard's Department of Linguistics as the Old Curiosity Shop of linguistic research. One French etymologist entitled his book *The Museum of French Expressions*. In that shop or museum, there are some antiques that can no longer be found in everyday language.

The word *beck*, for instance, was used from the fourteenth to the nineteenth centuries to describe a gesture of command. In modern English it is fossilised in the nineteenth-century phrase *to be at someone's beck and call*, 'to be constantly at someone's service'. Other examples are *hue* (HUE *and cry*), *loggerhead* (*at* LOGGERHEADS), *mettle* (*to be on one's* METTLE), *petard* (HOIST *with one's own petard*), *scot-free* (*to get off* SCOT-FREE), *trice* (*in a* TRICE) and *umbrage* (*to take* UMBRAGE), all now fallen from common usage, except in everyday phrases. Further examples of obsolete words that live on in idioms can be found in COUPLINGS, page 294.

There are, however, words still commonly used in English which have lost some of the shades of meaning they once had. Sometimes these obsolete meanings are preserved in idiomatic phrases.

Take the word *pain*, for instance. Today it means 'physical suffering', such as the hurt you experience when you cut yourself with a knife, but it does have earlier senses. For instance, it once meant 'punishment', so when we use the phrase *under* or *on pain of death*, we are referring to this former meaning.

Pain also once meant 'trouble' or 'effort'. This sense is evident in the expressions *to take great pains to do something* or *to be at pains to do something* or *for one's pains* which all emphasise the work we have put into accomplishing a thing.

For similar senses of the word *mind*, see IT'S ALL IN THE BLOOD, page 114.

*When Oprah Winfrey, known for having **a Midas touch**, sang the praises of TiVo last year, the company's stock shot up more than 10 percent over a few days.*
SAN JOSÉ MERCURY NEWS, 12 JUNE 2004

Midas inherited his kingdom from Gordius. For more about him see GORDIAN *knot*. For details of how Midas passed on his wealth, see *as rich as* CROESUS. For other idioms derived from ancient legends, see page 317.

middle of the road
a position mid-way between two extremes, a safe position; inoffensive, bland

There are sound reasons for choosing the middle of the road. According to Philip Thicknesse, who in 1777 wrote a book called *A Year's Journey* describing his travels around France and Spain, *It is necessary...to keep in the middle of the road, so as not to be too suddenly surprised;* while a report in the *Rocky Mountain News* for 17 July 1892 advocated the middle of the road *because side tracks are rough, and they're hard to walk.*

In the United States by the late nineteenth century *middle of the road* was a political phrase, coined to describe a person or policy that took no risks, that avoided extremes. It was particularly applied to the moderates of the Populist party (originally the People's Party) established in 1891 to advance agrarian issues: *The only honest Populist is the 'middle-of-the-road' Populist* (Congressional Record, 10 December 1896). The phrase remains a political one. Harold Wilson, British Prime Minister in the 1960s and '70s, claimed: *I'm at my best in a messy, middle-of-the-road muddle.* From the second half of the twentieth century, it has also been used to describe arts and entertainment popularly produced to achieve wide appeal.

*Our arts are in decline, made bland and packaged as an unadventurous, **middle-of-the-road** 'product' for mass consumption.*
THE TIMES, 27 MARCH 2004

*Mr Verhofstadt established his free market credentials early in his political career, though he is now seen as a **middle-of-the-road** politician.*
THE INDEPENDENT, 27 MAY 2004

millstone: a millstone around one's neck
a heavy burden, a great responsibility

And whoever welcomes a little child like this in my name welcomes me. But if anyone causes one of these little ones who believe in me to sin, it would be better for him to have a large millstone hung around his neck and to be drowned in the depths of the sea. These are the words of Jesus recorded in Matthew 18:5–6. Here, the *large millstone* refers to one pulled round by a donkey, and not the small domestic kind used by women at home. The figurative use of *millstone* to denote a 'heavy burden' probably comes from this biblical source and dates back to the eighteenth century.

*Unlike in the Fifties, we are no longer an imperial power. This is a plus for us since the colonies were so often **millstones about our necks**...*
DAILY MAIL, 31 MAY 2002

For another idiom with a similar meaning, see *an* ALBATROSS *around one's neck*. For other idioms from the Bible, see page 317.

mince: not to mince matters/one's words
to speak frankly, to be brutally honest

The allusion, current since the sixteenth century, is to chopping up cheaper, stringier cuts of meat finely in order to make them easier to chew and digest.

Thomas Churchyard expresses the connection between meat and message well: *Ear he obtaind the thing he sought, howe he his tong could fiell. To talk and mince the matter well, the better to disgeast* (*The firste parte of Churchyardes chippes*, 1575). About a hundred years later, the now much more common negative form was found. Someone who *does not mince matters* makes no attempt to soften his tough message. It is not until the early nineteenth century that the variant *not to mince one's words* is first found.

*As usual, an indignant Kim **does not mince words** and awards domestic delinquent Georgina 'the prize for the dirtiest, rottenest hovel'.*
DAILY MAIL, 12 NOVEMBER 2003

mind: to mind one's Ps and Qs
to take great care how one speaks; be on one's best behaviour

Speculation abounds about the origin of this phrase, which has been in use since at least the second half of the eighteenth century.

Some hold French dancing masters responsible for the expression for constantly reminding their pupils to pay close attention to the execution of their *pieds* and *queues*.

Others say the phrase may have arisen from the old custom in alehouses of hanging a slate behind the counter on which '*p*' or '*q*' (*pint* or *quart*) was written against the name of each customer according to how much he had drunk. The accounts would be settled on payday. The landlord had to keep a careful record of his *p's* and *q's* and the customer had to ensure that only the ale he had consumed was marked up.

There are also stories from the nursery and schoolroom, of children being told *mind your please's and thank-you's* or instructed to be careful not to muddle their *p's* and *q's* when learning to write

their letters. Similarly typesetters had to be careful not to mistake a *p* for a *q* when composing text, although the letters *b* and *d* pose a comparable problem.

These stories are all purely speculative. Even if they sound plausible in themselves, it is sometimes difficult to reconcile them with the actual meaning of the expression they are supposed to have birthed. But, until a piece of real evidence is uncovered, speculation of this kind is as good as it gets.

*We should be proud of our unique identity rather than apologetic about it. It's liberating to be here. We can talk without **minding our Ps and Qs**.*
THE DAILY TELEGRAPH, 12 MARCH 2003

*We English are renowned for having good manners. We **mind our P's and Q's**, give up our seats on buses and wait our turn in line. I like the fact the English have retained courtesy as part of our make-up. I can't abide people who think they have the right to jump the queue when I was clearly next in line.*
HUDDERSFIELD DAILY EXAMINER,
11 APRIL 2005

moment of truth, the
a crisis point

Ernest Hemingway explains the origin of this phrase in *Death in the Afternoon* (1932), a novel about bullfighting: *The whole end of the bullfight was the final sword thrust, the actual encounter between the man and the animal, what the Spanish call the moment of truth.*

The moment of truth, then, is a translation of the Spanish *hora* or *momento de la verdad*, which speaks of the kill, the climax of the whole fight. Hemingway was doubtless responsible for bringing the phrase to the attention of the English-speaking world, which then used it until the 1950s with a real understanding of its origins: *A good detective story should be like a good bull-fight...*

The author plunges the unexpected explanation into [the reader] like a sword; the moment of truth, as the Spaniards call it (*New Statesman*, 15 January 1949).

Since the 1950s, however, the phrase has stood alone, its bullfighting origins largely forgotten.

Arguably, the most wrenching scene in the '20/20' story is when Jessica cradles her newborn in the hospital and the adoption contract is placed on her bedside table. It's Jessica's **moment of truth***: Does she honor her commitment to give up her baby, or does she back out as allowed?*
MILWAUKEE JOURNAL SENTINEL,
1 MAY 2004

Monita McGhee's **moment of truth** *came as she checked out of an Austin, Texas, hotel. She happened to see a co-worker's bill and noticed that it was 15 percent less than hers, even though both rooms had been the same.*

'My colleague had requested the senior discount, and I hadn't,' the Dallas woman said. Since turning 50 more than a year earlier, she had resisted asking for any of the thousands of discounts available to 50-plus adults. McGhee, the new director of the Area Agency on Aging, didn't want to take advantage of special offers that she thought were needed more by elderly consumers.

'But I'm not reluctant any longer, even at Denny's,' she said.
DALLAS MORNING NEWS, 12 MAY 2005

monkey: a monkey on one's back

a drug addiction; a burdensome problem

In the second half of the nineteenth century one's *monkey* was one's temper and the phrases *to get one's monkey up* and *to have a monkey on one's back* meant 'to get angry'. These are now obsolete, but in 1930s America the phrase *to have a monkey on one's back* was used by addicts, particularly of heroin, to describe their addiction, the allusion being to an inability to shake off the clinging creature. More recently the idiom has also been applied to 'a weighty problem that refuses to be shifted'.

As a new biography published next week makes clear, Chesney Henry Baker Jnr... had **a monkey on his back** *of gorilla-like proportions. According to the author...the trumpeter was on 6g of heroin a day by the time he died. And that's not counting the cocaine, codeine, barbiturates, alcohol and hash Baker used as a regular top-up.*
THE INDEPENDENT, 24 MAY 2002

Hughes, like Sanchez, wants to see an end to that depressing run of 14 matches without a win and no goals in 1,242 minutes – an embarrassing statistic which Sanchez describes as **a monkey on his back***.*
THE DAILY TELEGRAPH,
17 FEBRUARY 2004

Now owned by Whitbread, the David Lloyd clubs act as a performance benchmark, business enemy and reminder of Lloyd Senior's huge success – something that has been both a springboard for [Lloyd's son] Scott's career and **a monkey on his back***.*
THE DAILY TELEGRAPH, 25 APRIL 2004

month: in a month of Sundays
an interminable period of time

In the first half of the nineteenth century, when this phrase was coined, the biblical injunction to labour for six days and rest on the Sabbath was taken more seriously and activities on Sundays were restricted, at least for the better-off. For some the day seemed to drag by in tedium; a whole month of Sundays was an unimaginable stretch of time. In modern use, if a person says that something will *not* happen *in a month of Sundays*, it means that it will not happen in the foreseeable future.

But far more alluring to them were the temples we visited in Ponda, the heartland

of Hinduism in this state. Here was more life and colour than they would find **in a month of Sundays** *in a Renaissance church.*
THE DAILY TELEGRAPH, 1 APRIL 2000

She will never vote for you **in a month of Sundays***!*
THE GUARDIAN, 12 JUNE 2004

moon: once in a blue moon
very rarely, hardly ever

Way back in the sixteenth century, to say that the moon was blue meant that an event was absurd, and could not happen. As William Barlowe, the Bishop of Chichester, ironically put it:

> *Yf they saye the mone is blewe,*
> *We muct beleve that it is true.*
> (*Rede Me and Be Nott Wrothe,* c. 1526)

At exactly that period, there was a proverb in use with the same meaning but which held the moon to be made of green cheese: *They would make men believe...that the moon is made of green cheese* (Richard Brightwell, pseudonym of John Frith, *A Pistle to the Chr[iste]n Reader,* 1529). Blue or green, it was absurd, and as a consequence could never happen. That seems to be the earliest meaning – 'never'.

None the less the moon does, on rare occasions, appear blue when atmospheric conditions are exactly right or an event such as the eruption of Krakatoa (1883) occurs and dust particles fill the sky. A number of such instances have been recorded over recent centuries. People recognised this, and so *once in a blue moon* came to mean 'hardly ever', a use which dates from the mid-nineteenth century. The phrase may also have been influenced by the expression *once in a moon* (here referring to a phase of the moon), which had existed since at least the early seventeenth century and meant 'once in a while, every now and again'.

Blue moon alone was not recorded as a figurative expression until the first half of the nineteenth century when it meant 'for a long time', as in *I haven't seen you this blue moon* or *He won't come till a blue moon*. In 1874 James Greenwood wrote in *The Wilds of London*:

She's agin my coming out, and takes on a bit; but it don't do to let a woman get the upper hand of you, so I sez, 'If you jaw till a blue moon it Won't alter me. You go to bed and get your bit of rest like you ought to, and I'll go out, which rainin' pitchforks I'd as life and liefer do than lay there being gnawed.'

In the USA, there has been another development in the meaning. It has been the subject of extensive research. *Blue moon* in a technical sense is first found in the *Maine Farmers' Almanac* of 1937, but then through an influential misunderstanding came to mean a month in which there were two full moons (which actually happens a little under every three years).

It is quite a story – 'never' to 'hardly ever' to 'for a long time' to 'rarely' to (in the USA) 'less than every three years'. Would Bishop Barlowe have believed it?

My position is not that of an anti-smoker. If you want to smoke in my house, fine. Or over lunch. I may even join you **once in a blue moon***.*
THE SPECTATOR, 30 JUNE 2001

For more idioms about the moon see *over the* MOON and MOONSHINE, page 204.

moon: over the moon
highly delighted

Someone who is *over the moon* is elated. The phrase was frequently used in the 1970s by footballers and their managers to express their delight at victory. This overuse was seized upon by the satirical magazine *Private Eye* which proceeded to ridicule televised post-match interviews with the result that both *over the moon* and its counterpart *sick as a* PARROT have become football clichés: *Football fans who like a flutter will either be over the moon or as sick as a parrot. It all depends on what the commentators have to say during tonight's European Championship match between England and Croatia* (*The Times*, 21 June 2004).

The phrase *over the moon* alludes to feeling so high with excitement that one imagines being able to jump or fly over the moon would be easy. A character in John Vanbrugh's play *The Relapse* (1696) talks of leaping over the moon, and, in the well-loved nursery rhyme, whose earliest known date in print is 1765, there is an enormously happy cow who does just that:

> *Hey diddle diddle,*
> *The cat and the fiddle,*
> *The cow jumped over the moon.*
> *The little dog laughed*
> *To see such sport,*
> *And the dish ran away with the spoon.*

*I first traced my mother in 1974 through the Salvation Army but, when I met her, I didn't think much of her… My mother was **over the moon** when I traced her for the second time.*
GOOD HOUSEKEEPING, APRIL 2001

*A long-serving school janitor has been awarded the MBE. Eric Ross, 49, who works at Grange Primary in Bo'ness, West Lothian, said: 'It is a tremendous honour. I am **over the moon**.'*
THE DAILY TELEGRAPH,
31 DECEMBER 2003

For more idioms about the moon, see *once in a blue* MOON and also MOONSHINE, page 204.

moot point, a

an issue which is open to various interpretations or viewpoints, to which no satisfactory answer is found

The word *moot* means 'meeting'. It ultimately derives from a prehistoric Germanic word *motam*, 'meeting'. In Anglo-Saxon and early medieval England a *moot* signified in particular a local 'judicial assembly'. The term was also used to describe the arguments, discussions and litigation that took place in such meetings. During the sixteenth century law students at the Inns of Court would argue hypothetical cases for practice and these debates, too, were known as *moots*. The phrase *moot case* or *moot point* arose around this time to describe a 'law-case proposed for discussion'. By the eighteenth century the expression was no longer confined to debatable points of law but was being more generally applied to instances where there were various interpretations but no definitive answers.

The contemporary sense of *moot* in American English is 'academic', 'irrelevant', as in this example from the *Wisconsin State Journal* of 3 April 2005: *It is clear that Wisconsin is one of the most highly taxed states. Whether third or fifth is a moot point when considering there are 50 states…*

Is Mr Davies saying that Asian teenagers are the target audience for the bilge that Dyke has been putting on our screens? Does he believe that Asian teenagers would rather watch Porn Star *than the proceedings of the party conferences, which are now to be axed from the principal channels? It is **a moot point**.*
THE DAILY TELEGRAPH,
14 MARCH 2002

There has never been a pop record quite like Bob Dylan's 'Like A Rolling Stone'. For one thing, at close on six minutes, it was

Moonshine

For centuries the moon has appeared to man to be distant and remote, quite untouchable and unreachable. So the moon has come to have the extended metaphorical sense of the unattainable, that which it is futile to pursue. John Lyly captures this sense in a reworking of a Latin proverb: *Eager Wolves bark at ye Moone, though they cannot reach it* (*Euphues and His England*, 1580). In *Julius Caesar* (1599), Shakespeare has a dog *bay at the moon*, and this idiom is still current, sometimes as the variant *howl at the moon*.

The moon's inaccessibility is the very reason it has been passionately desired and sought after. In 1550 Nicholas Udall wrote of men who *will cry to have a piece of the moon* (*Answer to Commoners of Devonshire and Cornwall*). In his poem *The Princess* (1847), Tennyson wrote *I babbled for you, as babies for the moon*. Five years later, Charles Dickens described Mr Skimpole in *Bleak House* as *a mere child in the world, but he didn't cry for the moon*, while in his novel *Democracy* (1880) American author Henry Adams asked: *Is it not better to be a child and to cry for the moon and stars?* References such as these indicate that the idiom *to cry for the moon* alludes to children who innocently ask for the unreachable because they want it as a plaything.

A more common variant *to ask for the moon* dates from the early twentieth century. A nice example of its use comes from J B Priestley's *Angel Pavement* (1930):

To have a little place of his own with a garden and a bit of music whenever he wanted it, that wasn't asking too much. And yet for all the firm's increased turnover and its rises, he couldn't help thinking it was really like asking for the moon.

A related expression is *to promise the moon*, that is, 'to make a promise one cannot possibly carry out'. The expression is often applied to the exaggerated pledges of political parties at election time, or to promises of large amounts of money. The website for the charity Children in Need advises applicants for grants to prepare a careful budget and show how the money would be spent. *You don't need to promise the moon*, it says, *just tell us what you can realistically achieve*.

What could be more romantic than two lovers hand in hand in the moonlight, the subject of numerous popular songs? But a moonlit night isn't always so idyllic. The hours of darkness can be the perfect cover for illegal deeds, with the moon providing just enough light to carry out the task, but not enough to make detection easy. There are strong connotations here of illegality – a far cry from the sugary sentimentality of romance in the moonlight. There are a couple of expressions that reflect this sense:

twice as long as the average single but it also, at a stroke, expanded the vocabulary of pop music.

Whether it's worth a whole book, however, is **a moot point**, although if anyone can carry off such a conceit it's Greil Marcus, the high priest of rock journalism.

BIRMINGHAM POST, 30 APRIL 2005

mountain: to make a mountain out of a molehill

to make a small problem or grievance seem much greater than it really is

The ancients had a variety of phrases to encapsulate the idea of blowing up a trifling matter out of all proportion. One such was the Latin *to make a triumphal arch out of a sewer*, a favourite of Cicero's, and another was the Greek *to make an elephant out of a fly*, an expression which has

Moonlighting is an American term, also common in Britain. It was coined in the nineteenth century to describe the carrying out of a dishonest deed under cover of darkness. By the mid-twentieth century it had come to mean doing a second paid job in addition to one's regular work, and with this sense was borrowed into British English. While there is nothing particularly wrong with extra employment, *moonlighting* often implies that the second job is not declared to the authorities, in order to avoid paying taxes.

Doing a *moonlight flit* is another instance of taking advantage of darkness and the dim light of the moon, this time to disappear quickly and secretly from one's lodgings to avoid paying the bills (see *to* DILLY-DALLY). The phrase was generally common in the nineteenth century, but there is an earlier example of it in James Kelly's *Complete Collection of Scotish Proverbs* (1721).

An alternative idiom with the same meaning, dating from at least the early nineteenth century, was *to shove* (later *to shoot*) *the moon*, and this was still current in the first half of the twentieth century: *I remember how surprised she was at my asking her instead of removing the clothes on the sly, shooting the moon being a common trick in our quarter* (George Orwell, *Down and Out in Paris and London*, 1933). By the second half of the fifteenth century, however, it was also used figuratively, its metaphorical sense of 'airy, empty nonsense' suggested by the ethereal and ephemeral quality of moonlight.

But now to return to the theme of illicit dealings. During the eighteenth century *moonshine* was the term smugglers used for brandy brought from France to England, their shipments shrouded in darkness. Thereafter, it was used for any smuggled spirit. In nineteenth-century America, the temperance movement forced a number of states to pass prohibition laws, and those desperate for a drop of the hard stuff would distil liquor illegally at dead of night. They called their products *moonshine*. This term is still current, although the illicit liquor is attracting some surprising customers these days: *According to the Wildlife Department, elephants attracted to the villages by the smell of moonshine frequently attacked the liquor bins, got drunk and then trampled anyone who got in their way* (*The Daily Telegraph*, 14 June 2004). And the trade is supplying its markets by ingenious means. In Lithuania, in 2004, border guards unearthed a lengthy pipeline intended to carry *moonshine* from the neighbouring, authoritarian state of Belarus.

For more information on the moon, see also *once in a blue* MOON and *over the* MOON.

---

passed into French as *faire d'une mouche un éléphant*. The English phrase, with its pleasing alliteration, dates from the sixteenth century, with an early mention in Thomas Becon's *Catechism* (1560).

*All parents get bad tempered sometimes. I tell you that you're **making a mountain out of a molehill**.*
ANN WIDDECOMBE,
THE CLEMATIS TREE, 2000

*Junior Foreign Minister Conor Lenihan shamed himself and Ireland with his racist outburst yesterday… Some people might think this is **making a mountain out of a molehill** – but they are people not at the receiving end.*
DAILY MIRROR, 19 MAY 2005

For other idioms drawn from Greek and Roman writers, see page 318.

mouth: to make one's mouth water

to cause one to anticipate something with relish; to tempt, tantalise

These craftie foxes...espying their enemies a farre of, beganne to swalowe theyr spettle as their mouthes watered for greediness of theyr pray. So wrote Richard Eden in *Decades of the Newe Worlde* (1555), a translation of Spanish historian Peter Martyr's work. *The craftie foxes* in the passage are, in fact, slobbering cannibals, their salivary glands running in anticipation of a human feast. By the mid-seventeenth century, mouths were figuratively watering for things other than food: *The Mountains of Gold* did it for Cortez, the conquistador of Mexico (North's *Plutarch: Additional Lives*, 1657), while, a century or so later, Tristram Shandy's uncle Toby salivated for a puff on his beloved pipe (Laurence Sterne, *Tristram Shandy*, 1759–67).

*With smooth lines, tactile fabrics and colours **to make your mouth water**, European designers are in vogue at contemporary furnishing fairs worldwide.*
DAILY RECORD, 9 JULY 2002

*And, by God, there she was – a drop-dead gorgeous screen goddess in a 1940s swimsuit, stretched out in the California sun. My jaw dropped. Her home movies had a cast that would have **made MGM's corporate mouth water**.*
THE DAILY TELEGRAPH,
12 OCTOBER 2002

mud: one's name is mud

one's reputation has been discredited; one is (temporarily) out of favour

From the early eighteenth century *mud* was a slang term for *a Fool, or Thick-Scull Fellow* (*Hell upon earth: or, the character of the Poultrey compter. By a late prisoner confin'd in that place*, 1703). Over a century later John Bee, in his slang collection *A Dictionary of the Turf* (1823), defined mud as *a stupid twaddling fellow*, but went on to say that *And his name is mud* was *a jeering comment upon the conclusion of a silly speech, or a preposterous leader in the* Courier *newspaper.* Sometime between then and the end of the century, the phrase seems to have undergone a subtle change in meaning from 'object of derision' to 'object of contempt'. Interestingly, *mud* is sometimes written with an initial capital letter, suggesting that in the popular mind there is some sense of a character named *Mud*. There is no evidence of this, however.

The arts world was divided between shock and hilarity last night at the news that the latest novel from the best-selling author Fay Weldon has been sponsored by the Italian jewellery firm Bulgari – with a requirement in her contract for at least a dozen mentions of its products.
Weldon told the New York Times: *'When the approach came through I thought, oh no, dear me, I am a literary author. You can't do this kind of thing; **my name will be mud** forever. But after a while I thought, I don't care. Let it be mud. They never give me the Booker prize anyway.'*
THE GUARDIAN, 4 SEPTEMBER 2001

But deep in the corridors of the MoD, people still bear grudges against the group [BAE] that some officials refer to as Big And Expensive Systems. The disastrous projects to develop the Nimrod attack aircraft, the Typhoon jet, the nuclear-powered Astute submarine and the Brimstone anti-tank missile, which last year cost £3bn in overruns according to the NAO, stir up passions not normally seen in mild-mannered civil servants.
*'To say that **BAE's name is mud** would be a gross understatement,' said one senior source close to the MoD.*
THE INDEPENDENT ON SUNDAY,
25 JANUARY 2004

mug's game, a

a foolish activity that gives no pleasure or profit

Mug has been a slang term for a stupid or inadequate person since the mid-nineteenth century. The term was particularly applied to one who was easily duped: *The method of plucking the mug varies according to circumstances* (*The Sporting Times*, 3 August 1889). *Mug's game* to denote 'a foolish pursuit or activity' has been in use since the early twentieth century.

If inflation is destroying the value of money, then saving is **a mug's game** *and borrowing is sensible.*
THE MAIL ON SUNDAY, 31 AUGUST 2003

Economic forecasting is, most of the time, **a mug's game**. *Economists are alleged to have forecast ten of the past three recessions.*
THE SCOTSMAN, 3 NOVEMBER 2003

mum's the word

don't say anything about it, keep the secret

Mum has meant 'silence' through an inability or unwillingness to speak since the fourteenth century, the word being imitative of the sound made when the lips are firmly pressed together. The idiom itself, a pledge or command to secrecy, dates from the 1660s. An earlier form, *mum is counsel*, goes back to the mid-sixteenth century. Another variant *to keep mum* dates only from the first half of the nineteenth century.

Recently *mum's the word* has become a well-worn and therefore clichéd headline used by journalists reporting on anything at all to do with the family: *Mum's the word: After a rocky patch Charlotte Church and her mum are close again* (*Daily Mail*, 27 May 2004). The pun has worn rather thin.

Can you keep a secret, ladies and gentlemen? I think Jeremy may have had a few. Ssshhh. **Mum's the word**.
THE DAILY TELEGRAPH,
16 NOVEMBER 2003

WHO WILL OCCUPY MONROE STREET'S 'GROCERY PALACE'?
Those closest to the negotiations between potential grocers seeking to lease ground-floor retail space at the Monroe Commons multi-use development and Monroe Neighbors LLC are **keeping mum**.
CAPITAL TIMES, 11 MAY 2005

See POSTER PROPAGANDA, page 208.

mumbo jumbo

nonsense, something that has no meaning (said of jargon or a system of belief)

In July 1734, Francis Moore left England for West Africa as a writer in the service of the Royal African Company, a trading company that dealt in commodities such as gold, beeswax, ivory and slaves. In his *Travels Into the Inland Parts of Africa* (1738), he tells of Mumbo Jumbo, a spirit invented by the men of the villages along the Gambia river to keep their womenfolk in order:

The women are kept in the greatest subjection; and the men, to render their power as compleat as possible, influence their wives to give them an unlimited obedience, by all the force of fear and terror. For this purpose the Mundingoes have a kind of image eight or nine feet high, made of the bark of trees, dressed in a long coat, and crowned with a whisp of straw. This is called a Mumbo Jumbo; and whenever the men have any dispute with the women, this is sent for to determine the contest, which is almost always done in favour of the men. One who is in the secret, conceals himself under the coat, and bringing in the image, is the oracle on these occasions.

Poster propaganda

> *If you've news of our munitions,*
> KEEP IT DARK.
> *Ships or 'planes or troop positions,*
> KEEP IT DARK.
> *Lives are lost through conversation,*
> *Here's a tip for the duration,*
> *When you've private information,*
> KEEP IT DARK.

This rhyme, penned for a security poster during World War II, urged the British population to keep any information they might have about the war effort secret. The phrase *to keep dark*, used by Shakespeare in *All's Well that Ends Well* (c 1603), was doubtless given a boost by finding itself on the billboards of wartime England. Other idiomatic phrases urging secrecy, which appeared under the general slogan *Careless Talk Costs Lives*, were also pressed into service. Posters bearing pictures of hats carried the instruction *Keep it under your hat*, a phrase dating from the nineteenth century. And the command *Keep mum* appeared on several different posters (see MUM'S *the word*).

One of these showed cartoons of a variety of everyday social scenes and bore the punning slogan *Be like Dad, keep Mum*. Another, intended for officers' messes, showed a sexy young woman, probably a spy, lounging in a chair and carried the caption *Keep mum, she's not so dumb*.

For the duration of the war, everyone was expected *to do their bit* towards the war effort. The phrase *to do one's bit* was coined in the second half of the nineteenth century with the sense 'to make one's small contribution to the larger whole' and became a favourite wartime expression. Everyone had a part to play, even if it was only by *keeping mum* and exercising thrift.

World War II posters introduced *Make-do and mend*. This was a combination of a relatively new phrase, *to make do,* meaning 'to manage with whatever scant resources are to hand', and a very old one, *to make and mend*, which goes back to Langland's *Piers Plowman* in the fourteenth century. These posters, intended to encourage recycling and careful use of precious resources, showed Mrs Sew and Sew happily patching cloth, a lady going through her wardrobe and two little figures made of cotton reels, cards of darning wool and scissors. The population were also cautioned against throwing leftover food away with the punning slogan *Better pot-luck with Churchill today than humble pie with Hitler tomorrow – don't waste food* (see *to eat* HUMBLE *pie*).

In fact, people were encouraged to use up or recycle most things, except information – and germs. In an effort to keep the nation and the forces healthy and productive, the Ministry of Health issued posters showing men sneezing heavily in crowded places, to the disgust of the people around them. These posters carried the still-familiar catchphrase *Coughs and sneezes spread diseases – trap the germs in your handkerchief,* along with the additional caption *Help to keep the nation fighting fit*. *Fighting fit* was a military term dating from the second half of the nineteenth century and meant, quite literally, 'fit enough to fight'. Since the end of World War II, however, the country as a whole has been fortunate enough to know a prolonged period of peace. *Fighting fit* is still used but the expression is now more generally applied and has come to mean 'extremely healthy'.

Any man over the age of 16 who was given access to *Mumbo Jumbo* was forced to swear not to divulge the secret to any woman lest this means of domination should be lost.

In 1799 the Scottish explorer Mungo Park, who had sailed up the Gambia river on a mission to chart the course of the Niger, published *Travels in the Interior Districts of Africa*. In his book he tells of being shown a Mumbo Jumbo costume, describing the idol as *a strange bugbear...much employed by the Pagan natives in keeping their women in subjection*. Park's book was very popular and references to Mumbo Jumbo as an African deity soon began to appear in English literature. By the end of the nineteenth century *mumbo jumbo* was established as a colloquial expression for 'unmeaning jargon', appearing in Farmer and Henley's *Dictionary of Slang* (1896) with that definition. No one has been able to ascertain for sure which language the idiom was originally borrowed from, although the OED suggests Mandinka, spoken by over a million people in modern-day Senegal, Gambia and Guinea-Bissau.

*The Pythia apparently sat, out of sight, balanced on Apollo's tripod; the prophetic vapours emerged from the ground underneath her, entered her vagina and finally came out of her mouth bearing an answer to the question. Exactly what form this answer took is now a matter of debate. Some ancient observers claim that it was all mad **mumbo-jumbo**; others suggest she spoke at least some intelligible phrases.*
THE INDEPENDENT, 2 JANUARY 2004

*Like Gillian Bowditch...I have only contempt for new-age **mumbo-jumbo** such as feng shui and astrology.*
THE SCOTSMAN, 12 FEBRUARY 2004

See also *a load of old* CODSWALLOP.

murder: to scream/shout/cry blue murder

to shout aloud in alarm or distress

The French oath *morbleu*, a euphemism for *mort dieu*, 'God's death', has been in English as a comic exclamation since the seventeenth century. It is a contraction of Middle French *mort bleu*, which appropriately translates not as 'blue death' but as 'blue murder', since various contemporary English words (meaning 'slaughter, murder') share a common origin and meaning with the French *mort*. *Blue murder* is listed in John Camden Hotten's *Dictionary of Modern Slang, Cant, and Vulgar Words* (1859) with the definition *a desperate or alarming cry*, showing that it had been current enough to merit inclusion. It is now used as an intensifier, mainly with *scream* and *shout* and *cry*, to emphasise the ferocity of the shriek.

*Sarah comes across remarkably unsympathetically, hogging the family's precious resources, **screaming blue murder** and – quite probably – duping and manipulating most if not all of those who cared for her into believing she wasn't eating.*
THE DAILY TELEGRAPH, 2 MARCH 2003

*The air-raid siren **screams blue murder** as I run across a deserted Westminster trying to escape a nuclear attack.*
THE GUARDIAN, 14 JULY 2004

For some other instances of *blue murder*, see GIVING IT TO THEM HOT AND STRONG, page 176.

mustard: as keen as mustard

enthusiastic over a cause or undertaking

See under *to cut the* MUSTARD.

Since the introduction of the congestion charge, Ken Livingstone's Transport For

London (TFL) have been **keen as mustard**
to promote the idea of cycling in the capital.
THE BIG ISSUE, JANUARY 2004

*Glamorgan believe the signing of India Test
captain Sourav Ganguly will spark a
dramatic turnaround in their Frizzell
County Championship fortunes...*
   'Sourav's **as keen as mustard***, and
can't wait to get started,' revealed Derrick.*
WESTERN MAIL, 26 MAY 2005

mustard: to cut the mustard
to come up to standard

Mustard, a condiment noted for its zest
and piquancy, has been in figurative use
since the seventeenth century when *as
keen as mustard* was coined to describe a
person full of enthusiasm for a cause or
undertaking. Around the turn of the
twentieth century *mustard* was a slang
term in American English denoting 'the
best of anything'. It was the ingredient
that made all the difference: *I'm not
headlined in the bills, but I'm the mustard in
the salad dressing just the same* (O Henry,
'The Phonograph and the Graft', in
Cabbages and Kings, 1903). This is probably the origin of the term *to cut the
mustard*, meaning 'to come up to expectations'. It is first recorded in 1902, also
in O Henry ('Cupid à la Carte'): *By
nature and doctrines I am addicted to the
habit of discovering choice places wherein to
feed. So I looked around and found a proposition that exactly cut the mustard. I found a
restaurant tent just opened up by an outfit
that had drifted in on the tail of the boom.*
   There are, however, other theories
as to the idiom's etymology. One of
these alludes to the common practice
of adding vinegar to mustard to 'cut'
its sharp flavour; another says it is a
corruption of the synonymous military
idiom *to pass* MUSTER, meaning 'to
pass inspection', '*to make the* GRADE'.
There is now a tendency to use the
expression in negative contexts, as in
the examples below.

*In terms of adding value to your home, a
separate dining room no longer* **cuts the
mustard***. 'The kitchen has taken over as
the top room in the house,' says Graham
Harris.*
GOOD HOUSEKEEPING, APRIL 2000

*I'm also learning to be a computer expert,
because a few pictures cut from a magazine
and some nice handwriting no longer* **cut
the mustard** *when it comes to school
projects. Now it's got to be downloaded
images from the internet with 60 different
typefaces.*
GOOD HOUSEKEEPING, FEBRUARY 2002

muster: to pass muster
to come up to standard, to bear
scrutiny

The word *muster* derives from the Latin
monstrare, 'to show' and, from the early
fifteenth century onwards, was used to
describe the assembling of troops for
inspection. The phrase *to pass muster*
(originally *to pass the musters*) dates from
the sixteenth century and meant 'to
undergo a successful military inspection'. There is an instance from the same
date where the expression is used figuratively but this idiomatic sense seems not
to have become widespread till the first
half of the eighteenth century.

*Jasper Jackson...leads an enviable life,
spending most days at a desk in his attic flat
and buying his dinner from a bizarre pair of
shopkeepers called Roy Sr and Roy Jr (who
are so aghast at his lifestyle that they put up
the prices daily to see if he notices). Too
uptight* **to pass muster** *as a lovable rogue,
he extols the virtues of the liberated life
without quite enough conviction.*
THE INDEPENDENT, 6 JULY 2003

*Nearly 70 percent of the Erie Parking
Authority's older, mechanical parking
meters failed state certification testing,
and must be replaced. Raymond Massing,
the authority's executive director, said
timing devices inside 750 of the 1,085*

mechanical meters tested by inspectors from the state's Department of Agriculture couldn't **pass muster**.
ERIE TIMES-NEWS, 11 MAY 2005

See also *to cut the* MUSTARD.

mutton dressed as lamb

an older woman dressed in clothes more suited to a younger one

The idiom could be comparing old meat with young meat, or a sheep with a lamb. *Mutton* has long been derogatory when applied to women. From the early sixteenth century onwards it was a slang term for a 'prostitute', and the phrase *to hawk one's mutton*, meaning 'to solicit', is surprisingly modern, dating back only as far as the first half of the twentieth century. It has the sense of offering one's flesh for profit.

But *mutton* was also sometimes used to denote 'a sheep', a sense that was obsolete by the nineteenth century, except for humorous effect, and this jocular tone would fit well with the light-hearted early-nineteenth-century idiom *mutton dressed as lamb*. However, there is also the matter of *to dress*. Meat has been *dressed*, that is 'prepared for cooking', since at least the early fourteenth century. The expression thus suggests preparing an older cut of meat to look and taste like young lamb. Today, *dressed* in this phrase carries the idea of 'wearing', the phrase referring to older women inappropriately decked out in the fashions and clothing of the young.

Most of us find it tougher to steer a line between wanting to grow old at least a little disgracefully and the very female fear of being **mutton dressed as lamb**.
THE TIMES, 16 OCTOBER 2001

I recently chucked out clothes that I wore in younger days, telling myself: 'I'm never going to wear that rara skirt again!'

Luckily, my husband, Grant, would never let me leave the house looking like **mutton dressed as lamb**.
DAILY MAIL, 20 NOVEMBER 2001

If you're 18 and on the pull this is your shop. Pelmet skirts, noisy prints, Lycra everything, ubiquitous midriffs. No quality but bags of fun. Anyone over 24 will end up looking like **mutton dressed as lamb**, *and if you're big-busted or big-bottomed, don't bother.*
THE TIMES, 28 FEBRUARY 2002

mutual admiration society, a

a pair or group given to praising and promoting each other's interests

Mutual admiration society is first recorded in the New York literary magazine *The Knickerbocker* in 1845. A little later it is found in the writings of the American philosopher, essayist and poet Henry David Thoreau (1817–62), in a journal entry dated 27 February 1851:

The lecturer is wont to describe the Nineteenth Century, the American [of] the last generation, in an off-hand and triumphant strain, wafting him to paradise, spreading his fame by steam and telegraph, recounting the number of wooden stopples he has whittled. But who does not perceive that this is not a sincere or pertinent account of any man's or nation's life? It is the hip-hip-hurrah and mutual-admiration-society style.

Within seven years the phrase was taken up by American poet and jurist Oliver Wendell Holmes and from this period onwards was current on both sides of the Atlantic, often as a satirical barb to describe any group where the members are overly effusive and self-promoting in their reciprocal esteem.

We all know how much Mrs Thatcher admired Reagan and that, from the

*latter's arrival in office in 1981, they formed a powerful **mutual admiration society**.*

THE GUARDIAN, 8 JUNE 2004

Helen Mirren has taken Scarlett Johansson under her wing. The two award-winning actresses are serving on the Venice Film Festival jury – and their blossoming friendship is obvious for all to see.

*'They seem to have become **a mutual admiration society** – and it's based on respect for each other's work,' Marc Mueller, the festival's director, told me when I remarked on how the two women were making each other laugh.*

DAILY MAIL, 3 SEPTEMBER 2004

THE BUSH–PUTIN MUTUAL ADMIRATION SOCIETY

When President Bush and Russian President Vladimir Putin came out to meet the press yesterday, it was not to engage in the sparring match some had anticipated. It was more of a celebration of mutual admiration.

WASHINGTON POST, 25 FEBRUARY 2005

· N ·

nail: a nail in one's coffin

the shortening of life by shock, anxiety or bad habits; a severe blow to a plan or undertaking that hastens its end

An early, if not the original, use of the phrase occurs in an ode penned by John Wolcot who, under the pen-name Peter Pindar, was noted for his gift for comic verse in the second half of the eighteenth century:

Care to our coffin adds a nail, no doubt;
But every grin so merry draws one out.
(Expostulatory Odes, Ode xv, 1792)

In the nineteenth century drunkards began calling their drink *a nail in the coffin* and, perhaps inspired by this vivid metaphor, Lucy Page Gaston, the American founder of the Anti-Cigarette League at the turn of the twentieth century, is said to have coined the term *coffin nail* for a 'cigarette'. The League's slogan was 'Ban the Coffin Nail'.

Smoking, heavy drinking and stress are, of course, routes to an early demise and the literal hammering down of the coffin lid but, in the second half of the nineteenth century, the scope of the *coffin nail* idiom was widened to include any event which hastened the premature end of projects, plans and businesses: *This dispelling of the illusion of cheapness should prove a nail in the coffin of Co-operative stores (Society*, 7 February 1885). Both senses are current in modern English.

And so...Mackintosh retreats from the centre of the British stage. It could be seen as **the final nail in the coffin** *of the*

giganticist movement in musical theatre that he, Lloyd-Webber and Claude-Michel Schonberg pioneered.
THE GUARDIAN, 23 JULY 2001

The college's bid for university status failed last year, thus heralding **the final nail in its coffin.**
THE TIMES EDUCATIONAL
SUPPLEMENT, 27 JUNE 2003

'Tobacco puts **nails in the coffins** *of 120,000 people a year in this country. Banning the advertising of tobacco has put* **nails in the coffin** *of the tobacco industry. Acting on second-hand smoke would put* **a further nail in that coffin,'** *[the Government's chief medical officer] said.*
THE INDEPENDENT, 4 JULY 2003

nail: (to pay) on the nail

(to pay) at once, without delay, especially with regard to making a prompt cash payment

Outside the Corn Exchange in Bristol stand four bronze *nails*, pillar-like counters upon which merchants are said to have struck bargains and money was exchanged in full public view. There is another set of nails in Limerick. It has been supposed that the expression *to pay on the nail* derived from deals thus struck in the sixteenth century but, in truth, the expression appears to be somewhat older than the nails themselves.

A likely explanation is that the current phrase goes back to common European terms and practices of the early Medieval period. French, for instance, has the expression *sur l'ongle*, meaning 'precise', 'exact', though the nail here is definitely a fingernail, bringing into question the sense of *nail* in the English idiom. Anglo-Norman used the phrase *payer sur l'ongle*, 'to pay on the nail'. This phrase seems to have been derived from a European drinking custom of the period: the fuller form of *sur l'ongle* is *boire la goutte sur l'ongle*, 'to drink the drop on the fingernail'. This is a reference to *supernaculum*, a Modern Latin word translating as 'on the nail'. It is used in English from the late sixteenth century through to the mid-nineteenth.

The French also have the expression *faire rubis sur l'ongle*, 'to make a ruby on the fingernail'. This is the custom of draining the cup until there remains only sufficient wine to form a red bead on the drinker's fingernail. If the drop rolls off, the drinker must refill his cup. There is ample evidence to show that this drinking custom had also been adopted by the English, and there are similar idioms in both German and Dutch.

These terms, reflections of widespread European practices, certainly seem to be the likeliest source of (*to pay*) *on the nail*.

By degrees the flippancy of journalism will become a habit and the pleasure of being paid on the nail, and more especially of being praised on the nail, grow indispensable.
THE INDEPENDENT, 2 JULY 2000

Ryanair says it has the cash to pay on the nail.
THE GUARDIAN, 7 AUGUST 2001

namby-pamby
sentimental and insipid

Namby Pamby was a nickname for Ambrose Philips, who penned dainty pastoral verse in the first half of the eighteenth century. Alexander Pope, who had written some poems in a similar vein, was a harsh critic of Philips' verse, maintaining that his own was far superior. Literary society of the day was divided in its allegiance, though there were some big guns of the period, Swift and Gay in particular, in Pope's camp. It was not only a literary matter, for Philips, a confirmed Whig, was fair game for those of a Tory persuasion. When, therefore, Philips produced a poem written for the infant daughter of Lord Carteret which was especially cloying in its sentimentality, its publication sent dramatist and critic Henry Carey – a supporter of Pope – scurrying for his pen. It was he who coined *Namby Pamby* in a 1725 poem of that name. Its target was immediately evident from its dedication: *Namby Pamby: or, a panegyrick on the new versification address'd to A----- P----*, and the title was a rhyming play on the name Ambrose. The first stanza of the poem concludes:

> *Let your little Verses flow*
> *Gently, Sweetly, Row by Row:*
> *Let the Verse the Subject fit;*
> *Little Subject, Little Wit.*
> *Namby-Pamby is your Guide;*
> *Albion's joy, Hibernia's pride.*

Pope was quick to join the attack and make use of the nickname – in the *Dunciad* of 1728, for instance. Dr Johnson was gentler in his assessment of Philips' poetry, however. In his *Life of Philips* (in *The Lives of the English Poets, 1779–81*), he writes: *The pieces that please best are those which, from Pope and Pope's adherents, procured him the name of Namby Pamby.*

Brought up in a tough Scottish working class environment where emotions were seen as namby-pamby and suppressed as people got on with the job of surviving, she found a way of expressing herself through her music.
GOOD HOUSEKEEPING, JUNE 2002

First, we need to ask if we're giving enough recognition to the importance of making Scotland an attractive place to live. 'If we'd had this debate 20 years ago, I bet this wouldn't have been an important issue,' Turner said. 'Who would have thought that namby-pamby things like museums, cafes and nurseries would be so important for economic success?'
THE SCOTSMAN, 29 JUNE 2004

For other idioms drawn from literature, see page 319.

neck: in this neck of the woods

in this district or neighbourhood

This phrase is American in origin. The word *neck* has been used to describe 'a narrow stretch of land' from the first half of the seventeenth century. *Neck of the woods* was used to describe 'a woodland settlement' by the mid-nineteenth century and, by the first half of the twentieth century, the phrase had broadened out to refer to a particular area or neighbourhood in any location.

*At that particular moment, she rather wished she had not moved anywhere. Particularly not to the same **neck of the woods** as Mrs Blunt.*
MAVIS CHEEK, MRS FYTTON'S COUNTRY LIFE, 2000

*Village greens and garden fetes being rather thin on the ground **in my urban neck of the woods**, I went to Shropshire in search of the proper tea ceremony, for there tradition is still a part of everyday life.*
THE GUARDIAN, 12 JUNE 2004

nectar of the gods

a delicious drink

The gods of the ancient world feasted on ambrosia and drank *nectar*, a sweet beverage made from fermented honey: Zeus

himself is said to have been brought up on honey from the queen bee. Delicious drinks have been compared to nectar since the sixteenth century.

*The alchemy that transforms the local grapes into '**the nectar of the gods...**'*
THE DAILY TELEGRAPH, 7 JULY 2003

For other idioms derived from ancient legends, see page 317.

needle: like finding/looking for a needle in a haystack

a near-impossible search for something

This clever simile has been in use since the first half of the sixteenth century, although its earliest appearance was as *a needle in a meadow* and then *a needle in a bottle of hay*, *bottle* being an old word for a 'bundle of hay or straw' (from Old French *botel*, a diminutive form of *botte*, meaning 'bundle'). The *haystack* dates from the second half of the eighteenth century.

*Finding a vulnerable child in a large shire authority can be **like finding a needle in a haystack**.*
THE TIMES EDUCATIONAL SUPPLEMENT, 5 MARCH 2004

*For fans of Philippine cuisine who live in western New York, the discovery of Ly-Lou's Pearl of the Orient is **like finding the needle in the haystack**. To my knowledge, it is the only Filipino eatery in Rochester.*
ROCHESTER DEMOCRAT AND CHRONICLE, 30 JUNE 2004

The Coast Guard also will rate the security of each foreign port and target ships that recently docked where security was inadequate.
*'This really helps the whole **needle-in-a-haystack** problem by helping you target ships that present the higher risk,' Coast Guard spokeswoman Jolie Shifflet said.*
NEW YORK NEWSDAY, 2 JULY 2004

nest egg, a

part of one's savings put aside as a reserve for the future

A common country trick in days gone by to encourage hens to lay more eggs in the same place was to put a porcelain egg in the nest, or leave behind just one of the eggs laid. In this literal sense, *nest egg* goes back to the early fourteenth century. In the same way, a small sum of money set aside for future use is an inducement to the saver to add to it and watch it grow. This use of the term dates from the seventeenth century.

So all else has failed and you are desperate to find a way to save on living costs. Simply commit a white-collar crime (lie in court, let's say). No need to worry about housing benefit or income support, the State will provide for all your needs – and in the meantime you can work on that bestseller as a nest egg for when you get out.
THE TIMES, 26 JULY 2001

It was the early 1980s. We were in Shaun's first parish, in Barnet, and kicking ourselves: our nest egg was mouldering away, and property prices going berserk.
THE DAILY TELEGRAPH,
8 OCTOBER 2001

nest: to feather one's nest

to provide for one's future financial security and comfort, often at the expense of others

The allusion is to birds making their nests soft by lining them with feathers. The phrase, which dates from the second half of the sixteenth century, is usually used in a critical tone to suggest that those who are *feathering their nests* are doing so dishonestly or at the expense of others. John Bunyan used it in this way in *A Pilgrim's Progress* (1680): *Mr Badman had well feathered his Nest with other men's goods and money*.

From the recent tales of those feathering their nests, it appears they are preparing for their own futures at the expense of the state's future.
CHARLESTON DAILY MAIL, 7 JUNE 2004

nest: to foul the/one's own nest

to prejudice someone's/one's own interests

A proverb which teaches *It is a foul bird that defiles its own nest* has been in existence for almost a thousand years. It alludes to the housekeeping birds do, keeping their nests free from excreta. The proverbial *nest* was understood as either a person's country:

Where's the use o' vilifying ane's country?... It's an ill bird that files its ain nest (Walter Scott, *Rob Roy*, 1818)

or his family:

It becometh not any woman to set light by her husband, nor to publish his infirmities: for they say, That is an evil bird that defileth her own nest (Henry Smith, *Sermons*, c. 1591).

In modern usage, however, one can foul not necessarily one's own but any nest one chooses to visit, as the examples below show.

Civil servants learn to keep out of politics. It is the people imported by Labour who have been fouling the nest. Some of them are simply not house-trained.
THE OBSERVER, 16 JUNE 2002

Complacently, it was assumed that as long as extremists simply ranted, they represented no great threat – and that they would not foul the nest by attacking their British safe haven.
THE DAILY TELEGRAPH,
19 NOVEMBER 2002

nettle: to grasp the nettle

to face a problem with determination

The stinging nettle is covered with fine hairs that contain formic acid and other irritants and cause much discomfort when lightly touched. Nevertheless, the plant has been used for centuries for its medicinal and nutritive qualities. The Roman poet Petronius had a slave regularly beat him about his lower body with a bunch of nettles in the belief that the treatment would increase his virility. The ancients also held that the plant was efficacious against typhoid, rheumatism, late periods and fits. In one of his poems (1745) John Gay advises *Nettle's tender shoots, to cleanse the blood*, and John Wesley in his *Primitive Physick* (1747) urges *Take an ounce of nettle juice*. Nettles have been enjoyed as a soup or vegetable for centuries. When cooked they lose their sting and are highly nutritious, a good source of iron and magnesium. In his diary, Samuel Pepys records enjoying some nettle porridge one February day in 1660. But how did intrepid cottagers gather this stinging plant? Aaron Hill's poem 'The Nettle's Lesson' (1743), tells the secret:

> *Tender-handed stroke a nettle,*
> *And it stings you for your pains;*
> *Grasp it like a man of mettle,*
> *And it soft as silk remains.*

This characteristic of the nettle has been used metaphorically and proverbially since the sixteenth century. William Secker, in *The Nonesuch Professor* (1660), comments that *Sin is like a nettle, which stings when it is gently touched, but hurts not when it is roughly handled*, and in his *Vocabulary of East Anglia* (1830), Robert Forby has *Nip a nettle hard and it will not sting you* – i.e. *strong and decided measures prevail best with troublesome people*. The familiar idiom *to grasp the nettle* dates from the second half of the nineteenth century.

*In this instance someone who had been shown almost certainly to be guilty of murder walks free. But it could equally work the other way... [Home Secretary] Jack Straw may not feel able **to grasp the nettle** himself. But he should refer the issue to the Law Commission. A change in this rule would not only be popular but right in principle.*
THE TIMES, 30 MAY 2000

*My guess is that Dukie also takes that view, but has not begun to think the problem through, let alone **grasp the nettle**.*
THE TIMES, 16 NOVEMBER 2001

nine days'/nine-day wonder, a

something arousing great initial interest that quickly fades

Chaucer reminds us that *A wonder last but nyne night never in toune* (*Troilus and Criseyde*, c. 1380). The expression predates Chaucer by over half a century, subsequently appears in a sixteenth-century proverb collection and is alluded to by Shakespeare in two of his plays. But why should interest last for nine days? There are a number of explanations.

One theory is that the phrase originates from the Catholic 'Novena', festivals of nine days' duration, in which the statue of the saint being honoured is carried through the streets, accompanied by relics and votive offerings. According to Hargrave, the Latin root is *novenus*, 'nine each', which not uncommonly was confused with *novus*, 'new, wonderful', thus perhaps reinforcing the *wonder* element of the English phrase.

There may be something in this, as the medieval cult of saints is fairly well documented for England. St Edmund was widely venerated, and St George's popularity was at its highest in the fifteenth and sixteenth centuries. From

1415 St George's Day was raised in status to a level (technically called a *festum duplex*) such that it was on a par with Christmas Day, and it was celebrated with 'ridings' or parades featuring a model dragon and actors portraying the roles of St George and St Margaret. In fact, the cult of the saints was getting out of hand, so that in 1536 Henry VIII restricted it to those appearing in the New Testament plus St George, and processions with images were banned.

A second theory lies in the pervading influence of English proverbs. Charles, Duke of Orleans, was captured at Agincourt and wrote various poems in English. One, probably from around 1450, includes this line: *For this a wondir last but dayes nyne, An oold proverbe is seid.* The 'old proverb' in question could be an abbreviation of the one recorded subsequently by John Ray (1670): *A wonder lasts but nine days, and then the puppy's eyes are open.* Puppies are born blind, their eyes remaining sealed for about nine days until they are opened to the reality about them. Early users would have recognised this allusion, though the connection has long since been lost.

Or else the Duke's 'old proverb' may refer to another lost proverb. A Scottish saying, also in Ray (1678), echoes Chaucer's fourteenth-century usage: *Wonder lasts but nine nights in a town*, possibly a reference to urban populations being less credulous than their country cousins.

By the way, the Italians, according to one of their proverbs, marvel at wonders for just three days.

Former Tory Minister Edwina Currie said yesterday the scandal over her affair with John Major was a 'nine-day wonder' and would soon blow over... The people concerned had 'moved on' and the book was

unlikely to damage the Tory Party. Mrs Currie said: 'This will all blow over. This is nine days wonder territory.'
BIRMINGHAM POST, 5 OCTOBER 2002

*Anti-globalisation is not a **nine-day wonder** that ended on September 11.*
THE GUARDIAN, 11 NOVEMBER 2002

nineteen: to talk nineteen to the dozen
to talk rapidly, very quickly; incessantly

This phrase was coined in the second half of the eighteenth century to describe the speed of a person's speech. It implies that for every twelve words uttered at normal speed, the speaker can fit in nineteen. But why nineteen? The answer is that no one knows. A story that eighteenth-century engines fuelled by just 12 bushels of coal could pump an impressive 19,000 gallons of water out of a mine is unlikely. The suggestion that nineteen was chosen because it was one short of a round number, and therefore unexpected, is as good as any. A second sense emphasises the speaker's constant, apparently unstoppable, flow of words, rather than their speed. The idiom can now be found in a range of extended contexts: fists can fly, hearts can beat, all *at nineteen to the dozen*.

*Interview nerves can be crippling and however calm and composed you might feel, when the curtain goes up it's easy to lose it. Some of us freeze, others **talk nineteen to the dozen**.*
THE GUARDIAN, 13 DECEMBER 2003

*Saturday night and more often than not you'll see a pair of boozy blokes brawling, teeth gritted, fists flying **nineteen to the dozen**.*
WALES ON SUNDAY, 24 OCTOBER 2004

nip: to nip in the bud
to prevent a problem from growing and developing by dealing with it at an early stage

The allusion is to a plant early in the growing season, whose development can be retarded by nipping off the buds or shoots. Figurative use of *to nip* with the sense 'to arrest the development of something' dates from the sixteenth century: *It is much better to nip misorder in the verie ground, that it may not take hold, then when it is growen up, then to hacke it downe* (Richard Mulcaster, *Positions Concerning the Training Up of Children*, 1581). The full figurative phrase *to nip in the bloom* dates from the late sixteenth century and the familiar variant *to crush* or *nip in the bud* from the early seventeenth century.

During the sixteenth century, anyone abandoned to his difficulties was said *to be left in the briars*, a briar being a thorny bush. By the eighteenth century the phrase *to nip the briar in the bud* was current. James Kelly lists it in his *Scotish Proverbs* (1721), adding: *It is good to prevent, by wholesome correction, the vicious inclinations of children*.

HAY FEVER. **NIP IT IN THE BUD.**
HEADLINE, DAILY MIRROR,
24 MAY 2001

Counselling services are strapped for cash, while in many institutions personal tutors – who are perfectly placed **to nip problems in the bud** *and prevent unhappiness developing into something more serious – are thin on the ground.*
THE INDEPENDENT, 5 JUNE 2003

no holds barred
without restraint or restriction; forceful, without regard for fair play

This is a wrestling term and refers to a *no-holds-barred contest*, where the usual rules and restrictions are lifted and the competitors are permitted to use any means they can to throw their opponents and keep their shoulders pinned to the floor. The phrase dates from the first half of the twentieth century.

I MAKE GOD KNOWS HOW MUCH MONEY A YEAR
A **no-holds-barred** *interview with Elton John in the magazine.*
THE SUNDAY TELEGRAPH,
9 SEPTEMBER 2001

Jackie Rowley, Mr Kennedy's spokeswoman, called the questions 'personal and unpleasant'. But, she added: 'He was not upset by the interview. It was a **no-holds-barred** *interview – that is Jeremy's style.'*
DAILY EXPRESS, 19 JULY 2002

The show's witty **no-holds-barred** *girl-talk about men, sex and relationships has, she says, challenged an age-old taboo.*
GOOD HOUSEKEEPING, AUGUST 2002

Nod: the land of Nod
sleep

The Bible tells how Cain, after killing his brother Abel, was exiled from the land he worked and from God's presence. He then dwelt *in the land of Nod* (Genesis 4:16). It was Jonathan Swift who, in his witty *Complete Collection of Polite and Ingenious Conversation* (1738), made a pun on Cain's place of refuge and the verb *to nod*, meaning 'to become drowsy', 'to fall asleep'.

For anyone who faces a nightly struggle to get to sleep, it is a dream come true. A Japanese firm has invented a 'sleep room' which is designed to lull the worst of insomniacs into **the land of nod** *within 30 minutes.*
DAILY MAIL, 12 JUNE 2004

The Beeb shove most of the World Championship stuff they didn't show live during the day into their graveyard Snooker Extra *programme and the late-night leftovers are perfect for snoozing to before you drift off to sleep, writes Steve Palmer. You sometimes get the feeling the commentators realise that their job is to send the nation to* **the land of nod**.
THE RACING POST, 21 APRIL 2005

nose: as plain as the nose on your face
totally obvious

See under *as plain as a* PIKESTAFF.

The connection between the colour of your eyes, the quality of your sleep and the food you should eat may not be obvious to you or me. But to practitioners of the ancient Eastern healing system Ayurveda, the relationship is as plain as the nose on your face.
THE DAILY TELEGRAPH,
11 AUGUST 2004

Some things in life are as plain as the nose on your face and one of them is that the government is gearing up for yet another stealth tax. You can almost see the Chancellor rubbing his hands.
COVENTRY EVENING TELEGRAPH,
21 JANUARY 2005

nose: to pay through the nose
to pay an exorbitant price for something

A rather grisly explanation is that, following their successful invasion of Ireland in the ninth century, the Danes imposed a hefty tax upon the people. Those who did not pay it suffered the penalty of having their noses slit. Apart from the fact that there is no historical evidence for this, it seems unlikely that such a remote origin should be responsible for a phrase which was not current until the second half of the seventeenth century.

More contemporary with the phrase is the clever theory based on seventeenth-century slang. *Rhino* was a slang term for money (*rhinocerical* meant 'rich') but *rhinos* is also the Greek word for 'nose'. *To bleed* meant 'to lose a lot of money' or 'to have money extorted' (hence the current idiom *to bleed someone dry*). Since noses bleed, a victim could be said to be *paying through the nose*.

The real reason the summer rentals are so exorbitant is that people are prepared to pay through the nose not to be near anyone else.
EVENING STANDARD, 5 JUNE 2002

See also SPLITTING ONE'S SIDES, opposite.

nutshell: in a nutshell
expressed concisely, in a few words

According to Pliny in his *Naturalis Historia* (c. AD 77), there once existed a copy of Homer's *Iliad* so small that it could be contained within the shell of a nut. This claim gave rise to the Latin proverb *in nuce Ilias*, 'an Iliad in a nutshell', a phrase employed by many writers from the sixteenth century onwards. In the dedication to his *Schoole of Abuse* (1579), Stephen Gosson writes that the title of his book promises much though the volume itself is small. He goes on to list *small things that contain great wonders, among them the whole worlde...drawen in a mappe; Homers Iliades in a nutte shell; a Kings picture in a pennie.*

From the second half of the seventeenth century phrases such as *to reduce to a nutshell, to lie in a nutshell*, were used to express 'weighty matters greatly condensed'. The familiar idiom *in a nutshell*, meaning 'in a few words', is a development of this and dates from the first part of the nineteenth century. As so many readers lack time, or patience, publishers have often included the idiom in book and series titles as an inducement to master complex material concisely. Perhaps they should heed the warning of an anonymous writer of a century ago: *You said that this put the matter in a nutshell. I distrust nutshell propositions* (*Westminster Gazette*, 8 September 1909).

Splitting one's sides

Did you hear the story about the dog who went to the local flea market and stole the show? Or perhaps you heard the one about the young man who stayed up all night trying to work out where the sun went when it set. It finally dawned on him.

Comedians and those who write jokes for Christmas crackers are very grateful for one particular characteristic of idioms, for they get their laughs from its operation. Just about all idioms have a straightforward literal meaning and an idiomatic meaning.

Part of the art of the comedian lies in leading you to expect one interpretation and then suddenly forcing you to switch over to the other. For instance, the first part of one Christmas cracker joke goes: *I told him not to give the game away...* At this point we understand this to mean that one person is idiomatically telling another not to let out a secret or reveal something hidden. The second part of the joke continues: *so he decided to sell his herd of zebra instead.* This totally changes our expectation, as it now seems the first person was advising the second, who turns out to own a herd of game, to insist on getting a purchase price for the zebras rather than letting them go for nothing. Very weak, you might think. But that is the nature of this type of humour.

If those were terrible plays on words, there are others that are even worse:

> *I've got my husband to the point where he eats out of my hand.*
> *It saves such a lot of washing up.*

> *'Waiter, bring me something to eat. I could eat a horse!'*
> *'You couldn't have come to a better place, sir.'*

> *What goes 'Ha Ha Bonk?'*
> *A man laughing his head off.*

> *What lies on the sea bed and twitches?*
> *A nervous wreck.*

On the same principle, humorous verse often gets its effects by playing on the tension between the literal and the idiomatic, as in this limerick, penned by Arnold Bennett:

> *There was a young man of Montrose*
> *Who had pockets in none of his clothes.*
> *When asked by his lass*
> *Where he carried his brass,*
> He said, *'Darling, I* pay through the NOSE.*'*

The opening shot of Thirteen *has its adolescent heroine framed against her bedroom wall, flanked on one side by a teddy bear, on the other by a pin-up male torso. It's her predicament in a nutshell: one moment, LA girl Tracy is all ankle-socks and ponytails, the next she's discovering sex, drugs, theft, body piercing and self-mutilation.*
THE INDEPENDENT, 7 DECEMBER 2003

Songwriter, storyteller, son of Texas; that in a nutshell is Jimmie Dale Gilmore, a troubadour of ethereal voice and old-time sensibility.
PORTLAND PRESS HERALD,
13 FEBRUARY 2005

For other idioms drawn from Greek and Roman writers, see page 318.

offing: in the offing

very likely to happen, imminent

From the sixteenth century, offing meant the part of the sea most distant from land but still visible from it. In his *Seaman's Grammar* (1627) Captain John Smith, a leading figure in the settlement of Virginia, defines *offing* as *the open Sea from the shore*.

The first use of the phrase *in the offing* in 1779 takes the idea of geographical distance and applies it to time. The perspective is that the *offing* is far away and so the time reference is to the far future. This sense is now obsolete. From the early nineteenth century, the perspective shifted: any vessel discernible from the shore is not very far away, relative to the whole ocean, and so by the same metaphorical extension the term *in the offing* began to be used to denote 'something likely to happen soon'.

*He refuses to talk about the state of his marriage although, at a recent stand-up gig, he intimated that a reconciliation might be **in the offing**.*
THE DAILY TELEGRAPH,
26 NOVEMBER 2003

*Ratzinger is an insider's insider, a networker, and a strong-willed politician, so it's unlikely great changes are **in the offing** in the Roman Catholic church. That's why he was elected: to make sure there wouldn't be many.*
PHILADELPHIA INQUIRER, 20 APRIL 2005

For other nautical idioms, see A LIFE ON THE OCEAN WAVES, page 24.

oil: to pour oil on troubled waters

to soothe a quarrel, to calm a heated argument

That stormy waters could be quelled by pouring oil onto them was known at least as far back as the first century AD. Pliny reported the fact and Plutarch later wrestled with the science: *Why does pouring oil on the sea make it still and calm? Is it because the winds, slipping over the smooth oil, have no force, nor cause any waves?* (*Moralia: Quaestiones Naturales*, c. AD 95).

But English knowledge of the fact might have become known through Bede's account of a miracle performed by Bishop Aidan (*Ecclesiastical History*, completed 731). A priest by the name of Utta was charged with escorting King Oswy's bride across the sea. Before he left he was approached by the bishop, who gave him a phial of holy oil. The bishop prophesied that there would be a fierce storm at sea but promised Utta that, if he were to cast the oil upon the water, the storm would immediately cease and the journey home would be safe and calm. The storm arose, as Bishop Aidan foretold; the waves began to fill the vessel and the sailors were in despair, but Utta remembered the oil and the sea was calmed.

However, metaphorical reference to oil on water dates back only to around the middle of the nineteenth century, possibly through the published experiments of the American scholar Benjamin Franklin, who *had when a Youth, read and* smiled at Pliny's Account of a Practice among the Seamen of his Time, to still the Waves in a Storm by pouring Oil into the Sea (letter to William Brownrigg, 7 November 1773). Franklin determined to investigate and discovered that there was truth in the ancient practice, as he reports in the same letter:

At length being at Clapham, where there is, on the Common, a large Pond, which I observed to be one Day very rough with the Wind, I fetched out a Cruet of Oil, and dropt a little of it on the Water. I saw it spread itself with surprising Swiftness upon the Surface, but the Effect of smoothing the Waves was not produced; for I had applied it first on the Leeward Side of the Pond where the Waves were largest, and the Wind drove my Oil back upon the Shore. I then went to the Windward Side, where they began to form; and there the Oil tho' not more than a Tea Spoonful produced an instant Calm, over a Space several yards square, which spread amazingly, and extended itself gradually till it reached the Lee Side, making all that Quarter of the Pond, perhaps half an Acre, as smooth as a Looking Glass.

Franklin's experiments, collected under the heading *Of the Stilling of the Waves by means of Oil*, could well be the inspiration for the current idiom.

Ms Langford-Wood says the idea of the book is not to apportion blame but **to pour oil on troubled waters**.
THE TIMES, 15 NOVEMBER 2001

If there's trouble in the workplace then the chances are that Peter Richards will want to be in the thick of it. Not that he's a troublemaker, you understand. Quite the opposite. Richards' role in life is **to pour oil on troubled water**.
LIVERPOOL DAILY POST,
25 FEBRUARY 2004

For other idioms drawn from Greek and Roman writers, see page 318.

over: to go over the top
to go too far, to behave immoderately

The phrase originated in the trench warfare of the First World War. To mount an attack, soldiers had first to climb out over the trench parapet before charging into no man's land, the territory between allied and enemy positions. Initially *to go over the top* was used euphemistically and meant 'to engage in dangerous action'. Since then, the meaning and range of contexts in which it is used have broadened enormously. *To go over the top* means 'to behave immoderately', and anything excessive can now be described as *over the top*: a fashion, a remark or behaviour, for example.

The phrase has also caught on in the entertainment world to describe performances or material that push the limits of good taste. To exploit this meaning, and thereby gain an audience, a risqué 1982 television comedy show took the title *OTT*, an abbreviation that is still current. There is a growing tendency for *OTT* to be used adjectivally, rather than as part of the fuller earlier phrase, and of course much of the force of the military origin has been lost.

At lunchtime I spot a free bench space in the busy square outside the office. As I sit down, the lunching workman sitting next to me just stares…Workman's mate joins him. 'Blimey, what on earth's that bird wearing?' he says. 'Bit **O.T.T.** *innit?'*
DAILY MIRROR, 13 OCTOBER 2001

Where was the famous deep decolletage, the tight corsetry, the **over-the-top** *fur trim? True, there was a flash of well-tanned thigh. But this was the rarely seen demure Dell'Olio.*
THE DAILY TELEGRAPH, 22 JULY 2004

Academically able but far too sharp for their own good. Too pushy and **over-the-top***, they like the sound of their own voice,*

dominate the conversation, try too hard to impress and have to win at any cost.
THE DAILY TELEGRAPH, 2 AUGUST 2004

The Eurovision Song Contest – it's embarrassing, it's glam and it's downright outrageous. It has had 31 female and just six male winners. And Israel's Dana International was a bit of both!
Famous for its kitsch nostalgia, flamboyant glamour and OTT costumes, Eurovision is the by-word for cheesy pop. But it is adored by millions – last year 11 million viewers watched it in Britain – that's an unbelievable 54% of watchers tuning in.
THE SUN, 23 MAY 2005

For other idioms derived from the army and warfare, see page 317.

over-egg: to over-egg the pudding

to exaggerate grossly, to spoil something by going much too far

Adding too many eggs to a pudding is excessive, it simply spoils the mixture. This British culinary metaphor dates from the late nineteenth century.

Looking fit and agile, he invests old songs like 'Never Going Back Again' and 'Big Love'...with the vigour and urgency of someone clearly delighted to be back in the spotlight. That said, he had a tendency to over-egg the pudding a little bit, cranking out a few seemingly interminable wailing guitar solos...
THE TIMES, 21 NOVEMBER 2003

The Dons sold everything they could and began the long process of paying off their debts rather than declaring bankruptcy.
'I don't want to over-egg the pudding. We survived. No one died,' says Monty. 'But for the record, the worst thing was not the loss of creature comforts but the humiliation. I felt a complete and utter fool.'
WISCONSIN STATE JOURNAL,
14 MAY 2005

• P •

paddle: to paddle one's own canoe

to be independent, to get along by one's own efforts

This phrase was coined in the American West in the first half of the nineteenth century. It was brought to general attention as a recurring line in an inspirational poem by Sarah Bolton which was published in *Harper's Monthly* in May 1854:

> *Voyager upon life's sea,*
> *To yourself be true;*
> *And, what'er your lot may be,*
> *Paddle your own canoe.*
>
> *Leave to Heaven, in humble trust,*
> *All you will to do;*
> *But if you succeed, you must*
> *Paddle your own canoe.*

This extract gives a fair idea of the subject and tone of the rest.

Ginola thinks he would make an excellent manager, although he emerges from an entertaining book essentially as a supreme individualist, forever destined **to paddle his own canoe** *while always keeping an eye out for the sharks which, as he admits, infest his nightmares.*
THE SUNDAY TIMES, 1 OCTOBER 2000

paint: to paint the town red

to go out on a spree, to indulge in excessive revelry

This phrase is American slang and dates from the second half of the nineteenth century. Its origin is a mystery which has given rise to a number of colourful suggestions. One authority points out that *to paint* was a slang term for 'to drink', and hazards the suggestion that the term is a reference to the red nose and flushed cheeks caused by excessive alcohol.

Others say that the phrase alludes to revelling cowboys having a good time by shooting up a town and issuing a defiant warning that they would *paint it red* if anyone tried to stop them. Yet another source points out that red is a loud and cheerful colour that matches the mood of anyone out for a good time.

There are many more intriguing but unconvincing stories, even an unlikely English challenger for the earliest honours. Melton Mowbray's official web site claims: *'Painting the Town Red' means having a good time today, but in 1837 it meant precisely what it says. At that time, Melton Mowbray was the metropolis of fox hunting and the eccentric Marquis of Waterford and friends decided after a day's hunting to 'redecorate' the town. Several buildings, the toll gate and the unfortunate toll keeper, plus some local police constables were all painted bright red! So, when anyone refers to 'Painting the Town Red' it reflects boisterous times in Melton Mowbray.*

Robbie Savage may live up to his name on the football pitch but when it comes to after-match fun he's boring. The midfield ace doesn't drink or smoke and would rather have a quiet night in than **paint the town red***.*
DAILY MIRROR, 4 JANUARY 2003

Sick of eating out alone and entranced with ordinary domestic contentment, her lover has installed a roast and carrots in his fridge in the hopes of a home-cooked meal. But his mistress arrives with finery expecting **to paint the town red**, *and interprets his insistence on dining in as horror of being seen with her in public.*
THE ECONOMIST, 5 JULY 2003

pale: beyond the pale
outside civilised society or limits, beyond acceptable conduct

Pale comes from Latin *palum*, meaning 'a wooden stake'. Use of the word was later extended to refer to a fence made up of such stakes and from there to a territory which was under a particular authority or jurisdiction. As early as the second half of the fifteenth century, the word *pale* was used figuratively to denote a sphere of influence or activity. The phrase *beyond the pale* is a metaphorical extension of the notion of life within the pale being civilised and, beyond it, barbaric. It dates from the mid-seventeenth century.

Some claim that the designation of various areas as Pales over the centuries is the real origin. There was, for instance, an *English Pale* around the part of Ireland under English rule in the fifteenth century, and another, the *Pale of Calais,* around Guînes, Marck and Calais, from 1360 to 1558. However, the OED dismisses this derivation as being unsupported by the historical evidence.

The angry scenes which followed Le Pen's arrival in Cheshire also made it clear that his own views are **beyond the pale** *for a lot of people.*
DAILY MIRROR, 28 APRIL 2004

pan: to pan out (well/badly)
to work out, to turn out well/badly

See *to do one's* LEVEL *best.*

[40] is the life expectancy estimated for Leo – given to us on the day he was diagnosed. Although it is only a guide, and it depends how Leo's health **pans out**, *my heightened emotional state at the time has soldered it permanently onto my psyche.*
THE GUARDIAN, 29 OCTOBER 2002

Super league clubs have been stepping up their preparations for the new season. So have I: I have been consulting some of the game's deepest thinkers in bars throughout the rugby league world to find out how things will **pan out** *in 2005.*
LIVERPOOL ECHO, 15 JANUARY 2005

Pandora's box
a seemingly harmless situation fraught with hidden difficulties

Prometheus had offended Zeus. In revenge Zeus ordered Pandora, the first mortal woman, to be created. She was presented to Epimetheus who fell helplessly in love with her, despite being warned by his brother, Prometheus, never to accept gifts from the untrustworthy Zeus. As a wedding present Zeus presented Pandora with a beautiful box which she was told never to open. Over time, however, her curiosity grew stronger and stronger until, one day, she turned the key and lifted the lid to peep inside. At that moment, all the problems and wickedness which afflict mankind were loosed to do their worst and have done so ever since. All that was left in the bottom of the box was Hope.

References to the mythological *Pandora's box* date back to the sixteenth century; figurative senses from somewhat later.

*King Abdullah, a key partner in the war against terror, warned Mr Blair that military strikes will open a '***Pandora's box***' and trigger an Arab uprising.*
DAILY MIRROR, 30 JULY 2002

*Australia's evangelical churches may be booming, but the country still embraces staunchly liberal values. Yes, Tony Abbott, the health minister (and a former monk), has been allowed, from time to time, to raise the subject of abortion. But no one seriously believes that the Howard government is going to open that **Pandora's box**.*
THE ECONOMIST, 5 MAY 2005

For other idioms derived from ancient legends, see page 317.

paper: to paper over the cracks

to resolve a problem only superficially or temporarily, to provide a veneer of normality or success

The allusion is to papering a wall without bothering to first prepare the surface. The metaphor was used by Otto von Bismarck, First Minister of Prussia, to describe the Convention of Gastein of 1865. Relationships between Prussia and her neighbour, Austria, were tense and war was brewing. The Convention was a holding operation during which both sides began to prepare for the inevitable conflict. An article in the *Encyclopaedia Britannica* of 1910 later referred to *paper over the cracks* as Bismarck's phrase.

At the end of last year, the government announced a £44m initiative to help fill teaching vacancies in hard hit areas. Headteachers at the time warned that it would be difficult to avoid using the money to 'paper over the cracks' using supply staff.
THE GUARDIAN, 24 APRIL 2002

America's treasury secretary, John Snow, tried hard at the weekend meetings to emphasise his government's desire for a co-operative approach on Iraq. For their part, those countries which had been firmly opposed to military intervention, *particularly France and Germany, have also worked hard to paper over the cracks. They never wanted to be seen as apologists for Saddam Hussein: their objection was to the strategy adopted to disarm and topple him.*
THE ECONOMIST, 14 APRIL 2003

paper tiger, a

a person, country or organisation that is apparently powerful but actually ineffective

The expression is Chinese and was popularised by Chairman Mao Tsetung, who used it in an interview with the American correspondent Anna Louise Strong in August 1946: *All reactionaries are paper tigers. In appearance, the reactionaries are terrifying, but in reality they are not so powerful. From a long-term point of view, it is not the reactionaries but the people who are really powerful.* However, there are a number of references to the expression in English and American texts dating back over a hundred years before that. Even up to the 1970s the context was a direct allusion to the Chinese proverb, but since then it has been applied more generally.

*Two months after announcing a flurry of charges in what was spun by Soho Square as a much-needed clampdown against violent behaviour, the FA was once again shown to be nothing more than **a paper tiger**.*
DAILY MAIL, 20 MARCH 2002

*The ease with which the most militarised dictator was toppled in Iraq shows that these regimes are all **paper tigers** once faced with US mega-might.*
THE GUARDIAN, 16 APRIL 2003

parrot: as sick as a parrot

extremely disappointed

Sick, meaning 'ill, unwell', goes back at least 1200 years to Anglo-Saxon English. A more metaphorical sense, 'subject to a deep feeling' (such as disappointment) that could give the appearance of physical sickness, is a mere thousand or so years old. With a long and venerable history, there have inevitably been many coinages and novel uses. For instance, similes comparing one's feelings of nausea with those of a domestic animal date from the early eighteenth century with *sick as a dog*. Other comparisons include *cats* and *horses*. The most recent, *sick as a parrot*, describes not physical nausea but profound emotional disappointment. It dates from the late 1970s and, for a while, became a favourite idiom of defeated sportsmen, particularly football players and their managers (see *over the* MOON). It is now a much parodied cliché.

But why should it be a parrot as opposed to any other animal? The figurative phrase may well allude to a real illness. In the early 1970s there were reports of people falling seriously ill with a disease known as psittacosis, or parrot fever, which affects cage birds and can be passed on to man. But although real victims of psittacosis respond well to antibiotics, there is no rapid cure for a disappointed footballer.

*A few weeks ago Motson described Alan Shearer as being '**sick as a parrot**' after missing a penalty, and the Newcastle player had to call on an array of veterinary experts and gastric specialists to effect a recovery.*
THE OBSERVER, 4 MARCH 2001

*Oh, the hard life of a choreographer. You toil over your ideas. You rehearse your dancers, you chivvy and make compromises with them. You invite critics, knowing full well some might be hostile, but any publicity is better than none. It's all enough to make you **as sick as a parrot**...*
THE INDEPENDENT, 7 MAY 2003

parting shot, a
a final, pithy or wounding remark, to which the listener has no chance of replying

Originally *a Parthian shot*, the expression refers to the war tactics of the Parthians, an ancient people of south-west Asia. These skilled mounted archers would feign retreat then, twisting round in their saddles, fire backwards with deadly accuracy onto the enemy in pursuit. In 53 BC the armies of Crassus, then Roman governor of Syria, were shot to pieces by the wily Parthians at Carrhae in modern Turkey, thus bringing his dreams of military glory to an end. It was one of the greatest losses in Roman military history, with 20,000 killed and 10,000 captured from a force of 42,000. This disaster meant that Parthian military strategies were well known to Ovid: *Flee: by flight the Parthian is still safe from his foe* (*Remediorum Amoris*, c. 1 BC).

The term *Parthian shot* was in regular use in English from the nineteenth to the early twentieth century, when the variant *parting shot* gained currency. *Parthian shot* is, however, still occasionally found.

*Tusa's blistering attack on Matthew Evans (58), for his 'glib', 'New Labour speak' may also, one suspects, be at least partly **the Parthian shot** of the retiring man for the colleague with a few potent years left.*
THE GUARDIAN, 6 SEPTEMBER 2000

Occasionally, things can even turn violent. Take the case of Gary Coch, now a commentator for American television, who got so upset at hitting a bad drive that he threw the club in the general direction of his caddie. It bounced off the turf and caught him in the testicles. After hitting another bad shot at the next hole, he pretended to throw the club again. The caddie flinched and jumped out of the way. 'Got you that

time,' Coch said. The caddie, unamused, picked up the driver, snapped it across his knee and promptly walked off the course. 'Ay, and now I've got you as well,' was his **parting shot**.
THE GUARDIAN, 24 JULY 2001

...his face still bears the marks of a parting shot from fellow jailbirds: a black eye and two angry-looking scabs on his cheek.
DAILY MIRROR, 19 JUNE 2004

For another idiom about warfare in the ancient world, see PYRRHIC *victory*, and for other idioms drawn from ancient life and history, see page 317.

pastures new
a change of place or activity; a moving on to fresh opportunities

The idiom is part of the last line of *Lycidas* (1637), a poem by John Milton:

> *At last he rose, and twitch'd his mantle blue;*
> *Tomorrow to fresh Woods, and Pastures new.*

Surprisingly, usage dates only from around the beginning of the twentieth century. The voice of the poet still rings out, however: in normal English one would expect *new pastures*, not the *pastures new* of the contemporary idiom.

My colleague and deputy James Robinson leaves the Financial Sunday Express *this week for* **pastures new**. *I would like to thank him for his tremendous support over the past couple of years and wish him well in his new job.*
SUNDAY EXPRESS, 9 NOVEMBER 2003

I realise I still need the city, but I'm leaving for **pastures new**.
THE INDEPENDENT, 12 JULY 2004

For other idioms drawn from literature, see page 319.

pecking order, the
a hierarchy of authority and dominance

A strict hierarchy known as *the pecking order* operates within the hen coop. It is dominated by one particular hen who has the right to peck all the others to get her own way without being pecked back. The other hens all have their places below her and know that they may assert themselves by pecking any bird lower in the order but never one above. Inevitably there is one lowly creature who is dominated by all her sisters. Similar patterns of dominance exist both in human society as a whole and within the groups and organisations it divides itself into and, by analogy, these structures have come to be known as *pecking orders*. The literal use of the phrase dates from the 1920s; the metaphorical uses from the mid-1950s.

There's nothing you can do to change it, but where you come in the family **pecking order** *has far-reaching effects when it comes to shaping your personality, relationships and even your career.*
GOOD HOUSEKEEPING, FEBRUARY 2003

Griet enters the financially precarious Vermeer household at the bottom of the **pecking order**, *quickly put in her place by Vermeer's haughty wife Catharina.*
THE DAILY TELEGRAPH,
18 JANUARY 2004

peg: a round peg in a square hole/a square peg in a round hole
a person whose talents or character are totally unsuited to the demands made on them

There is a whole philosophy behind the *round peg in a square hole* idiom. The Reverend Sydney Smith explains it thus: *If you choose to represent the various parts in life by holes upon a table, of different shapes, ...and the persons acting these parts by bits of wood of similar shapes, we shall generally find that the triangular person has got into the square hole, the oblong into the triangular, and a square person has squeezed himself into the round hole* (Sketches of Moral Philosophy, 1806).

It is not known who the originator of the concept was, but it caught popular imagination. *A round man cannot be expected to fit a square hole right away*, wrote Mark Twain. *He must have time to modify his shape* (Following the Equator, 1897). For the journalist and political writer Albany Fonblanque, however, it was a case of *once a round peg always a round peg*. Fonblanque found neither the Prime Minister, Sir Robert Peel, nor his Chancellor, Lord Lyndhurst, well suited to their particular roles: *Sir Robert Peel was a smooth round peg, in a sharp-cornered square hole, and Lord Lyndhurst is a rectangular square-cut peg, in a smooth round hole* (England Under Seven Administrations, 1836). Perhaps they should have changed places.

*He had felt pushed into an office job by his father's expectations. The stress of feeling like **a round peg in a square hole** was making him miserable. Finally, Martin decided to re-train as a tradesman, where he could actually see his work and feel proud of what he had achieved.*
THE OBSERVER, 6 APRIL 2003

*There is a reason why expressions like **'putting a square peg in a round hole'** exist. They are simple reminders not to repeat mistakes, and to find solutions that fit the problem, not just those that are closest at hand.... Inevitably, the future will always hold more changes, making it difficult to choose a sufficient peg that will fit any hole (be it square or round) for any decent length of time.*
WALL STREET AND TECHNOLOGY,
1 APRIL 2005

penny: the penny dropped
the joke, remark or point of the argument has suddenly been understood

The phrase dates from around the middle of the twentieth century. The allusion is to the penny slot machines found on piers and in penny arcades popular from the end of the nineteenth century. They are motionless and unresponsive until the penny drops inside but then they come to life. Similarly a person who does not understand a joke or remark made to him does not react as one would expect until *the penny drops*.

The penny, it seemed, suddenly dropped. Ian finally understood the full implications of her actions.
MAVIS CHEEK, MRS FYTTON'S
COUNTRY LIFE, 2000

*In his late teens '**the penny dropped**' that he was illegitimate.*
THE TIMES, 27 MARCH 2004

*I racked my brains to think where I had seen all this before... Then **the penny dropped**.*
THE INDEPENDENT, 16 JULY 2004

pickle: in a pickle
in a difficult situation, in a mess

Pickled and salted vegetables and meat were an important part of the diet in the Middle Ages. There would be little fresh food to be had in the long hard winter months and pickled produce allowed for some variety. The idiom dates from the sixteenth century. The Dutch expression *in de pekel zitten*, 'to sit in the pickle', explains the sense of the English, as *pekel* is the brine or vinegar in which the food was preserved. Having a bath of brine surely counts as being in a predicament. And it can be tragic, as this recent bizarre news story from the *Times of India* of 28 May 2005 shows: *Tragedy struck a migrant family twice in a week, when four persons died of asphyxiation in a pickle-*

*making pit in the Pandesara area here on
Friday morning. Two members of the same
family, which is into pickle-making business
[sic], had died in the same pit on Tuesday.*

*One shouldn't feel too sorry for famous folk:
most of them are narcissistic fools **in a
pickle** of their own making.*
THE DAILY TELEGRAPH,
26 SEPTEMBER 2004

*A lot of us who like to start the dinner
ritual with a glass of white wine –
especially in warm weather – are finding
ourselves **in a pickle**. We are too proud to
drink chardonnay because it tastes too
much like an oaky crème brûlée, and
besides, trendy folks have been moving
away from chardonnay for several years
now. The hipper call these days is for
sauvignon blanc or pinot grigio.*
VIRGINIAN PILOT, 4 MAY 2005

See GIVING IT TO THEM HOT AND
STRONG, page 176.

pie: as easy as pie
very easily done

Around the middle of the nineteenth
century *pie* emerged as an American
slang term to denote 'something to be
sought after', 'a treat', 'a bribe' (see PIE
in the sky). After all, what child has not
been bribed or treated with a promise
of a slice of pie? Towards the end of
that century *pie* also came to signify
'something easily accomplished', an
allusion no doubt to the ease with
which a tasty piece of pie is eaten. The
idiom *as easy as pie*, which reinforces
this sense, dates from the 1920s.

The Daily Mirror *once hired butler
Harold Brown for a glittering cocktail
party in Mayfair. It was **easy as pie** and
his discreet presence cost us the princely
sum of thirty quid.*
DAILY MIRROR, 5 DECEMBER 2002

pie in the sky
heavenly rewards; an unrealistic dream,
ambition or goal

Joel Emmanuel Haggland was born
into poverty in Gavle, Sweden, in
1879. In 1902 he emigrated to the
United States to seek his fortune, but
opportunities were scarce and Joel,
along with many thousands of others,
simply exchanged the gruelling poverty
of one country for that of another. In
1910 Joel, now known as Joe Hillstrom
and later as Joe Hill, joined the
Industrial Workers of the World, or
'Wobblies' for short, a recently formed
labour organisation set up to bring the
poor together into 'One Big Union'
bent on the denunciation of capitalism
and the distribution of company profits amongst the low-paid.

Upon joining the Wobblies, every
new member was given a *Little Red
Songbook* (variously known as *The IWW
Songbook,* and *Songs of the Workers*) containing songs of protest set to the tunes
of familiar hymns or popular songs. Joe
Hill, a self-taught musician with a certain gift, contributed many songs and
poems to the movement. One of these,
The Preacher and the Slave, written in
1911 to the tune of *In the Sweet Bye and
Bye,* attacked the Salvation Army
whose Christian message seemed to
support the status quo by preaching a
heavenly recompense in exchange for
earthly endurance:

*Long haired preachers come out ev'ry night,
Try to tell you what's wrong and what's
right;
But when asked, how 'bout something to
eat, (Let us eat)
They will answer with voices so sweet;
(Oh so sweet)*

CHORUS
*You will eat (You will eat)
Bye and bye (Bye and bye),
In that glorious land above the sky*

(Way up high);
Work and pray (Work and pray),
Live on hay (Live on hay),
You'll get pie in the sky when you die
(That's a lie).

Pie in the sky was therefore 'heavenly reward'. This specific sense grew in fertile ground since, after originating in American slang, from the mid-nineteenth century *pie* was used figuratively to denote 'something to be sought after', 'a prize', 'a favour' (see also *as easy as* PIE).

The phrase *pie in the sky* with its catchy rhyme was first used idiomatically in the 1920s to refer in a derogatory way to 'heavenly rewards', just as Hill had originally intended, but by the 1940s it was also being used to denote 'wishful thinking', 'an unrealistic ambition' or, particularly in political contexts, 'a fanciful promise that is unlikely to be fulfilled'.

*Last week Julie Keeble and Luke Zalewski, the current British champions who managed only 21st place in the recent world championships, announced their early retirement. Their coach, Garry Hoppe, also resigned, saying he had become disillusioned with the skating authorities and their '**pie-in-the-sky** predictions' of future success.*
THE DAILY TELEGRAPH,
21 AUGUST 2000

*One royal biographer suggested that Sir Felix Cassel (born in 1869) was the son of Edward VII, but Harold Cassel dismissed the idea as '**pie in the sky**'.*
THE DAILY TELEGRAPH,
21 SEPTEMBER 2001

pig: to buy/sell a pig in a poke
to buy something without inspecting it carefully first, then find it defective/to sell something off as better than it really is

The poke in this idiom is a small sack. (The word is a Middle English borrowing from Old French. *Pocket* is its diminutive.) A favourite scam at markets or country fairs in medieval times was to put a stray cat in a bag and pass it off as a piglet. The trusting customer would only discover his error when he got his purchase home. Buyer beware.

The phrase is recorded in John Heywood's *Proverbs* (1546). In Europe it was semi-proverbial and all the languages, Romance and Germanic, have *cat* instead of *pig*, English being the exception: Italian, for instance, has *comprare gatta in sacco*, 'to buy a cat in a sack'. In one of his *Essays* (1580), the French philosopher Montaigne caught the spirit of the proverb when he perceptively remarked that when women get married they *achetent chat en sac*, they 'buy a cat in a bag'.

This is a recurrent thought down the centuries: '*Wimmin's a toss up,*' said Uncle Pentstemon. '*Prize packets they are, and you can't tell what's in 'em till you took 'em 'ome and undone 'em. Never was a bachelor married yet that didn't buy a pig in a poke. Never. Marriage seems to change the very natures in 'em through and through. You can't tell what they won't turn into—nohow* (H G Wells, *The History of Mr Polly*, 1910).

Stephen Smith believes the popularity of owning a property in France can only increase as transport links between the two countries improve. 'But an unscrupulous vendor knows full well that it is far easier to sell a pig in a poke to a trusting buyer from abroad.'
THE INDEPENDENT, 10 AUGUST 2001

See also *to let the* CAT *out of the bag*.

pigs might fly

said disbelievingly about something
that is very unlikely to happen

An expression of incredulity that was
current from at least the early seventeenth to the nineteenth centuries was
pigs fly in the air with their tails forward –
the clever old things. Thomas Fuller in
his *Gnomologia* (1732) has the more
recognisable *That's as likely as to see an
Hog fly*, while *Pigs may fly but they are
very unlikely birds* is listed in the nineteenth century as a Scottish proverb.
The ability of pigs to fly was a subject
for discussion proposed by the Walrus
in Lewis Carroll's *Through the Looking
Glass* (1871):

> 'The time has come,' the Walrus said,
>   'To talk of many things:
> Of shoes – and ships – and sealing-wax –
>   Of cabbages – and kings –
> And why the sea is boiling hot –
>   And whether pigs have wings.'

Carroll's line inspired P G Wodehouse
to entitle one of his books *Pigs Have
Wings* (1952) and introduced the temporary variant *maybe pigs have wings*.

*A government with vision should be promoting
foreign languages as a key to greater
intercultural competence. That's about as
likely as a week with four Thursdays. Which,
for the benefit of monolinguals, is the French
for* **pigs might fly***.*
THE GUARDIAN, 12 MARCH 2002

*The new baby was making Rosemary feel
sick and she thought how wonderful it would
be if Victor suddenly woke from his snore-
laden sleep and said to her, 'Can I get you
something, dear?' and she would say, 'Oh,
yes, please, I would like some tea – no milk
– and a slice of toast, lightly buttered,
thank you, Victor.'* **And pigs would fly***.*
KATE ATKINSON, CASE HISTORIES, 2004

pikestaff: as plain as a pikestaff

totally obvious, evident; easy to
understand

This phrase began as *plain as a packstaff*
in the first half of the sixteenth century,
a packstaff being the sturdy pole upon
which a pedlar carried his load and sup-
ported it when he stopped to rest. The
reference is to the surface of the wood,
worn plain through constant use.

> *Not, riddle like, obscuring their intent;
> But, packe-staffe plaine, uttring what thing
>   they ment,*

wrote Bishop Joseph Hall in the
prologue to one of his *Satires* (1597).
The variant *plain as a pikestaff*, that is 'a
staff used in walking', dates from the
late sixteenth century.

Other current phrases expressing
the obvious are *as plain as the* NOSE *on
your face*, which dates from the sixteenth century, and *as plain as* DAY,
which was coined in the nineteenth.

It is **plain as a pikestaff** *to me that note-
keeping was woefully poor. If the notes had
been properly written up the doctors would
have known the problems they would have
been facing.*
DAILY MAIL, 3 OCTOBER 2001

'In this particular case on the video it's **as
plain as a pikestaff** *that you were
enjoying yourself,' he said.*
THE TIMES, 6 SEPTEMBER 2002

pin money

money given for a woman's incidental
expenses; money earned by a married
woman for her personal use on
incidentals and luxuries

In past centuries pins were essential
items for fastening together various
parts of a fashionable lady's attire.
Before machinery permitted large-scale
manufacture in the eighteenth century,
however, the pin industry was a slow

and labour-intensive one. Pins were, therefore, luxury items and a woman would be given an allowance, known as *pin money*, with which to buy them. Sometimes a sum of money would be left in a will to cover this necessary expense: *I give my said doughter Margarett my lease of the parsonadge of Kirkdall Churche...to by her pynnes withal* (York, 1542). Such was the cost and scarcity of pins in the fourteenth and fifteenth centuries that Parliament legislated to restrict their sale to just the first two days of the year.

In time *pin money* became a sum settled upon a wife at her marriage to cover all her personal expenses. The financial dependency of women through the centuries has kept the term alive to denote 'money given to a wife by her husband for her private needs'. Since the second half of the twentieth century, however, *pin money* has come to refer to a woman's own earnings which, when they are surplus to the family's day-to-day requirements, go towards little luxuries.

Childminding, however, suffers from an outdated and unflattering reputation that's proving hard to shift. 'A lot of people still think we're nice ladies around the corner looking after children for a bit of **pin money**,*' says Gil Haynes, the director of the National Childminding Association.*
THE DAILY TELEGRAPH, 12 JUNE 2003

Gloria's career began as a part-time presenter on BBC Radio Northern Ireland working for **pin money** *and fitting the job around the school run with her three young children, Caron, Paul and Michael.*
THE GUARDIAN, 13 MARCH 2004

pin: to pin something on someone
to attach blame to someone

See under *to wear one's heart on one's* SLEEVE.

The lawyers and judges who flocked to Equitable Life now find themselves facing the prisoners' dilemma, where twin defendants hope that if neither speaks both will be acquitted, but if one squeals he may **pin it on the other** *and get off.*
THE DAILY TELEGRAPH, 6 JANUARY 2001

Shortly after that our offices were trashed. The computer screens were all kicked in but nothing was taken. **We couldn't pin it on** *Van Hoogstraten but I remain convinced it was him*
THE GUARDIAN, 23 JULY 2002

pink: in the pink
in the best of health; to the highest degree (of something)

In the 1570s, the agricultural writer Thomas Tusser began to refer to the plants of the dianthus family as *pinks*, and other herbalists subsequently followed his lead. It is thought that the word may have come from the Dutch name for the flowers *pink oogen*, 'small eyes'. (In the second half of the seventeenth century, *pink-coloured* was used to describe something of the same hue as the dianthus, hence the modern English colour term *pink*.)

From the thirteenth century on, *flower* was used to denote 'the perfect embodiment of some outstanding quality' (*the flower of chivalry*, for instance), and later 'the very best example of something'. Shakespeare, in *Romeo and Juliet* (1592), substituted *pink* for *flower* in a spot of playful banter between Mercutio and Romeo, with Mercutio claiming to be the paragon of a courteous man:

MERCUTIO: *Nay, I am the very pinck of curtesie.*
ROMEO: *Pinke for flower.*

Thereafter *pink* often replaced *flower* in such contexts, and phrases such as *the pink of elegance*, *the pink of perfection*, *in the pink of taste* and, of course, *in the pink of health* became widespread. Such locutions still occur in modern English, although they are becoming rare now. An exception is the reference to good health, mostly found in the condensed phrase *in the pink*, common from the beginning of the twentieth century.

'Oh, a place in Notting Hill is what I would really like,' he said. 'But it's too expensive and there is no one to help me.'

*Looking back, I am not certain whether I didn't do the wrong thing at this juncture. But I was a good deal moved. I said that financially speaking I was **in the pink** and that I might be able to assist if he wanted me to.*
THE ECONOMIST, 19 OCTOBER 2000

*Everyone was sick as dogs, although the dogs themselves were **in the pink**, feeding on the Christmas dinners that no one could keep down.*
THE DAILY TELEGRAPH, 5 JANUARY 2002

For other idioms from Shakespeare, see WILLIAM SHAKESPEARE, page 152.

pipe: put that in your pipe and smoke it
put up with that if you can; that's the situation, whether you like it or not

In use since the early nineteenth century, this idiom alludes to the gentleman who retires to his favourite armchair to smoke his pipe and reflect on life. The phrase, however, functions as a crushing retort to the smoker; instead of sweet tobacco, he is being given unwelcome information or a challenging remark to puff upon and consider. John Galsworthy used the idiom to good effect in *To Let* (1921): *The noble owner put his opinion in his pipe and smoked it for a year.*

*I always thought what a woman wanted was an end to gender generalisations, and **you can put that in your Mars and Venus pipe and smoke it**...*
THE GUARDIAN, 16 APRIL 2004

*Having a real enemy to fight gives you the chance to find the best in yourself – to rise up and show the demons what you are made of, and to know that every day that you live as richly as you can is a triumph... Every day, I carry in me the knowledge that my life is a gift I must use fully and wisely. My life is still extraordinary, not least because it is still mine to be lived. And I really did live happily ever after. So **put that in your pipe and smoke it**, demons!*
EMMA BOWES-ROMANELLI,
BETWEEN ANGELS AND DEMONS, 2004

pipe: to pipe down
to stop talking

Instructions to the crew on board ship were made by the boatswain sounding a pipe or whistle. Admiral William Smyth in his *Sailor's Word-Book* (1867) defines *pipe down* as *The order to dismiss the men from the deck when a duty has been performed on board ship*. Clamour on the decks then fell as the men went below. The term was put to more general use in the nineteenth century; *Dialect Notes* (1900) records it as meaning *to stop talking*. Nowadays the idiom is often used as a command with the sense 'shut up!'

*David Hope, the Archbishop of York, last night told Church of England evangelicals to **pipe down** and listen to other sections of Anglicanism. They should chatter less and contemplate more, he said.*
THE GUARDIAN, 22 SEPTEMBER 2003

For other nautical idioms, see A LIFE ON THE OCEAN WAVES, page 24.

pitched battle, a
a fierce fight or dispute

This military term, coined in the sixteenth century, originally referred to a planned encounter, a battle fought on a site chosen in advance by both sides. By the second half of the eighteenth century, however, *pitched battle* was used idiomatically to denote any furious fight or argument in a wide range of contexts.

*By 3pm things were turning ugly. The protest plunged into violence with **a pitched battle** between hunt supporters and police.*
THE DAILY TELEGRAPH,
19 SEPTEMBER 2004

*A village football club is facing **a pitched battle** with neighbours over plans for a new playing field.*
NEWCASTLE JOURNAL, 19 MAY 2005

plain sailing
a trouble-free situation or course of action

This nautical term originated as *plane sailing* which, since the seventeenth century, was a simplified method of charting the position of a vessel by assuming that she was progressing along a plane surface rather than following the earth's sphere. The phrase began to be used figuratively in the first half of the nineteenth century. Later, Admiral William Smyth referred to this idiomatic use of a nautical term in his *Sailor's Word-Book* (1867): *Plane-sailing is so simple that it is colloquially used to express anything so easy that it is impossible to make a mistake.* The term, even amongst seafarers, was often misspelt as *plain sailing*, and this is now the accepted form of the idiom.

*You're pretty lucky as a sports person if you have **plain sailing** for your whole career.*
THE DAILY TELEGRAPH,
29 SEPTEMBER 2001

*Teachers of seven- and eight-year-olds are now being given more training, so you must find out how much phonics your daughter will be getting. You can back this up at home, but be aware that it isn't entirely **plain sailing**. 'C-a-t spells cat' is easy, but when you get on to, say, the different 'oo' sounds in 'look' and 'loop', it gets more complicated.*
THE INDEPENDENT, 2 SEPTEMBER 2004

For other nautical idioms, see A LIFE ON THE OCEAN WAVES, page 24.

pleased: as pleased as Punch
extremely pleased

In the second half of the seventeenth century, a puppet show of Italian origin became popular in England: Samuel Pepys records his enjoyment of several entertainments. Polecenella, the name of the principal character, was anglicised as Punchinello which, by the early eighteenth century, had been shortened to Punch. The puppet performances were the forerunners of the famous Punch and Judy shows that are still played to children at the seaside today. In the traditional tale Mr Punch is a serial murderer despatching in turn his baby, his wife, a policeman, a doctor, a lawyer, the hangman and the Devil. His glee at defeating every enemy, temporal and spiritual, who crosses his path is jubilantly expressed in the recurrent phrase 'That's the way to do it'. It was Mr Punch's renewed elation at every success that inspired the phrase *as pleased as Punch*, coined in the early nineteenth century.

*I remember being **pleased as Punch** at getting full marks at primary school for an exercise which involved excising 'Scotticisms' from a piece of text.*
THE TIMES EDUCATIONAL
SUPPLEMENT, 27 OCTOBER 2000

See ALLITERATIVE SIMILES, opposite.

Alliterative similes

One day the American writer and editor Christopher Morley and his friend, the poet William Rose Benét, were strolling down the street when they noticed a shop-window display featuring two identical wigs on stands. *They are alike as toupees in a pod*, quipped Morley. The idiom on which Morley based his clever pun began life in the sixteenth century as the rather cumbersome *as alike as one pease is to another*, a form that persisted until well into the nineteenth century. The neater *as like as two peas* dates from the second half of the nineteenth century with *as like as two peas in a pod* appearing around the turn of the twentieth. Although the latter is quite lengthy, its rhythm and alliteration allow it to trip happily off the tongue.

Alliteration and rhythm make a phrase memorable and easy to say. Consider *as pleased as* PUNCH, for instance. The substitution of *happy* or *content* for *pleased* would destroy the balance and sound of the phrase. Similarly *as fit as a* FIDDLE would not work if *fit* were replaced by *healthy*.

Alliteration is often the key to the survival of one particular turn of phrase from amongst others like it. This is undoubtedly the case with *as dead as a* DOORNAIL, which remains current while *as dead as mutton, a mackerel, a herring* and *a nit* are all now obsolete. Or consider the triumph of *as cool as a cucumber*, a phrase from the first half of the eighteenth century, over the variant *as cold as a cucumber*. *Cool* and *cucumber* share not only their initial letter, but also a vowel with a similar sound and length.

This book also contains entries for *as busy as a* BEE, *as* BOLD *as brass*, *as dead as a* DODO and *as* MAD *as a March hare*, but there are many more. Here are just a few of them.

As bright as a button describes someone who is alert and intelligent. The punning phrase probably alludes to a burnished metal button, and dates from the first half of the nineteenth century.

As good as gold came into use towards the middle of the nineteenth century. It refers to a person on their very best behaviour, like Jane:

> Gentle Jane was good as gold.
> She always did as she was told.
> She never spoke when her mouth was full,
> Or caught blue-bottles their legs to pull.
> (W S Gilbert, *Patience*, 1881)

As hot as hell is American in origin, and replaces the earlier *hot as blazes*. It dates from the early twentieth century.

As pretty as a picture is also American and dates from the second half of the nineteenth century. Any young lady described by the phrase would be pretty enough to sit for an artist and have her portrait displayed on the drawing room wall.

As right as rain dates from the late nineteenth century and generally means that everything is as it should be, everything is going to plan. More particularly it refers to a person's restored health or wellbeing, as in *Rest and you'll be right as rain in the morning*. As to why *rain* should be *right*, it is hard to fathom, unless falling rain represents normality. Whatever the inspiration behind the simile, W L Phelps (quoted in Stevenson, 1949) was quite right when he wrote that *The expression 'right as rain' must have been invented by an Englishman* (*The Country or the City*).

For more on our fondness for alliterative idioms, see COUPLINGS, page 294.

plug: to pull the plug on something/someone

to withdraw one's support for a project or a person

The *plug* in this idiom refers to a stopper which, in an old type of water-closet, sealed the lavatory pan and had to be pulled out to allow the contents to drain away. *To pull the plug* therefore meant in its first uses from the mid-nineteenth century 'to flush the toilet': *It was not...an agreeable drawing... She took it...into the nearest lavatory, dropped it in and pulled the plug on it* (Dorothy L Sayers, *Gaudy Night*, 1935).

The phrase began to be used figuratively in the first half of the twentieth century to describe an action which effects a sudden release: the discharge of bombs from a plane, for instance. It is not a long step from this to the contemporary sense of 'to withdraw support'. This is sometimes in the context of life support machines (where a plug can literally be pulled from an electric socket), but more often of projects that are failing and so forfeit financial backing.

But before you **pull the plug** *on your sponsored swim, remember that school events do more than just raise money. They provide an outlet for pupil energy, and a chance to involve parents and foster community spirit.*
THE TIMES EDUCATIONAL
SUPPLEMENT, 27 JUNE 2003

point: the point of no return

the crucial moment in an undertaking beyond which there is no point in, or possibility of, turning back

An article in a 1941 issue of the *Journal of the Royal Aeronautical Society* described this phrase as a *fatalistic expression* that intrigued the layman. It went on to explain that the *point of no return* was *merely a designation of that limit-point, before* which any engine failure requires an immediate turn around and return to the point of departure, and beyond which such a return is no longer practical. Figurative use dates from the late 1940s.

At Gamblers Anonymous, it's the working classes, not the chattering ones, who share sob stories of financial ruin, who've re-mortgaged their houses to meet dodgy loans, and stretched their credit limits beyond **the point of no return**.
SCOTLAND ON SUNDAY, 18 JULY 2004

In describing the Iranians as on the cusp of a **'point of no return**,' *officials said, Sharon was arguing to Bush that once Iran solved some remaining technical hurdles, there would be no effective way of stopping it from ultimately building a weapon, even if that day was years away.*
INTERNATIONAL HERALD TRIBUNE,
14 APRIL 2005

For other fatalistic expressions, see *to* BURN *one's boats/bridges* and *the* DIE *is cast*.

poker-faced

straight-faced, expressionless

The allusion is to the bland expression of the poker shark, determined not to betray his hand. In an article on the playing of poker, the *Encyclopaedia Britannica* for 1885 rated a *good 'poker-face'* as essential for success in the game. The phrase was extended in the first quarter of the twentieth century to any situation necessitating 'an expressionless countenance'.

[The Sting] was a tale of double-dealing, con tricks and **poker-faced** *bluffs.*
THE SUNDAY TIMES, 4 MAY 2003

[Johnny] Cash plugged straight into the myth of the Old West – the star-crossed cowhand, the **poker-faced** *loner, the mysterious man in black.*
DAILY MIRROR, 15 SEPTEMBER 2003

*Cut to the 1960s, to the work of Allan Jones, Keith Arnott and the lesser-known Bruce Lacey, and you immediately recognise that sculptors are beginning to let their hair down. **Poker-faced** monumentality is disappearing.*
THE INDEPENDENT, 7 MARCH 2005

For other idioms derived from poker, see page 320.

pot: to go to pot

to be ruined, to deteriorate, to go downhill

The idiom, originally often in the form *to go to the pot*, dates back to the first half of the sixteenth century. The figure is of meat being cut up for the cooking pot and was originally used only of people who were being literally destroyed. *Then goeth a part of ye little flocke to pot, and the rest scatter,* wrote William Tyndale of persecuted Protestant Christians (*Answer unto Sir Thomas More's Dialogue,* 1531), while in his *History of Whiggism* (c 1680), Edmund Hickeringill tells of *Poor Thorp, Lord Chief Justice, saying that he went to Pot, in plain English, he was Hang'd.*

Not until the nineteenth century was the idiom more widely applied – to failing empires, potatoes and the like: *The potato is really going to pot… Constitutional disease and the Colorado beetle have preyed too long upon its delicate organism* (*Cornhill* magazine, July 1889). Renton Nicholson in his *Swell's Night Guide to the Great Metropolis* (1846) neatly defines the phrase thus: *Gone to pot, become poor in circumstances, gone to the dogs.*

*The man who won Celebrity Fit Club has seen his diet **go to pot** during his holiday in Positano, Italy.*
DAILY MIRROR, 18 JULY 2003

[Marlon Brando] was so beautifully made that maidens swooned and young men fell
*at his feet. So what did he do? Year by year he let himself **go to pot**, over-eating until he was grossly overweight.*
THE TIMES, 6 JULY 2004

pound of flesh, a

a full, legal entitlement which one exacts out of vengeance or to the detriment of the other party

In Shakespeare's *The Merchant of Venice* (c. 1596) Antonio borrows from the moneylender, Shylock, promising to give him a pound of his flesh if the sum is not repaid on time. When Antonio's ships are wrecked, he is unable to meet the payment and Shylock takes him to court. Portia, disguised as an advocate, defends Antonio. She tells Shylock he is entitled to his pound of flesh but warns him that, in taking it, he must not spill a single drop of blood since there was no mention of blood in the bond: *Then take thy bond, take thou thy pound of flesh.* The phrase has been used idiomatically by writers since the second half of the nineteenth century.

*Chuck your girlfriend in a very humiliating way in front of your soon-to-be ex-wife. It will save you a fortune and in all likelihood keep you out of court. My guess is your wife won't want you back and having received her '**pound of flesh**' will quietly dissolve into the backdrop of your life. Then you can return to the woman you love, beg her forgiveness and live happily ever after having spent the money you've saved on a fabulous holiday to make up for your abusive treatment.*
THE OBSERVER, 27 OCTOBER 2002

So-called 'vulture' funds pick over the non-performing bonds discarded by disheartened investors. In the summer of 2002, a few months after Argentina stopped honouring its debts, a brave buyer could have purchased a distressed bond in the secondary market for 20 cents on the dollar or less. On February 25th, he could have swapped it for crisp peso-denominated paper worth 35 to 37 cents: a tidy annualised return of 25% or more.

*Not every vulture will settle for such quick pickings. The more patient among them will hold out for their full **pound of flesh** in the courts.*
THE ECONOMIST, 3 MARCH 2005

For other idioms from Shakespeare, see WILLIAM SHAKESPEARE, page 152.

Pyrrhic victory, a
a victory won at too great a price

Ambitious Pyrrhus, king of Epirus, had invaded Italy, having been encouraged by a Delphic oracle to help defend the Greek cities threatened by the expanding Roman empire, and needing no further excuse. Although he met with initial military success, the Romans rejected his peace proposals. Pyrrhus was forced to invade Apulia, his troops engaging with the Roman army at the Battle of Asculum (279 BC). Once again Pyrrhus was successful, but the price this time was the lives of his finest soldiers and ablest officers. According to Plutarch (*Lives: Pyrrhus, AD 75*), when congratulated on his

victory, Pyrrhus lamented *Another such victory over the Romans and we are undone* – hence the term *Pyrrhic victory* for a battle won at too great a cost. The idiom has been in use since the second half of the nineteenth century. Strictly, of course, *Pyrrhic* should be written with a capital letter, but nowadays the rule is more relaxed.

*It would be **a pyrrhic victory** of epic proportions should the keys to No 10 come at the price of a deeply divided Labour party.*
THE GUARDIAN, 8 SEPTEMBER 2004

*No doubt a deal will be done some time next year and Mr Paisley will duly be appointed first minister. It may, however, be a **pyrrhic victory**. He is not in good health and will by then be in his 80th year. Although he will claim to speak for unionism, many of his own supporters will believe he has sold out, while moderate unionists will hold him in contempt for his past behaviour and present opportunism.*
THE ECONOMIST, 9 DECEMBER 2004

For another idiom from warfare in the ancient world, see PARTING *shot*. For other idioms drawn from ancient life and history, see page 317.

quantum leap/jump

a dramatic advance, a positive stride forward

The origin of the expression lies in the work of Planck and Einstein, who introduced the concept and term of the *quantum* at the beginning of the twentieth century. From the 1920s, *a quantum jump* referred to the instantaneous movement of a particle from one state or place to another. *Quantum jump* is subsequently found in various technical senses, though more figuratively only in the 1950s. The now more common *quantum leap* is not recorded till 1970. In both cases, the sense is 'a major advance, a significant step forward', in any field.

In the story of Giovanni Medici, head of the papal army, who died in 1526 of cannon wounds on the banks of the Po, Mr Olmi finds a portent for the destructive power of warfare today. The world of war, he seems to be saying, took **a quantum leap** *in that period – the kind of blind technological advance in destructiveness that we have become all too accustomed to.*
THE ECONOMIST, 18 APRIL 2002

Fixed supplies, stalled discoveries, and sharply increased consumption will drive prices in the near future to an oil-price tipping point.
    The wisest way to anticipate and mitigate this risk would be to implement an immediate **'quantum jump'** *into energy conservation and hydrogen development… To be sure, even this quantum jump strategy will likely require 15 to 20 years*

to achieve broad displacement of current oil sources by hydrogen.
THE FUTURIST, 1 MARCH 2005

queer: in Queer Street

in debt

Queer Street was an imaginary nineteenth-century street populated by people suffering from all sorts of difficulties, from illness or unemployment to financial worries. Since lack of money is at the root of so many other problems, it is not surprising that *in Queer Street* had come to mean 'in debt' by the twentieth century.

Forget Tannadice, Kerrydale or Firhill Street, almost every club in the SPL is **in Queer Street**. *According to the latest reports, half the clubs in the league are 'technically insolvent' and the top 12 together owe a massive £160 million.*
GLASGOW DAILY RECORD,
24 SEPTEMBER 2003

Never fear. I bring tips for belt-tightening that should see you out of **Queer Street** *in two shakes of a bailiff's fist.*
THE GUARDIAN, 31 JANUARY 2004

queer: to queer someone's pitch

(intentionally) to spoil someone's chances of success, to make life difficult for someone

To queer the pitch was a common turn of phrase amongst hawkers, tradesmen and showmen in the nineteenth century when something occurred to interfere with their business. In his *Circus Life and Circus Celebrities* (1875), Thomas Frost explains: *The spot they select for their performance is their 'pitch' and any interruption of their feats, such as an accident, or the interference of a policeman, is said to queer the pitch.* The phrase began to be used more generally to mean 'to spoil someone's chances of success in an undertaking' early in the twentieth century.

*Neither Olazabal nor Ken Schofield, the executive director of the European Tour, would become embroiled in why so few of the top players wanted to come to the oldest tournament on mainland Europe. Fair enough, they do not want **to queer their pitch** with the leading draws on tour, but global expansion certainly seems to be hurting Europe.*
THE DAILY TELEGRAPH, 5 MAY 2004

Metro, *the morning daily distributed free to rail commuters in major cities, was started by the* Mail *group merely **to queer the pitch** for any would-be rival to its* London Evening Standard.
NEW STATESMAN, 17 MAY 2004

quick: the quick and the dead
the living and the dead

The Authorised Version of the Bible (1611) uses *quick* in the ancient sense outlined in the following entry. New Testament passages speaking of God's judgement declare that *he will come to judge the quick and the dead*, a phrase that was later used in the Apostles' Creed. But coinage of the phrase cannot be attributed to the Bible scholars, even if

familiarity with their work was responsible for preserving the expression. They were simply employing a coupling that had been in use since the days of King Alfred back in the ninth century and was already well established in the language.

*The German intelligence service is resuming its familiar role in the Middle East: acting as a negotiator between Israel and Hizbollah guerrillas to swap hostages and prisoners – both **the quick and the dead**.*
THE INDEPENDENT, 17 DECEMBER 2000

See also *to be cut to the* QUICK.

quick: to be cut to the quick
to suffer deep emotional hurt

Quick comes from the Old English word *cwicu*, meaning 'living', and in this phrase refers to the most sensitive, living flesh on the body, such as that protected by the fingernails and toenails. Someone who has been figuratively *cut to the quick* feels inner pain as intense as if this tender flesh had been pierced. The phrase is an old one appearing as *touched to the quick* in John Heywood's proverb collection (1546), a form that persisted until at least the mid-nineteenth century.

*Firstly Mamillius – son of Sicilia's king Leontes – dies tragically young, **cut to the quick** by his parents' marital bust-up.*
THE INDEPENDENT, 28 MAY 2001

See also *the* QUICK *and the dead*.

· R ·

Rs: the three Rs

the basic subjects taught at school:
reading, writing and arithmetic

This expression is commonly attributed to Alderman Sir William Curtis (1752–1829) who rose to become Lord Mayor of London. A firm believer in education, he once proposed a toast at a public dinner given by the Board of Education with *The three Rs – Riting, Reading and Rithmetic*. The wording was ascribed to Sir William's generally agreed illiteracy. However, a correspondent with *Notes and Queries* claims to have known someone present at the dinner. Sir William, it appears, had a limited education but was very shrewd. He chose the particular wording as a joke, and it was received with great applause and merriment. His political opponents, however, seized on the phrase and used it to portray Sir William as an ignoramus.

Most private schools were, and are, very much better than most state schools (and particularly in the area of south London where I live). They are better at teaching everything, from **the three Rs** *to music, drama, woodwork and sport.*
THE DAILY TELEGRAPH, 31 MAY 2000

ETON SPELLING MISTAKE
That venerable educational institution Eton College is advertising for a dame to help with the pastoral care of boarders. The role, it promises, will be 'totally fulfiling [sic]'. So much for **the three Rs**.
THE DAILY TELEGRAPH, 11 AUGUST 2000

Children who once tended livestock are learning their **three Rs** *now in the community of Nturumeti. Nursery school enrolment has increased from 18 children to 68...*
TEARTIMES, WINTER 2001

rack: to rack one's brains

to stretch the brain beyond its normal limits, in order to remember something, to find something appropriate to say, etc

The *rack* was an instrument of torture. It consisted of a frame with a roller at each end. The victim was strapped to these and would endure agony as they were turned little by little, stretching the joints of his arms and legs. From the sixteenth century onwards the *rack* was a favourite figure for expressing something that caused intense suffering. *To rack one's brains* likens the mental pressure of stretching one's thoughts or memory to this physical torture. The phrase dates from the second half of the seventeenth century but in 1583 the composer William Byrd is quoted as saying *Racke not thy wit to winne by wicked waies.*

I wish to point out that, as fund-raising manager for Hearing Concern, I **rack my brains** *daily to think of ways of raising money.*
THE DAILY TELEGRAPH, 25 APRIL 2001

There, see, I knew that if I **racked my brains** *hard enough I would be able to find something about this place that wasn't quite up to scratch.*
SCOTLAND ON SUNDAY,
9 SEPTEMBER 2004

rain: to rain cats and dogs
to rain hard, extremely heavily

It's raining cats and dogs!
I know – I've just stepped into a poodle.

The joke is an old one, as is the picturesque expression, and there are a number of theories to account for it.

The most vivid suggests that drainage in the streets in bygone centuries was so inadequate that during storms the bodies of stray animals were washed along in the flood. Swift's *Description of a City Shower* (1709) gives us a flavour of what it was like:

Now from all parts the swelling kennels
[gutters] flow,
And bear their trophies with them
as they go.

The 'trophies' are numerous, but amongst them:

Drown'd puppies, stinking sprats, all
drench'd in mud,
Dead cats and turnip tops, come tumbling
down the flood.

The earliest written example of the phrase as we know it comes in Swift's *Polite Conversation* (1738), and it might be supposed that he was merely referring to his earlier verse. If so, Swift could be the author of the metaphor. However, some credit needs to be given to Richard Brome in the previous century, who wrote in a slightly different form: *It shall raine…dogs and polecats* (*The City Wit*, 1653).

Alternatively, some authorities have suggested that the phrase may be a corruption of the Greek word *catadupe*, meaning 'cataract' or 'waterfall', which had been borrowed into English from French and was in the contemporary vocabulary. The original figure would then have been of rain coming down like a waterfall. Still others suggest a connection with Norse mythology, in which witches in the guise of cats rode upon storms and the storm-god Odin was accompanied by a dog.

Funk (1950) is rather more down-to-earth, speculating that the din of a thunderstorm was like cats and dogs having a scrap.

*It's **raining cats and dogs** and you can't get a taxi. But what do you do? Well, in the real world you get wet.*
THE SUNDAY TIMES, 30 MARCH 2003

Just threaten to wash the car, or invite the neighbours round for a barbecue.
*Guaranteed **to rain cats and dogs**.*
GLASGOW DAILY RECORD, 24 JUNE 2004

rank and file, the
the common people, those not in leadership; the ordinary membership of a political party

Rank and file has described the way a body of soldiers is drawn up for inspection since the sixteenth century: *rank* is a line of men standing side by side in close order and *file* a line standing one behind the other. The men in question are private, non-commissioned soldiers who carry out the orders of those in command. Its figurative use, to describe the ordinary members of a large organisation or political party, dates from the late eighteenth century. With the growth of the Trades Union Movement, the expression was frequently heard in the twentieth century. Playwright Alan Bennett uses this fact to humorous advantage in *Habeas Corpus* (1973):

MRS WICKSTEED: *I'm going to my cake-decorating class. I don't really want to, but we're electing a new secretary and it's like everything else; if the **rank and file** don't go, the militants take over.*

*According to the Police Federation, respect for **rank-and-file** police is being damaged by over-reliance on speed cameras.*
THE INDEPENDENT, 25 MAY 2004

If the views of **rank-and-file** *Conservatives still count for anything, the contest for the Tory Party leadership is now all but over, with David Davis established as clear favourite to succeed Michael Howard... The poll's findings also make clear whom* **rank-and-file** *Tories are determined to blackball.*
THE DAILY TELEGRAPH, 1 JUNE 2005

For other idioms derived from the army and warfare, see page 317.

rare: a rare bird

an exceptional person or occurrence

In one of his *Satires* (c. AD 120), the Roman writer Juvenal described chastity as *Rara avis in terris nigroque simillima cygno*, 'A bird as rare upon the earth as a black swan'. References to the black swan as a figure for something wondrous and seldom found began in the fourteenth century. *The Ladies Dictionary* (1694) illustrates this use of the phrase to good effect: *Husbands without faults (if such black Swans there be)*. Meanwhile, from the early seventeenth century onwards, other writers began to use *rara avis* in a similar way: *A good nurse for neurotic patients is a rara avis indeed* (*Tuke's Dictionary of Psychological Medicine*, 1892). Late in the nineteenth century still others translated the latter into English. George Bernard Shaw, in his role as music critic for the *Star*, described the perfect dancer as *the rarest of rare birds* (21 February 1890).

Of these phrases, *black swan* is extinct (perhaps because black swans were perceived as not so rare after all – Captain Cook discovered them in Australia), *rara avis* becoming rare, and *rare bird* current and quite common.

Most people seem remarkably ignorant about the very existence of the inner-city bungalow, but this **rara avis** *of the urban property scene is suddenly making a bit of a splash...*
THE DAILY TELEGRAPH, 25 MAY 2002

PR skills in the book trade can ensure so much orchestration that an apparently 'unpromoted' book is thrust before the public at every turn, so the author of a really spontaneous success is **a rare bird**.
THE INDEPENDENT, 13 SEPTEMBER 2003

For other idioms drawn from Greek and Roman writers, see page 318.

read: to read between the lines

to discover the intended or real meaning beyond the obvious

The phrase refers to a method of cryptography in which secret messages were concealed in alternate lines of a text so that they could be discovered only when extracted from the whole. The idiom dates from the middle of the nineteenth century. It can be used not only of texts, letters and the like, but also of the spoken word where the speaker is holding back from giving the complete picture.

She had been interviewed once before, in 1991, in an unpleasantly trivial way just after Greene died, and I was expecting the encounter to be difficult, a process of **reading between the lines** *combined with outright refusal to talk about anything she regarded as too intimate about her life with Greene.*
THE GUARDIAN, 27 MARCH 2004

red herring, a

anything which diverts (usually intentionally) attention away from the main argument

This is a nineteenth-century expression, but its origins are earlier. A herring that has been dried, salted and smoked turns a red-brown colour. These cured fish have a particularly strong smell so, as far back as the seventeenth century, they were sometimes used to train hounds to follow a scent: *The trailing or dragging of a dead Cat, or Fox, (and in case of necessity a Red-Herring) three or four miles…and then laying the Dogs on the scent* (Cox, *Gentlemen's Recreations*, 1686).

Of course, a *red herring* would be equally useful to anyone who wanted to lure hounds away from the quarry; hunt saboteurs are proposed by some, for instance, while others have suggested escaped prisoners or people training hounds to remain focused on the real scent. It would be a matter of simply drawing a red herring across the path. This diversionary tactic is now the main sense of the idiom. More recently, however, speakers who wander off the subject in pursuit of a personal hobby horse might be accused of following a *red herring*.

I like The Hound of the Baskervilles *because it is a detective story, which means that there are clues and **Red Herrings***.
MARK HADDON, THE CURIOUS INCIDENT OF THE DOG IN THE NIGHT-TIME, 2003

A question of colour

Some years ago there was a fascinating piece of research done by two anthropologists, Berlin and Kay, in America. After looking at ninety-eight different languages they found that, contrary to contemporary views, there were universal basic colour terms. Some languages had as few as two basic colour terms, whereas others could have up to eleven. Not only that, but languages acquire colour terms in a fixed order. For instance, any language with only two basic colour terms, such as Jale in New Guinea, must have black and white. A language with three basic colour terms must have black, white and red. One with five colour terms must have black, white, red, green and yellow, and so on.

The evidence seems strong that this is how languages, following these general principles, acquire their basic colour terms. Idioms including colour terms, however, show some characteristics that are difficult to explain in terms of these universals of language. Perhaps that is not surprising, since one fundamental characteristic of an idiom is that it breaks the rules of language. Rather, the evidence from them points to each language expressing a unique world view by the way it slices up reality into its own relative categories. For instance, why do we say *to be in the* RED in English, yet *to be in the green* in Italian? Why is a *blackleg* in English a *yellow* in French and Spanish? And why is *to be in someone's* BLACK *books* in English *to be in the green book* of somebody in Spanish?

One particularly interesting example is that of the *blue joke* or 'dirty story'. In Spanish this can be a *red story* or a *green joke*. Yet in French a *blue tale* means a 'fairy story', while a *green story*, or even a *green* as a noun, is the equivalent of our *blue story*. But a German who tells *blue tales* is lying – perhaps telling a *white lie* (see BLACK AND WHITE, page 311)?

So individual are languages, so much do things change from one language to another, that several authorities have suggested that a good test to decide if a given phrase is an idiom or not – and this applies to all idioms, not just colour ones – is to see if it translates directly into another language. If it does, it's not an idiom. If it does not, it is. Better ways to decide what constitutes an idiom are considered in WHAT IS AN IDIOM? (page 4). However, the translation test highlights the peculiarity and idiosyncrasy of different languages as a basic criterion for definition, which in turn lends support to what is known technically as the Sapir-Whorf hypothesis. It argues that languages – and, it seems from the limited evidence above, idioms also – are the unique product of their immediate context and do not obviously obey universal rules.

*Wind power, being inherently inefficient, is considered by many as an interim energy solution at best... References to the number of homes supplied with electricity from wind power are a disingenuous **red herring**.*
THE TIMES, 29 MARCH 2004

*Katy Gardner's campus chiller will appeal to those who like a touch of creepiness, but not too much sleuthing... A cosy psycho-drama conducted over canteen latte and chocolate muffins. The **red herrings** win the day.*
THE INDEPENDENT, 4 JUNE 2004

red: in the red
in debt, overdrawn

The idiom dates from the 1920s. It is American in origin and comes from accounting where debit and negative balances were traditionally written in red ink. It is, of course, possible to get *out of the red*, in which case one's account would be *in the black*, black being the colour of ink used to record credit.

NEARLY HALF OXFORD'S COLLEGES IN THE RED
HEADLINE, THE GUARDIAN, 7 JULY 2004

*The major market indicators are still firmly **in the red** for this month, which is not a good sign for the rest of the year. Since 1945, the Standard & Poor's 500-stock index has had 21 down Januarys while the Dow Jones industrial average has had 19; in about two-thirds of the cases, a negative January was followed by a down year.*
THE NEW YORK TIMES, 27 JANUARY 2005

See also *in the* BLACK.

red-letter day, a
a day to celebrate, a day of special significance

During the fifteenth century it became customary to mark all feast days and saints' days in red on the ecclesiastical calendar whilst other days were in black. These were days for rejoicing and celebrations and so people began to refer to days which had particular significance for them personally as *red-letter days*: *To sit at the same table with Grattan* [a respected Irish politician], *who would not think it a memorable honour, a red letter day in the almanac of his life?* (Samuel Taylor Coleridge, *Letter*, 1811).

*Put the date in your diary now. Sunday, July 4, will be **a red letter day** for armchair sports fans following the announcements yesterday that next year's British Grand Prix and a cricket one-day international between England and New Zealand will be on the same day as the climax of Euro 2004 and the men's singles final at Wimbledon.*
THE DAILY TELEGRAPH,
12 SEPTEMBER 2003

*It's my daughter's tenth birthday this week – **a red-letter day** for all of us.*
THE TIMES, 14 JUNE 2004

red tape
excessive bureaucracy, form-filling

The phrase originates in the former practice of tying together papers and official documents with red tape. This procedure goes back to the seventeenth century, as instanced by an advertisement in the *Public Intelligencer* (6 December 1658), which offered a reward for *a little bundle of papers tied with a red tape which were lost on Friday last*. Possibly it was Sydney Smith who first used the term to satirical effect. Discussing the philosopher Sir James Mackintosh, he writes: *What a man that would be, had he a particle of gall, or the least knowledge of the value of red tape! As Curran said of Grattan, 'he would have governed the world.'* (*Lady Holland's Memoir*, 1855)

Modern usage has reinforced the use of *red tape* as a condemnatory phrase, often the insult of a frustrated person doing battle with officialdom.

Red Tape *watch. Burgess Hill town council is thought to be close to a decision that has taken months of discussion, a six-page report, thousands of pounds and a vote at a full committee…the council has been through these procedures to decide what to do about a desk in the tourist information department blighted by too much direct sunlight. Councillors will vote next week and a resolution looks imminent. They are expected to decide to move the desk.*
THE INDEPENDENT, 13 MARCH 2002

Reilly: to live the life of Reilly

to lead a luxurious and trouble-free existence

The idiom originates in Irish-American ethnic songs of the late nineteenth century. One of these, 'Is That Mr Reilly?' (1880), by the comic Pat Rooney, ponders what Mr Reilly's life would be like if only he were a wealthy man. The actual phrase, however, is from a song by Harry Pease, 'My Name Is Kelly', written in 1919, in which the character of the title makes reference to Mr Reilly's contented existence:

> *Faith and my name is Kelly,*
> *Michael Kelly,*
> *But I'm living the life of Reilly*
> *just the same.*

The phrase was soon picked up by American novelists before beginning to appear in British texts around the middle of the twentieth century.

The example below from the *Daily Telegraph* shows a common anglicised spelling of Reilly, which may also have been influenced by the humorist and poet James Whitcomb Riley. That Riley gained minor celebrity status in the latter part of the nineteenth and early twentieth centuries with poems

such as 'Little Orphan Annie' (1885), and many of his themes illustrated the idiomatic *life of Riley*.

*It's obvious to all that Nicky could travel around the world on his chunky bank account **living the life of Reilly**.*
THE PEOPLE, 10 AUGUST 2003

*My old man was strict with me in a good way, but all of a sudden I was 19, 20, 21 and I had money. I liked it far too much and **led the life of riley**.*
THE DAILY TELEGRAPH,
24 SEPTEMBER 2004

rhyme: neither rhyme nor reason

without any good sense

This phrase is a translation of part of a line from a celebrated fifteenth-century French farce, *Maistre Pathelin* (c. 1464), by an unknown dramatist: *En toy ne ryme ne raison*, 'in you neither rhyme nor reason'. The phrase was taken up by the English poet John Skelton (?1460–1529) and, according to one of Francis Bacon's apophthegms, was used by Sir Thomas More in a witty remark to a friend who had taken the trouble of putting a rather indifferent book into verse: *Yea, marry, now it is somewhat, for now it is rhyme; whereas before it was neither rhyme nor reason* (c. 1535).

Shakespeare made abundant use of the phrase, Ben Jonson employed it, and in 1678 it was included in John Ray's collection of English proverbs.

*The fact is that there really is **no real rhyme nor reason** why one place becomes a hotspot and another doesn't.*
THE GUARDIAN, 12 JULY 2003

For other idioms drawn from literature, see page 319.

ride: to ride roughshod over

to behave in an arrogant and domineering manner towards someone

Horses which were *roughshod* had shoes from which the nail-heads projected a little. Practically speaking, this helped to prevent their feet from slipping on loose ground or in wet or icy weather. From the seventeenth century on, cavalry horses were also *roughshod* to inflict greater injury upon fallen enemy soldiers as they galloped over them; hence the phrase *to ride roughshod over*, used figuratively from the early nineteenth century.

*Enough of this leader who cares nothing for international opinion, acts unilaterally with no attempt at consensus-building, **rides roughshod over** all who disagree, and stubbornly guards his own country's influence on the world stage at the expense of others.*
METRO, 20 FEBRUARY 2003

*She is so sure of herself that she has a tendency **to ride roughshod over** people who lack the desire or willpower to stand up to her.*
DAILY MAIL, 19 MAY 2003

*Unions warned ministers yesterday **not to ride roughshod over** civil servants' feelings in radical moves to cut jobs and save money.*
DAILY EXPRESS, 16 MARCH 2004

For other horsey idioms, see page 319.

ring: to ring a bell

to remind someone of something, to jog someone's memory

Speculation abounds as to what kind of ringing bell jogs the memory. Some say that the bell is that which attracts the attention of a clerk, receptionist or servant. The idea here is that, in the same way, something seen or said may suddenly focus our attention on a person or event stored away in our memory.

Others think it may simply be the doorbell or a telephone ringing. Another theory points to a bell which rings in a shooting gallery at the fair when a bull's eye is scored. This is dismissed by Funk (1955), who feels the expression would then logically have to be *to ring the bell*. Instead he proposes a bell which sounds a more nostalgic note and suggests a school or church bell.

The OED even hints that the bell might be that used by Ivan Pavlov, the Russian physiologist, who conditioned dogs to salivate at the ringing of a bell. Certainly the dates of Pavlov's experiments in the early twentieth century and the coining of the phrase fit, as does the notion of a bell triggering a response.

What this all boils down to, though, is that no one really knows how the expression came about.

FIRST CALLER: *Hiya, First Minister. I'm Wendy from Paisley. I used to be a powerful executive minister, do you remember me?*
FIRST MINISTER: *Hi, Wendy. The name seems **to ring a bell**. Do go on.*
DAILY EXPRESS, 19 JANUARY 2004

There's a scene in Tony Parsons' novel Man and Boy *where the child is puzzled when his newly single dad offers him the sugary cereal, the one saved for holidays, instead of the no-fun everyday breakfast his mum usually gives him. It **rings bells** with every parent who has had to negotiate a deal: the sweetest cereals are allowed for 'special' occasions, like Saturdays.*
THE INDEPENDENT, 3 APRIL 2004

ring: to ring the changes

to do things in as many different ways as possible for the sake of variation; to reiterate the same message in different ways

The allusion here is to bell ringing and, in particular, to change ringing, an art peculiar to the English which was fully developed by the seventeenth century. *To the musical Belgian,* wrote Dorothy L Sayers in her novel *The Nine Tailors* (1934), *it appears that the proper thing to do with a carefully tuned ring of bells is to play a tune upon it. By the English campanologist…the proper use of the bells is to work out mathematical permutations and combinations.* Changes are the different orders in which bells in a peal of four or more can be rung. The more bells there are in the church belfry, the greater the number of possible changes. In a tower boasting twelve bells it would be possible to ring a total of 479,001,600 changes (taking some 40 years to perform). Four bells would permit just 24 (taking just 30 seconds). Change ringing relies on the skilful handling of the bell rope, on precision timing and on an excellent memory, since the patterns are memorised, not written down. *Ring the changes* has been in figurative use since the seventeenth century.

His violinist is superb; his wind-player **rings the changes** *between flute, folk-oboe, and jew's harp.*
THE INDEPENDENT, 1 JANUARY 2004

You can also **ring the changes** *by using wholegrain mustard instead of horseradish.*
DAILY EXPRESS, 5 APRIL 2004

ring: to ring true/false
to give the appearance of being genuine and authentic, or not

When coins were made of pure metal, and not alloys as they are today, it was possible to test whether or not they were genuine by the sound they made when dropped on a solid surface. *The ring of a sovereign or of a shilling is a criterion of the genuineness of the coin,* wrote Alexander Bain (*The Senses and the Intellect,* 1855). This was a long-established practice, as Samuel Pegge pointed out in his *Anonymania* of 1796 (published 1809): *Ringing, or sounding, money, to try if it be good, is not modern.*

The test has been figuratively applied to character, words and actions since around the middle of the nineteenth century. Anything that passes the test may also be said to have a *ring of truth* to it.

Given this administration's shameful record of dissembling and manipulation, his allegations have **a ring of truth**.
DAILY MAIL, 23 JUNE 2003

Bernard Shaw called the role of the Countess 'the most beautiful old woman's part ever written' and, while I prefer to think of Dame Judi as timeless rather than old, she certainly makes Shaw's words **ring true**.
SUNDAY EXPRESS, 14 DECEMBER 2003

There are a few moments that **ring false** – *unfortunately, they tend to be when the drama is most heightened.*
THE SUNDAY TIMES, 4 JANUARY 2004

riot: to read someone the riot act
to quell rowdy or objectionable behaviour by remonstrating and making the consequences clear; to reprimand someone forcibly

When the Stuart queen Anne died in 1714, in order to secure a Protestant succession, the crown of Great Britain passed to George I of the House of Hanover. British Catholics demanded that Charles Edward Stuart, descendant of the deposed Catholic monarch James II, should be king and rioted in protest. Threats of a Jacobite uprising were brewing in Scotland and, in 1715, the nervous British government attempted to quell anti-Hanoverian demonstrations by passing the Act for Preventing Tumults and Riotous Assemblies. The act made it unlawful for twelve or more people to disturb the public peace through riotous behaviour. An unruly crowd could be ordered to disperse by a magistrate reading aloud the following proclamation: *Our Sovereign Lord the King chargeth and commandeth all persons being assembled immediately to disperse themselves, and peaceably to depart to their habitations or to their lawful business.* Those who had not obeyed the command an hour later were sentenced to imprisonment with hard labour.

The phrase *to read the riot act* was first used figuratively in the early nineteenth century. The Riot Act was still law; there are mentions of it in Charles Dickens's *Barnaby Rudge* (1840) and, on 13 November 1887, it was read to a mass of unemployed people outside Parliament in London. Indeed, the Act was not repealed until 1973.

She is listed in Christine Hamilton's Book of Battleaxes *and not averse to hauling her managers dripping from the shower* **to read them the riot act**.
DAILY TELEGRAPH, 18 NOVEMBER 2000

river: to sell someone down the river

to betray someone, usually for one's own profit

The phrase was coined in the southern states of North America, where an illegal trade in slaves continued, even after a bill had been passed to abolish it in 1808. The southern states relied heavily on slave labour to work their prosperous cotton and sugar plantations. Unwanted slaves from the north would be transported down the Mississippi river to be sold into the harsher conditions of the deep south: *'...you's a nigger en a slave dis minute; en if I opens my mouf ole Marse Driscoll'll sell you down de river befo' you is two days older den what you is now!'* (Mark Twain, *Pudd'nhead Wilson*, 1894). Figurative use dates from the early twentieth century.

The picture presented was of a loyal Beckham being **sold down the river** *by an uncaring, shifty United board.*
THE DAILY TELEGRAPH, 19 JUNE 2003

Arabella Weir, Germaine Greer, Sheila Hancock and Jenny Eclair are some of the respected – and witty – women who get it all off their chests in the book Grumpy Old Women. *They rant about everything from thongs to children's parties, but also make the point that 20 years after being told they could have a career and a perfect family, 'it now feels like we were* **sold down the river** *on the having-it-all idea. The only "all" we seem to have now is all the work.'*
WESTERN MAIL, 16 FEBRUARY 2005

rob: to rob Peter to pay Paul

to benefit one person or enterprise at the expense of another; to pay off one debt by incurring another

According to Peter Heylyn in his *History of the Reformation of the Church of England* (1661), the estates of the abbey church of St Peter fell into decay in the period 1540–50, under the only Bishop of Westminster, Thomas Thirlby. When Thirlby resigned his seat, the see was dissolved and St Peter's Westminster, which then became part of the diocese of London, was required to surrender many of its holdings to finance repairs to St Paul's cathedral. *From hence first came*, wrote Heylyn, *that significant By-word (as is said by some) of Robbing Peter to pay Paul*. The story sounds convincing but no real evidence has been uncovered to support these accusations, and Heylyn obviously had an axe to grind, having been appointed treasurer of Westminster Abbey in 1637. In fact,

It's not cricket!

The vocabulary of general English is enlarged, even enriched, by the assimilation of words from the jargon, slang, cant or argot of subcultures in society. The special lexicons of business, the military, jazz musicians and thieves amongst many others have contributed words and phrases that are used far beyond their original confines, often with a somewhat different meaning (see A LIFE ON THE OCEAN WAVES, page 24). It would be surprising, then, if cricket, that most English of games, had not given the language several colourful idioms.

For instance, the wicket is the area in the middle of the ground where all the action takes place. In ordinary informal British English *to be* or *to bat on a sticky wicket* means 'to be in a difficult situation'. It refers to the problems faced by a batsman when performing on a wicket that has been saturated by rain.

The quickest way to score runs in cricket is to hit the ball up in the air and right out of the playing area. For that, you score six runs, you *hit the ball for six*. In general English, however, the expression has a different meaning. You might hear, for instance:

My wife's death hit me for six; it took me months to recover.
The news knocked me for six; I just didn't believe it.

The sense here is that the event or happening overwhelmed me, shattered me, dealt me as severe a blow as the batsman hitting the ball over the boundary.

There are quite a few more idioms from cricket: *off one's own bat*, for instance, which means 'on one's own, independently, without help or assistance'. Or *hat trick*, now used to denote a triple victory in many sports, but originally honouring a bowler who, having taken three wickets with three successive balls, was rewarded with a new hat. And then, of course, there's that lovely, now rather dated, phrase *it's not cricket*, meaning 'it's not fair play, it's not acceptable or honourable', gleaned from cricketing handbooks of the second half of the nineteenth century:

If you have ever gone to the cinema only to find that you are stuck behind a couple slurping each other's faces throughout the movie, then, perhaps, you will agree with me that this sort of behaviour is just not cricket (The Observer, 5 September 2004).

he was using a phrase that had been in English since the fourteenth century to support his argument.

The religious reformer John Wyclif gives us the earliest known reference to the idiom: *Lord, hou schulde God approve that thou robbe Petur, and gif this robbere to Poule in the name of Crist?* (*Selected Works*, c. 1380). Sixteenth-century examples admit variants: *to rob saint Peter therewith to clothe saint Paul, to unclothe Peter to clothe Paul* and *to borrow of Peter to pay Paul*, for instance. Nor are idiomatic expressions linking the two apostles confined to English. French has *descou-vrir S Pierre pour couvrir S Pol* (to strip St Peter to clothe St Paul), and German has the equivalent.

So how was the phrase originally coined? It may be that, apart from the fact that their names are pleasingly alliterative, both Peter and Paul were very prominent in the early church and, as such, deserving of equal regard. Indeed, papal seals affixed to bulls bear the figures of both saints as well as the name of the reigning pope. To detract in any way from one to honour the other would in effect be robbing him of that equal standing to which he was entitled. Outside the world of the early apostles, however, the practice certainly finds favour, as George Bernard Shaw ironically remarked in *Everybody's Political What's What* (1944): *a government that robs Peter to pay Paul can always depend on the support of Paul.*

*The idea of the National [Theatre] colonising the cool and thus depriving smaller, fringey theatres of their biggest attractions smacks to me of **robbing Peter to pay Paul**. Will it genuinely create new younger audiences or merely move them from one space into another? We shall see.*
THE MAIL ON SUNDAY, 12 AUGUST 2001

*If the money for IVF is ring-fenced, it may be a good move. However, if it is not, it may be a case of **robbing Peter to pay Paul**. It is possible that cancer patients, especially, may lose out as a result.*
THE INDEPENDENT, 27 AUGUST 2003

rock: between a rock and a hard place
in a dilemma, between two unpalatable alternatives

According to an American book of dialect notes published in 1921, to be *between a rock and a hard place* meant 'to be bankrupt'. The phrase seems to have arisen in Arizona during a period of financial nervousness earlier that century. Its meaning is no longer so exact, however, for by the second half of the twentieth century the idiom had come to denote 'being in a situation of any sort in which a choice has to be made between two equally undesirable alternatives'.

*Mr Watkins, who had an unblemished 35-year career, said: 'We are caught **between a rock and a hard place**. There does not seem to be anything you can do without being at risk of prosecution. If you decide to restrain a child, you face a possible action for assault. If you do nothing, it's criminal negligence. What do you do?'*
THE TIMES EDUCATIONAL SUPPLEMENT, 2 NOVEMBER 2001

*The diplomats are caught **between a rock and a hard place**, accused of recklessly endangering lives if they fail to release intelligence of terrorist attacks…or of inflicting economic harm by advising business travellers to stay at home when nothing actually happens.*
THE TIMES, 16 JANUARY 2003

For idioms with a similar meaning see *a* CATCH-*22 situation* and *between the* DEVIL *and the deep blue sea*.

rooftops: to cry/proclaim/shout something from the rooftops
to make something known publicly

In Luke 12:2–3 Jesus warned that everything hidden through hypocrisy will one day be made known: *that which ye have spoken in the ear in closets shall be proclaimed upon the housetops*. Of course, in Palestine it was an easy matter to climb up the stairway to the flat roof and make a public proclamation. It is rather more difficult on the pitched roofs of Europe. Nevertheless, the phrase has been idiomatic in English since the second half of the nineteenth century. It remained faithful to the wording of the Authorised Version of the Bible until the second half of the twentieth century, when *housetops* was replaced by *rooftops* and *shout* became more common than *proclaim*.

*Another pupil at Forest School is the son of two state school head teachers. His mother, a girls' school headmistress who asked not to be named, said: 'I work in a fairly Left-wing local authority so I don't **shout it from the rooftops**.'*
THE DAILY TELEGRAPH, 8 JUNE 2003

Gordon Brown has not just a chancellor's but also a puritan's hatred of tax avoidance. That shows in this year's budget, which includes the broadest swipe ever taken at Britain's huge tax-avoidance

business... At present, to overturn a scheme, the Inland Revenue must first find out about it – and tax advisers hardly **shout their latest ploys from the rooftops**. *Then they must challenge it.*
THE ECONOMIST, 18 MARCH 2004

For other idioms from the Bible, see page 317.

ropes: to know/learn the ropes

to know/learn how to perform a task skilfully; to understand the workings of an organisation; to become conversant with the tricks and dodges of a job

This is a nautical term, first recorded in the nineteenth century. The rigging on a vast sailing vessel was a complicated system of ropes which sailors had to become familiar with because *to handle a ship, you must know all the ropes* (Thomas Chandler Haliburton, *Wise Saws*, 1843). From this nautical context the phrase was applied to other areas of expertise by the mid-nineteenth century. It can on occasions carry connotations of knowing all the tricks of the trade, so as to turn things to one's own advantage.

Shivaun's father Solomon Woolfson gave up a promising career as a barrister **to learn the ropes** *at the family firm, a lock factory, determined to make it a success.*
DAILY EXPRESS, 27 MARCH 2002

These kids are savvy. These kids **know the ropes***. I mean, when we first met this school, I went in and Amy and I were introducing ourselves and explaining, to put the kids at ease, that we were going to be shooting a film. And I said, 'This is a documentary film. Does anyone know what a documentary is?' And this little boy from the back of the room raises his hand, and I call on him, and he said, 'Do you guys have a distribution deal in place yet?'*
NATIONAL PUBLIC RADIO, 15 MAY 2005

For other nautical idioms, see A LIFE ON THE OCEAN WAVES, page 24.

Rubicon: to cross the Rubicon

to take a step or decision from which there is no turning back

In ancient times the little river Rubicon made up part of the boundary separating Italy and Cisalpine Gaul, the province governed by Julius Caesar. When Pompey was appointed sole consul in 52 BC he turned the Senate against Caesar, who was ordered to lay down his command. Caesar's army was fiercely loyal and, secure in this, he decided to lead it across the Rubicon. This was a flagrant violation of the Lex Cornelia Majestatis, a law which forbade a general to enter Italy under arms and was tantamount to a declaration of war. Once the Rubicon was crossed there could be no turning back. *To cross the Rubicon* has been idiomatic in English since the first half of the seventeenth century.

Over the centuries river courses have changed but attempts have been made in modern times to identify the Rubicon and this has caused a number of disputes in the region. In 1933 Mussolini tried to resolve the question once and for all by renaming the little town Savignano di Romagna as Savignano sul Rubicone, claiming that the bridge there marked the exact spot where Caesar's successful campaign against Pompey began. Unlike Caesar, however, Mussolini was unsuccessful and the disputes continue to this day.

The whole business of selecting embryos for a particular purpose changes the nature of parenthood. If you select a child to match your desire, even for the sake of another, you have **crossed a Rubicon***. You have made the child a product of your will, rather than a gift from your being.*
IDEA, JANUARY/FEBRUARY 2002

*George Bush has, for the first time, taken an overt protectionist step against China – the popular scapegoat for job losses in America's industrial heartland. Until this week, the White House had restricted itself to bellicose rhetoric, usually to do with the value of the Chinese currency. Now it has **crossed the Rubicon**.*
THE ECONOMIST,
22 NOVEMBER 2003

For another idiom arising from the same episode, see *the* DIE *is cast*. For other idioms drawn from ancient life and history, see page 317.

rule: a/the rule of thumb

guesswork, rough calculation, estimate based on experience rather than careful calculation

Old ways of measuring die hard. Horses are still measured in hands, and until British decimalisation of 1971 people were only measured in feet and inches. This latter practice has a venerable history. In Roman times it was estimated that the measure of the last part of the thumb above the top joint would fit roughly twelve times into the larger measure of a foot. Thus the foot was split into twelve 'inches' (the French called them *pouces*, meaning 'thumbs') and remained a standard measure for centuries. Careful measuring required a standard rule but, where an estimated length would do, the thumb sufficed.

A *rule of thumb* has been in figurative use since the late seventeenth century.

*So, even if you have a queen-size bed, be careful not to attach a padded headboard that's too short – **the rule of thumb** is for the height of the board to measure at least two thirds of the bed's width.*
THE TIMES, 17 JULY 2004

*Don't go abroad until you're on top of your teaching and able to prepare and deliver your own work confidently. As **a rule of thumb**, you'll need at least two years' teaching in the UK.*
THE TIMES EDUCATIONAL
SUPPLEMENT, 27 JULY 2004

rule: to rule the roost

to be dominant, to display one's authority

In the hencoop the cock makes an obvious display of his dominance over the hens to show that he *rules the roost*. The origins of this phrase are not so transparent, however. As early as the fifteenth century *rule the roast* was current and, in Britain, remained so until the late nineteenth century. This has led to speculation, by no means proved, that the expression refers to the master of the house who presided over the carving of the roast meat at table. At first sight, a quotation from Thomas Nabbes's *Microcosmus* (1637) might seem to confirm this theory: *I am my ladies cooke, and king of the kitchen, where I rule the roast*. The line is not unambiguous, however, in spite of the culinary context. It is even possible that Nabbes might have been playing with words, for, on another tack, it has been pointed out that *roast* or *rost* were also alternative spellings for *roost*, which was originally pronounced with a long *o*. This takes us away from the kitchen and back to the hen run.

The modern form *to rule the roost* dates back to the eighteenth century. So far, earliest known written records are of American origin, the very earliest appearing in a document dated 1769 and quoted in the William and Mary College *Historical Magazine* (1908): *They say she rules the Roost, it is a pity, I like her Husband vastly*. Was American usage assuming a hen run origin for the phrase or simply substituting the modern *roost* for the archaic *roast* that lingered in British English? The debate continues. The influence of American over British English meant that, by the twentieth century, British English had finally admitted *rule the roost*, to the extent that, by 1926, the lexicographer and grammarian Henry Fowler pronounced in his *Modern English Usage* that *most unliterary persons say roost & not roast; I have just inquired of three such, & have been informed that they never heard of rule the roast, & that the reference is to a cock keeping his hens in order.*

She split the filing system in two, choosing to file by author primarily, then chronologically, rather than let simple dates rule the roost.
ZADIE SMITH, WHITE TEETH, 2000

Our Government will soon hold EU presidency. Let not ambivalence rule the roost.
DAILY MIRROR, 13 SEPTEMBER 2003

However, in the field the United States rule the roost with all but one top placing – Finland having a large lead in another of their traditionally strong events, the javelin.
THE TIMES, 13 JULY 2004

·S·

sack: to get the sack/to give someone the sack
to be dismissed/to dismiss someone from their job

At one time a journeyman kept all his tools in a sack and took them with him to his job where he would leave them with his employer. If he were dismissed, whether through his own fault or lack of work, he would literally *get the sack*, that is, his employer would return his sack of tools. The phrase was probably a variant of *to get the bag*. Written references to this date from the early nineteenth century and slightly pre-date those for *to get the sack*. A similar expression was current in Middle Dutch and in French from the early seventeenth century. Nowadays the English phrase is often replaced by the simple verb *to sack*.

If he's late for school, they'll grumble; but if he's late for work, he'll get the sack.
THE GUARDIAN, 16 OCTOBER 2001

I didn't get back to work until Wednesday where I proceeded to get the sack for refusing to stop singing, but did I care?
DAILY MIRROR, 17 NOVEMBER 2003

sackcloth: (in) sackcloth and ashes
(a visible expression of) penitence

The phrase alludes to the ancient Hebrew custom, made familiar through the Bible, of wearing *sackcloth and ashes* as a sign of mourning or penitence. The *sackcloth* was black, coarse goathair which was used to make grain bags. To wear it was a sign of humility.

The Hebrew word for sackcloth was *saq* and the Greek *sakkos*. The English word *sack* ultimately comes from these.

There are significant numbers of references in English, beginning with Wyclif's *Sermons* (c. 1375): *Do penaunce in aishen and hayre*. Thereafter, each of the early English translations of Scripture has variants of it in key passages, such as Jonah 3:6 and Matthew 11:21. Needless to say, it is also found in Shakespeare. It is not until the nineteenth century that the expression is found more freely in general contexts expressing a sense of regret and sadness.

*This lady, I understood, should have stayed at home covered in **sackcloth and ashes**, for her husband was in prison for embezzlement.*
THE MAIL ON SUNDAY,
11 NOVEMBER 2001

*One shareholder, outraged at the collapse in Granada's share price, called for 'a bit more **sackcloth and ashes**' from the board.*
DAILY MIRROR, 20 MARCH 2003

For other idioms from the Bible, see page 317.

salad days
one's days of youth and inexperience

Green has been used to mean 'youthful' since the fifteenth century, the allusion being to the bright, fresh shoots of young spring foliage. In Shakespeare's *Antony and Cleopatra* (1606), Cleopatra speaks of her *salad days, when I was green in judgement, cold in blood.* The metaphor was put into general use in the second half of the nineteenth century and in 1977 was spoken by another queen, this time Elizabeth II on the occasion of her Silver Jubilee when, in her speech at the Guildhall, she renewed her pledge to serve the people: *My Lord Mayor, when I was twenty-one I pledged my life to the service of our people and I asked for God's help to make good that vow. Although that vow was made in my salad days, when I was green in judgement, I do not regret nor retract one word of it.*

*Having grown up at last in his medium – film is the one life [Steven Spielberg] has known – the wunderkind, who turned 56 in the week his newest film opened, can indulge in nostalgia about his **salad days**.*
THE ECONOMIST, 9 JANUARY 2003

*Britain's over-50s have proved as glum about the young, and as forgetful of their own **salad days**, as the mass of predecessors who have lamented the decline of civilisation on approach to late middle age.*
THE GUARDIAN, 1 OCTOBER 2004

For other idioms from Shakespeare, see WILLIAM SHAKESPEARE, page 152.

salt of the earth, the
(of a person or persons) unpretentious yet praiseworthy, fundamentally good

The expression is a biblical one and can be found in the Sermon on the Mount (Matthew 5:13) where Jesus says: *Ye are the salt of the earth: but if the salt have lost its savour, wherewith shall it be salted? It is thenceforth good for nothing, but to be cast out, and to be trodden under foot of men.*

Salt is essential to flavour and preserve food. The Hebrews obtained their salt supply from the Dead Sea and from the Hill of Salt (Jebel Usdum) nearby. It was rock salt and subject to chemical changes which meant that the outer layer, besides being full of impurities, had very little flavour. Moisture and high temperatures caused it to deteriorate and be thrown out. Jesus, however, was calling on his disciples to be good salt that would permeate the world with the flavour of God's kingdom. Biblical connotations of good salt are virtues such as loyalty and purity, precisely the qualities of someone today described as *the salt of the earth*.

Apart from a period in the nineteenth century, when it was used flippantly to refer to people of rank and importance, the phrase *salt of the earth* has been used to denote 'a person or persons of exceptional good character' since the fourteenth century:

Sire, quod the lord, ye woot what is to doone.
Distempre yow noght, ye be my confessour;
Ye been the salt of the erthe and the savour.
For goddes love, youre pacience ye holde!
(Chaucer, *The Summoner's Tale,*
c. 1386.)

*This is typical of Roger. Straight as a die, **salt of the earth**, he is a thoughtful, big-hearted man.*
DAILY MIRROR, 22 MARCH 2003

*It is not just the film footage that is frequently black and white: so are the characters. Every member of the working class is downtrodden and **the salt of the earth**; and every employer or landlord is an ogre with a heart of ice.*
THE TIMES, 17 SEPTEMBER 2003

For other idioms from the Bible, see page 317.

salt: to be worth one's salt
capable, deserving of one's position or salary

Salarium (from Latin *sal*, 'salt'), from which our word 'salary' derives, was 'salt money', a sum paid to a Roman soldier so that he could buy salt to flavour his meals and remain healthy. Someone who is *worth his salt* is capable, efficient and deserving of his salary, privilege or position. In spite of its Roman origins, however, the idiom is not a particularly old one, dating back to only the first half of the nineteenth century and coined from the origins of the word *salary*.

Jonathan Swift turns the absurdities of party politics in the reign of Queen Anne into a saga of bizarre invention and a narrative style that any contemporary novelist **worth his salt** *can only envy.*
DAILY MAIL, 13 FEBRUARY 2004

Every French king **worth his salt** *kept a mistress. They were open about it and proud of it.*
DAILY MIRROR, 25 JUNE 2004

For other idioms drawn from ancient life and history, see page 317.

salt: to take something with a pinch/grain of salt
to be sceptical about something, to entertain doubts

Some etymologists find the origin of this phrase in Pliny's *Naturalis Historia* (c. AD 77) in which the author recounts how Pompey, after capturing the palace of Mithridates VI, finds in the king's desk a formula for an antidote to poisoning. Apparently a walnut, two dried figs and twenty leaves of rue, all mixed together *cum grano salis* (with a grain of salt) and eaten on an empty stomach, guaranteed protection. The Latin phrase, sometimes shortened to *cum grano*, was often used in English until well into the nineteenth century: *I know this speech must be understood cum grano salis* (Richard Baxter, *Christian Concord*, 1653).

Even so, other authorities take this suggestion *with a pinch of salt*, pointing

out that Pliny intended the phrase to be taken literally and that nowhere in classical Latin does the word *salt* appear as a figurative expression of scepticism.

Indeed, all the evidence supports the OED's statement that *cum grano salis* is a modern Latin coinage dating back no further than the seventeenth century. Funk suggests that, just as a sprinkling of salt makes a meal more palatable, so a doubtful story or excuse goes down more easily with *a pinch of salt*.

The GHI has tried out a dozen cleaning tips, both ancient and modern, so you know which are worth using and which you should take **with a pinch of salt.**
GOOD HOUSEKEEPING, JANUARY 2003

The good guest takes his/her hosts at their face value. He takes stories about others from mutual friends **with a pinch of salt** *and a spoonful of cynicism. It may be no more than gossip.*
THE TIMES, 8 NOVEMBER 2003

For other idioms drawn from ancient life and history, see page 317.

sandboy: as happy as a sandboy
pleased with life

Happy, jolly or *merry as a sandboy* dates back to the first quarter of the nineteenth century. *Sandboys* made their living from digging up sand and then hawking it around city streets where people would buy it to scour pots and pans or to throw down on the floors to absorb spills in taverns or butchers' shops. Although Jon Bee, in his slang reference *Dictionary of the Turf* (1823), describes the sandboys as 'urchins', the appendage *boy* could easily apply to a full-grown man, as it does today in terms such as *backroom boy* or *stable boy*. Since their work was gruelling and the living meagre, it is surprising that sandboys should be described as happy.

Jon Bee's definition gives us a clue to their proverbial cheerfulness. *As jolly as a sandboy,* he writes, *designates a merry fellow who has tasted a drop.* In other words, sandboys liked their beer.

The tavern theme is taken up by Dickens in *The Old Curiosity Shop* (1841) when Mr Codlin, the Punch and Judy man, repairs for the night to *The Jolly Sandboys...a small roadside inn of pretty ancient date, with a sign, representing three Sandboys increasing their jollity with as many jugs of ale...*

'This is what I have been waiting for for a long time...I'm **as happy as a sandboy** *and my expectations are good.'*
EVENING STANDARD, 11 JULY 2002

The course she preferred was academic, immensely varied, demanding and tremendous fun; she got a good degree and is now **happy as a sandboy** *working in arts publicity.*
THE INDEPENDENT, 11 AUGUST 2002

scot-free: to go/get off scot-free

to escape punishment or having to take the consequences of one's misdeeds

Scot means 'payment'. It was the name given to municipal taxes as early as the thirteenth century. People paid according to their means. The very poor were exempt from payment and went *scot-free.* Similarly a *scot* was a tavern score or contribution towards entertainment. *To go scot-free* was to be let off or to have one's bill paid by a drinking companion. The phrase was used figuratively by William Tyndale in his *Exposition of I John* (1531) to describe Christ's act of atonement: *The poore synner shulde go Skot fre,* and it is this sense of being allowed to go free and unpunished, though deserving penalty, that is current today.

The mammoth may have died out as the climate warmed up at the end of the last

Ice Age, which coincided roughly with man's arrival, but the experts are reluctant to blame hunting... However, we do not **escape scot-free** *from blame. A different group of scientists...point the finger at 'hyperdisease' – the name given to viruses which cross the species-barrier between one type of animal and another.*
DAILY MAIL, 24 OCTOBER 2001

They have somehow managed to turn terrorising the elderly into a nightly sport and **get away scot free.**
SUNDAY EXPRESS, 14 MARCH 2004

See also THE OLD CURIOSITY SHOP OF LINGUISTICS, page 198; for other idioms from the Bible, see page 317; for idioms drawn from Tyndale's translations, see WILLIAM TYNDALE, page 270.

scratch: to come/be/bring up to scratch

to meet/bring up to the required standard

The expression was originally *come up to the scratch, the scratch* being a sporting term for a line scratched in the earth that served as a starting place for contestants.

Early boxing knew none of the sophistication of the sport today. Bouts took place in the open air and contestants fought with their bare fists. Both began the bout with their left foot on the *scratch.* The fight was not divided up into rounds but went on until one contestant was knocked down. The fighters were then permitted a thirty-second break before being given a count of eight during which they had to *come up to the scratch* once more. A fighter who was unable to do so was no longer fit for the fight. Today, if a boxer is not dedicated enough to submit to a rigorous training programme, it is unlikely that he will ever *come up to scratch,* that is reach a high enough standard to be selected to fight.

Outside sporting contexts, the phrase *up to the scratch* is used from the mid-nineteenth century onwards, but it is nearly another hundred years before the current contemporary form *up to scratch* prevailed.

*'Ultimately the bond of all companionship,' he says at one point, 'whether in marriage or in friendship, is conversation.' Sadly neither Wilde's wife nor his chosen companion **came up to scratch** in that department.*
THE INDEPENDENT ON SUNDAY,
12 NOVEMBER 2000

*England's most senior surgeon has attacked the 'dreadful' state of the NHS under Labour, warning that Government spending plans will not **bring it up to scratch**.*
DAILY MAIL, 7 DECEMBER 2001

*She'd been the same at school, her work books were never smudged, her illustrations and maps were always finely drawn, everything underlined and tabulated and indexed, and she'd worked so hard and so methodically that even when the quality of her work hadn't been **up to scratch** her teachers gave her good marks.*
KATE ATKINSON, CASE HISTORIES, 2004

For a different idiom with the same origin, see *to* TOE *the line*. For other boxing idioms, see PACKING A PUNCH, page 45.

scratch: to scratch the surface
to deal with a matter very superficially

Scratches are only superficial marks on any surface. Since the seventeenth century *to scratch* has been used to mean 'to furrow the soil lightly', shallow preparation that is not adequate for most cultivation, and it is probably this sense that has been drawn upon for the idiom. Figurative use dates back to the early twentieth century.

*Mr Farquhar said recently IU [Interactive University] had 'only begun **to scratch**
the surface'* of the global e-learning market, which is estimated to be worth around £15 billion.*
EVENING NEWS, 20 MAY 2004

*Our few days in St Petersburg had been too brief to do anything other than **scratch the surface** of Peter the Great's northern capital, still gleaming from its 300th anniversary refurbishment.*
THE INDEPENDENT, 12 JUNE 2004

scratch: to start from scratch
to start from the very beginning with no help or advantage

In a number of sports there exists a handicapping system which allows the less good an advantage over the skilled. The point from which the most accomplished start is *scratch*. In the second half of the nineteenth century this starting point for the best player is found in tennis, athletics, cycling and other sports. Still today, a *scratch golfer* plays against opponents with handicaps, who are 'given' a specified number of strokes in order to make the contest more even.

By the 1920s the contexts extended beyond sport to anyone who began without advantage. James Joyce in *Ulysses* (1922) writes of a *poor foreign immigrant who started scratch as a stowaway and is now trying to turn an honest penny*. Today, the meaning has widened still further to include starting from the very beginning of a project or plan, often after an initial failed attempt.

*Opposition appears to be growing to the council's plans. This week the Friends of Inverleith Park vowed to fight the scheme, and the campaign group Save Inverleith Park is mobilising objectors... The council is trying to respond to the concerns of the objectors – after all it faces being forced **to start from scratch** and look for yet another site in the city.*
EVENING NEWS, 6 NOVEMBER 2004

*On Thursday, the secretary general of the United Nations, Kofi Annan, did what was once unthinkable: He told the UN Commission on Human Rights that the best way to improve the organization was simply to throw it away and **start from scratch**...*
INTERNATIONAL HERALD TRIBUNE,
9 APRIL 2005

For a similar use of *scratch* in a boxing context, see *to come up to* SCRATCH.

sea change, a
a profound change, a metamorphosis

The expression is from a song sung by the spirit Ariel in Shakespeare's play *The Tempest* (1611). The song describes the metamorphosis wrought upon Ferdinand's father by the sea:

> *Full fathom five thy father lies;*
> *Of his bones are coral made:*
> *Those are pearls that were his eyes;*
> *Nothing of him that doth fade*
> *But doth suffer a sea-change*
> *Into something rich and strange.*

The phrase has been used since the early twentieth century to describe anything which has undergone a radical transformation. It is currently a favourite with politicians hoping to convince the electorate that the old has gone and major changes for the better are on the way.

*And with all this passion comes **a sea change** in her emotional life: she feels more open than she has for a long time to the prospect of finding lasting love again.*
GOOD HOUSEKEEPING, JUNE 2002

*In May 1979, after his government had lost a confidence vote in the Commons, James Callaghan confided to an adviser: 'There are times, perhaps every 30 years, when there is **a sea change** in politics... I suspect there is such **a sea change**, and it is for Mrs Thatcher.' He was right, and his ministerial career was soon over.*
THE ECONOMIST, 21 MARCH 2005

For other idioms from Shakespeare, see WILLIAM SHAKESPEARE, page 152.

seamy side, the
the lowest, most degraded side of life

The phrase is Shakespeare's and alludes to the wrong side of a garment with all the seams and loose threads exposed to view. It comes from *Othello* (1604) where Emilia, speaking to her husband Iago, says:

> *Some such Squire he was*
> *That turn'd your wit, the seamy-side without,*
> *And made you to suspect me with the Moor.*

The expression was picked out in the first half of the nineteenth century to describe the baser and more shameful side of life.

*The people who paid up to £95 for a ticket didn't stump up their cash to hear Minnelli's fantastic three-octave voice. They paid because Minnelli is the living embodiment of both Hollywood's glitz and glamour and – thanks to her struggles with drugs and alcohol – **the seamier side** of showbiz.*
THE GUARDIAN, 4 APRIL 2002

Little remembered today, Wolff's debut created a sensation in literary circles that left her a well-regarded author for years after.
Part of it was her unlikely arrival on the publishing scene. But mostly it was what she wrote, a tale of a poor, rough-hewn family who lived and spoke in ways that left readers and critics astonished that this demure young lady could have conjured up such raw lives and gritty language.
*'Little Miss Wolff was 22 at the time and as thoroughly informed about **the seamy side** of life in a Midwestern factory town as if she had spent 50 years*

in police courts, reformatory schools, honkey tonks and slums,' a New York Times *reviewer wrote.*
ORANGE COUNTY REGISTER,
30 MARCH 2005

For other idioms from Shakespeare, see WILLIAM SHAKESPEARE, page 154.

shambles: in a shambles
in complete chaos, disarray

This is a favourite expression of politicians when criticising the policies and performance of another party. *Shambles* comes from the Old English *scamel*, meaning 'stool', and in the singular form *a shamble* was a little counter or bench where a butcher displayed his goods. In medieval towns, each street would be occupied by a particular trade or guild. Several British towns, Nottingham and York among them, still have streets named *Shambles* which would once have had a whole row of butchers' stalls. From here *shambles* was used to describe a slaughterhouse and, figuratively, in the late sixteenth century, a place of carnage and bloodshed. Modern usage, originating in America in the 1920s, has weakened the sense to 'a state of disorder, a total mess'.

*What **the shambles** really exposes is Britain's amateurism at managing large projects.*
THE TIMES, 4 MAY 2004

*Government schools are **in a shambles** so Mugabe is trying to put the blame on the private schools.*
THE GUARDIAN, 8 MAY 2004

sheep: to separate the sheep from the goats
to separate the good from the bad

This phrase comes from the Bible. Matthew 25:32 reads: *And before him shall be gathered all nations: and he shall separate them one from another as a shepherd divideth his sheep from the goats.* Sheep and goats were equally valued in Palestine for their provision of cheese, milk and meat. Just as sheep were kept for their wool, the goats' hair could be twisted into ropes or woven into cloth. Goatskins were made into bottles to hold water or wine.

There is a figurative distinction made between the animals, however. In biblical parables sheep are helpless creatures in need of care, guidance and protection. Goats, on the other hand, are wayward animals and often represent sin or condemnation (e.g. a scapegoat). And so it is with this parable in Matthew: the sheep are those who belong to God and the goats are those who are judged unworthy.

Idiomatic use of the biblical phrase only dates back to the first half of the twentieth century. Early examples show that it need not necessarily refer to people. *No two persons can agree on what is good art, so it is not possible to make a sheep-and-goat division between religious and individualistic art,* wrote Herbert Read in *The Meaning of Art* (1931), while Noel Coward, in his play *Future Indefinite* (1954), speaks of *stilling anxieties by segregating them, by separating the sheep from the goats.*

*The A level is not only, it seems, inexorably headed towards a 100 per cent pass rate, but more than one in five of those passes is of the highest rank. A qualification that was originally intended **to separate the sheep from the goats** has been degraded into a mass herding system.*
THE TIMES, 18 AUGUST 2003

*One of the biggest headaches for the amateur gardener is the mind-boggling number of different plants for sale. The RHS Plant Finder, for example, lists more than 73,000, with many species – such as roses, fuchsias and daffodils – having hundreds of cultivars to choose from. In the face of such profusion, **how do you sort the sheep from the goats**? Not easy...*
THE INDEPENDENT ON SUNDAY,
21 NOVEMBER 2004

See also *to separate the* WHEAT *from the chaff*. For other idioms from the Bible, see page 317.

sheets: three sheets to the wind
very drunk

On board a sailing ship, *a sheet* is a rope fastened to the bottom of a sail which is pulled in or let out to expand the sail or to change direction. If the sheet is left free, the sail will flap about and the ship will not be under tight control. A sheet and sail in this condition are said to be *in the wind*. The more sails there are *in the wind*, the more unstable the ship; like a drunken sailor, in fact. In the nineteenth century sailors would measure their degree of intoxication by alluding to the number of *sheets in the wind*: *Though S. might be thought tipsy – a sheet or so in the wind – he was not more tipsy than was customary with him. He...seldom went up to the town without coming down three sheets in the wind* (Richard Henry Dana, *Two Years before the Mast*, 1835).

The phrase, now modified as *three sheets to the wind*, is still current but slipping from regular usage.

*Jonathan was an excellent journalist and my mentor in the trade. I first met him at a Nairobi nightclub called Lips. **Three sheets to the wind**, he had his arms out wide and seemed to be buying the entire bar*

a beer... 'Drinking to excess doesn't make you sexier,' said a notice above the bar. 'Or richer,' I read, 'or more sophisticated...' 'Just drunk,' the notice concluded.
AIDAN HARTLEY,
THE ZANZIBAR CHEST, 2003

*Apparently scientists were working on a tablet that would allow KGB agents to drink adversaries under the table and steal secrets without getting **three sheets to the wind** themselves, but it didn't quite work.*
THE GUARDIAN, 20 JANUARY 2004

For other nautical idioms, see A LIFE ON THE OCEAN WAVES, page 24.

shell-shocked
in a state of shock

Shell shock is a medical condition suffered by those traumatised by being under fire in war. The phrase arose during the First World War and was extended to describe victims of any kind of sudden shock (divorce, redundancy, bereavement) in the 1970s. Nowadays it can apply to those jolted by quite trivial events: a victory or defeat at sport, for instance, or even having to get up early.

*The 12-year-old Teen Queen wants to be on the stage...forcing her **shell-shocked** mother to get up at 5am to queue around the block and rub shoulders with dolled-up mums for whom fame is anything but a four-letter word.*
THE TIMES, 10 APRIL 2004

*The defending Totesport League champions appeared to be still **shell-shocked** after their C&G Trophy defeat by Ireland...*
THE INDEPENDENT, 10 MAY 2004

For other idioms derived from the army and warfare, see page 317.

shilly-shally, to
to be undecided, to vacillate

The original form of this late seventeenth-century expression of indecision was *shall I, shall I*. This became *shill I, shall I* at the turn of the eighteenth century, but was soon reduced to *shilly-shally*. It was first used as an adverb (*Why should I stand shilly-shally?*) and then as an adjective (*...this constitution was a shilly-shally thing*), and even as a noun (*...marriages should be driven like bargains without shilly shally*) before being used from the late eighteenth century as a verb, as it is today.

*All the relentless **shilly-shallying** and buck-passing about the replacement stadium has long buried any residual affection for the original.*
THE DAILY TELEGRAPH,
9 DECEMBER 2002

*I hate the way people **shilly-shally** around and then moan because things don't turn out the way they want.*
DAILY MIRROR, 13 JANUARY 2004

A similar phrase is WILLY-NILLY. See also COUPLINGS, page 294.

ships (that pass) in the night
people who meet fleetingly

The idiom comes from a narrative poem, *The Theologian's Tale; Elizabeth* one of the *Tales of a Wayside Inn* (1863) by Henry Wadsworth Longfellow. Elizabeth Haddon tells the passing traveller John Estaugh, an old acquaintance, that the Lord has permitted her to love him. John has no such assurance but goes on his way promising to seek guidance for himself:

Ships that pass in the night, and speak each other in passing;
Only a signal shown and a distant voice in the darkness;

So on the ocean of life we pass and speak one another,
Only a look and a voice; then darkness again and silence.

Longfellow's work was widely read in the English-speaking world. Twenty years after the publication of the poem, *Ships that Pass in the Night* was chosen by Beatrice Harraden, suffragette and popular novelist, as the title of a novel about an ill-fated love affair between two tuberculosis patients in a sanatorium. From then on the phrase became idiomatic for a brief or doomed love affair. It was soon to be found in yet another suffragette publication when Gertrude Colmore used it as a chapter heading in her novel *Suffragette Sally*. This time, the ships destined for a brief encounter were two Suffragettes in Holloway gaol.

*I tried to arrange things in the house so that the two of them never collided. **Ships in the night** was what I hoped for.*
MARGARET ATWOOD,
THE BLIND ASSASSIN, 2000

Incidentally, Beatrice Harraden was amongst a number of suffragettes who refused to pay tax as a means of protest. One of her objections was against forcible feeding. See *to play* CAT *and mouse*.

For other idioms drawn from literature, see page 319.

shipshape: (all) shipshape and Bristol fashion
neatly in place and ready, immaculately organised

Bristol had, for many centuries, been an important port. The phrase *all shipshape and Bristol fashion* was used as a boast among seamen proud of their vessels. It meant that the ship was well organised and maintained and ready for the open sea. The adjective *ship-shape* (originally *ship-shapen*) was already in use amongst sailors in the first half of the seventeenth century to describe an orderly vessel. *Bristol fashion* was an addition noted in the first half of the nineteenth century. According to Admiral William Smyth, the phrase was coined *when Bristol was in its palmy commercial days...and its shipping was all in proper good order* (*Sailor's Word-Book*, 1867). The implication here is that, by the time the Admiral had compiled his dictionary, the port's fortunes and standards were failing. By then, however, the idiom had passed into popular usage; it is still current, though its use is waning.

*Expect Mrs Bush has the White House **shipshape and Bristol fashion** by now – after all, she's been there for a week, and any evidence of Democratic occupation will have been Cloroxed away.*
THE TIMES, 27 JANUARY 2001

Whose bright idea was it to turn parts of Liverpool city centre into a slalom course? I know they're relaying the pavements. I know some disruption is inevitable. And I know how much our beloved city council like a laugh. But closing off some of the streets behind Church Street to pedestrians – and then not telling them about it – is a joke too far.
  *I recently wrote how I hoped that Liverpool city centre would be **shipshape and Bristol fashion** in time for 2008. I hope this week's evidence isn't the shape of things to come.*
LIVERPOOL ECHO, 9 APRIL 2004

See also COPPER-*bottomed*. For other nautical idioms, see A LIFE ON THE OCEAN WAVES, page 24.

shirt: to keep one's shirt on
to keep calm

This is an American expression which dates from the mid-nineteenth century. Men who were spoiling for a fight would first remove their shirts to keep them from being soiled and torn. The phrase is usually found in the imperative *Keep your shirt on*, words that would have been on the lips of anyone present who preferred talking things over to fisticuffs. The phrase soon became a general plea for someone who was getting agitated to remain calm.

*[Peter Robinson] was spotted by one of my ever-growing legion of spies, on board a BA flight from Toronto on Thursday. He was not a happy bunny. First, his Club class television didn't work; then his food wasn't up to scratch... It was all he could do **to keep his shirt on**, I'm told.*
THE DAILY TELEGRAPH, 12 MAY 2001

shoestring: (to live) on a shoestring
to manage on very little money, to live on an unpredictable, low income

On a shoestring was first used in America in the late 1800s when it referred to a business operated on a very restricted budget. Its origins are open to interpretation. One suggestion is that funds are so reduced that there is only sufficient money to buy a shoelace. Webster's Dictionary mentions that shoelaces were amongst the articles commonly carried by street vendors. Perhaps living or running a business *on a shoestring* refers to the lowliest business of all – that of the street salesman who has food to eat or buys new stock only if his sales of these humble items are sufficient. Or it might simply be that the appearance of a shoelace is suggestive of thin, meagre resources.

It's shamingly shoddy television made on a shoestring for enormous profit.
DAILY MAIL, 29 MAY 2002

For years, Kenneth and Talita – former members of a survivalist cult led by a woman called Ma Prophet – seem to have lived on a shoestring, with only occasional employment.
THE DAILY TELEGRAPH,
22 DECEMBER 2003

shrift: to give/get short shrift
to treat someone brusquely without hearing them out/to be dismissed out of hand

A shrift is a confession made to a priest, after which absolution is given. In past centuries criminals were given short shrift, routinely hurried through confession before being executed. In Shakespeare's *Richard III* (1597), Ratclif, supervising the execution of Hastings, says: *Come, come, dispatch; the duke would be at dinner; make a short shrift, he longs to see your head.* The phrase has been used figuratively to describe giving or receiving curt, unsatisfactory treatment since the early nineteenth century.

Shrift comes from the verb *to shrive*, meaning 'to hear confession'. The past tense is *shrove*, hence *Shrove Tuesday*, the holiday immediately before Lent, when people went to confession, then made merry with sport and feasting.

[Britney Spears] the blonde shantoozy from Louisiana just got short shrift from Los Angelenos who, furious about being kept awake by filming of her new video, turned nasty.
THE TIMES, 23 MARCH 2002

The three parties agree on less government, but not nearly as much less as Mr Fortuyn wanted. His demand for elected mayors, in place of today's appointed ones, was accepted; his ideas for direct democracy got short shrift.
THE ECONOMIST, 13 JULY 2002

Lord Goddard...he claimed gave short shrift to counsel and had even less time for the appellants.
THE TIMES, 29 APRIL 2004

Being only human, doctors sometimes will give short shrift to this part of their job because they want to get on with making money again.
CLINICAL PSYCHIATRY NEWS,
1 MAY 2005

silly season, the
the months of August and September when Parliament is not in session

For most of the year newspapers reported the news, informing the population about political debate and decision. When Parliament rose for the months of August and September, the *silly season*, sometimes also known as the *big* or *giant gooseberry season*, began. Deprived of Parliament for its steady provision of newsworthy items such as political rows, leaks to the press, errors of judgement and interference in the affairs of other countries, desperate nineteenth-century journalists were forced to make much of giant gooseberries, sightings of the Loch Ness monster and the like, to keep the paper in print. The *silly season* still comes round each year, but the British public is now fed a year-round diet of trivia and so hardly notices.

In America, by contrast, newspapers prefer a bizarre 'human interest' story to see them through the silly season. And human interest doesn't come much more bizarre than the tale of Jason Black, Frances Schroeder and their newborn babe.
THE TIMES, 9 AUGUST 2001

The silly season, like the football season, appears to be getting longer. It never used to start in earnest, if earnest is the right word for silliness, until August. That was when otherwise sober newspapers and television

news bulletins would devote slightly too much space to a report that the world's biggest Scotch egg had been made at a factory near Kidderminster. But halfway through July, we are already into silly season *stories, and a classic of the genre is this week's news that Scotland has laid claim to King Arthur, of Camelot fame.*
THE INDEPENDENT, 13 JULY 2004

silver: to be born with a silver spoon in one's mouth
to be born into a rich family; to be born lucky

Some authorities claim that the expression originates in the traditional practice of godparents giving their godchild a spoon as a christening gift: only the rich could afford a silver one. It might, however, simply be a reference to the kind of spoon used to wean a child, the modest alternative to a silver spoon being one made of horn, wood or pewter, for, as the early eighteenth-century proverb goes, *Every man is not born with a silver spoon in his mouth, only one born to riches or good fortune*. The proverb was cited by Peter Motteux in his free translation of Miguel Cervantes' seventeenth-century classic *Don Quixote* (1712) and also in two proverb collections of the same period. Life is not fair, as Oliver Goldsmith pointed out in this telling contrast: *One man is born with a silver spoon in his mouth, and another with a wooden ladle* (*The Citizen of the World*, 1762), while William Hazlitt quoted an amended version of the original along the lines of 'Wealth is wasted on the rich': *They who are born with silver spoons in their mouths, don't know how to use them* (*English Proverbs*, published posthumously in 1869).

David Blunkett is a grouch, a scold, a street-fighter hardened by struggle. He had no silver spoon in his mouth, *not even the gift of sight.*
THE TIMES, 11 DECEMBER 2001

Sophie [Countess of Wessex], as we all know, was not born with a silver spoon in her mouth, *just her foot.*
DAILY EXPRESS, 7 AUGUST 2002

sink: to sink or swim
to fail or survive, without external help

The phrase refers to the water-ordeal, the centuries-old practice of judging whether or not a person was a witch by casting her into a lake or pond to see if she would sink or swim. The belief was that water would not accept anyone who had rejected the water of baptism, so if the victim drowned she was innocent and if she survived she was guilty and condemned to death. Either way, the outcome was the same, though drowning was probably gentler. As early as the fourteenth century Chaucer had *Ye rekke not whether I flete [float] or sink* (*Compleynte Unto Pite*, 1369), and he used the phrase again in *The Knight's Tale* (c. 1386).

The modern variant dates from the sixteenth century, and in 1774 John Adams famously used it in conversation with Jonathan Sewall. Sewall was trying to convince his friend not to join the congress which was being assembled in the American colonies. Adams would not be swayed and confirmed his commitment with the words:

I know that Great Britain has determined on her system, and that very fact determines me on mine. You know I have been constant and uniform in opposition to her measures; the die is now cast; I have passed the Rubicon; to swim or sink, live or die, survive or perish with my country is my unalterable determination.

In the end Mr Adams swam, eventually rising to become the second President of the United States in 1797.

The small farmer will never be satisfied, if he is merely plonked down amid modern conditions and left to **sink or swim**, *isolated and unadvised.*
IRISH UNIVERSITY REVIEW,
22 MARCH 2003

They gave me a mini-interview over the phone – I wasn't prepared for it at all but for me that was better; it was **sink or swim** *without time to think about it overnight and get worried.*
THE INDEPENDENT, 1 AUGUST 2003

sitting duck, a
an easy target

Someone described as *a sitting duck* is vulnerable to verbal or physical attack. A literal *sitting duck* makes an easy target for the huntsman. The phrase came into figurative use around the middle of the twentieth century in military contexts. *Sitting target* is a common variant.

Sometime in the late 8th century, however, the Vikings realised there was a much easier way to acquire luxury goods. The monasteries they dealt with in Britain, Ireland and mainland Europe were not only extremely wealthy but also situated on isolated coastlines and poorly defended – **sitting ducks** *for men with agile ships.*
TIME, 22 MAY 2000

The selection of the North-East as the first Anglian area in which to test-bed the rise and rise of regional devolution was supposed to be a **sitting duck** *for the cause of English assemblies. Instead it proved to be a dead duck. The voting was 696,519 votes against an elected assembly, 197,310 in favour.*
DAILY MAIL, 11 NOVEMBER 2004

skeleton: a skeleton in the cupboard/closet
a painful or shameful secret

Some speculate that this idiom may refer back to the actual discovery of a skeleton boarded up in a dark corner of some fusty cupboard. Others suggest its roots lie in the study of anatomy and the illegal activities of the body snatchers. It is more likely that this is simply a vivid nineteenth-century allusion to a murder victim who has been shamefully concealed in a cupboard. The years may roll by but the evidence never quite disappears; the skeleton is always there to bring the dreadful deed out into the open again. The expression was used by Thackeray for an article in an 1845 edition of *Punch* magazine, and again ten years later in *The Newcomes* (1855). The OED says that it is known to have been current earlier, though gives no evidence. Subsequently the phrase appeared in the works of other nineteenth-century writers and poets. There is a tendency to drop the mention of cupboard or closet, and just refer to *the skeleton*. As Shaw put it, *if you cannot get rid of the family skeleton, you may as well make it dance* (in H Pearson, *Bernard Shaw*, 1942).

Strewth, imagine writing a biography about a national treasure who makes it roundly clear that he wants nothing to do with it, or you, and whose friends and colleagues feel constrained not to co-operate… [Alexander] Games admits a cobble-job, but he has done it skilfully enough, producing an unacademic, modest primer for the fans. If there are **any skeletons in [Alan] Bennett's cupboard,** *Backing into the Limelight leaves their dust undisturbed.*
THE SUNDAY TELEGRAPH,
9 SEPTEMBER 2001

Fictitious visits to her long-lost aunt Eliza are convenient cover for the lovers' trysts – until a family funeral means Dilys really does have to track down Eliza and in the process discovers several **skeletons in the family cupboard**.
GOOD HOUSEKEEPING, MARCH 2002

William Tyndale
(1494–1536)

William Tyndale was a man of courage and genius. As a theologian, he embraced the Reformation, skilfully using scripture to argue against the established church. As a linguist, in 1522 he set about translating the Bible into English so that the common citizen, *the boy that drives the plow*, could have access to its truths.

Tyndale was hindered in his efforts and forced to take refuge on the continent, working in secret on his translations in Hamburg and Wittenburg and finally printing his New Testament in Cologne and Worms in 1525–6. Copies which reached England were condemned by the bishops and burnt, but Tyndale persevered. There followed translations of the Pentateuch in 1530 and Jonah in 1531.

In 1534 Tyndale eventually settled in Antwerp, where he was betrayed by an English spy, a man called Philips whom he had unwittingly befriended. He was imprisoned at Vilvorde, found guilty of heresy and, in October 1536, was strangled and burnt at the stake. His last words were, *Lord, open the king of England's eyes*, a prayer which was answered three years later, when Henry VIII consented to the publication of the Great Bible in English and made it mandatory that all parish churches should possess a copy. Ironically, the Great Bible was mostly Tyndale's work. In 1537 his friend John Rogers, working under the cover name Thomas Matthew, printed a complete Bible. This contained all of Tyndale's translations (he had prepared manuscripts of a further nine Old Testament books), work by Tyndale's associate Miles Coverdale and Rogers's prefaces and marginal notes. Known as Matthew's Bible, this text eventually won the king's approval for publication.

Tyndale's translations are remarkable because, instead of working from the Latin texts of the Vulgate, as John Wyclif and his followers had in the late fourteenth century, he went back to the original Hebrew and Greek. He understood that the simplicity of these texts could be rendered into lively, straightforward English prose:

They will say it cannot be translated into our tounge it is so rude. It is not so rude as they are false lyers. For the Greeke tounge agreeth more with the English, then wyth the Latin. And the properties of the Hebrue tounge agreeth a thousand tymes more wyth the Englishe, then wyth the Latyn. The maner of speaking is both one, so that in a thousand places thou needest not

---

*What they want is...someone whose sexual **skeletons are dangling from his rearview mirror rather than hanging about in the closet**...*
EVENING STANDARD, 10 JANUARY 2003

*Vermeer had a number of **skeletons lurking in his family closet**. His maternal grandfather...was implicated in one of the greatest money-forging scandals of early 17th-century Holland.*
THE DAILY TELEGRAPH,
18 JANUARY 2004

skid: on skid row
homeless, down-and-out

In the logging towns of the Pacific Northwest of the United States in the nineteenth century, *a skid road* denoted a sturdy timber track, greased with oil, down which the logs were slid to the mill. By about 1880 the parts of town where the loggers lived, which were characterised by brothels, run-down bars and shabby hotels, had come to be known as *Skid Road*, a term which was subsequently corrupted to *Skid Row*. The Depression of the 1930s ruined the *but to translate it into the English, worde for worde, when thou must seeke a compasse in the Latin, and yet shalt haue much worke to translate it welfauouredly, so that it haue the same grace & sweetnesse, sence & pure understanding with it in the Latin, & as it hath in the Hebrue. A thousand partes better maye it be translated into the English, then into the Latin.*

At a time when people spoke vernacular English and dialects and there was no recognised standard English, Tyndale succeeded in providing a translation of such clarity and beauty that when, for political purposes, King James I ordered a new translation to be prepared in 1607, Tyndale's text could hardly be improved upon. Eighty per cent of the Authorised or King James Version (1611) is Tyndale's work. His sense of linguistic rhythm and balance is evident in familiar verses, such as these:

Ask, and it shall be given you; seek and ye shall find; knock and it shall be opened unto you; for whosoever asketh receiveth; and he that seeketh findeth; and to him that knocketh, it shall be opened (Matthew 7).

In him we live and move and have our being (Acts 17).

The spirit is willing, but the flesh is weak (Matthew 26).

Centuries of familiarity with the Bible have led to biblical phrases being borrowed into everyday idiomatic speech. Here are just a few, inspired by William Tyndale:

let there be light (Genesis 1)
eat, drink and be merry (Ecclesiastes 8 and Luke 12)
a prophet has no honour in his own country (Matthew 13)
ye of little faith (Matthew 14)
to fall from GRACE (Galatians 5:4)
a man after his own heart (1 Samuel 13)
signs of the times (Matthew 16)
the fat of the land (Genesis 45)

flowing with milk and honey (Exodus 3)
the powers that be (Romans 13)
my brother's keeper (Genesis 4)
a law unto themselves (Romans 2)
FILTHY *lucre* (Titus 1:7)
fight the good fight (1 Timothy 6)
to GIRD *up one's loins* (1 Kings 18)
to kill the FATTED *calf* (Luke 15)
to fall by the WAYSIDE (Matthew 13)

See also *the* APPLE *of one's eye; to go* SCOT-FREE; *a* WOLF *in sheep's clothing.* For a further list of idioms from the Bible, see page 317.

---

livelihood of millions of workers and the phrase *Skid Row* was then commonly applied to a run-down slum in any town where the destitute hung out. Sadly, it remains so today: *At 50 square blocks, 11,000 inhabitants – 7,000 of them living in 65 single-room-occupancy hotels – Los Angeles' Skid Row is perhaps the nation's largest* (*National Catholic Reporter*, 12 October 2001).

*Like an ageing dowager eking out her last years **on skid row**, an empty gin bottle in her hand, the West Pier is a tragic sight.*
THE DAILY TELEGRAPH, 17 MAY 2003

skin: by the skin of one's teeth
just about, by the narrowest of margins

This evocative phrase is biblical but it is also a misquotation. Job 19:20 reads: *My bone cleaveth to my skin and to my flesh, and I am escaped with the skin of my teeth*. Job meant that *all* he had escaped with was the skin of his teeth; that is to say, nothing at all. Everything had been taken away from him: his family, his possessions, his friends and his health. The misquotation *by the skin of my teeth* leads to a different interpretation of the phrase from the original: that the speaker has just about escaped, that it was a very close run thing. Nevertheless, the misquotation has been idiomatic since the nineteenth century and is here to stay.

*It was assumed that after winning the presidency **by the skin of his teeth**, Bush would have to move towards the centre.*
THE TIMES, 23 APRIL 2001

*He escapes only **by the skin of his teeth** from St Nazaire in a coal barge, witnessing the aftermath of the sinking of the cruise ship* Lancastria, *with perhaps as many as 11,000 evacuated troops on board...*
DAILY MAIL, 18 JUNE 2004

For other idioms from the Bible, see page 317.

sleep: to sleep like a top
to sleep soundly

How does a spinning top sleep? Miss A E Baker in her *Glossary of Northamptonshire Words and Phrases* (1854) has the answer: *A top sleeps when it moves with such velocity, and spins so smoothly, that its motion is imperceptible.* The simile dates from the second half of the seventeenth century and replaces the earlier *to sleep like a swine/hog/pig*, in use since Chaucer's day and doubtless referring to the snoring of which only someone who is dead to the world is capable.

Dead to the world, incidentally, dates back to the late nineteenth century, predating the common simile *to sleep like a log*.

*Last night, he **slept like a top** ('the melatonin kicked in nicely') and, today, he has treated himself to a light lunch designed to clear the palate.*
THE DAILY TELEGRAPH, 19 MAY 2002

sleeve: to have something up one's sleeve
to keep a resource concealed but in reserve

The phrase brings to mind the magician who keeps any number of surprises hidden up his sleeve to amaze his audience. Instead, the expression goes back to the sixteenth century when sleeves were cut wide, so it was quite easy to stow, or even secrete, things away in their folds. One gentleman admitted to having *contrary Edicts from the King in his sleeue* (F de L'Isle, *Legendarie*, 1577). In his *Arte of English Poesie* (1589) George Puttenham put the phrase to good figurative use in a description of the dissembling courtly poet who, *the better to winne his purposes & good aduantages, now and then has a iourney or sicknesse in his sleeue, thereby to shake of other importunities of greater consequence*.

In more recent times, as well as the magician who might want to secrete things up his sleeve, so does a card sharp. Students of the history of poker claim that the expression *to have a card up one's sleeve* goes back to the bad old days of their game.

The current general use simply means to have a resource, or surprise, ready to be brought into action when the situation demands.

*Irene [Worth] is due back here and will give a week of Recitals in London in April. Don't know which of the many she seems **to have up her sleeve**.*
GIELGUD'S LETTERS: JOHN GIELGUD IN HIS OWN WORDS, ED. RICHARD MANGAN, 2004

*The government's spending binge means that the economy is 'extraordinarily vulnerable' to any fall in oil prices or in production, according to Orlando Ochoa, an economist at the Catholic University. Even so, Mr Chávez **has cards up his sleeve**. He appears set on selling Citgo, a big refiner and marketer of gasoline in the*

*United States and a subsidiary of
PDVSA. Second, officials have proposed
that the government should be able to spend
the central bank's 'excess' reserves.*
THE ECONOMIST, 12 MAY 2005

See also *to laugh up one's* SLEEVE.

sleeve: to laugh up one's sleeve

to laugh to oneself, to enjoy a
private joke

Earliest written records of the phrase *to
laugh in one's sleeve* date from the very
early sixteenth century when the
sleeves on fashionable garments were
wide enough to hide a secret smile,
whether of scorn or of mirth. The modern variant *to laugh up one's sleeve* dates
from the twentieth century.

*Minimalism has always been rather
mistrusted in Britain, as though,
puritanically, we suppose that the artist is in
some way short-changing us on handiwork,
or **laughing up his sleeve** because no one
dares to say that the Emperor has no clothes.*
THE TIMES, 1 MAY 2004

See *to have something up one's* SLEEVE.

sleeve: to wear one's heart on one's sleeve

to make one's (amorous) feelings
obvious

The phrase as we know it comes from
the first scene of *Othello* (1604) where
Iago feigns devotion to Othello:

> *I will wear my heart upon my sleeve
> For daws to peck at.*

But Shakespeare was simply reworking
an existing sixteenth-century figure *to
pin someone* or *something on one's sleeve*,
meaning 'to have a firm attachment to
someone or something'.
  Striking as Shakespeare's turn of
phrase is, it did not become idiomatic

until the nineteenth century. The
expression *to pin something on one's
sleeve*, however, remained in constant
use, developing in the seventeenth
century a further strand of meaning:
'to fasten something objectionable on
a person'. Thus, Thomas Middleton in
his play *Women Beware Women* (1626)
has *You were pleased of late to pin an error
on me*. And this sense has survived into
modern English in the curtailed version *to* PIN *something on someone*.

*True social conscience involves not **hearts
on sleeves**, but policies of tough love.*
DAILY MAIL, 7 JANUARY 2002

*[Princess Diana] was a professional
'victim' – of infidelity and eating disorders
– and **wore her heart on her sleeve**.*
THE DAILY TELEGRAPH,
23 FEBRUARY 2004

For other idioms from Shakespeare, see
WILLIAM SHAKESPEARE, page 152.

soft soap

flattery

The likening of smooth flattery to slippery, semi-liquid soft soap is American
in inspiration and dates from the first
half of the nineteenth century when,
according to John Bartlett in his
Dictionary of Americanisms (1848), it
was considered *a vulgar phrase, though
much used*.

*My Life by Bill Clinton: The memoirs of
a colourful president show a woeful lack of
philosophical insight and an excess of
sentimentality and **soft soap**.*
THE INDEPENDENT, 27 JUNE 2004

son of a gun, a

a man, affectionately considered; a
disagreeable scoundrel

This is one of those terms that conveys
affection,   admiration   or   contempt

depending on the speaker, the tone of voice and the context. When it was coined towards the end of the seventeenth century, however, the sense was deprecatory. At that time it was not unknown for some navy wives, usually those of officers, to accompany their husbands on board their warships. These women were generally useful. When battle raged they would often busy themselves with chores or with tending the wounded. Testimony of life aboard a warship also suggests that sometimes the captain, in contravention of all regulations, permitted prostitutes to sail. A reason for this is that press-gangs operated up to 1814 and sailors were confined to their ships at all times. So, to avoid desertions, captains allowed prostitutes aboard when in port. Some did not go back ashore.

Inevitably, then, childbirth occurred on board, though normally only recorded if the child's mother was entitled to ship's rations. *One woman bore a son in the heat of the action; she belonged to Edinburgh*, wrote John Nichols, a seaman aboard the HMS *Goliath* during the Battle of the Nile on 1 August 1798. Apparently a favourite place for a woman to give birth was between the broadside guns, where she might be shielded by a tarpaulin and present no inconvenience to the busy crew. A sailor's boy child thus birthed (and particularly if the father was unknown) was called *a son of a gun* and the event gave rise to the salty doggerel:

> *Begotten in the galley and born under a gun.*
> *Every hair a rope yarn, every tooth a marlin spike,*
> *Every finger a fishhook,*
> *And his blood right good Stockholm tar.*

That, at least, is the favourite etymology, and one faithfully reported by Admiral William Smyth in his *Sailor's Word-Book* (1867). All this does, however, raise some knotty questions. Why, for instance, are there no recorded examples of the phrase in a nautical context? And why is there no equivalent term for girl babies?

The alternative suggestion, that the phrase is a more acceptable form of the abusive *son of a bitch*, is much more sensible, if rather less colourful. *Biche-sone* occurs as an insult in the fourteenth-century text *Of Arthour and of Merlin*. In Shakespeare's *King Lear* (1606) Kent calls Oswald *the Sonne and Heire of a Mungrill Bitch*, and a century later, the form of the expression as we know it today was in full use. The euphemistic variant *son of a gun* dates from the same period, the word *gun* probably chosen because it created a pleasing rhyming phrase.

*Tyson recalls: 'I knocked him right out of the ring. Boom. Bang. But he came back for more. Even at 16 or 17 he was tough. He's a tough **son of a gun**. I knew then he was a special fighter and one day I would meet him in the pros.'*
THE GUARDIAN, 20 JANUARY 2000

*The Day One crew are pretty damn sharp. Byrne is a smooth-talking **son-of-a-gun** in his three-quarter-length coat...*
EVENING STANDARD, 8 MARCH 2000

*She might have been a 19-year-old rookie last year but as her car came to a crumpled halt she screamed to her team on the radio: 'I'll kill that **son of a gun**!' – a reference to the rival she felt had triggered the shunt. Tough driving has followed the tough talk.*
THE OBSERVER, 27 MAY 2001

See also *to show a* LEG.

song: to go for a song

to be sold very cheaply, below the true value

When Edmund Spenser wrote his allegorical romance *The Faerie Queene* (1590) in honour of Elizabeth I, the queen was both flattered and impressed. She ordered her treasurer, William Cecil, to pay the poet the generous sum of £500 for his work. Cecil, less taken with the poetry than his mistress, was heard to exclaim *'What! All this for a song?'*

Sadly, although the story is appealing, Cecil's meaning is the opposite of that of the idiom. The origins of the phrase are probably far more down-to-earth, referring either to the price of old ballads, which in Elizabethan times were available cheaply at fairs, or to the coins given to itinerant entertainers, or both.

With the high street sales in full swing and the grim winter temperatures starting to bite, now is the time to get your anorak at a bargain price... If they're available for half-price (or less) in the sales up West, they must be going for a song on the market stalls of Watford.
THE DAILY TELEGRAPH, 5 JANUARY 2004

sour grapes
comfort sought in despising what one would like for oneself but cannot have

In one of Aesop's fables entitled 'The Fox and the Grapes', the fox finds herself unable to reach the succulent grapes growing high on a vine above her and, in a fit of pique, declares that they are sour. The idiom has been in use since the eighteenth century.

This was what made Grandma furious. She said that Ivy looked like Olive Oyle in the Popeye *cartoons, or like a stick of liquorice. And that she was common. But it was all sour grapes.*
LORNA SAGE, BAD BLOOD, 2000

He never disguised the pain he suffered when Rachel Hunter walked out on him after nine years of marriage. Rod Stewart was said to be heart broken and depressed. But if the ageing rocker was tasting sour grapes over her blossoming romance with Robbie Williams, he was hiding it well yesterday.
DAILY MAIL, 27 MAY 2002

For other idioms derived from fables, see page 318.

sow: to sow one's wild oats
to spend one's youth in dissipation

The vices of youth are varnished over by the saying, that there must be a time for 'sowing of wild oats'.

So wrote William Cobbett in 1829. The excuse was not a new one. For at least three centuries before that, young men had made light of their youthful dissipation and sexual indiscretions with the same phrase. The allusion is to the young and impulsive lad who wastes his time broadcasting wild seed, a fitting metaphor for sexual promiscuity. Like the weeds they are, *wild oats* take hold rapidly but are extremely difficult to get rid of, rather like the consequences of such youthful folly.

He was not just seeking to sow a few wild oats; he was turning his back on everything his father, his community, and his very upbringing, had taught him.
ROB PARSONS, BRINGING HOME THE PRODIGALS, 2003

He then worked alone for a time, and, having apparently sown more than his fair share of wild oats, married a wealthy young woman from Mechelen and found an unusual state of rest and quiet.
SUNDAY TELEGRAPH, 11 APRIL 2004

spade: to call a spade a spade

to use the real name, not a euphemism; to be blunt or offensive

Even the great Renaissance scholar Erasmus could make mistakes, and his error with this idiom means that we now call spades spades, and not tubs tubs. The ancient Greeks had a popular proverb for plain speaking, *to call figs figs, and a tub a tub*. In his *Sayings of Kings and Commanders* (*Moralia III*), Plutarch (AD c. 50–125) quoted Philip of Macedon as saying *The Macedonians are by nature a rough and rustic people who call a tub a tub*. When the Dutch scholar Erasmus drew upon this in 1500 for his *Adagia*, a collection of Greek and Latin proverbs traced back to their origin, he confused the similar sounding Greek words for *spade* and for *tub*. Erasmus' version stuck and *to call a spade a spade* has been in popular use ever since.

Although the expression can be forceful enough, it was strengthened still further from the beginning of the twentieth century with uses like this one: *The man in the chair is the ebullient Kelvin McKenzie, the former editor of* The Sun *who delights in upsetting the thinking classes. He likes to call a spade a bloody shovel and worse…*(*Birmingham Evening Mail,* 7 June 2003)

We both come from Hull, you know, where they **call a spade a shovel** *and where they possess the most beautiful bridge in the world, spanning the Humber.*
GOOD HOUSEKEEPING, JUNE 2002

Money managers, and anyone else with a vested interest in maintaining confidence in equities, want to play down any sense of alarm. So instead of **calling a spade a spade,** *and a crashing stock market a crashing stock market, they talk of 'volatility'.*
THE TIMES, 29 MAY 2004

Any claim to pretensions fails to impress in the North. They still believe in **calling a spade a shovel** *and keeping your feet on terra firma, whether your grandad's a rock star or your mum's on the screen at the local cinema.*
EXPRESS ON SUNDAY, 27 JUNE 2004

For other idioms drawn from Greek and Roman writers, see page 318.

spanner: to throw a spanner in the works

to upset the smooth running of something, to disrupt a plan or activity

The phrase *to throw a monkey wrench into the machinery* was coined around 1900 and is probably of American origin. *A monkey wrench* is a type of spanner with a movable jaw which fanciful people in the early nineteenth century likened to that of a monkey. It was a common strategy of low-paid workers, enduring bad conditions, to sabotage industrial machinery. Indeed, the word *sabotage* itself arose during the Industrial Revolution of nineteenth-century France when frustrated workers threw their *sabots* (clogs) into the works.

The phrase became current on both sides of the Atlantic. On 16 October 1931, the popular British national newspaper the *Daily Express* reported that Mr Lloyd George, the leader of the Liberal party, had *hurled a monkey wrench last night into the creaking and decrepit machinery of Liberalism*.

Although British English introduced the word *spanner* into the phrase in the 1930s, making the spoken idiom easier on the tongue, American English stayed with the *monkey wrench*. In 1974 Edward Abbey wrote *The Monkey Wrench Gang*, the story of a group of eco-terrorists waging war against technology through sabotage. This has given rise to the American English term *monkeywrenching* to describe the destructive tactics of eco-warriors.

Children are questioned continually about the way they are thinking about the problems they are given to work out. And halfway through each session, they are presented with a 'spanner in the works' designed to turn their thinking on its head.
THE TIMES EDUCATIONAL SUPPLEMENT, 15 FEBRUARY 2002

Most Nevadans loathe the plan for a nuclear dump at [Yucca] mountain, which has been shoved down their throats by the federal government. The process of preparing the site has been going on for nearly 20 years. Over $5 billion has already been spent on it. And the Bush administration seemed determined to put the dump into operation in 2010. But a surprising court ruling has suddenly thrown a spanner in the works.
THE ECONOMIST, 14 JULY 2004

spick and span
clean and neat, in perfect order

The phrase has its origins in an Old Norse word, *spannyr*, which meant 'fresh chip of wood', being a compound of *span*, 'a chip of wood', and *nyr*, 'new'. Middle English had the phrase *span-new* to describe brand new items or clothes, and this remained current into the second half of the nineteenth century. *Spick*, meaning 'spike' or 'nail', was added to form the extended alliterative expression *spick and span new* in the late sixteenth century. The phrase appears to have been influenced by the synonymous Dutch word *spiksplinterernieuw*, which described a wooden ship that had just been built, new in every plank and nail. Again, this new emphatic form persisted until the late nineteenth century.
    The seventeenth century, however, saw the emergence of the now familiar shortened form *spick and span*. Its primary sense was 'brand new'. Samuel

Pepys records it in his diary for 15 November 1665: *My Lady Batten walking through the dirty lane with new spicke and span white shoes.* Apart from one isolated earlier example, the contemporary sense of 'neat and trim' only predominates towards the middle of the nineteenth century.

The internal restoration [of St Paul's Cathedral, London] will be done by Christmas. By then the West Front will also be revealed in its new glory. As for the rest, that will be spick and span for the 300th anniversary of the 1708 topping-out ceremony, God, and a heavenly host of generous bankers, willing
THE TIMES, 10 JUNE 2004

Wisteria Lane, home of the now-infamous Desperate Housewives, *seems the suburban-American ideal: spacious, spick-and-span timber houses, neat white picket fences, emerald-green lawns and colourful blooms jostling in the flowerbeds. Life, it would seem, is perfect.*
THE MAIL ON SUNDAY, 22 MAY 2005

See COUPLINGS, page 294.

spoke: to put a spoke in someone's wheel
purposely to hinder someone's plans or success

Since the spokes are an essential part of any wheel, it is unclear why the insertion of a spoke should hinder progress. Unless, of course, the *spoke* is a stave of some sort that is thrust through the wheel of a cart to prevent it turning. The Dutch have the identical expression *een spaak in 't wiel steeken*. This may have been borrowed into English in the sixteenth century and the word *spaak*, meaning 'bar' or 'stave', mistranslated as 'spoke'.

Some financial planning experts say that it could take investors 10 to 15 years to

*benefit from China's potential and that doubts over the country's political stability could yet **put a spoke in the wheel**.*
THE MAIL ON SUNDAY, 19 AUGUST 2001

*It's not all plain sailing in a construction director's working week. Things are going great for the Sunderland builder...out of the blue, there was an unexpected **spoke in the wheel**. A job which both parties were looking forward to came unstuck.*
NEWCASTLE JOURNAL,
19 SEPTEMBER 2003

sponge: to throw in the sponge

to give in, to admit defeat

The phrase was originally *to throw up the sponge*. It goes back to the days of prize-fighting in the mid-nineteenth century. When a fighter had taken enough punishment and was ready to admit defeat, his corner would toss into the ring the sponge used to refresh him between rounds. Today *to throw in the* TOWEL, a later gesture of defeat, is perhaps more commonly heard. Its figurative use dates back to the early twentieth century.

*Available to every university student is a tutor or adviser to help him or her choose and change courses, and in more than just the academic sense. Please, make an appointment with your tutor to discuss alternatives before you **throw in the sponge**.*
THE TIMES, 27 MARCH 2004

*If you stop to think about it, when most people get tired, what happens? They just **throw in the sponge**. They would like to do this, or do that, or perform at a high level, but they are too tired to do it.*
CARRIL AND WHITE, THE SMART TAKE FROM THE STRONG, 2004

For other boxing idioms, see
PACKING A PUNCH, page 45.

spot: to hit the spot

to be just what was needed (usually referring to food or drink)

Since this American phrase was coined to express satisfaction with food or drink, one must assume that the *spot* is that specific place in the brain where yearning for a particular taste begins. First references in the second half of the nineteenth century have *go to* or *touch the spot*. Hit the spot dates from the early twentieth century and, with the advent of radio, was used in the very first advertising jingle to be broadcast in the 1930s:

> *Pepsi-Cola hits the spot,*
> *Twelve full ounces, that's a lot,*
> *Twice as much for a nickel, too,*
> *Pepsi-Cola is the drink for you.*

The tune was so catchy that listeners throughout America phoned radio stations requesting them to play it, and sales of Pepsi surged ahead of those of its close competitor, Coca-Cola.

*After these hefty Filipino meals...a garishly colorful Filipino sundae...**hits the spot**. It's juicy, cold and refreshing.*
SAN FRANCISCO EXAMINER,
12 NOVEMBER 2003

*The chicken is coated in a deliciously sweet satay sauce – only for the sweetest of tooths. Both dishes looked not just tempting but substantial, and **hit the spot** perfectly.*
EDINBURGH EVENING NEWS,
21 FEBRUARY 2004

spots: to knock (the) spots off

to defeat with ease, to be much better than

That the idiom is American, dating from the middle of the nineteenth century, is certain. Less certain is its origin. It probably refers to shooting contests where the target would be a playing card, the idea being to hit as many of the *spots* (the symbols for spades, clubs, diamonds or hearts) on the card as possible.

*Good glass extensions can **knock the spots off** timber or wrought-iron conservatories if you want to give your home a contemporary edge.*
EVENING STANDARD, 23 JUNE 2004

*Wholly unexpectedly, the spa at Elveden Forest **knocks spots off** other, supposedly more luxurious spas.*
THE TIMES, 3 JULY 2004

For a similar expression, see *to knock/beat into a* COCKED *hat.*

spout: up the spout
in trouble, ruined, out of action

The *spout* was a type of lift found in a pawnbroker's shop. Articles to be pawned were put into it and hauled up to the rooms above where they were stored. Belongings that had gone *up the spout* were out of service, totally useless to the owner until they were redeemed. Figurative use dates from the 1820s. During the first half of the twentieth century the phrase became a euphemism for 'pregnant', an allusion to intercourse and its consequences.

*The Queen Mother's funeral was a masterpiece of timing and ceremony, and proved that even if our transport and health service are **up the spout**, we can still get it right when the occasion demands.*
THE PEOPLE, 14 APRIL 2002

*'I don't want to be sensible, I don't want to grow up. I want to stay in Never-Never Land. I want to find my Wendy and get her **up the spout**.' Blue rebel Lee Ryan wants to be the next Peter Pan.*
DAILY EXPRESS, 10 OCTOBER 2003

*After a virus in 2001 which caused vestibular damage, I became severely deaf with my sense of balance, gravity and acceleration totally **up the spout**.*
THE TIMES, 21 JUNE 2004

square: back to square one
to be back where one started with a project or plan

A favourite story to explain this idiom goes back to the days before televised sport when soccer enthusiasts would huddle around the wireless listening to live commentary. In the 1920s the *Radio Times* printed a plan of the pitch which was divided into squares, each with a number. These were referred to in the course of the commentary to show where the action was taking place. Playing the ball back to square one meant losing maximum territorial advantage and, by extension, it meant 'back to the beginning'. The difficulty with this theory is that the football grid was abandoned around 1940 and no record of the phrase predating 1960 has so far been found.

There is, however, a simple and plausible alternative origin, that of a board-game such as Snakes and Ladders where players are sent back to the start if they land on a certain square. Etymologist Eric Partridge supports the first suggestion but says the commentators' cries of *back to square one* were influenced by the snakes and ladders theory.

*Others said that if our bid was turned down, we would be **back to square one** and not have lost anything in the process.*
THE SUNDAY TIMES, 30 MAY 2004

*Along the way she [Amma Asante] suffered the usual rejections and broken promises, but then got a commission from Channel 4 for seven scripts... The drama ran for two series, but then there were a couple of changes of controller, and it was not recommissioned: Asante went **back to square one** and spent much of her time writing and learning her craft.*
THE GUARDIAN, 8 NOVEMBER 2004

stalking horse, a

a person or pretext designed as a cover for an ulterior action or motive or person, a mask for the true purpose

The problem of any huntsman is how to get close enough to the game to shoot at it. In the Middle Ages horses were trained to provide cover for fowlers, who hid behind them whilst stealthily creeping up on their quarry. Later, real horses were replaced by movable screens made in the shape of a horse. Figurative allusion to the *stalking horse* began in the late sixteenth century. In Shakespeare's *As You Like It* (1599), the Duke comments that the court jester, Touchstone, *uses his folly like a stalking-horse, and under the presentation of that he shoots his wit.*

In America, since the mid-nineteenth century, the expression has been used in the political arena, as here: *Some pundits have speculated that Wesley Clark's entry into the presidential race makes him a stalking horse for Hillary Clinton* (*National Public Radio*, 26 September 2003).

In Britain, the most famous political *stalking horse* of recent decades was Sir Anthony Meyer who, in 1989, challenged Margaret Thatcher for the Conservative Party leadership. Although she won by 314 votes to 33, 60 of her MPs refused to back her. This evidence of weakening support eventually provoked her downfall. Obituaries on Sir Anthony's death in January 2005 all referred to his sobriquet, *the stalking horse.*

British politicians continue unabated in their enthusiasm for such tactics. This time it is Tony Blair potentially under attack: *Those who want to see a challenge to Mr Blair cite the famous 'stalking horse' precedent created in 1989 [of Sir Anthony Meyer]... One MP was adamant last night that a volunteer stalking horse had come forward – but would not name him. 'It is someone with no ambition and no enemies within the party,' it was claimed* (*The Guardian*, 23 March 2002).

The idiom is also found widely in business contexts: *Just last week, One Equity Partners announced it was acting as a stalking horse in a bidding process designed to rescue Polaroid from bankruptcy* (*Financial Times*, 23 April 2002).

*Later, when we actually talked to some of the boy gang from the grammar school...they told us that they'd known straight away...that Gail was using me – dreamier, curvier, blonder – as her **stalking horse**, to hunt down boys she wanted.*
LORNA SAGE, BAD BLOOD, 2000

For other horsey idioms, see page 319.

steal: to steal a march (on)

to gain a furtive advantage

In Tudor times a *march* was the distance an army on the move could be expected to cover in a single day. *To gain a march* upon the enemy was to be one day's march ahead of him. *To steal a march* meant to travel when the enemy would not expect it: by night, for instance, or by leaving early. The phrase began to be used figuratively in the eighteenth century.

*Judy Macdonald, the careers tutor, felt that, on past experience, fewer good places were coming into clearing and therefore it was very much the early bird that would catch the best slots. The school installed extra computers and planned to collect results from its Royal Mail sorting office at 7.30am, to allow its pupils **to steal a march** on the rest of the country.*
THE OBSERVER, 22 AUGUST 2004

George Osborne, the Shadow Chancellor, has hinted that the Tories could adopt the 'flat tax' being embraced in Eastern Europe to outflank Labour at the next election... Introducing a flat rate of tax

*would **steal a march** on the other parties in Britain.*
THE INDEPENDENT, 21 JUNE 2005

For other idioms derived from the army and warfare, see page 317.

sterner: made of sterner stuff
having a firm resolve; inflexible, unyielding

This idiom comes from Shakespeare's *Julius Caesar* (1599). Ambitious Caesar returns to Rome after a successful military campaign amidst fears that he will allow himself to be crowned king. To prevent this, friends of the republic conspire to murder him in the Senate House. At Caesar's funeral, his friend Mark Antony rouses the anger of the people against the conspirators in a carefully crafted speech:

> *Did this in Caesar seem ambitious?*
> *When that the poor have cried, Caesar*
> *hath wept;*
> *Ambition should be made of sterner stuff.*

*Richards, Wood and Watts seem to be **made of sterner stuff** and have shown few signs of sickness or exhaustion during the gruelling tour.*
SUNDAY EXPRESS, 7 SEPTEMBER 2003

*Would your mother be prepared to abseil down the side of a 300ft tower block?…It obviously depends on the mother: mine was flattened by a day at Legoland, but these families are **made of sterner stuff**.*
THE TIMES, 10 JULY 2004

For other idioms from Shakespeare, see WILLIAM SHAKESPEARE, page 152.

stiff: to keep a stiff upper lip
to remain calm and self-reliant in the face of problems or danger; to be in control of one's emotions

*A **stiff upper lip** refers to the ability to keep one's features, especially one's mouth, under control so that they do not betray the turmoil of emotion within. It is said to be a particularly British characteristic, as all the contemporary examples quoted below affirm. Strange, then, that the earliest references are found in American works such as John Neal's *The Down-Easters* (1833), William Thompson's *Chronicles of Pineville* (1845), Harriet Beecher Stowe's *Uncle Tom's Cabin* (1852) and Canadian author Thomas Chandler Haliburton's *The Clockmaker* (1837–8).

*Keeping a **stiff upper lip** and martyrishly not wanting to make a fuss about yourself is an extremely British and peculiar way of dealing with things.*
THE DAILY TELEGRAPH, 20 APRIL 2000

*It makes you want to weep. That's the trouble with the English, they might want to weep but yesterday, as they moped away, there were only metaphorical tears cascading past those **stiff upper lips**.*
THE GUARDIAN, 23 JULY 2001

*Britons are dropping the **stiff upper lip** and loosening their grip on their emotions. But many do not feel as happy as they believe they ought to be.*
THE TIMES HIGHER EDUCATION SUPPLEMENT, 19 DECEMBER 2003

*From Tom Brown to Billy Bunter, schoolboys are trained to **keep a stiff upper lip**… That may be the spirit that built the British Empire… New Men are supposed to engage with their emotions.*
THE TIMES, 2 JULY 2004

stone: to leave no stone unturned
to make every effort possible to accomplish an aim

After the defeat of the Persians by the Greeks at Plataea (479 BC), Polycrates set about looking for treasure rumoured to have been left in the tent of the Persian general, Mardonius. Unable to find it, he resorted to the oracle at Delphi, which instructed him *to move every stone*. Polycrates resumed his search and found the treasure.

Move every stone rapidly became proverbial to the ancient Greeks, Aristophanes calling it *the old proverb* (*The Thesmophoriazusae*, 410 BC). In the sixteenth century, the Renaissance scholar Erasmus rendered the phrase as *leave no stone unturned* in his *Adagia* (1500), a collection of Latin and Greek proverbs that was frequently referred to by English writers. The phrase was then used so often in English that, by 1559, Thomas Becon described it as *a common proverb* (*New Catechism*).

The original meaning of the expression, 'an exhaustive search', is still current, but it may be used more widely to embrace 'sparing no expense or effort to achieve a goal'.

*But it was Sam who had made sure they were able **to leave no stone unturned** when it came to coping with Jeremy's disability.*
ANN WIDDECOMBE,
THE CLEMATIS TREE, 2000

*Sir John has already vowed **to leave 'no stone unturned'** in his inquiries and will have talks with both MI5 and MI6 chiefs.*
DAILY EXPRESS, 26 JUNE 2004

For other idioms drawn from ancient life and history, see page 317.

---

storm in a teacup, a
a petty disagreement, much fuss made about something of little importance

Excitabat fluctus in simpulo is a neat little metaphor used by Cicero (*De Legibus*, begun 52 BC). Translated it reads 'He whipped up waves in a wine ladle.' The phrase was cited by Erasmus in his *Adagia* (1500). From the seventeenth century onwards,

several distinguished people have played with the expression: The Duke of Ormond, in a letter to the Earl of Arlington (1678), wrote of *a storm in a cream bowl*; Grand Duke Paul of Russia described an insurrection in Geneva as *a tempest in a glass of water* (c. 1790); and, in an edition of *The Gentleman's Magazine* dated 1830, Lord Thurlow spoke of *a storm in a wash-hand basin*. *Storms in teacups* do not appear to have brewed until the first half of the nineteenth century.

*I have to confess that when the council first proposed giant wheelie bins for the New Town, I thought the protests would amount to **little more than a storm in a fine bone china tea cup**. Little did I realise that the row would not only reach the royal ears of Prince Charles, but escalate into a full-blown international incident.*
EDINBURGH EVENING NEWS,
1 MAY 2004

EUROPEAN UNION'S WOES
A STORM IN A TEACUP?
*'I don't see any major strategic changes in direction' if the Constitution dies, says Mark Leonard, director of political studies at the Centre for European Reform, a think tank in London. 'I think this is **a storm in a teacup**. People won't remember it in 10 years' time.'*
CHRISTIAN SCIENCE MONITOR,
3 JUNE 2005

For other idioms drawn from Greek and Roman writers, see page 318

---

strain: to strain at a gnat and swallow a camel
to be preoccupied with the trivial rather than the important, with details rather than major matters

This biblical expression meaning 'to fuss over insignificant matters while accepting glaring faults' can be found in Matthew 23:24. Jesus criticises the scribes and Pharisees for their bad example to the people in meticulously observing less important areas of law whilst failing to observe the weighty issues of justice, mercy and faithfulness. The law, says Jesus, should be kept in its entirety: *These ought ye to have done, and not to leave the other undone. Ye blind guides, who strain at a gnat, and swallow a camel* (Authorised Version, 1611).

The expression is commonly thought to describe someone who has difficulty in swallowing a gnat but none at all in swallowing a camel. In fact the original Greek text does not read *strain at*, as the Authorised Version has it, but *strain out* and refers to the practice of straining wine before it was drunk to remove the tiny insects which bred in it while it was fermenting.

This leads to an intriguing question. The earliest translations into English, those of Wyclif and Tyndale, have the correct rendering of the original. As the box on WILLIAM TYNDALE (page 270) points out, eighty per cent of the Authorised Version comes from Tyndale's work. So why did it introduce a 'wrong' translation?

There seem to be two explanations. One is very simple; *at* is a misprint for *out*, and there is plenty of evidence for misprints in that era, even in texts of very high standing such as the Bible. The second explanation is the one preferred by the OED. There are late sixteenth-century texts which show that *strain at* for *strain out* was already part of idiomatic English immediately before the Authorised Version was translated. Those responsible for it were, therefore, deliberately using a turn of phrase current at the time, even though it is not a faithful translation. The translators of the New International Version of the Bible (1973) have made no such concessions to current usage and correctly translate the words *strain out* but, of course, *strain at* is such a part of our

idiomatic language that the expression's misleading wording will remain.

*The National Union of Students went along with the abolition of the maintenance grant and its replacement by loans. After that, objecting to tuition fees, which are not paid by the really hard up, is **to strain at the gnat after swallowing the camel**.*
THE INDEPENDENT, 13 JANUARY 2000

*Parliament having **swallowed the camel** of including unmarried partners within the protection given to married couples, it was not for the court **to strain at the gnat** of including such partners who were of the same sex as each other.*
THE TIMES, 14 NOVEMBER 2002

For other idioms from the Bible, see page 317.

straw: a straw poll
a superficial, informal test of opinion

It is difficult to imagine a time when public opinion polls were not an ingredient in elections. *Straw polls* originated in the United States. In 1824 reporters from the *Harrisburg Pennsylvanian* decided to question the people of Wilmington, Delaware, to try to establish their preferred presidential candidate. The idea caught on. The terminology for these soundings was *straw vote* from around the middle of the nineteenth century, with *straw ballot* and the eventual winning form *straw poll* appearing in the early 1930s.

The term alludes to the custom of throwing a straw up into the air to determine the direction and strength of the wind. Figurative reference to this rural practice is much older than the *straw poll*, however. In his collection of Spanish maxims, the seventeenth-century Jesuit philosopher and writer Baltasar Gracián makes reference to it: *Echar al aire algunas cosas, para examinar*

Proverbs and idioms

Proverbs exist in all languages and written collections of them date back to the earliest times. A good example is the Book of Proverbs in Jewish sacred writings, which is of course also found in the Old Testament of the Christian Bible.

Proverbs are universally held in high esteem, whereas idioms have had to struggle for recognition. Perhaps this is a little surprising, as there is some overlap between idioms and proverbs. Proverbs can be defined as 'memorable short sayings of the people, containing wise words of advice or warning'. Many idioms share at least some of these characteristics. For example, are *a stitch in time saves nine* or *more haste, less speed* better considered as proverbs or idioms? Or *better late than never*; *the more, the merrier*; *out of sight, out of mind*; *seeing is believing*? Idioms or proverbs? Proverbs, probably, but two idiom experts feel they can class them as idioms without, as they put it, 'stretching the definition too far'.

To add to the confusion, idioms can become proverbs and proverbs can become idioms. Take, for example, the idiomatic phrase – idioms are normally phrases, whereas proverbs are whole sentences – *to cry for the moon* (see MOONSHINE, page 204), meaning 'to ask for the impossible'. This could easily become a full sentence (proverb?) with a kernel of wisdom: *Don't cry for the moon* or, better, *Only fools cry for the moon*. Similarly, habitual shortening of established proverbs creates a phrase (idiom?) that eventually stands alone, its proverbial origin often forgotten. An example of this is *new broom*, used since the late eighteenth century to refer to a new appointee who makes noticeable changes to the previous routine. *New broom* is a phrase (idiom?) gleaned from the existing proverb *New brooms sweep clean*. Yet another instance is *the last/final* STRAW.

For a more detailed account of the nature of an idiom, see WHAT IS AN IDIOM?, page 4. For full information on proverbs, see our Dictionary of Proverbs, from the same publisher.

---

la aceptación, 'Throw matters into the air to find out how things will be received' (*Oráculo manual y arte de prudencia*, 1647). John Selden repeats the wisdom in *Table Talk: Libels* (c. 1654): *Take a straw and throw it up into the Air, you shall see by that which way the wind is.*

If you took a **straw poll** of 20 women, the chances are that one, maybe two would be brave enough to admit to having problems.
GOOD HOUSEKEEPING,
SEPTEMBER 2002

A **straw poll** of agents suggests that about 5% of clients refuse to budge on price, even when it becomes clear that their home has been overvalued.
THE SUNDAY TIMES, 14 DECEMBER 2003

straw: the last/final straw
an insignificant event which brings about a final crisis or collapse

The last straw is an abbreviation, since the second half of the nineteenth century, of the still current proverb *It's the last straw that breaks the (laden) camel's back*. This was first recorded by Dickens in *Dombey and Son* (1848), but is not the original proverb. In the seventeenth and eighteenth centuries people spoke of *the last feather that breaks the horse's back*. A number of languages, among them French, Spanish and Arabic, have proverbs which express the same idea in a similar way: that eventually a minute, and seemingly insignificant, increase in weight, effort or volume will bring about disaster. It seems a highly relevant expression for today's high-pressure, high-stress lifestyles.

*Jim Bradley, 45, said he had a furious row with his wife Sharon after telling her she had to leave at short notice for Sweden. Having already been forced to move house twice in two years because of his job, this was **the last straw** and she stormed out of their home.*
DAILY MAIL, 22 MARCH 2002

*For Diane Hoare, a strong and proud woman, being plagued by nuisance calls from Diana was **the final straw**. In October 1993 she decided to contact the police.*
KEN WHARFE & ROBERT JOBSON,
DIANA: A CLOSELY GUARDED
SECRET, 2002.

***The final straw** was my inability to deal with the wall-climbing machine – a sadistic device shaped like an upended tank track.*
GOOD HOUSEKEEPING, MARCH 2004

See also PROVERBS AND IDIOMS, opposite.

swan song, a
a farewell appearance, performance, statement or work

The ancients believed that swans were mute but that, upon death, they sang a song of pure joy because they were about to go to Apollo, the god of poetry and song, whose servants they were. Chaucer mentions the legend several times in his works and Shakespeare, too, makes references to it. In the early seventeenth century, English composer Orlando Gibbons took the fable as inspiration for one of his madrigals:

*The silver swan who, living, had no note,
when death approach'd, unlock'd her silent throat;
Leaning her breast against the reedy shore,
thus sung her first and last, and sung no more.
Farewell, all joys;*

*O Death, come close mine eyes;
More geese than swans now live,
more fools than wise.*

Indeed, the legend has inspired writers and poets from the Middle Ages to the nineteenth century, when the term *swan song* was coined to describe an artist's final great work or a farewell performance of any kind.

*While the rest of the Beach Boys toured their greatest hits, Brian Wilson stayed at home in his studio and created pop's enduring masterpiece – and his **swansong**.*
THE OBSERVER, 2 MAY 2004

For other myths derived from fabled animal behaviour, see page 318.

sword of Damocles, the
impending doom, an imminent threat

Damocles' story is an ancient one recorded in the works of Horace and Persius, amongst others. The story tells of Dionysius, ruler of Syracuse around 400 BC, who, night and day, was compelled to listen to the sycophantic murmurings of Damocles lauding his happiness, power and riches. The exasperated Dionysius finally invited Damocles to taste this good fortune for himself, urging him to take the king's own seat at the banqueting table. Damocles accepted eagerly and was enjoying the feast when, glancing upwards, he was horrified to see a large sword suspended above his head by a single hair. This, explained Dionysius, was a symbol of the insecurity which everyone holding power and position is forced to live with. *The sword of Damocles* has been used as a simile of impending doom since the mid-eighteenth century.

His choice of reed provoked the wrath of English Heritage, whose rules can be enforced by the courts. The organisation threatened to sue unless he tore down his

new roof and replaced it with local
materials.

'My new roof looked exactly the same as
it did before and was more cost efficient,'
said Mr Ridge. 'But for three years, I had
English Heritage and the local council
hovering over my shoulder. It was like a
£20,000 sword of Damocles over my
family's heads.'
THE DAILY TELEGRAPH,
7 SEPTEMBER 2003

Ever since Iain Duncan Smith was elected
Conservative leader, **the sword of
Damocles** has hung over his head.
THE GUARDIAN, 4 OCTOBER 2003

See also *to hang by a* THREAD and, for
other idioms derived from ancient
legends, see page 317.

· T ·

tale: thereby hangs a tale

there is a story to tell about this

Thereby lyeth a tale is recorded in the early sixteenth century but the witty pun in *thereby hangs a tale* was possibly coined by Shakespeare. If so, he was very pleased with it, for he used it in a number of his plays – *The Taming of the Shrew* (c. 1592), *The Merry Wives of Windsor* (1597), *As You Like It* (1599) and *Othello* (1604) – thus ensuring its idiomatic status.

*The only interesting thing about him, biographically, is that he was born in von Ribbentrop's bedroom. And **thereby hangs a tale** he's happy to relate.*
THE GUARDIAN, 25 AUGUST 2001

Most of this summer there has been room enough and to spare for him to share the trug with the only other object in it – a packet of seeds.
    ***Thereby hangs a tale.** A tale of – what should I say? – of recalcitrance and rescue? Of abandonment and retrieval?*
    Although this seed packet has been the only one in the trug, the awful fact is that a whole bagful of similarly unopened seed packets has resided in a cupboard. Not a single seed has been sown.
CHRISTIAN SCIENCE MONITOR, 19 SEPTEMBER 2003

For other idioms from Shakespeare, see WILLIAM SHAKESPEARE, page 152.

talk: to talk the hind leg off a donkey

to talk incessantly

This bit of nonsense, used to emphasise extreme loquaciousness, is first recorded as *to talk a horse's hind leg off*. In an issue of his *Political Register* for 1808, William Cobbett referred to the phrase as a *vulgar old hyperbole*, one in common use amongst uneducated people, so it may in fact date from the eighteenth century. During the nineteenth century dogs also lost their back legs to the garrulous, John Benwell declaring that *to talk a dog's hind leg off* was *a Yankee phrase* (*An Englishman's Travels in America*, 1853), while Anthony Trollope considered it to be Australian (*John Caldigate*, 1879). The *donkey* earned a place in the expression in the second half of the nineteenth century, and is the only member of the animal trio to survive.

*Henri didn't dare explain that Valentina could **talk the hind leg off a donkey**, and that she was an intrusive and, in every sense, extreme personality.*
PATRICK RAMBAUD, THE BATTLE, 2001

*Iphigenia can **talk the hind leg off a donkey**, and poor old Thoas...doesn't stand a chance against her ardent torrent of persuasion.*
THE INDEPENDENT, 7 DECEMBER 2003

tarred: to be tarred with the same brush

to be marked with the same faults or unpleasant characteristics

The verb *to tar* was used figuratively from the early seventeenth century with the sense 'to make dirty, to besmear (as if daubed with tar)'. The Elizabethan writer and courtier Sir John Harington uses it thus in one of his *Epigrams* (c. 1612): *To purge the vapours that our cleare sight tarres*. The phrase *to tar with the same stick* occurs in Sir Walter Scott's *Rob Roy* (1818), and *You are all tarred with the same brush*, said the sensible people of Maidstone appears in William Cobbett's *Rural Rides* (1823), the sense being 'You are all exactly the same, just as bad as each other'.

The book's greatest limitation, though, is its failure to grapple intelligently with the issue of transcendence. This is not at all the same as religion, though here **tarred with the same brush**.
THE ECONOMIST, 17 MAY 2003

Cycling's efforts to rid itself of the image of being a drug-ridden sport took another knock yesterday... Jesus Manzano claimed that before riding the seventh stage to Morzine in the Alps he was injected with 50 millilitres of an unknown substance by Kelme team doctors. Vicente Belda, Kelme's sporting director, said: 'He is not telling the truth and he cannot **tar the entire peloton with the same brush.'**
THE DAILY TELEGRAPH, 25 MARCH 2004

There have been mutterings that the vast majority of Muslims, who are decent and law-abiding people, are being **tarred with the same brush** *as the extremists.*
DAILY EXPRESS, 3 APRIL 2004

tenterhooks, on

under strain, in a state of agitation or suspense

Much of England's wealth in past centuries was gained from the woollen industry. Wool was spun and woven into cloth and was then exported to Holland, where it was finished before being marketed. Cloth which had just been woven, washed and beaten, to cleanse and thicken it, was taken to the tenterground. This was a field containing rows of wooden frames known as *tenters* (from the Latin *tendere*, 'to stretch'). The cloth would be stretched out taut on a tenter and secured there by the selvedges on *tenterhooks* to dry. This process gave rise to a number of figurative phrases from the first half of the sixteenth century onwards. The expression *on tenterhooks* to describe someone who feels tense while awaiting the outcome of a situation, dates from around the middle of the eighteenth century and supersedes the seventeenth-century idiom *to be on (the) tenters*.

Let's hope that Luciano Pavarotti goes on for ever; or at least a few seasons more. Of course, he's holding us **on tenterhooks**. *When his name didn't appear on next season's schedules at the New York Met for the first time in years, doubts were raised...*
THE INDEPENDENT, 13 MARCH 2002

The night before Christmas won't be the same this year. Instead of hanging up the stockings and retiring early, we'll be up all night, waiting **on tenterhooks** *for a small squeak from a distant world. It will tell us that our British space probe, Beagle 2, has landed safely on Mars to begin its search for life.*
THE INDEPENDENT, 26 NOVEMBER 2003

tether: at the end of one's tether/rope

at the point of frustration; at the end of one's inner resources or powers of endurance

A tether is a rope which restricts the freedom of a grazing animal to wander, one end being fastened around the animal's neck, the other to a stake. The expression alludes to the frustration of the animal that would browse further afield but has come to the end of its freedom to do so. The phrases *at the end of one's tether* and *at the end of one's rope* date from the seventeenth century.

*Have you ever been a victim of crime? I once had £1.20 stolen at work. I knew who it was so I had him brought to my office and we had a long talk. I've also had my car broken into three times and I'm **at the end of my tether** about it. I've considered doing something drastic to stop it.*
MINETTE WALTERS IN GOOD
HOUSEKEEPING, MAY 2001

*Two hours into the shift I already feel I am **near the end of my rope**. Fay and I aren't coming close to making the inmates do what they are supposed to do, and I am uncertain about whether I should use my power to compel them.*
THE GUARDIAN, 30 JULY 2001

*'I've never felt suicidal but I know that **end-of-tether** feeling that can be an early signal that all is not right.'*
EVENING STANDARD,
26 NOVEMBER 2001

thick: through thick and thin
no matter what the difficulties, through good times and bad

This phrase came into use in the fourteenth century to describe the different types of ground that a traveller or a horse and his rider might need to traverse, from dense thicket to thinner woodland:

> *Through thicke and thinne,*
> *Both ouer Hill and Plaine*
(Guillaume du Bartas, *Devine Weekes and Workes*, trans. Joshua Sylvester 1608)

By the sixteenth century the expression was also being figuratively applied to the determination to stick with a course of action and, later, with a friendship or allegiance, no matter what difficulties might be encountered: *Kyng Richard... purposed to goo thorow thicke and thinne in this mater* (Richard Grafton in *The Chronicle of John Harding...with a Continuation in Prose to this Our Own Time*, 1543).

*Mentor...thinks Archie. For him, it's always been Samad... **Through thick and thin**. Even if the world were ending. Never made a decision without him.*
ZADIE SMITH, WHITE TEETH, 2000

*The curious character of the president has made assessment harder. On the one hand, Mr Bush claims to be an uncompromising and direct leader. He has stuck with his policies **through thick and thin**: what you see is what you get.*
THE ECONOMIST, 7 OCTOBER 2004

thin: the thin end of the wedge
a first step along a path of increasingly damaging consequences

A *wedge* is a V-shaped chunk of metal or wood which is hammered into a fault or crack in a stone or log to prise it apart. Insertion of the thin, tapering end of the wedge has shattering consequences. The figure has been current since around the middle of the nineteenth century.

*But some fear that the changes now being introduced are **the thin end of the wedge**, and that once the principle of change has been accepted, the old system based on need might eventually be replaced by one based on the ability to pay.*
THE ECONOMIST, 12 JUNE 2003

Scientists have created the ultimate pet: genetically modified fish that glow in the dark. In future, there will be no need for aquarium lights – fluorescent fish will provide their own illumination... But the prospect of GM pets has outraged pet

dealers... *'This is **the thin end of the wedge**,' said Keith Davenport, chief executive of the Ornamental Aquatic Trade Association. 'You could put all sorts of different genes in animals and do all sorts of damage.'*
THE OBSERVER, 15 JUNE 2003

thinking: to put on one's thinking cap

to take time to consider, to mull things over

From the seventeenth to the nineteenth centuries, a person with something to think over would put on a metaphorical *considering cap*. *Thinking cap* dates from the late nineteenth century.

*Solving murders used to be perfectly straightforward. The clues were there for all to see among the shoals of red herrings. All Sherlock Holmes had to do was puff on his pipe and **put on his thinking cap**.*
DAILY MIRROR, 9 MAY 2000

*Charlie had **put his thinking cap on**. For some time he had wanted to build a trapping cabin. In his new plan, I could build the cabin and use it for my adventure, after which it would be returned to him.*
THE SCOTSMAN, 13 SEPTEMBER 2004

third: to give someone/get the third degree

to give/get a gruelling interrogation, sometimes accompanied by brutal treatment

There are three degrees in Freemasonry, the third being the sublime degree of Master Mason. The questioning of a candidate presenting himself for admittance to this rank is said to be intensive and therefore an ordeal to be endured. In the United States in the late nineteenth century, *third degree* began to be used generally to denote 'a rigorous interrogation' of any sort. By the turn of the twentieth century the phrase was being specifically applied to aggressive questioning, accompanied by rough treatment at the hands of the police. Today it may still on occasion have this same sense, but more usually describes rigorous questioning of any sort, such as that given to a politician about his policies, for instance.

*We are wafted up to the 28th floor and the Windows Bar where we **get the third degree** from the receptionist – who are we, why are we here?*
THE DAILY TELEGRAPH,
12 OCTOBER 2002

SPYMISTRESS NOT SPOOKED WHEN **GIVEN THIRD DEGREE** BY AUDIENCE
The former head of MI5 Stella Rimington had her diplomacy tested at her event yesterday, not by her interviewer,
Woman's Hour's *Jenni Murray, but by fierce interrogators in her audience.*
THE INDEPENDENT, 13 OCTOBER 2004

thorn: a thorn in the flesh/side

a person or thing which causes persistent pain or annoyance

The Old Testament tells how, as the children of Israel prepare to invade Canaan, the Lord speaks to them through Moses, commanding them to drive out all the inhabitants and warning them that, if they do not, those whom they allow to remain will be *barbs in your eyes, and thorns in your sides, and shall vex you in the land wherein ye dwell* (Numbers 33:55). In the New Testament, the apostle Paul speaks of being afflicted with an ailment, *a thorn in the flesh* (II Corinthians 12:7), to keep him humble and dependent on Christ. The biblical phrase was borrowed for general idiomatic use in the first half of the nineteenth century.

Jonty Driver who, 40 years ago, was such
a thorn in the flesh *of the old apartheid
gang in South Africa…that he was banged
up in solitary for five weeks.*
THE DAILY TELEGRAPH, 16 MARCH 2002

Another **thorn in the flesh** *of Beijing
leaders was the Falun Gong chapter in
Hong Kong…the Falun Gong Hong Kong
chapter is legally registered and often
practices in open areas and regularly
protests in front of the CGLO building in
Hong Kong.*
JOURNAL OF CONTEMPORARY ASIA,
1 MAY 2004

For other idioms from the Bible, see
page 317.

thread: to hang by a thread
to be in a perilous state

The idiom alludes to a sword suspended by a single hair above the head
of the sycophant Damocles. Since the
sixteenth century anything which is in
a precarious state and in danger of
falling into ruin has been described as
hanging by a thread.

*The failure of the world's leading industrial
nations to resolve their deep differences on
trade left the future of global liberalisation
talks in Cancun, Mexico, later this year*
hanging by a thread *last night.*
THE GUARDIAN, 3 JUNE 2003

Kevin Keegan's future is **hanging by a
thread***. He's apparently lost the backing
of several flannel-slacked suits, who will
kick him out if City go down.*
THE GUARDIAN, 1 APRIL 2004

For the full story, see under *the*
SWORD *of Damocles.* For other idioms
derived from ancient legends, see
page 317.

thumbs: to give someone the thumbs up/down
to show approval/disapproval of
something, to give a project the go-
ahead/to reject a project

Whilst it may be stated with confidence
that this expression has in some way
emerged from the use of the thumb to
judge gladiatorial contests in Roman
arenas, there is some uncertainty over
what the signals actually were. Most
authorities agree that Roman gestures
meant the opposite of our modern use
of *thumbs up* and *thumbs down.* Athough
the 'thumbs up' (*pollice recto*) signifies
approval to us, it was not the gesture a
gladiator on the point of defeat wanted
to see; equally, the 'thumbs down' (*pollice verso*) did not mean certain death but
that the crowd believed the defeated
gladiator had struggled successfully
enough for his life to be spared.

Up to 1907, all the quotations in
the OED, except for one, support the
meaning of the gestures that is outlined above. The citation in 1906, and
ones from that decade onwards, are all
in line with the contemporary use of
thumbs up for approval and *thumbs down*
for disapproval. So where did our present-day interpretations come from?
The most likely source is a well-known
painting by the nineteenth-century
French artist, Jean-Léon Gérôme, entitled *Pollice Verso* (1872). It depicts a
victorious gladiator standing astride
his defeated foe and looking up into
the crowd for their verdict. The crowd
have their thumbs down and it is evident that the fallen gladiator will die.
It seems that Gérôme simply made an
error, and influenced the language in
consequence.

*But however tasty your child's packed lunch,
it will still* **get the big thumbs down** *if it is
in an old Tupperware box. A trendy lunch
box has to be on your shopping list too.*
DAILY EXPRESS, 26 AUGUST 2003

But we should still be wary. Science has
given Atkins only a tentative thumbs
up*.*
THE TIMES, 22 MAY 2004

For other idioms drawn from ancient
life and history, see page 317.

thunder: to steal someone's thunder

to upstage someone, to take the credit
properly belonging to someone else

The expression is attributed to playwright and critic John Dennis
(1657–1734), who discovered that, by
rattling a sheet of tin, he could make
the sound of thunder for dramatic
effect in his play *Appius and Virginia*
(1709). The play was not well
received, the poet Alexander Pope
being one of its most cutting critics,
and closed down after only a short
run. The sound effects were more
successful, however, and Dennis was
infuriated to hear his thunder repro-
duced not long afterwards in a
production of *Macbeth*, when it is
reported that he leaped to his feet in
anger crying *See how the rascals use me!*
They will not let my play run, and yet they
steal my thunder! The idiom *to steal*
someone's thunder dates from the beginning of the twentieth century.

When Lord Runcie was enthroned as
Archbishop of Canterbury in 1980, Lord
St John of Fawsley had to lobby in Cabinet
to get Budget day moved so that it wouldn't
*clash with the ceremony and **steal his***
thunder. *The Exchequer has had its*
revenge: the pre-Budget statement was
timed perfectly to clash with the memorial
service held in his honour in Westminster
Abbey yesterday.
THE DAILY TELEGRAPH,
9 NOVEMBER 2000

You might also manipulate the timing. If
they have an event or product roll-out, time
your announcement to coincide roughly
*with theirs – **steal their thunder**.*
THOMAS MCKNIGHT, WILL IT FLY?, 2003

tie the knot, to
to get married

He has tied a knot with his tongue he can't
untie with his teeth is an old proverb
dating back to at least the sixteenth
century and still in limited use in the
early twentieth. The warning is clear:
the bonds of matrimony so easily tied
are not so easily loosened. By the early
eighteenth century the first part of the
proverb, *to tie the knot*, was being used
with the sense 'to perform the marriage ceremony'. During the twentieth
century it came to mean 'to get married', the warning note sounded by the
old proverb long forgotten.

The recently-divorced star has denied
*intentions to **tie the knot** with current*
squeeze Penelope Cruz...
THE INDEPENDENT ON SUNDAY,
14 DECEMBER 2003

See PROVERBS AND IDIOMS,
page 284.

tilt: to tilt at windmills
to face an imagined evil; to pursue an
ideal with little hope of its realisation

In *Don Quixote*, the classical Spanish
novel by Miguel de Cervantes, Don
Quixote attacks some windmills in the
belief that they are monstrous giants.
When his lance becomes entangled in
one of the whirling sails, the knight
and his horse are snatched up and
sent rolling over the plain, the act
of chivalry leading only to injury.
The book was published in 1605 and
such was its popularity that, by 1622,
references to Don Quixote's battle

with the windmills had started to appear in English literature with the expression *to have windmills in one's head,* meaning 'to have a head full of fanciful notions'. The form *to tilt at windmills* dates from the second half of the nineteenth century.

*The small size of the Czech market means Sparta will never have the television revenue to buy the best players, as big clubs do. For clubs like it, the quest for glory abroad is increasingly **a tilt at windmills**.*
THE ECONOMIST, 23 DECEMBER 2000

*I always recognised…the challenge we faced. What good is it being Spanish if you cannot **tilt at windmills**?*
CARRIL AND WHITE, THE SMART TAKE FROM THE STRONG, 2004

For other idioms drawn from literature, see page 319.

time: (just) in the nick of time
at exactly the right moment; at the very last minute, only just in time

In the middle of the sixteenth century the phrase *in the nick* was coined to mean 'the precise moment' when something happened or had to be done. It was probably derived from *nick* in the now obsolete sense of 'the mark', 'the exact spot aimed at'. *In the nick of time* was an extension of the phrase dating from the beginning of the seventeenth century. Its sense was also 'at precisely the right moment', though more modern use is 'at the last possible second'.

*Michele's nagging ('Get in touch with your body, for God's sake') had driven me to the doctor. Our GP provides a 'well-man check-up' for men turned 50… I ask: 'Is this really a good use of scarce NHS resources?' 'It's preventative medicine,' the doctor says cheerily. 'Have we caught you **in the nick of time**?'*
THE DAILY TELEGRAPH, 7 MARCH 2002

*For all his faults, the father loved the boy and expressed that love by spiriting the delinquent out of Denver. In the boy's memory, it was **just in the nick of time**.*
DENVER ROCKY MOUNTAIN NEWS, 14 FEBRUARY 2003

tit for tat
retaliation; the exchange of blow for blow, insult for insult, etc

In use since the sixteenth century, this is a corruption of the fifteenth-century alliterative expression *tip for tap*, which literally means 'blow for blow'.

*The Notorious B.I.G. was gunned down at traffic lights in Los Angeles, and since then theories about who pulled the trigger and why have tormented his family. Rival gangs, **tit-for-tat** shootings, allegedly corrupt and incompetent police officers have all featured.*
THE GUARDIAN, 25 JUNE 2005

*Even if you succeed in gripping your opponent, at some point you may still find yourself under attack. In this situation, your first priority should be to Avoid **Tit-for-Tat**. When competing with stronger players, meeting force with force is a quick route to defeat. Resisting every move will wear you down, put you on the defensive, and recast the competition as a trial of strength – the game that you're least likely to win. So rather than get dragged into a war of attrition, stay on the offensive and respond to attackers on your own terms.*
YOFFIE AND KWAK, JUDO STRATEGY, 2003

See COUPLINGS, page 294.

toe: to toe the line
to submit to authority, regulations, etc

The phrase comes from running, where every competitor in a race is expected to submit to the rules and put a toe on the starting line with everyone else. It dates from the early nineteenth century.

But in order to do that, she's going to have to toe the line a bit. For all its laid back air, Hollywood is the most old-fashioned town in the world, immutable in its rules and rituals, and utterly unforgiving to those who do not play by them.
THE DAILY TELEGRAPH,
24 JANUARY 2002

I was a single parent and needed the job so I toed the line. But I was persistently humiliated and openly criticised by my boss.
GOOD HOUSEKEEPING, NOVEMBER 2002

For a different idiom from the same origin, see *to come up to* SCRATCH.

Topsy: to grow like Topsy
to grow without attention or help

Topsy is a lively little slave girl in Harriet Beecher Stowe's anti-slavery novel *Uncle Tom's Cabin* (1852). Asked where she was born and who her parents are, Topsy denies she was ever born and says she has no parents. The questioning continues:
'Have you ever heard anything about God, Topsy?'
The child looked bewildered, but grinned as usual.
'Do you know who made you?'
'Nobody, as I knows on,' said the child, with a short laugh.

Couplings

English has a number of idiomatic couplings which are both alliterative and tautological. That is, they are made up of two words beginning with the same letter and meaning the same thing, which have been put together for emphasis. *To go to rack and ruin* is an example dating from the sixteenth century. *Rack* is another variant of *wrack* and *wreck*, all three words meaning 'destruction, devastation': the same as *ruin*, in fact. Then there is *part and parcel*, both terms meaning 'an essential portion of a larger whole', a coupling that began in the fifteenth century as a legal term to emphasise the inclusion of every clause in an act of law or every piece of property in an estate. Much older than both of these is *might and main*, meaning 'with all one's strength'. *Main*, which meant 'physical strength, power', has been used as an intensifier with *might* since at least the tenth century. Other examples are BAG *and baggage*, CHOP *and change* and HUM *and haw*.

Other couplings may not be tautological but still reflect the English fascination with the alliterative phrase (see ALLITERATIVE SIMILES, page 237). TIT *for tat*, DILLY-DALLY, WILLY-NILLY, SHILLY-SHALLY, *hither and thither* and *kith and kin* all come into this category.

Many of the words in these couplings are now obsolete except for their presence in these phrases (for more see THE OLD CURIOSITY SHOP OF LINGUISTICS, page 198). *Rack, chop,* and *main* are no longer used in these senses. Neither is *tip*, the original element in TIT *for tat*, nor *nill*, found in the rhyming phrase WILLY-NILLY, nor SPICK, nor *span*, nor *hither* nor *thither*. Similarly *kith* is now only found when coupled with *kin*. In the ninth century, *kith* meant one's 'homeland' and hence one's 'fellow countrymen'. It was put together with *kin* in the fourteenth century to make the alliterative phrase *kith and kin*, one's 'acquaintances and kinsfolk', one's 'friends and relatives'.

Most of these alliterative couplings are centuries old, but English still turns them out. FOOTLOOSE *and fancy free* is an American coinage dating from the nineteenth century. Also from that century comes *rough and ready*, a favourite phrase to describe something that is just about good enough for its intended purpose. And from the twentieth century comes *mix and match*, coined in the 1940s when the vogue for women's separates came in.

The idea appeared to amuse her considerably; for her eyes twinkled, and she added, 'I 'spect I grow'd. Don't think nobody never made me.'

Topsy is one of the more endearing characters in this well-known book and, before long, anything that grew by itself without any real planning or assistance was said *to grow like Topsy*.

In this it perfectly mirrors, and complements, the state of popular culture. When I left these shores, the icon of the new flippant, irreverent, anything-goes, infantile, self-referential, self-absorbed celebrity culture was Chris Evans. Since my return he has been barely visible but no matter, the syndrome he represents has **grown like Topsy***. There is no longer one Chris Evans but a huge cast of them.*
THE GUARDIAN, 5 OCTOBER 2002

But the [Co-operative] movement that started in the modest surrounds of the Shears Inn **grew like Topsy***, became ever stronger and served the needs of ordinary working people for generations. The aim was to improve social conditions.*
HUDDERSFIELD DAILY EXAMINER, 9 APRIL 2005

For other idioms inspired by literary characters, see *(little)* GOODY-*two-shoes* and MAN/GIRL *Friday*.

touch wood
words spoken to avoid bad luck and be blessed with good luck

The words *touch wood* in Britain and *knock on wood* in the United States, by which the speaker hopes to stave off a reversal of present good fortune, are almost always accompanied by the speaker rapping on something wooden. Winston Churchill, tongue in cheek, said that he rarely liked *to be any considerable distance from a piece of wood*. Churchill, growing up in the latter part

of the nineteenth century, would have been acquainted with the childhood game Touch Wood, common then and still found today, in which players are safe only when literally touching wood. Although the phrase is quite modern, with records dating back only to the early twentieth century, it may allude to the times of the druids when it was believed that spirits lived within the trees. Or it may come from country witchcraft of some sort. Perhaps people seeking particular help were encouraged to rap on a tree to implore the spirit's aid or protection from misfortune. A reference to this sort of practice comes in a poem penned in 1900 by American writer Nora Archibald Smith:

*They'd knock on a tree and would timidly say
    To the Spirit who might be within there
            that day:
    Fairy fair, Fairy fair, wish thou me well;
    'Gainst evil witcheries weave me a spell!*

while an English proverb, published in an early twentieth-century edition of *Notes and Queries*, has *Touch wood, it's sure to come good*.

Dancing, drumming, blowing cows' horns and roasting bulls, the people of the Nuba mountains, a black African enclave in central Sudan, celebrated the ceasefire. They are enjoying the first properly monitored break in the shooting in this region for 19 years. Announced on January 23rd, it has held, **touch wood***, for two weeks.*
THE ECONOMIST, 7 FEBRUARY 2002

I've had a scare with the calf problem. It cropped up in Madrid at the weekend and I came straight home for physiotherapy. **Touch wood** *it's going to be OK.*
DAILY EXPRESS, 24 JULY 2004

towel: to throw in the towel

to give in, to admit defeat

See *to throw in the* SPONGE.

I'm very Catholic and I'm generally a woman of my word…it was really hard to throw in the towel because I'm one of those people who will fight and fight and fight to make something work – to the end.
GOOD HOUSEKEEPING, JUNE 2000

*He…stood on the tee leaning on his club with his head down, the whole world on his shoulders. Woods is not one **to throw in the towel**, but he seemed to give up after that.*
THE GUARDIAN, 23 JULY 2001

trice: in a trice

in an instant

The word *trice* is now obsolete, except for this expression. It dates from the fifteenth century when it was first found in the phrase *at a trice* (later *with* or *in a trice*), which literally meant 'at one single tug or pull'. That is all it takes to pinch the bedclothes:

Sometime thy bed-felowe is colder then is yse,
To him then he draweth thy cloathes with a trice.
(Alexander Barclay, *Egloges*, 1515)

The phrase was rapidly put to figurative use and meant 'instantly', the sense it retains to the present day.

*Although the days were leisurely and long, it felt as if everything had gone by **in a trice** when it came to our final dinner.*
THE GUARDIAN, 24 FEBRUARY 2004

See THE OLD CURIOSITY SHOP OF LINGUISTICS, page 198.

trip: to trip the light fantastic

to dance

This idiom comes from John Milton's *L'Allegro* (1632), where the poet uses *trip on the light fantastic toe* to describe a fanciful dance:

Haste thee Nymph and bring with thee
Jest and youthful Jollity…
Sport that wrinkled Care derides,
And Laughter holding both his sides.
Come, and trip it as ye go
On the light fantastick toe.

In the nineteenth century, Benjamin Disraeli, British prime minister and novelist, picked out Milton's phrase to describe one of the accomplishments of Mr St Ledger, who prided himself on *his light fantastic toe* (*Vivien Grey*, 1826) and, by the end of that century, the expression was familiar enough to appear in a song about dancing in the streets of New York:

East side, west side, all around the town,
The tots sang 'Ring-a-rosie,'
'London Bridge is falling down.'
Boys and girls together, me and Mamie O'Rourke
Tripped the light fantastic
On the sidewalks of New York.
(James W Blake, *The Sidewalks of New York*, 1894)

Today *to trip the light fantastic* is usually a humorous cliché for 'to dance'; however, it is developing a range of new contexts from football to athletics to politics – anywhere, in fact, where light and deft footwork might be called for.

*Cole **tripped the light fantastic** through the visitors to shoot across Darren Ward.*
THE PEOPLE, 5 JANUARY 2003

*The lively set can **trip the light fantastic** on the largest dancefloor at sea in the Queen's Room.*
DAILY EXPRESS, 15 MARCH 2003

Without an ideological bone in his body – his whole speech was about the realities of power – he can **trip the light fantastic toe** *at home and abroad.*
THE TIMES, 1 OCTOBER 2003

For other idioms drawn from literature, see page 319.

trumps: to come up/turn up trumps

unexpectedly to produce just what is needed at the last moment; to turn out well after all

Trump is a corruption of *triumph*, the name of a sixteenth-century card game similar to whist. A *triumph* or *trump* was any card in the suit which, for the duration of the hand, out-ranked the other three. A trump card was therefore a valuable one to hold. The idiom in the form *to turn up trumps* dates from the seventeenth century and alludes to someone with a mediocre hand unexpectedly turning up a trump card and finding his luck suddenly revived.

The Greeks may be struggling to finish many of their Olympic venues in time for the Games next summer but in sailing they have already **come up trumps***. The Agios Kosmas Olympic Sailing Centre…is a vast and impressive facility that, if anything, is too big and too expansive for the task for which it was built.*
THE TIMES, 22 AUGUST 2003

If the UK weather **comes up trumps***, cool off under this hardwood tilting parasol.*
DAILY MIRROR, 17 APRIL 2004

truth: to be economical with the truth

to lie

It seems to be a universal human response to avoid a blunt statement and, by softening things, try to make the situation better for oneself. A clever choice of words might just help. *To be economical with the truth* came to prominence on 18 November 1986, and has been widely used since then. The British Cabinet Secretary, Sir Robert Armstrong, was giving evidence in an Australian court, in an attempt to muzzle the former assistant director of MI5 Peter Wright by preventing the publication of his book *Spycatcher*. The transcript reads:

LAWYER: *It [the letter] contains a lie?*
ARMSTRONG: *It was a misleading impression. It does not contain a lie.*
LAWYER: *What is the difference between a misleading impression and a lie?*
ARMSTRONG: *A lie is a straight untruth.*
LAWYER: *What is a misleading impression – a sort of bent untruth?*
ARMSTRONG: *As one person said, it is perhaps being 'economical with the truth'.*

Armstrong's reference here is to the political philosopher Edmund Burke, who used the phrase at the end of the eighteenth century, although one authority ascribes it to Pepys some 125 years earlier.

Just six years after Armstrong, the former Defence Minister, Alan Clark, demonstrated in Court the now semi-proverbial standing of the phrase. In a similar effort to mitigate his own dishonesty, note his self-serving choice of words. He was answering a question about lying over arms sales to Iraq, and confessed thus:

LAWYER: *That could not be the case, to your knowledge?*
CLARK: *Well it's our old friend 'being economical', isn't it?*
LAWYER: *With the truth?*
CLARK: *With the* actualité.

The proud-to-be-Welsh actress Catherine Zeta-Jones is upset at rumours circulating in Hollywood that she has been **economical with the truth** *about her age.*
THE TIMES, 14 JULY 2004

turkey: to talk turkey

to get down to business, to discuss frankly

The story goes that a white man was out hunting with a Native American companion. At the end of the day they sat down together to divide the bag. Adopting a reasonable tone the white man said, 'Now, either I'll take the turkey and you can take the buzzard or you can have the buzzard and I'll take the turkey.' But the Indian, as sharp witted as his companion, replied, 'Now talk turkey to me.' The source of the story is unknown and details vary, but the tale is credited with the origin of this American phrase, in use since at least the 1840s.

*We really **talk turkey** – discussing the latest fashions, makeup, diet and exercise fads – and get geared up for the months ahead.*
THE MAIL ON SUNDAY, 25 APRIL 2004

See also *to go* COLD *turkey*.

two-faced

hypocritical, saying one thing and meaning another

Two faces under one hood was the original expression of duplicity. It was in use in this form from the end of the four-teenth until well into the nineteenth century. The earliest record is from *The Romaunt of the Rose*, a translation dating from around 1365 of a French poem: *Two hedes in one hood at ones*. A late example comes in the form of a rhyming couplet in Bohn's *Handbook of Proverbs* (1855):

> *May the man be damned and never*
> *grow fat,*
> *Who wears two faces under one hat.*

Double-faced and *two-faced* date from the sixteenth and seventeenth centuries respectively.

***Two-faced** people say one thing to your face and something else behind your back. They make ingratiating remarks to you but criticise you to other people, and vice versa… An extraordinary characteristic of **two-faced** people is that they can never bring themselves to believe that their cover has been blown. So they carry on being deceitful, in the words of an old pop song, 'never saying what they mean, never meaning what they say'.*
HONEY: PROBLEM PEOPLE, 2002

*It is a **two-faced** country that preaches European unity, yet seeks to maintain division and dominance.*
THE TIMES, 9 APRIL 2004

See also JANUS-FACED.

·U·

ugly duckling, an

a gauche, awkward child who blossoms into a beauty

This expression comes from *The Ugly Duckling* (1844), one of Hans Christian Andersen's tales in which a swan's egg is mistakenly hatched by a duck who cannot understand how she could have produced such an ungainly child, so different from the rest of her brood. The cygnet, scorned for its dull feathers and its clumsiness, hides away in shame all winter, but then emerges from the reeds as a beautiful swan. *Ugly duckling* has been idiomatic since the second half of the nineteenth century.

In the mid-twentieth century, Danny Kaye starred in a film about the life of Hans Andersen which produced a hit song, 'The Ugly Duckling'; his musical account of Andersen's fairy tale is kept alive for a new generation on DVD and MP3 downloads.

*The Beeb will be introducing more positive portrayals of care leavers in its programmes and this is a welcome step… It's time to tell the world: we are not **ugly ducklings** but fine swans.*
THE BIG ISSUE, 2 FEBRUARY 2004

*Never without make-up herself, Estée insisted that even the **ugliest ducklings** could be swans with the right cosmetics.*
DAILY MIRROR, 27 APRIL 2004

*Gawky, bespectacled Sylvia, her teeth recently caged in ugly orthodontic braces, had greasy hair, a hooting laugh and the long, thin fingers and toes of a creature from outer space. Well-meaning people called her an **'ugly duckling'**…imagining a future Sylvia casting off her braces, acquiring contact lenses and a bosom, and blossoming into a swan.*
KATE ATKINSON, CASE HISTORIES, 2004

umbrage: to take umbrage (at)

to take offence

The word *umbrage*, meaning 'shadow' or 'shade', came into English by way of Old French *umbrage* and Latin *umbra*, in the fifteenth century. It is now obsolete, surviving only in the seventeenth-century phrase *to take umbrage*, which presumably alludes to the dark shadow of ill-feeling that settles upon anyone who takes offence at another's words or actions.

Susan still feels that any woman working in science has an uphill struggle. 'Senior women who say there is no problem are either deluded or lying,' she told the scientific journal The Lancet.

*Ouch! No doubt some 'senior women' **took as much umbrage at** her words as the 'dysfunctional nerds' she castigated earlier. But has she herself encountered much discrimination?*

'Certainly, yes!'
INTERVIEW WITH PROFESSOR SUSAN GREENFIELD, DIRECTOR OF THE ROYAL INSTITUTION OF GREAT BRITAIN, IN GOOD HOUSEKEEPING, APRIL 2000

Busted are the current darlings of an increasingly important market – the six- to 12-year-olds. They are unusual in

appealing to boys as much as girls, and
took umbrage *recently when someone*
referred to them as a boy band.
THE MAIL ON SUNDAY,
27 NOVEMBER 2003

See THE OLD CURIOSITY SHOP OF
LINGUISTICS, page 198.

up and running

functioning as it ought, operating
without defect

Computers, particularly in their early
days, were notorious for *going down* and
ceasing to operate. As soon as the technical experts have put them right, they
should (hopefully) be *up and running*.
The expression has been in use since the
late 1970s. It is tautological. A computer is either *down*, 'not running', or
up, 'running'. So to declare it *up and run-*
ning is emphatic over-kill. The contexts
in which the expression is found are
becoming more and more general, as the
following quotations illustrate.

Plans to launch a lifeline to pensions
victims have been welcomed, but it will take
a lot of time, trouble and diplomacy to get
a rescue fund **up and running**.
THE SUNDAY TELEGRAPH, 8 JUNE 2003

A £20m project to improve Wilton Power
Station is **up and running**. *The project,*
which created around 85 jobs during
construction, involved 200,000 hours
of work and recently began generating its
first electricity.
MIDDLESBROUGH EVENING GAZETTE,
11 JANUARY 2005

upper crust, the

the aristocracy, higher social circles

Upper crust, a phrase which alludes to
the best part of a loaf of bread, the part
which has not touched the bottom of
the bread oven, was coined in the nineteenth century by Thomas Chandler

Haliburton, a much respected and
highly influential Canadian businessman and judge. Haliburton hankered
after political and social reform but, as
a prominent conservative, felt unable
to give his opinions free rein. Instead,
he created Sam Slick.

Sam first appeared in 1835 in a
series of anonymous sketches published in the *Nova Scotian* newspaper.
As his name implies Sam was indeed
slick, a cheery but artful itinerant
Yankee clockmaker who invariably got
the better of his Nova Scotian customers. An astute observer of Nova
Scotian life, Sam did not hesitate to
speak his mind, thus voicing
Haliburton's true opinions. And it was
from Sam's mouth that the phrase
upper crust was first uttered. In *The*
Clockmaker (1837–8) Sam, on his travels, calls in on an old woman who is
unable to offer him lavish hospitality
having had a grand tea party the day
before: *I actilly have nothin' left to set*
afore you; for it was none o' your skim-milk
parties, but superfine uppercrust real jam,
and we made clean work of it.

In 1843, Haliburton sent his alter
ego to Britain as a member of an
American diplomatic mission, a visit
recorded in the humorous fiction *The*
Attaché, or, Sam Slick in England. This
enabled Haliburton to satirise Britain, a
land where all the prominent political
figures were aristocratic: *I want you to see*
Peel, Stanley, Graham, Sheil, Russell,
Macaulay, Old Joe, and so on. These men
are all upper-crust here. In fact *upper crust*
is used several times in the work to
describe either high society or objects
and events associated with them.

Six years later James Fenimore
Cooper, an American novelist whose
works, like those of Haliburton, were
eagerly read on both sides of the
Atlantic used the phrase in *The Ways of*
the Hour (1850), and the idiom's
launch was confirmed.

*[The Earl of Cardigan] is clearly a colourful character. He has been convicted on a couple of firearms offences and is secretary of the local Conservative Party. He is assisting its parliamentary candidate and the party's chairman, Michael Ancram, during the election campaign. Having met the delightful Mr Ancram on several occasions, I cannot imagine he has much in common with this aggressive boor. Is the party so desperate for help that it enlists **upper-crust** morons like this one?*
THE INDEPENDENT, 27 MAY 2001

*Is there another city on the planet where the needs and desires of today's **upper crust** are fulfilled so exquisitely by the legacies of yesterday's working class? Case in point, as Rod Serling would say: the Elysian Cafe.*

The Elysian originally opened about 1897. 'During Prohibition,' its current owners, Joyce and Eugene Flinn, wrote me recently, 'the business operated as a speakeasy disguised as, of all things, a beauty parlor.'

Two years ago, staring at the old cafe's stained but gloriously filigreed plaster-and-horsehair ceiling, he had an epiphany: why not recreate the place as a bistro?

Voilà. The Elysian reopened last July. And its season, unlike the Yankees', has been a success in every way.
THE NEW YORK TIMES,
26 DECEMBER 2004

For other idioms drawn from literature, see page 319.

upper: to have/get/gain the upper hand

to gain the advantage, to win control

The upper hand has been idiomatic since the fifteenth century. It is probably an alteration of the earlier, and now obsolete, *over hand*, which dates from the turn of the thirteenth century. The phrase is thought to come from a drinking or gambling game where one player holds the bottom of a stick with one hand and his opponent grasps the same stick just above it. Play continues, hand over hand, until the top of the stick is reached by the winner.

*In the battle of the sexes, females have **the upper hand** when it comes to education – at least they do in the world of chimpanzees. Researchers at the Gombe National Park in Tanzania found that female chimpanzees learnt certain hunting and gathering skills from their mothers much faster than their male counterparts – who prefer to spend their time playing.*
THE SCOTSMAN, 15 APRIL 2004

*The working world is becoming increasingly feminine. The number of female civil servants has doubled in a decade; the proportion of female managers has risen from one in 10 to one in four; women now outnumber men among newly-qualified solicitors and doctors. Even in the City, women make up 41 per cent of the workforce. Eventually, sheer weight of numbers will give us **the upper hand**.*
THE DAILY TELEGRAPH, 18 JULY 2004

· V ·

vale of tears
life with all its troubles and sorrows

Mountain tops and valleys have long been used to describe emotional highs and lows. During the medieval period, literature records the *vale of aduersite* (John Lydgate, *Troy Book*, 1412–20), *vale of trowbull of woo and of hevynes* (*The Vision of Tundale*, fifteenth-century version), and *vale of wepynge* (Richard Misyn, *The Fire of Love*, 1435). The *vale of tears* dates from the middle of the sixteenth century. It has been identified with the biblical *Valley of Baca*, often translated as the 'Valley of Weeping', mentioned in Psalm 84:6, and thought to be symbolic of arid places crossed by pilgrims on their way to Jerusalem. The eighteenth-century poet William Cowper, who struggled with depression for most of his life, often described this world as a *vale of tears*, and Shelley, in his 'Hymn to Intellectual Beauty' (1816), penned the sombre lines:

Spirit of BEAUTY, that dost consecrate
With thine own hues all thou dost shine upon
Of human thought or form, where art thou gone?
Why dost thou pass away and leave our state,
This dim vast vale of tears, vacant and desolate?

At least the Victorians understood that life is a *vale of tears* and you just had to get through it without drowning.
THE DAILY TELEGRAPH,
18 SEPTEMBER 2004

The deaths of five Irish girls in Monday's horrific road accident has turned the picturesque grounds of a Co Meath convent school into a *vale of tears*. Hundreds of pupils drifted through the grounds of Loreto Convent, which four of the five dead girls attended. But instead of lively chatter there was mostly silence yesterday, broken occasionally by sobs.
THE INDEPENDENT, 25 MAY 2005

veil: to draw a veil over
to avoid discussing, to hush up

The allusion is to discreetly concealing a shameful object or scene behind a veil. The earliest known example of the phrase occurs in Daniel Defoe's spirited satirical poem 'The True-Born Englishman' (1701), which criticised those prejudiced against William III because of his Dutch birth:

Satyr, be kind! and draw a silent Veil!
Thy native England's vices to conceal.

It has been in constant use ever since.

But [Sir Simon] Rattle the man still awaits his biographer. Several interviewees speak of his unknowability. And since, as Kenyon puts it, he 'would very understandably prefer to **draw a veil**' over the messy period during which he divorced his first wife (and effectively deserted his children), that veil is obediently drawn.
THE INDEPENDENT, 22 NOVEMBER 2001

Colin Montgomerie was today going into the second round of the US Open seeking to consolidate a challenge for the maiden major title that would **draw a veil** over

the traumas that have blighted his life in recent months. A high-profile divorce, a slump in form and allegations of cheating at a tournament in Indonesia have taken a toll on the seven-times European No1.
EVENING STANDARD, 17 JUNE 2005

vicious circle, a

one difficulty leading to another, which aggravates the first; a downward spiral of negative reactions

Logic has the concept of the *vicious circle*. It concerns an argument that assumes what is being proved. To put it another way, the argument for A depends on B, which depends on C, which in turn depends on A. However, we are not all logicians, and the layman understands the idiom less formally. The simple idea is that an action or event, A, triggers a reaction, B, and that makes A worse. This is the way a contributor to the *Daily Mirror* (15 June 2005) put it:

My weight problem started at puberty. From then on, I just got bigger and bigger. It was a vicious circle: the more I ate, the fatter I got and the more depressed I felt – which just made me eat more.

The logical fallacy is referred to in the third edition of the *Encyclopaedia Britannica* (c. 1792). The more day-to-day sense follows shortly afterwards in the first half of the nineteenth century. On a more optimistic note, since the mid-nineteenth century, there has been in circulation the *virtuous circle*, an ongoing cycle of positive reactions.

It is excellent that Mahmoud Abbas, Yasser Arafat's successor, is breaking out of the **vicious circle** *of the intifada, talking the armed factions into ceasing fire and so setting the scene not only for a tentative, reciprocal ceasefire from Israel but also for a meeting next week with Israel's prime minister, Ariel Sharon.*
THE ECONOMIST, 3 FEBRUARY 2005

· W ·

wagon: on the wagon

teetotal, abstaining from drinking alcohol

This idiom was coined against the backdrop of the Temperance Movement in the United States, which had been gaining in momentum throughout the nineteenth century and culminated in the Prohibition of 1920. Originating as *to be on the water wagon*, the phrase was inspired by the water carts used in towns and cities to dampen down the dusty streets. Those pledging to abstain from alcohol would rather avail themselves of the copious quantities of water on the cart than drink alcohol. The expression is recorded in *Dialect Notes* of 1904 and is, therefore, probably of nineteenth-century origin. The condensed form, *on the wagon*, dates from around 1906. And, since rehabilitation is a struggle, it is also possible to *fall off the wagon*: *It is better to have been on and off the Wagon than never to have been on at all* (B J Taylor, *Extra Dry*, 1906).

Limit the number of days that you shop each week, and limit the number of things you buy each time to one item only. That will force you to slow down and choose carefully.
Expect to fall off the wagon every now and again...
GOOD HOUSEKEEPING, JULY 2001

Giving up the booze proved tough. 'It wasn't easy...I fell off the wagon three times.'
DAILY MIRROR, 30 OCTOBER 2003

Going on the wagon and drinking booze-free drinks can help to protect your health.
THE TIMES, 29 MAY 2004

wall: to go to the wall

to give way under pressure; to suffer failure, ruin

When a person pursued into a blind alley hits the wall at the end, he can go no further. This picture of desperation has been in use since the sixteenth century in a number of expressions. *To have one's* BACK *to the wall* suggests there is no obvious escape. In the sixteenth century, Sir Thomas More, finding himself in a difficult situation from which he could see no way out, wrote: *I am in this matter euen at the harde walle, and see not how to go further* (*Works*, 1528). The lesser-used phrase *to be driven to the wall* means 'to be forced into a hopeless situation by circumstances': *That deede without words shall driue him to the wall. And further than the wall he can not go* (John Heywood, *Proverbs*, 1546). The familiar *to go to the wall* has a sense of having to give way, in conflict or under pressure, as does the old proverb, also from the sixteenth century, *the weakest go to the wall*. An extension of this idea dates from the mid-nineteenth century and refers to the failure of a business or institution. This is perhaps the predominant meaning today.

If we get a budget like this year again, there will be a lot of schools that will go to the wall.
THE INDEPENDENT, 24 MAY 2003

That may be no bad thing if small charities duplicating the work of others go to the wall.
THE GUARDIAN, 7 APRIL 2004

wall: to have one's back to the wall

to be under extreme pressure, resulting in failure or fight-back; to struggle against the odds

See under *to go to the* WALL.

*With his **back to the wall** after a bruising political year the prime minister put his bill to establish student 'top-up' fees at the front of the Queen's speech – ready for what could be a dramatic showdown with up to 100 labour rebels within weeks.*
THE GUARDIAN, 27 NOVEMBER 2003

*Saturday's loss in Christchurch still smarts. As we climbed on the team bus after the parliamentary visit, I could imagine the All Blacks chuckling to themselves. We didn't do ourselves justice, we let the fans down and it must not – cannot – happen again. It's **backs-to-the-wall** time.*
THE DAILY TELEGRAPH, 30 JUNE 2005

warpath: on the warpath

spoiling for a fight; in an aggressive or vengeful mood

Warpath originated amongst the North American Indians and denoted the route taken by a warlike tribe on its way to confront the enemy. First written references to it are in the second half of the eighteenth century. *On the warpath* began to be used figuratively in the second half of the nineteenth century, notably by Mark Twain, who, describing a young woman making an execrable fist of playing 'The Battle of Prague' on the piano, wrote: *She made it ALL discords, this time. She got an amount of anguish into the cries of the wounded that shed a new light on human suffering. She was on the war-path all the evening* (*A Tramp Abroad*, 1880).

*The Government has declared one of its key battles is the fight against child obesity and is **on the warpath** against unhealthy food.*
SUNDAY EXPRESS, 7 DECEMBER 2003

*Sir Alex Ferguson went **on the warpath** after watching Manchester United edge past Fulham, threatening his established stars with the axe… The United boss struggled to contain his anger after his side were forced to endure a barrage of late pressure from the Cottagers. Ferguson warned his senior players to up their game or face being dropped.*
LIVERPOOL DAILY POST,
21 MARCH 2005

For other idioms derived from the army and warfare, see page 317.

warts and all

(making) no attempt to hide defects

Portrait painters of the rich and powerful often soften craggy features and paint their subjects in a kind light. Oliver Cromwell, good Puritan that he was, would have none of this vanity. His order to Peter Lely, a Dutch painter who came to England in 1641, was: *I desire you would use all your skill to paint my picture truly like me, and not flatter me at all; but remark all these roughnesses, pimples, warts, and everything as you see me, otherwise I will never pay a farthing for it.* We are indebted to Horace Walpole and his *Anecdotes of Painting in England* (1763) for this report, from which the phrase *warts and all* was coined in the first half of the twentieth century.

Incidentally, those who know Lely's portrait will judge that Cromwell must have been well pleased with the result. So pleased, in fact, that he subsequently presented it to the Grand Duke of Tuscany, and it hangs in the Palazzo Pitti in Florence. There is, however, a possible twist to the tale.

Cromwell was painted a number of times in his lifetime. Robert Walker produced several portraits, Mascall an important late work, and Samuel Cooper some miniatures. It is thought by one authority, at least, that Lely copied Cooper, and so Cromwell's famous remarks may, after all, have been addressed to the miniaturist.

*She considered her children. They were part of her, **warts and all**, like her feet or her ears.*
MAVIS CHEEK, MRS FYTTON'S COUNTRY LIFE, 2000

*Not every flaw is a deal-breaker. Some things can be changed or buyers decide they can put up with them. But at least with a **warts-and-all** portrait there'll be no nasty surprises.*
FINANCIAL TIMES, 23–24 FEBRUARY 2002

*I really loved Diana, **warts and all**, and I cried the whole day of her funeral.*
THE GUARDIAN, 24 FEBRUARY 2004

*This whole thing has been a test of friendship, but the friendship has not changed one iota. This friendship has the benefit of longevity. It's **warts and all**.*
THE DAILY TELEGRAPH, 8 MARCH 2004

Waterloo: to meet one's Waterloo
to suffer defeat after initial success

The expression refers to the final and overwhelming defeat of Napoleon by the allied forces at Waterloo, ten miles south of Brussels, on 18 June 1815. The aftermath of the battle saw an end to Napoleon's dream of establishing France as a European empire. It brought about his abdication and his captivity on the island of St Helena until his death in 1821. Figurative application of *Waterloo* to denote 'a decisive contest' began the year after the victory. The phrase *to meet one's Waterloo* dates from the 1850s.

*In the early hours last Friday the polling industry patted itself on the back. Unlike 1992, when the pollsters **had met their Waterloo**, this year they did manage to pick the winner: Labour by a landslide.*
THE GUARDIAN, 13 JUNE 2001

For more on Napoleon, see BAPTISM *of fire* and *to* BEAT *a (hasty) retreat*.

wayside: to fall by the wayside
to drop out; to fail

Jesus told a parable about a sower who went out to broadcast some seed. Some of the seed fell on good soil, some amongst thorns, some on stony ground and some *fell by the way side, and it was trodden under feet, and the fowls of the air devoured it up* (Tyndale's translation, 1526, Luke 8:5). The seed represents the word of God sown abroad and the different soils the attitudes of hearers of the word. *The wayside* is descriptive of those who do not immediately understand the message and the birds represent the devil who snatches the word away before it can take root. Surprisingly this biblical phrase has been in idiomatic use only since the second half of the twentieth century.

*Under the proposal, developers would be taxed on the increase in the value of land once it has planning consent. The recommendation is a throwback to the 1970s when two similar schemes were launched and subsequently **fell by the wayside**.*
THE DAILY TELEGRAPH, 18 MARCH 2004

*1,200 veterans of the 10,000 believed to be in Normandy marched off round Arromanches. Some kept time faultlessly, some **fell by the wayside**.*
DAILY MAIL, 7 JUNE 2004

For other idioms from the Bible, see page 317. For more idioms drawn from Tyndale's translations, see WILLIAM TYNDALE, page 270.

weight: to pull one's weight
to do one's fair share

The idiom is from rowing, where each member of the crew is expected to row effectively in relation to his weight. An article in the *Daily News* dated 10 February 1897 explains the metaphor, showing its emergence into figurative speech: *In boating phraseology, he 'pulled his weight'…; he was not a mere passenger.* It was not long before the physical sporting contexts were extended to any sphere where a fair contribution to the collective effort was required.

Now he was back at work, lamentably failing to pull his weight and he knew he was ineffectual.
ANN WIDDECOMBE,
THE CLEMATIS TREE, 2000

Government can play its part by introducing forward-thinking paternity policies to give parents the choice of who stays at home. But ultimately the simpler solution involves a plea to Welshmen everywhere to pull their weight. Otherwise the stereotype of a nation of housework-shy men spoiled by their mams is in danger of stifling our claims to be an enlightened nation of equals.
CARDIFF WESTERN MAIL,
7 JULY 2004

wheat: to separate the wheat from the chaff
to separate the good from the bad, the valuable from the worthless

The expression refers to the farming practice of threshing corn in order to separate the worthless husks from the good grain. Someone who, figuratively speaking, *separates the wheat from the chaff* identifies what is worthwhile in an undertaking and discards that which is a waste of time.

A similar metaphor is used in the Bible. This time the *wheat* refers to

those who belong to Christ and are judged worthy and the *chaff* to those who have rejected him and have no place in his kingdom. Luke 3:17 records the words of John the Baptist: *His winnowing fork is in his hand to clear his threshing floor and to gather the wheat into his barn, but he will burn up the chaff with unquenchable fire.*

The entry *to separate the* SHEEP *from the goats* discusses another biblical analogy which conveys the same spiritual message. Both expressions, outside of agricultural and biblical contexts, seem to have gained a lease of life in the twentieth century in secular contexts, to describe the separating of something good from something bad.

The most depressing thing about second-hand shopping is searching through loads of horrible, mouldy-smelling clothes until you find a bargain. Wouldn't it be nice if someone else did some of the work, separating the wheat from the chaff?
THE OBSERVER, 24 NOVEMBER 2002

The first really capable search engine was AltaVista, unveiled by Louis Monier of Digital Equipment Corporation in December of 1995… That was because AltaVista successfully met two of the three requirements that later led to Google's success. First, it indexed a much larger portion of the web than anything that had come before… Second, AltaVista was fast, delivering results from its huge index almost instantly… Even so, AltaVista still lacked Google's uncanny ability to separate the wheat from the chaff.
THE ECONOMIST, 16 SEPTEMBER 2004

For other idioms from the Bible, see page 317.

wheel: the wheel has come full circle

we are back to the point of departure

There was a popular belief in the Middle Ages that one's fate was dependent on the whim of Fortune and her wheel. Everyone was aboard the wheel, whether at the bottom or the top, but fickle Fortune had only to nudge her wheel to reverse a man's happy circumstances or to raise him up again, regardless of his personal merits.

The wheel metaphor is an ancient one but was famously discussed in *On the Consolation of Philosophy* (c. AD 524), by the late Roman philosopher Boethius, which became an influential work in the Middle Ages. Boethius himself, who had enjoyed a brilliant political and academic career, wrote the *Consolation* from the misery of a prison cell, accused of treason. He puts these words into Fortune's mouth: *Inconstancy is my very essence; it is the game I never cease to play as I turn my wheel in its ever changing circle, filled with joy as I bring the top to the bottom and the bottom to the top. Yes, rise up on my wheel if you like, but don't count it an injury when by the same token you begin to fall, as the rules of the game will require.*

There are numerous references to Fortune's wheel in European literature of the Middle Ages and beyond. It finds its way into modern English idiom by way of Shakespeare who, in *King Lear* (1606) has Edmund say *The wheel is come full circle, I am here*.

The phrase *the wheel has come full circle* was taken up by writers in the first half of the twentieth century to describe circumstances that have inexplicably reverted to the way they once were. This example is from John Buchan's *Prester John* of 1910: *The hunters had become the hunted, the wheel had come full circle, and the woes of David Crawfurd were being abundantly avenged.*

In recent times the wheel has often been omitted from the idiom, reducing it to *to come full circle*.

*In common with many long-serving teachers, he feels that **the educational wheel has come full circle**. 'When I started, every lesson, every day was written up and advisers came to check that you were thoroughly prepared. Then came the days of greater flexibility and topic teaching, and now the formal side has made a comeback – and it's not necessarily a bad thing.'*
THE TIMES EDUCATIONAL SUPPLEMENT, 31 AUGUST 2001

*Ms Lux said Channel 4's breakfast shows had **come full circle** and it was time to return to a news agenda.*
THE GUARDIAN, 26 APRIL 2002

For other idioms from Shakespeare, see WILLIAM SHAKESPEARE, page 152.

wheel: to wheel and deal

to engage in political or commercial scheming

The entry for *wheel and deal* in Webster's *Third New International Dictionary* (1961) suggests that this rhyming phrase is derived from *(big) wheel*. This is an American slang term for a 'big shot', 'an influential businessman', which was already in existence when *to wheel and deal* and its derivative *wheeler-dealer*, meaning 'sharp operator', were coined around 1960. The allusion was presumably to a wheel turning and making the machinery of business or politics run smoothly. *To wheel and deal* often carries the implication that activities are at best shrewd, often touching upon the shady and dishonest.

*Certainly, capturing such a big fish would be entirely in keeping with Jordan's ability to **wheel and deal**...*
THE INDEPENDENT, 6 JANUARY 2004

*Ben Affleck plays a New York **wheeler-dealer** in* Jersey Girl *whose life changes when his wife dies and he has to bring up his daughter alone.*
SUNDAY MIRROR, 13 JUNE 2004

whipping boy, a
one who suffers the punishment for the wrongdoing of another, a scapegoat

Those who take the blame for the misdeeds of others have been alluded to as *whipping boys* since around the middle of the seventeenth century. A *whipping boy* was a child who shared the rich benefits of the nursery and schoolroom with a young prince, but who was beaten in his royal companion's place whenever the latter misbehaved. The whipping boy was necessary because it was an offence to strike a royal child whose family ruled by divine right. Edward VI's punishments fell upon Barnaby Fitzpatrick who was appointed his *proxy for correction* on 15 August 1551, and Mungo Murray suffered for Charles I.

Not all princes were spared the rod, however. George Buchanan, tutor of James I, punished his royal charge despite the presence of a whipping boy, and threatened to repeat the beating if he carried on being lazy. And the position undoubtedly opened later career advantages. James Worsley, for instance, whipping boy to Henry VIII, was knighted when Henry came to the throne and later appointed as Keeper of the Wardrobe and then Captain of the Isle of Wight.

It was the mid-nineteenth century before the expression was used figuratively in wider contexts.

A sense of public duty motivated Vanni Treves, at the age of 60, to take charge of Equitable Life. *Four months later, the dapper, wealthy Italian-born lawyer has found the troubled insurance company's policyholders are ungrateful for his public-spiritedness.*

*The new **whipping boy** for the increasingly furious 1m or so policyholders...of the once prestigious mutual insurer, he is not getting paid directly for his toil either.*
THE GUARDIAN, 11 AUGUST 2001

*Over the past 10 years, McDonald's has become **a whipping boy** for anybody with a gripe: anti-capitalists, the anti-fast-food lobby and opponents of advertising aimed at children.*
THE INDEPENDENT, 29 JUNE 2004

white elephant, a
an unwanted object of no great use or value

The royal white elephants of Southeast Asia were sacred animals symbolising power. The kings of Burma and Siam kept as many of these rare creatures as they could find in their stables, thus ensuring long and prosperous reigns. Death amongst the white elephants foretold disaster. The devious kings of Siam are said to have invented an ingenious way of ridding themselves of any courtier who irked them. They would present the hapless fellow with a white elephant. The cost of maintaining the creature, which was not permitted to earn its keep as a working animal, was excessive and gradually ruined its new owner.

Travellers' tales of the seventeenth century introduced the term *white elephant*: it began to be applied figuratively to 'something unwanted and without value' around the mid-nineteenth century. In a letter to her friend Jane Carlyle, dated 23 July 1851, the English novelist Geraldine Endsor Jewsbury, discussing a common acquaintance, wrote: *...what I have not got over is the seeing you so plagued as you were. If – were not so frightened of doing wrong, he would oftener do right, and anyway be less of a bother. His services are like so many white elephants, of which nobody*

can make use, and yet that drain one's grat-
itude, if indeed one does not feel bankrupt.

Later, during the twentieth century,
unwanted items of bric-à-brac would
be donated to the *white elephant stall* at
the local church bazaar or school fete.
But that is not to say that modern
white elephants are all diminutive. An
article in the *Daily Mail* for 27 October
1970 called a new rail link *the biggest
white elephant in all Africa* while, in the
twenty-first century, the London
Dome, built to celebrate the millen-
nium, was widely considered to qualify,
as the quotation from *The Independent*
below implies.

*If the Games do come to London, they
won't necessarily be a repeat of the Dome
debacle. And the 80,000 capacity stadium
to be built on the Hackney Marshes won't
necessarily be* **a white elephant**.
THE INDEPENDENT, 12 NOVEMBER 2003

*There is no use in pretending that the
Scottish Parliament has been nothing other
than* **a white elephant** *so far.*
EXPRESS ON SUNDAY, 23 MAY 2004

See BLACK AND WHITE, opposite.

whited sepulchre, a
a hypocrite, someone or something
outwardly presentable but inwardly
corrupt

This is a biblical expression coming from
the words Jesus uses in Matthew 23:27
when he condemns the scribes and
Pharisees for being outwardly orthodox
and beyond reproach but inwardly corrupt, full of self-indulgence and greed: *Ye
are like unto whited sepulchres, which indeed
appear beautiful outward, but are full of
dead men's bones, and of all uncleanness*
(Authorised Version).

In biblical times, contact with dead
bodies or tombs was considered
unclean, so Jewish sepulchres were
whitewashed to make them clearly visible to any passer-by who feared

defilement. It seems unlikely, however,
that Jesus would call such tombs beautiful since attractiveness was not the
reason for the whitewashing. It is more
likely that he was referring to the ornamental plasterwork which adorned the
sepulchres of the rich. The phrase has
been in figurative use since the second
half of the eighteenth century.

*The cinema has had fun depicting the
moral monstrosity of the men who, in
reality, have occupied that* **whited
sepulchre** *on Pennsylvania Avenue.*
THE OBSERVER, 17 DECEMBER 2000

*Yarm, which is considered by many to be
one of the nicest parts of Teesside, is: 'The
worst sort of town:* **a whited sepulchre**.
*Superficially it appears an attractive
market town in the industrial wasteland
of Teesside. However, spending any amount
of time there one will discover that no
resident has any taste or cultural
discernment. The pubs attract a crowd
similar to that found in the Costa del Sol,
complete with fake tan and skimpy clothes.
Weekends and Tuesday (singles night) are
even worse with fighting yobs and divorcees
on the hunt from out of town.'*
MIDDLESBROUGH EVENING GAZETTE,
4 AUGUST 2003

See BLACK AND WHITE, opposite,
and for other idioms from the Bible,
see page 317.

wild goose chase, a
a purposeless errand, a pointless
exercise, a waste of time

There was, in the late sixteenth and
early seventeenth centuries, a horseback
sport in which a rider would set out on a
random course, changing direction at
will, while the other participants came
behind at measured intervals, trying as
accurately as possible to follow in his
tracks. The sport, said to mimic the
flight of wild geese behind the leading

Black and white

Black has carried connotations of evil since the sixteenth century. This is reflected in such idioms as the *black arts, black magic, a black-hearted villain* and the way we say something is *as black as the devil* or *as black as hell*. They all have overtones of dark purposes and wrong-doing.

Black is also associated with illegality. There is the *black market* and an ever-increasing *black economy* whose transactions are never declared to the Inland Revenue. Much older expressions, such as *to fly the black flag* and *blackmail* (originally an illegal protection racket), contain the same idea of breaking the law.

Evil and illegality obviously bring moral censure and disgrace. Not surprisingly, then, there are plenty of phrases expressing this idea: *to be in someone's* BLACK *books*, *to* BLACKLIST, *to* BLACKBALL, or just *to black* someone, *a blackleg, the* BLACK *sheep of the family, a black mark* and so on.

Black is also associated with death in the Christian culture and this probably explains the gloomy connotations of the word in relation to human feelings. You can be *in a black humour* or *mood, look on the black side of things, paint things black* and claim that *things are looking black*. Other expressions connecting black with feelings are no better. *To give somebody a black look* and *to look as black as thunder* suggest anger and threat.

Recently, however, the use of such terms has become a somewhat sensitive issue amongst the black population because of the negative or sinister associations they carry. In Britain, the Trades Union Congress has produced a document advising members on the use of appropriate language in the areas of sex, age and race:

It is acceptable to use 'black' to describe colour, as in blackboard, black coffee and black bin bag. But the guide says terms such as black sheep, blacklist, black mark and black looks, although not linked to skin colour, reinforce a negative view of all things black (*The Daily Telegraph*, 24 May 2005).

White, on the other hand, has had generally positive connotations; a *white wedding*, for instance, or that old phrase *That's white of you*, meaning 'That's fair of you'. *White* has the power to turn something bad into something good. Lies, witches and magic all have negative associations, yet add the positive word *white* and they are rendered harmless, even beneficial. What wrong is there in *a white lie, a white witch* or *white magic*?

Conversely, there are quite a few negative expressions connected with *white*. A coward may be *white-livered*, be shown *the white feather* or surrender by waving *the white flag*. But such idioms usually tell of actual whiteness. The liver of a coward was once believed to be light in colour due to a deficiency of bile, a white feather in a game bird's tail revealed inferior breeding and a white flag was the recognised signal of a desire to negotiate with the enemy since the sixteenth century. Other examples are WHITE *elephant* and WHITED *sepulchre*.

---

bird, was called *a wild goose chase* or *race*. Shakespeare used it as a figure in *Romeo and Juliet* (1592):

Nay, if thy wits run the Wild-Goose chase,
I am done: For thou hast more of the
Wild-Goose in one of thy wits, then I am
sure I haue in my whole fiue

and it was used thus to denote 'an unpredictable course' or 'erratic, impulsive behaviour' throughout the seventeenth century. The sport turned out to be nothing more than a fad, however, and the origins of the phrase were soon forgotten, leaving Dr Johnson to define *wild goose chase* as *A pursuit of something as unlikely to be caught as a wild goose* in his well-known *Dictionary of the English Language* of 1755.

*Not a shot fired in anger. Not a terrorist captured or killed. Who can blame the Royal Marines in Afghanistan if they feel they have been sent half way round the world on **a wild goose chase** to satisfy the vanity of politicians?*
DAILY MAIL, 21 JUNE 2002

*In American English, a snipe-hunt is **a wild-goose-chase**.*
THE ECONOMIST, 10 AUGUST 2002

*On the morning of February 29, they sent poor Steve on **a wild goose chase** to keep him out of the way.*
SUNDAY PEOPLE, 29 FEBRUARY 2004

For other idioms from Shakespeare, see WILLIAM SHAKESPEARE, page 152.

willy-nilly: to do something willy-nilly

to do something whether one likes it or not; to do something carelessly, without thought

Willy-nilly arose in the early seventeenth century as a contraction of the much earlier phrase *will I, nill I* (similarly *will he, nill he; will ye, nill ye*). *Will* is a verb expressing the desire to do a thing and *nill*, long obsolete, expresses unwillingness, so the phrase means that a thing will be done whether it is in line with the will of the person concerned or against it. This remains one sense of the expression, although a new meaning, that of doing something without giving it much thought, is often found.

While we have our Harold Shipman, they had their William Palmer, trusted doctors who wantonly breached that

*trust by dispensing poison to patients **willy-nilly**.*
THE INDEPENDENT, 27 OCTOBER 2001

*He appears to have been handing out invitations **willy-nilly**...*
DAILY MAIL, 8 MAY 2004

*Their understanding is far superior to that of the people who dole out responsibilities **willy-nilly** because they can't think where else to place those duties.*
THE TIMES EDUCATIONAL
SUPPLEMENT, 1 OCTOBER 2004

A similar phrase is SHILLY-SHALLY. See also COUPLINGS, page 294.

wing: to take someone under one's wing

to provide someone with help, encouragement, protection

The allusion is to the mother hen who gathers her chicks protectively beneath her wings. There have been references to the wings of protection in English literature since the thirteenth century, but the figure is older. In the New Testament, for instance, Jesus laments over Jerusalem with the words: *O Jerusalem, Jerusalem, thou that killest the prophets, and stonest them which are sent unto thee, how often would I have gathered thy children together, even as a hen gathereth her chickens under her wings, and ye would not!* (Matthew 23:37, Authorised Version, 1611).

Thanks to the authority of the Bible through the intervening centuries, the phrase has maintained its currency till today.

*Born into the impoverished branch of the Austen family, Jane was **taken under the wing** of Francis Austen, only to be abandoned by her rich relatives upon his death.*
THE TIMES, 18 OCTOBER 2003

*Spektor, who came to America aged nine and was **taken under the wing** of a local piano professor, has since toured with Julian Casablancas.*
THE SUNDAY TIMES, 11 JULY 2004

For other idioms from the Bible, see page 317.

wolf: a wolf in sheep's clothing

someone who is not as pleasant and harmless as first appears

A wolf in sheep's clothing, wrote H F Kletzing at the end of the nineteenth century, *is a fitting emblem of the hypocrite. Every virtuous man would rather meet an open foe than a pretended friend who is a traitor at heart.*

Aesop tells a fable about a greedy wolf who, wrapped in a fleece, sneaks into the sheepfold by pretending to be one of the flock. Our present-day expression, like many others, may have come from Aesop's cautionary tales. In fact, the story was probably well-known in the ancient Mediterranean world. Jesus refers to a similar tale in Matthew 7:15. Tyndale's translation (1526) renders the verse: *Beware of false Prophetes which come to you in shepes clothinge but inwardly they are ravenynge wolves.*

The wolf in disguise has been alluded to in English literature since the fourteenth-century translation of the French poem *Roman de la Rose* (c. 1270). The phrase during the fifteenth and early sixteenth centuries was *a wolf in a lamb's skin* but, following Tyndale's clandestine translation of Matthew's gospel, the present-day variant *a wolf in sheep's clothing* began to appear. An early instance is found in Hugh Latimer's *Sermons and Remains* (1530): *The hypocrite-wolves clad in sheep's clothing.* After publication of Tyndale's New Testament was permitted in England in 1536, this became the commonly accepted idiom.

DISCOUNT DEALS: A WOLF IN SHEEP'S CLOTHING?

Homebuyers are enticed into discounted mortgage products every year... But what many of these customers fail to realise is that after paying an initial low discounted rate, they will move onto a higher standard variable rate. They would be far better off avoiding what appear to be attractive discount deals and, instead, picking a good low rate.
DAILY MAIL, 1 AUGUST 2001

For other idioms from the Bible, see page 317; for more idioms drawn from Tyndale's translations, see WILLIAM TYNDALE page 270; for idioms derived from fables, see page 318.

wolf: to cry wolf

to sound a false alarm

One of Aesop's fables tells of a shepherd boy who kept himself amused by crying 'Wolf! Wolf!' to alarm the villagers and make them rush to his rescue. Naturally they tired of this. One day wolves really did come among his flock but when he cried out for help no one took any notice. The idiom dates from the mid-nineteenth century. It remains in good use, having been the title of a popular book, of a movie and of two pop songs over recent decades.

*He has hinted that if he is defeated on this issue he will go. So let's defeat him and see what happens. One of these fine days, Tony Blair will **cry wolf** too often.*
DAILY MIRROR, 5 DECEMBER 2003

For other idioms derived from fables, see page 318.

wolf: to keep the wolf from the door

to ward off hunger, to provide the necessities of life

The *wolf* here is hunger. Since ancient times, the wolf has been a symbol of poverty and want. Fables depict the wolf as ravenously hungry, in desperate need of sustenance. The French say *manger comme un loup* – 'to eat like a wolf' – and the Germans have an expression *wolfshunger*. In English, a ravenous appetite was once commonly termed *a wolf* while, in modern English, *to wolf* means 'to devour one's food greedily'. *Keeping the wolf from the door*, then, signifies 'to ward off gnawing hunger', which our ancestors in the fifteenth century, who first used the phrase, would probably have understood far better than we do.

*Her mother, a resourceful and energetic woman, **kept the wolf from the door** by dressmaking.*
THE DAILY TELEGRAPH,
24 NOVEMBER 2001

*Many explorers are not motivated by money. I always try to make a living out of it but it is not easy... I have had **the wolf at the door** in the past due to two expedition failures in succession.*
EXPRESS ON SUNDAY, 25 MAY 2003

For other idioms derived from fables, see page 318.

wool: to pull the wool over someone's eyes
to deceive someone

The phrase refers back to a time when gentlemen wore wigs, *wool* being a humorous slang term for 'hair'. But why would anyone want to tip a gentleman's wig over his eyes? To prevent him from seeing something he shouldn't, presumably: a pickpocket, perhaps, or a prank of some sort. The earliest known references to the phrase are in American journals from the first half of the nineteenth century, and then in American literature in the second half.

In spite of this bank of evidence, some authorities think the phrase older and coined by the British. This stand would permit the speculation that, since British judges wear wigs, the expression may have been used in courts of law when lawyers, who had succeeded in a skilful deception, would boast of having *pulled the wool over the judge's eyes*. There is, however, no hard evidence for this.

*It's also helpful if you've been to London or New York, or to some of those places. If you've done that, then you know the world and nobody will be able **to pull the wool over your eyes**.*
ALEXANDER MCCALL SMITH,
THE KALAHARI TYPING SCHOOL
FOR MEN, 2002

*More than a million people are registered disabled with back pain but I am afraid many are lying. They get away with it because it is so easy **to pull the wool over the eyes** of the medical profession.*
THE SUNDAY TIMES, 2 MARCH 2003

writing: the writing is on the wall
downfall or disaster is imminent

In the book of Daniel, chapter 5, the Bible tells how Belshazzar, King of Babylon, showed his contempt of the Lord by holding a great feast where wine was served in goblets taken from the temple in Jerusalem. During the feast a human hand appeared, writing on the wall. The inscription read: *Mene, mene, tekel, upharsin*. The only one able to interpret the sign was the Jewish exile, Daniel, who voiced the Lord's anger and prophesied the downfall of Belshazzar and his kingdom. Just as Daniel had said, that very night Belshazzar was slain and his kingdom taken by a foreign power.

In 1720, Belshazzar's feast was alluded to in a poem called 'The Run upon the Bankers' by the satirist Jonathan Swift:

> *A baited Banker thus desponds,*
> *From his own Hand foresees his Fall;*
> *They have his Soul who have his Bonds;*
> *Tis like the Writing on the Wall.*

These days the message of imminent and inevitable doom is likely to apply to a failing enterprise, a politician, a sports team in danger of relegation or even society at large: *Mark my words, when a society has to resort to the lavatory for its humour, the writing is on the wall* (Alan Bennett, *Forty Years On*, 1968).

WRITING ON THE WALL FOR TRAVEL AGENTS

'Bucket-and-spade' travel agents could have virtually disappeared from the high street in five years' time as travellers turn to the internet.
THE GUARDIAN, 12 APRIL 2003

*They finished first and second in the championship but **the writing was on the wall** as Ferrari pushed hard to get on to the podium alongside these celebrated drivers. The turning point came at Silverstone on July 14, 1951, where Froilan Gonzalez won Ferrari's first race, the British Grand Prix.*
THE TIMES, 8 JULY 2003

For other idioms from the Bible, see page 317.

wrong: to have got out of the wrong side of the bed
to be bad tempered, grumpy

The wrong side of the bed is the left. According to Roman belief, omens seen on the left-hand side signified misfortune and anything to do with the left invited evil. Similar superstitions lurked in sixteenth- and seventeenth-century England when *to rise on one's right side* made everything well with the world. *Sure I rose the wrong way today. I have had such damned ill luck*, wrote Aphra Behn in *Town-Fop* (1676). Someone who is expecting to be dogged by disaster throughout the day would naturally be thrown into an irritable frame of mind from the outset and so, by the turn of the nineteenth century, *rising from the wrong side* or *getting out of bed on the wrong side* meant that they were disagreeable and grumpy.

*I am writing to defend Chuck Berry's incredible performance at the Playhouse last Sunday. Your critic Martin Lenon must have begun his Monday morning **on the wrong side of the bed** as there can be no other reason why he would malign one of the great music legends of our time.*
EVENING NEWS, 2 JULY 2004

*I woke up **on the wrong side of the bed** this morning. Grumpy, Grumpier and Grumpiest were waiting for me.*
TAMRA WIGHT,
THE THREE GRUMPIES, 2004

For related idioms, see *to put one's best* FOOT *forward, to set off on the right/wrong* FOOT. For other idioms drawn from ancient life and history, see page 317.

• Bibliography •

BREWER, Ebenezer Cobham, 1995
(15th edition, Adrian Room ed)
Dictionary of Phrase and Fable
(Cassell, London)

FARMER, J. S., 1890
A Dictionary of Slang, Vol 1
FARMER, J. S. and HENLEY, W. E.
**A further 6 volumes, 1891, 1893,
1896, 1902, 1904
Originally published as Slang and
its Analogues Past and Present**.
Edition used for this idiom dictionary:
Wordsworth Editions, Ware,
Hertfordshire, 1987

FUNK, Charles Earle, 1950
**A Hog on Ice and other curious
expressions** (Harper Bros,
New York)

FUNK, 1955
**Heavens to Betsy! and other
curious sayings** (Harper Bros,
New York)

GREEN, Jonathon, 1993
Slang Down the Ages
(Kyle Cathie, London)

Oxford English Dictionary,
2nd edition, 1989,
CD-ROM version 1.0d, 1993
(Oxford University Press, Oxford)

Oxford English Dictionary Online,
2005

PARTRIDGE, Eric, 1948
**A Dictionary of Forces' Slang
1939-1945** (Routledge &
Kegan Paul, London)

PARTRIDGE, Eric, 1950
A Dictionary of Cliches,
5th edition (Routledge &
Kegan Paul, London)

REES, Nigel, 1990
Dictionary of Popular Phrases
(Bloomsbury, London)

REES, Nigel, 2004
A Word in Your Shell-like
(Collins, Glasgow)

• Index of themes •

Idioms featuring alliteration and/or tautology
as busy as a BEE 27
as BOLD as brass 50
to DILLY-DALLY 99
as dead as a/the DODO 100
as dead as a DOORNAIL 104
as fit as a FIDDLE 120
FOOTLOOSE and fancy free 130
to HUM (hem) and haw 164
as MAD as a March hare 192
as PLEASED as Punch 236
to ROB Peter to pay Paul 251
to SHILLY-SHALLY 265
SPICK and span 277
TIT for tat 293
(to do something) WILLY-NILLY 312

See also ALLITERATIVE SIMILES, page 237, and COUPLINGS, page 294.

Idioms from ancient legends
ACHILLES heel 1
an APPLE of discord 8
not to have a CLUE 77
as rich as CROESUS 88
to cut the GORDIAN knot 140
HALCYON days 146
JANUS-faced 172
the MIDAS touch 198
NECTAR of the gods 215
PANDORA'S box 226
the SWORD of Damocles 285
to hang by a THREAD 291

Idioms from ancient life and history
to BURN one's boats/bridges (behind one) 59
the DIE is cast 98
DOG days 100
to FALL on one's sword 117
to FIDDLE while Rome burns 121
in the LAP of the gods 181
not to rest on one's LAURELS 182
a PARTING shot 228
a PYRRHIC victory 240

to cross the RUBICON 254
to be worth one's SALT 258
to take something with a pinch/grain of SALT 259
to leave no STONE unturned 281
to give someone the THUMBS up/down 291
to have got out of the WRONG side of the bed 315

Idioms from the army and warfare
BACKROOM boys 13
BAG and baggage 14
(when) the BALLOON goes up 16
a BAPTISM of fire 17
a BASKET case 19
to BEAT a (hasty) retreat 23
to BITE the bullet 37
to drop a BOMBSHELL 50
to go for a BURTON 61
a FLASH in the pan 123
a FORLORN hope 130
to run the GAUNTLET 133
to HANG fire 148
to play/wreak HAVOC 151
HOIST with one's own petard 157
everything but the KITCHEN sink 179
LAST-DITCH 181
to go OVER the top 223
the RANK and file 244
SHELL-SHOCKED 264
to STEAL a march (on) 280
on the WARPATH 305

See also POSTER PROPAGANDA, page 208

Idioms from the Bible
the APPLE of one's eye 8
a BESETTING sin 31
the BLIND leading the blind 42
to hide one's light under a BUSHEL 62
to turn the other CHEEK 72
FEET of clay 119
to HOPE against hope 159
at the eleventh HOUR 162
to put/get/set one's HOUSE in order 162
to KICK against the pricks 177

Idioms containing obsolete words
HUE and cry 163
at LOGGERHEADS 187
to be on one's METTLE 197
to go/get off SCOT-FREE 260
in a TRICE 296
to take UMBRAGE (at) 299

See also THE OLD CURIOSITY SHOP OF
LINGUISTICS, page 198

Idioms from poker
BLUE chip 46
to call someone's BLUFF 48
to pass the BUCK 57
to CHIP in 73
to hit the JACKPOT 170
POKER-FACED 238

Idioms from rhyming slang
to get down to BRASS TACKS 54
a load of old COBBLERS 79
a bit of how's your FATHER 118

See also HAVE A BUTCHER'S AT THIS,
page 80

Idioms that don't make sense
a CURATE'S egg 90
to be all FINGERS and thumbs 122

See also NONSENSICAL IDIOMS, page 124

Idioms from Shakespeare
BRAVE new world 55
to EAT someone out of house and home 111
to GILD the lily 135
it's (all) GREEK to me 142
the GREEN-EYED monster 142
HOIST with one's own petard 157
to LAY it on with a trowel 183
there is METHOD in one's madness 197
in the PINK 234
a POUND of flesh 239
SALAD days 257
a SEA change 262
the SEAMY side 262
to wear one's heart on one's SLEEVE 273
made of STERNER stuff 281
thereby hangs a TALE 287
the WHEEL has come full circle 308
a WILD goose chase 310

See also WILLIAM SHAKESPEARE, page 152

· Index ·